Practices of Looking

Marita Sturken and Lisa Cartwright's *Practices of Looking* is unquestionably the best introduction to the subject to have appeared in over a decade. It is a remarkably well-written, lucidly organized, and pedagogically astute book—few texts on visual culture in recent memory have been so well conceived and organized as to be suitable for an audience with no background in the subject; *Practices of Looking* is the exception. It's hard not to seem simply hyperbolic about this book, but the simple fact is this is an extremely fine accomplishment in every possible way.

> Donald Preziosi, Professor of Art History, University of California at Los Angeles,
> 2000–2001 Slade Professor of Fine Art at the University of Oxford

Practices of Looking explains contemporary theoretical debates in a lucid and highly engaging way. The numerous examples of visual culture from advertising, art, and various other media give the text a variety, liveliness and contemporary relevance that students will engage with. The authors are to be congratulated for an intelligent, clearly written, and engaging introductory text.

> Heather Dawkins, Professor of Art and Culture Studies, Simon Fraser University

Its strongest qualities are its timeliness as an introductory text in the field, its facility with each of the image practices it engages - from advertising to television, from cinema to a range of computer images - and its presentation of sophisticated methodologies and problems in an accessible manner. I was particularly impressed with its incorporation of current theoretical debates that have not been as well integrated in discussion of visual culture to date.

> Patricia White, Associate Professor of English and Film Studies, Swarthmore College

Written with stunning clarity, which nevertheless manages to convey a sense of the complexities at stake, this book will soon become indispensible for teachers seeking to introduce students to theoretical debates about visual culture within Marxism, structuralism, feminism, and postmodernism. It offers an impressively comprehensive survey of debates in the field, illustrated by accessible interpretations of up-to-date and familiar examples from contemporary visual culture.

> Jackie Stacey, Reader in Sociology and Women's Studies, Lancaster University

Textbook writers, lay down your cursors! At last we have a wide-ranging, supple, historical, and analytic approach to visual culture, full of lively examples, generously illustrated, and accessibly written. It is comprehensive, allusive, clear, well thought-out, and a pleasure to read.

> Toby Miller, Professor of Cinema Studies, New York University

CONSUMPTION AND OT

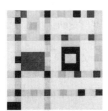

Practices
of Looking

An Introduction
to Visual Culture

Marita Sturken
and
Lisa Cartwright

OXFORD
UNIVERSITY PRESS

Oxford University Press, Inc., publishes works that further Oxford University's
objective of excellence in research, scholarship, and education.

Oxford New York
Auckland Cape Town Dar es Salaam Hong Kong Karachi
Kuala Lumpur Madrid Melbourne Mexico City Nairobi
New Delhi Shanghai Taipei Toronto

With offices in
Argentina Austria Brazil Chile Czech Republic France Greece
Guatemala Hungary Italy Japan Poland Portugal Singapore
South Korea Switzerland Thailand Turkey Ukraine Vietnam

Published by Oxford University Press, Inc.
198 Madison Avenue, New York, New York 10016
http://www.oup.com

Oxford is a registered trademark of Oxford University Press

ISBN-13: 978-0-19-874271-5
ISBN 0-19-874271-1

First printing 2001. First U.S. printing 2005.

Printing number: 9 8 7 6 5 4 3

Printed in the United States of America
on acid-free paper

Acknowledgements

Research for this book was supported in part by grants from the Zumberge Fund of the University of Southern California, and the James Irvine Foundation through the Southern California Studies Center (SC2) at USC. Christie Milliken, JoAnn Hanley, Amy Herzog, and Joe Wlodarz were extremely resourceful in their work on researching photographs. We are grateful to Amelia Jones, Toby Miller, Nicholas Mirzoeff, Jackie Stacey, and many other anonymous readers who provided very helpful and informed feedback on a previous draft. Our thanks to the many people who have shepherded this book at Oxford, including Andrew Lockett, Tim Barton, Sophie Goldsworthy, designer Tim Branch, and in particular Angela Griffin and Miranda Vernon, who have been efficient, attentive, and resourceful. Finally, we are grateful to Dana Polan and Brian Goldfarb for their advice and support throughout this project.

M.S. and L.C.

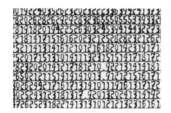

Contents

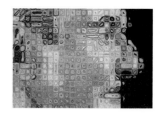

Introduction

The world we inhabit is filled with visual images. They are central to how we represent, make meaning, and communicate in the world around us. In many ways, our culture is an increasingly visual one. Over the course of the last two centuries, Western culture has come to be dominated by visual rather than oral or textual media. Even the bastion of the printed word, the newspaper, has turned to images—and color images by the end of the twentieth century—to draw in its readers and add to the meaning of its stories. Images have never been merely illustrations, they carry important content. For example, television, a visual and sound-based medium, has come to play the central role in daily life once occupied by the strictly aural medium of radio. Computers, originally equipped to generate text, numbers, and symbols, have been broadly adapted to generate and exchange more complex visual data. Hearing and touching are important means of experience and communication, but our values, opinions, and beliefs have increasingly come to be shaped in powerful ways by the many forms of visual culture that we encounter in our day-to-day lives.

On the one hand, this shift to the visual promotes a fascination with the image. On the other hand, it produces an anxiety about the potential power of images that has existed since the time of Plato. At the beginning of the twenty-first century, many older fantasies about the power of images seem to have come true thanks to technology. We are presented with a new set of challenges: to understand how images and their viewers make meaning, to determine what role images play in our cultures, and to consider what it means to negotiate so many images in our daily lives.[1]

Practices of Looking provides an overview of a range of theories about how we understand a wide array of visual media and how we use images to express ourselves, to communicate, to experience pleasure, and to learn. The term "visual culture" encompasses many media forms ranging from fine art to popular film and television to advertising to visual data in fields such as the sciences, law, and medicine. This book explores the questions, what does it mean to study these diverse forms together? How do shared understandings of these various forms of visual culture emerge? How does the visual intersect with aural and tactile media? We feel that it is important to consider visual culture as a complex and richly varied whole for an important reason: when we have an experience with a particular visual medium we draw on associations with other media and other areas of our lives informed by visual images. For example, when we watch a television show, the meanings and pleasure we derive from it might be drawn, consciously or unconsciously, from associations with things we have seen in movies, works of art, or advertisements. The experience of viewing a medical ultrasound image might evoke emotions or meanings more typically associated with viewing photographs or television images. Our visual experiences do not take place in isolation; they are enriched by memories and images from many different aspects of our lives.

Despite this cross-fertilization of visual forms, our cultures tend to "rank" different areas of visual culture according to systems of supposed quality and importance. For many decades, colleges and universities offered courses on the fine arts but did not consider popular media such as movies and television to be worthy of serious academic study. Today, in contrast, art historians include photography, computer graphics, mixed media, installation, and performance art among the practices they study. At the same time other fields, some of them new, have taken up a broader range of media forms. Since the 1950s, scholars in the field of communication have written important studies of radio, television, print media, and now the Internet. The disciplines of cinema, television, and media studies, which were instituted in the 1970s, have helped us to consider how movies, television programs, and media such as the World Wide Web have contributed to changes in culture over the course of this century. These fields have established the value of studying popular forms of visual media. The even newer field of science and technology studies has encouraged the study of visual technologies and the use of images in areas outside the arts and entertainment, such as the sciences, law, and medicine. Cultural studies, an interdisciplinary field that emerged in the late 1970s, has offered many ways of thinking about the study of both popular culture and the seemingly mundane uses of images in our daily lives. One of the aims of cultural studies is to provide viewers, citizens, and consumers with the tools to gain a better understanding of how visual media help us make sense of our society. Looking at images across disciplines can help us to think about the cross-fertilization that occurs among the different kinds of visual media. In the course of reading this book, the reader will encounter ideas drawn from cultural studies, cinema and media studies, communication, art history, sociology, and anthropology.

What is visual culture? Culture has been famously characterized by cultural theorist Raymond Williams as one of the most complex words in the English language. It is an elaborate concept, the meaning of which has changed over time.[2] Traditionally, culture was thought of as the "fine" arts: classic works of painting, literature, music, and philosophy. This idea of culture was defined by such philosophers as Matthew Arnold as the "best that has been thought and said" in a society, and was reserved for an elite, educated audience.[3] If one uses the term this way, a famous work by Michelangelo or a composition by Mozart would represent the epitome of Western culture. Thus, the idea of "high" culture has often been implicit within definitions of culture, with the notion that culture should be separated into the categories of high (fine art, classical painting, literature) and low (television, popular novels, comic books). As we will explore further in Chapter 2, high versus low was the traditional way of framing discussions about culture for much of history, with high culture widely regarded as quality culture and low culture as its debased counterpart.

The term culture, in what is known as the "anthropological definition," refers to a "whole way of life," meaning a broad range of activities within a society. Popular music, print media, art, and literature contribute to the daily lives of "ordinary people." So too do sports, cooking, driving, relationships, and kinship. This definition links the term "culture" to the idea of a popular or mass culture. However, while it expands the idea of what gets to count as culture in important ways, this definition does not fully make clear the focus of contemporary work that understands culture specifically as a meaning-producing process. This means foregrounding the practices of culture.

In this book, we are defining culture as the shared practices of a group, community, or society, through which meaning is made out of the visual, aural, and textual world of representations. Here, we are indebted to the work of British cultural theorist Stuart Hall, who states that culture is not so much a set of things (television shows or paintings, for example) as a set of processes or practices through which individuals and groups come to make sense of those things. Culture is the production and exchange of meanings, the giving and taking of meaning, between members of a society or group. Hall states, "It is the participants in a culture who give meaning to people, objects, and events. . . . It is by our use of things, and what we say, think and feel about them—how we represent them—that we give them a meaning."[4]

It is important to keep in mind that in any group that shares a culture (or set of processes through which meaning is made), there is always a range of meanings and interpretations "floating about," so to speak, with regard to any given issue or object at any given time. Culture is a process, not a fixed set of practices or interpretations. For example, three different viewers of the same advertisement who share a general view of the world may differently interpret its meaning, based on their respective experiences and knowledge. These people may share the same culture but still subject the image to different interpretive processes. These viewers may then talk about their responses, influencing one another's subsequent views. Some viewers might argue more convincingly than others; some might be regarded as having more authority than others. In the end, meanings are produced not in the heads of the viewers so much as through a process of negotiation among individuals within a particular culture, and between individuals and the artifacts, images, and texts created by themselves and others. Interpretations, then, are as effective as the visual artifacts (such as advertisements or films) that generate them in influencing a culture's or group's shared world view. Our use of the term "culture" throughout this book will emphasize this understanding of culture as a fluid and interactive process—a process grounded in social practices, not solely in images, texts, or interpretations.

Practices of Looking is concerned specifically with *visual* culture, that is, those aspects of culture that are manifested in visual form—paintings, prints, photographs, film, television, video, advertisements, news images, and science images. What separates visual culture from written text or speech? It is a paradox of the twentieth century that while visual images have increasingly come to dominate our culture, our colleges and universities traditionally have devoted relatively little attention to visual media. The fields mentioned earlier notwithstanding, higher learning remains largely a text- and symbol-based curriculum. We feel that visual culture is something that should be understood in an analytical way not only by art historians and other "image specialists," but by all of us who increasingly encounter a startling array of images in our daily lives. At the same time, many theorists of visual culture have argued that foregrounding the visual in visual culture does not mean separating images from writing, speech, language, or others modes of representation and experience. Images often are integrated with words, as in much contemporary art and in the history of advertising. Our goal is to lay out some of the theories that can help us to understand how images function in a broader cultural sphere, and how looking practices inform our lives beyond our perception of images *per se*.

Since the 1990s, there has been a move among scholars to focus on the study of visual culture across several disciplines. This has come about in part through the expansion of art history into social realms beyond art and through a cultural studies cross-fertilization between such fields as communication, cinema-television studies, and science studies. This has also been prompted by the study of new media such as the World Wide Web and digital imaging in many disciplines. It is essential to much of the interdisciplinary project of visual culture to mark boundary crossings between disciplines. Hence, it is important to understand, for instance, what it means when art images borrow from commercial imagery and advertising sells products through art.

The emergence of visual culture as a field of study has also been the subject of debate and controversy, in particular in relationship to the study of art history.[5] In this book, we examine a broad range of theoretical strategies for understanding how meaning is produced by and through images in their historical context. Our approach emphasizes less the distinction of art and more its interaction with other aspects of visual culture. It is thus one of the intentions of this book to demonstrate the ways in which art history can use other media as fruitful points of comparison. At the same time, we hope that *Practices of Looking* will offer ways for those interested in mass media to understand the relationship of media images to art. While this book examines many images from the history of painting, it has a particular emphasis on those images that since the mid-nineteenth century have been generated through cameras, such as photographs, films, and television images, and that gain meaning within and circulate among the realms of art, commerce, the law, and science.

This book takes as its distant inspiration John Berger's well-known book, *Ways of Seeing*. Published in 1972, *Ways of Seeing* is a model for the examination of images and their meanings across such disciplinary boundaries as media studies and art history. Berger's work was groundbreaking in bringing together a range of theory, from Walter Benjamin's concept of mechanical reproduction to Marxist theory, in order to examine images from the history of art and advertising. It is our goal to pay homage to many of the strategies of that book in updating such an approach to visual culture in the contemporary theoretical and media context. The terrain of images and their trajectories has become significantly more complex since Berger wrote his book. Technological changes have made possible the movements of images throughout the globe at much greater speed. The economic context of post-industrial capitalism has enabled a blurring of many previously understood boundaries between cultural and social realms such as art, news, and commodity culture. The mix of styles in postmodernism has aided in producing a context of image circulation and cross-referencing that prompts this kind of interdisciplinary approach.

The approaches of *Practices of Looking* can thus be understood in several different ways. One approach is the use of theories to study images themselves and their textual meanings. This is a primary, yet not the only, approach to understanding the dynamics of looking. It allows us to examine what images tell us about the cultures in which they are produced. A second approach is to look at the modes of responding to visuality, as represented in studies of spectators or audiences and their psychological and social patterns of looking. In this approach, the emphasis shifts from images and their meanings to viewers' practices of looking, and the various and specific ways people regard, use, and interpret images. Some of these approaches are about theorizing an idealized viewer, such as the cinematic spectator, and others are about considering what actual viewers do with popular culture texts. A third approach considers how media images, texts, and programs move from one social arena to another, and circulate in and across cultures, which is especially relevant in light of the escalation of globalization since the mid-twentieth century. This approach looks at the institutional frameworks that regulate and sometimes limit the circulation of images, as well as the ways that images change meaning in different cultural contexts. In these approaches, this book proposes a set of tools that can be used in deciphering visual media, and a means to analyze how and why we have come to rely so heavily on visual forms to make meaning in almost all areas of our lives.

Practices of Looking is organized into nine chapters that are intended to address issues of visual culture across various visual media and cultural arenas. Chapter 1, "Practices of Looking: Images, Power, and Politics," introduces many of the themes of the book, such as the concept of representation, the role of photography, the relationship of images to ideology, and the ways that we make meaning from and award value to images. It introduces the basic concepts of semiotics, the study of signs, and discusses aspects of image production and consumption that will be addressed in more depth in later chapters. It is one of the central tenets of this book that meaning does not reside within images, but is produced at the moment that they are consumed by and circulate among viewers. Thus, Chapter 2, "Viewers Make Meaning," focuses on the ways that viewers produce meaning from images, and discusses the concept of ideology in more depth. Whereas Chapter 2 analyzes many theories about how specific viewers and audiences make meaning of visual images, Chapter 3, "Spectatorship, Power, and Knowledge," examines those theories that consider an idealized viewer such as the spectator of cinematic and still images. It also addresses the concept of the gaze in both psychoanalytic theory and concepts of power. Here, we examine both concepts of how viewers identify with images, and the ways that images can be used as elements of discourse, institutional power, and categorization. Chapter 4, "Reproduction and Representation," explores the history of how visual technologies have affected ways of seeing. It begins by examining the development of perspective and concepts of realism that accompanied it, and then looks at how image reproduction has changed the meaning of images throughout history, including how these concepts have meaning in the contemporary context of the Internet and digital images. This historical tracing of these concepts is echoed in Chapter 5, "The Mass Media and the Public Sphere," which maps out many of the theories of mass media and the public sphere from their origins, examining the models of mass media that have ranged from propaganda to the idea of the media as a means of fostering democracy. This chapter addresses the question of what mass media means in the current media context of multimedia and cross-media cultural products. Chapter 6, "Consumer Culture and the Manufacturing of Desire," looks at the meanings of advertising images in relation to art about consumer culture. It discusses theories of ideology and semiotics as tools for understanding the strategies used in advertising images to add meaning to consumer products and to speak to consumers in the language of desire and need. In Chapter 7, "Postmodernism and Popular Culture," we look at a range of styles in contemporary art, popular culture, and advertising that have been defined within the contexts of modernism and postmodernism. We discuss the experience of modernity and its relation to the tenets of modern art, and the relationship between modernism and postmodernism both as philosophical concepts and styles of imaging. Chapter 8, "Scientific Looking, Looking at Science," returns to many of the concepts discussed earlier in the book on photographic truth to look at the relationship of images to evidence and the role of images in science. This includes the meaning of images in legal contexts, the politics of images of the body and the fetus, the meanings created by new medical imaging technologies, and the depiction of science in popular culture. The final chapter, Chapter 9, "The Global Flow of Visual Culture," looks at the ways that images travel in the contemporary context of globalization and diverse media convergence. This chapter examines how images change meaning when they move between cultures, models for thinking about the local and the global, and the role of the Internet and new media in changing the global flow of visual images. The book concludes with an extensive glossary of many terms used in the book. These terms are shown in italics in their first reference within each chapter. *Practices of Looking* aims to engage with a broad range of issues of visual culture by examining how images gain meaning in many cultural arenas, from art and commerce to science and the law, how they travel through different cultural arenas and in distinct cultures, and how they are an integral and important aspect of our lives.

Notes

1. For further discussion of this "pictorial turn," see W. J. T. Mitchell, *Picture Theory* (Chicago and London: University of Chicago Press, 1994), ch. 1.
2. Raymond Williams, *Keywords: A Vocabulary of Culture and Society,* Revised Edition (New York and Oxford: Oxford University Press, 1983), 87.
3. Matthew Arnold, *Culture and Anarchy* (New York and Cambridge: Cambridge University Press, 1932), 6.
4. Stuart Hall, "Introduction," in *Representation: Cultural Representations and Signifying Practices*, edited by Stuart Hall (Thousand Oaks, Calif. and London: Sage, 1997), 3.
5. See in particular the perspectives in *October*, 77 (Summer 1996), 25–70; and Douglas Crimp's response to them, "Getting the Warhol We Deserve," *Social Text*, 59 (Summer 1999), 49–66.

Further Reading

John Berger. *Ways of Seeing*. New York and London: Penguin, 1972.

Jessica Evans and Stuart Hall, eds. *Visual Culture: The Reader*. Thousand Oaks, Calif. and London: Sage, 1999.

Stuart Hall, ed. *Representation: Cultural Representations and Signifying Practices*. Thousand Oaks, Calif. and London: Sage, 1997.

Chris Jenks, ed. *Visual Culture*. New York and London: Routledge, 1995.

Nicholas Mirzoeff, ed. *The Visual Culture Reader*. New York and London: Routledge, 1998.

——*An Introduction to Visual Culture*. New York and London: Routledge, 1999.

W. J. T. Mitchell. *Picture Theory*. Chicago and London: University of Chicago Press, 1994.

1 Practices of Looking

Images, Power, and Politics

Every day, we are in the practice of looking to make sense of the world. To see is a process of observing and recognizing the world around us. To look is to actively make meaning of that world. Seeing is something that we do some-what arbitrarily as we go about our daily lives. Looking is an activity that involves a greater sense of purpose and direction. If we ask, "Did you *see* that?" we imply happenstance ("Did you happen to see it?"). When we say, "*Look* at that!" it is a command. To look is an act of choice. Through looking we negotiate social relationships and meanings. Looking is a *practice* much like speaking, writing, or signing. Looking involves learning to interpret and, like other practices, looking involves relationships of power. To willfully look or not is to exercise choice and influence. To be made to look, to try to get someone else to look at you or at something you want to be noticed, or to engage in an exchange of looks, entails a play of power. Looking can be easy or difficult, fun or unpleasant, harmless or dangerous. There are both con-scious and unconscious levels of looking. We engage in practices of looking to communicate, to influence and be influenced.

We live in cultures that are increasingly permeated by visual images with a variety of purposes and intended effects. These images can produce in us a wide array of emotions and responses: pleasure, desire, disgust, anger, curios-ity, shock, or confusion. We invest the images we create and encounter on a daily basis with significant power—for instance, the power to conjure an absent person, the power to calm or incite to action, the power to persuade or mystify. A single image can serve a multitude of purposes, appear in a range of settings, and mean different things to different people. The roles played by

Weegee, *Their First Murder*, before 1945

images are multiple, diverse, and complex. This image, of school children in the early 1940s who see a murder scene in the street, was taken by photographer Weegee (whose real name was Arthur Fellig). Weegee was known for his images of crimes and violence in the streets of New York, where he would listen to a police radio in order to get to crime scenes early. In this photograph, he calls attention both to the act of looking at the forbidden and to the capacity of the still camera to capture heightened emotion. The children are looking at the murder scene with morbid fascination, as we look with equal fascination upon them looking.

The images we encounter every day span the social realms of popular culture, advertising, news and information exchange, commerce, criminal justice, and art. They are produced and experienced through a variety of media: painting, printmaking, photography, film, television/video, computer digital imaging, and virtual reality. One could argue that all of these media— including those that do not involve mechanical or technological *means of production*—are imaging technologies. Even paintings are produced with the "technology" of paint, brush, and canvas. We live in an increasingly image-saturated society where paintings, photographs, and electronic images depend on one another for their meanings. The most famous paintings of Western art history have been photographically and electronically

Van Gogh painting
on coffee mug

reproduced, and many of these reproductions have been touched up or altered by means of computer graphics. For most of us, knowledge of famous paintings is not first-hand, but through reproductions in books and on posters, greeting cards, classroom slides, and television specials about art history. The technology of images is thus central to our experience of visual culture.

Representation

Representation refers to the use of language and images to create meaning about the world around us. We use words to understand, describe, and define the world as we see it, and we also use images to do this. This process takes place through systems of representation, such as language and visual media, that have rules and conventions about how they are organized. A language like English has a set of rules about how to express and interpret meaning, and so, for instance, do the systems of representation of painting, photography, cinema, or television.

Throughout history, debates about representation have considered whether these systems of representation reflect the world as it is, such that they mirror it back to us as a form of *mimesis* or imitation, or whether in fact we construct the world and its meaning through the systems of representation we deploy. In this *social constructionist* approach, we only make meaning of the material world through specific cultural contexts. This takes place in part through the language systems (be they writing, speech, or images) that we use. Hence, the material world only has meaning, and only can be "seen" by us, through these systems of representation. This means that the world is not simply reflected back to us through systems of representation, but that we actually construct the meaning of the material world through these systems.

Over time, images have been used to represent, make meaning of, and convey various sentiments about nature, society, and culture as well as to represent imaginary worlds and abstract concepts. Throughout much of history, for example, images, most of them paintings, have been used by religions to convey religious myths, church doctrines, and historical dramas. Many images have been produced to depict seemingly accurate renditions of the world around us, while others have been created to express abstract concepts and feelings such as love. Language and systems of representation do not reflect an already existing reality so much as they organize, construct, and mediate our understanding of reality, emotion, and imagination.

The distinction between the idea of reflection, or mimesis, and representation as a construction of the material world can often be difficult to make. The still life, for instance, has been a favored subject of artists for many centuries. One might surmise that the still life is simply about the desire to reflect, rather than make meaning of, material objects. In the still life on the next page, painted in 1642 by Dutch painter Pieter Claesz, an array of food and drink is carefully arranged on a table, and painted with an attention to each minute detail. The objects, such as the tablecloth, dishes, bread, carafe, and glass, are rendered with an attention to light and seem so lifelike that one imagines one could touch them. Yet, is this image simply a reflection of this particular scene, rendered with skill by the artist? Is it simply a mimesis of a scene, painted for the sake of demonstrating skill? Claesz worked in the seventeenth century, when Dutch painters were fascinated with the still life form, and painters painted many such works with attention to creating the illusion of material objects on canvas. The Dutch still life ranged in form from those that were straightforwardly representational to those that were deeply symbolic. Many were not simply about a composition of food and drink, but replete with allusions and symbolism, as well as philosophical ideas. Many works, such as this, were concerned with depicting the transience of earthly life through the ephemeral materiality of food. They call forth the senses through the

Pieter Claesz, *Still Life with Stoneware Jug, Wine Glass, Herring, and Bread*, 1642

depiction of foods which are associated with particular aromas, in which partially eaten foods evoke the experience of eating. In this work, the fare is simple, a reference to the everyday food of the common people, yet one can also see the potential religious allusions of bread, wine, and fish to Christian rituals.[1] Yet, even if we simply read this image as a representation of food without any symbolism, its original meaning was derived from its depiction of what food and drink meant in seventeenth-century Holland. Here, the language of painting is used to create a particular set of meanings according to a set of conventions about realistically depicting the material world. We will discuss concepts of realism more in Chapter 4. Here, we want to note that this painting produces meanings about these objects, rather than simply reflecting some meaning that is already within them.

Representation is thus a process through which we construct the world around us, even through a simple scene such as this, and make meaning from it. We learn the rules and conventions of the systems of representation within a given culture. Many artists have attempted to defy those conventions, to break the rules of various systems of representation, and to push at the definitions of representation. In this painting, for example, *Surrealist* painter René Magritte comments upon the process of representation. Entitled *The Treachery of Images* (1928–29), the painting depicts a pipe with the line in French, "This is not a pipe." One could argue, on the one hand, that Magritte is making a joke, that of course it is an image of a pipe that he has created. However, he is also pointing to the relationship between words and things, since this is not a pipe itself but rather the representation of a pipe; it is a painting rather than the material object itself. Philosopher Michel Foucault elaborates these ideas in a short text about this painting and a drawing by Magritte that preceded it.[2] Not only does he address the painting's implied commentary about the relationship between words and things, he also considers the complex relationship among the drawing, the painting, their words, and their *referent* (the pipe). One could not pick up and smoke this pipe. So, Magritte can be seen to be warning the viewer not to mistake the image for the real thing. He marks the very act of naming, drawing our attention to the word "pipe" itself, and its function in representing the object. Both the word "pipe" and the image of the pipe represent the material object pipe, and in pointing this out, Magritte asks us to consider how they produce meaning about it. Thus, when we stop and examine the process of representation, as Magritte

René Magritte, *The Treachery of Images* (*Ceci n'est pas une pipe*), 1928–29

asks us to do, a process that we normally take for granted, we can see the complexity of how words and images produce meaning in our world.

The myth of photographic truth

The rules and conventions of different systems of representation vary, and we attribute different sets of cultural meanings to each—such as paintings, photographs, and television images. Many of the images discussed in this book were produced by cameras and through photographic or electronic technologies. These images belong to the various worlds of fine art, public art, advertising, popular culture, alternative media, the news media, and science.

No matter what social role an image plays, the creation of an image through a camera lens always involves some degree of *subjective* choice through selection, framing, and personalization. It is true that some types of image recording seem to take place without human intervention. In *surveillance* videos, for instance, no one stands behind the lens to determine what should be shot and how to shoot it. Yet even in surveillance video, someone has programmed the camera to record a particular part of a space and framed that space in a particular way. In the case of many automatic video and still-photography cameras designed for the consumer market, aesthetic choices like focus and framing are made as if by the camera itself, yet in fact the designers of these cameras also made decisions based on social and aesthetic norms such as clarity and legibility. These mechanisms are invisible to the user—they are *black-boxed*, relieving the photographer of various decisions. Yet, it remains the photographer who frames and takes the image, not the camera itself. At the same time, despite the subjective aspects of the act of taking a picture, the aura of machine *objectivity* clings to mechanical and electronic images. All camera-generated images, be they photographic, cinematic, or electronic (video or computer-generated), bear the cultural legacy of still photography, which historically has been regarded as a more objective practice than, say, painting or drawing. This combination of the subjective and the objective is a central tension in camera-generated images.

Photography was developed in Europe in the early nineteenth century, when concepts of *positivist* science held sway. Positivism involves the belief that *empirical* truths can be established through visual evidence. An empirical truth is something that can be proven through experimentation, in particular through the reproduction of an experiment with identical outcomes under carefully controlled circumstances. In positivism, the individual actions of the scientist came to be viewed as a liability in the process of performing and reproducing experiments, since it was thought that the scientist's own subjectivity would influence or prejudice the objectivity of the experiment. Hence, machines were regarded as more reliable than humans. Similarly, photography is a method of producing images that involves a mechanical recording device (the camera) rather than hand recording (pencil on paper). In the context of positivism, the photographic camera was taken to be a scientific tool for registering reality and was regarded by its early advocates as a means of representing the world more accurately than hand-rendered images.

Since the mid-1800s, there have been many arguments for and against the idea that photographs are objective renderings of the real world that provide an unbiased truth because cameras are seemingly detached from a subjective, particular human viewpoint. These debates have taken on new intensity with the introduction of digital imaging processes. A photograph is often perceived to be an unmediated copy of the real world, a trace of reality skimmed off the very surface of life. We refer to this concept as the myth of *photographic truth*. For instance, when a photograph is introduced as documentary evidence in a courtroom, it is often presented as if it were incontrovertible proof that an event took place in a particular way. As such, it is perceived to speak the truth. At the same time, the truth-value of photography has been the focus of many debates, in contexts such as courtrooms, about the different "truths" that images can tell.

Camera images are also associated with truth-value in more everyday settings. A photograph in a family album is often perceived to tell the truth, such as the fact that a particular family gathering took place, a vacation was taken, or a birthday was celebrated. Photographs have been used to prove that someone was alive at a given place and time in history. For instance, after the Holocaust, many survivors sent photographs to their families from whom they had been long separated as an affirmation of their being alive. It is a paradox of photography that although we know that images can be ambiguous and are easily manipulated or altered, particularly with the help of computer graphics, much of the power of photography still lies in the shared belief that photographs are objective or truthful records of events. Our awareness of the subjective nature of imaging is in constant tension with the legacy of objectivity that clings to the cameras and machines that produce images today.

Yet, the sense that photographic images are evidence of the real also gives them a kind of magical quality that adds to their documentary quality. The images created by cameras can be simultaneously informative and expressive. This photograph was taken by Robert Frank in his well-known photographic essay, *The Americans*, which he created while travelling around the USA in the mid-1950s. The image documents a segregated group of white and black passengers on a city trolley in New Orleans. As a factual piece of evidence about the past, it records a particular moment in time in the racially segregated American South of the 1950s. Yet, at the same time, this photograph does more than document facts. For some contemporary viewers, this image is magically moving insofar as it evokes powerful emotions about the momentous changes about to occur in the American South. The picture was taken just before laws, policies, and social mores concerning segregation began to

Robert Frank,
Trolley–New Orleans,
1955–56

undergo radical changes in response to Civil Rights activism. The faces of the passengers each look outward with different expressions, responding in different ways to the journey. It is as if the trolley itself represents the passage of life, and the expressive faces of each passenger the way in which they confront and experience their life. The trolley riders seem to be eternally held within the vehicle, a group of strangers thrown together to journey down the same road, just as the Civil Rights era in the South brought together strangers for a political journey. Thus, this photograph is valuable both as an empirical, informational document and as an expressive vehicle. The power of the image derives not only from its status as photographic evidence but from its powerful evocation of the emotions of life's struggles. It thus demonstrates the photograph's capacity both to present evidence and to evoke a magical or mythical quality.

In addition, this image, like all images, has two levels of meaning. French theorist Roland Barthes described these two levels with the terms *denotative* and *connotative* meaning. An image can *denote* certain apparent truths, providing documentary evidence of objective circumstances. The denotative meaning of the image refers to its literal, descriptive meaning. The same photograph *connotes* more culturally specific meanings. Connotative meanings rely on the cultural and historical context of the image and its viewers' lived, felt knowledge of those circumstances—all that the image means to them personally and socially. This Robert Frank photograph denotes a group of passengers on a trolley. Yet, clearly its meaning is broader than this simple description. This image connotes a collective journey of life and race relations. The dividing line between what an image denotes and what it connotes can be ambiguous, as in this image, where the facts of segregation alone may produce particular connotative associations for some viewers. These two concepts help us to think about the differences between images functioning as evidence and as works that evoke more complex feelings and associations. Another image of passengers on a trolley might connote a very different set of meanings.

Roland Barthes used the term *myth* to refer to the cultural values and beliefs that are expressed at this level of connotation. For Barthes, myth is the hidden set of rules and conventions through which meanings, which are in reality specific to certain groups, are made to seem universal and given for a whole society. Myth thus allows the connotative meaning of a particular thing or image to appear to be denotative, hence literal or natural. Barthes argued that a French ad for Italian sauce and pasta is not simply presenting a product but is producing a myth about Italian culture—the concept of "Italianicity."[3] This message, wrote Barthes, is not for Italians, but is specifically about a French concept of Italian culture. Similarly, one could argue that the contemporary concepts of beauty and thinness naturalize certain cultural norms of appearance as being universal. These norms constitute a myth in Barthes's terms, because they are historically and culturally specific, not "natural."

Barthes's concepts of myth and connotation are particularly useful in examining notions of photographic truth. Among the range of images produced by cameras, there are cultural meanings that affect our expectations and uses of images. We do not, for example, bring the same expectations about the representation of truth to newspaper photographs as we do to television news images or to film images that we view in a movie theater. A significant difference among these forms is their relationship to time and their ability to be widely reproduced. Whereas conventional photographs and films need to be developed and printed before they can be viewed and reproduced, the electronic nature of television images means that they are instantly viewable and can be transmitted around the world live. As moving images, cinematic and television images are combined with sound and music in narrative forms, and their meaning often lies in the sequence of images rather than its individual frames.

Similarly, the cultural meanings of and expectations about computer and digital images are different from those of conventional photographs. Because computer images can look increasingly like photographs, people who produce them sometimes play with the conventions of photographic realism. For example, an image generated exclusively by computer graphics software can be made to appear to be a photograph of actual objects, places, or people, when in fact it is a *simulation*, that is, it does not represent something in the real world. In addition, computer graphics programs can be used to modify or rearrange the elements of a "realistic" photograph. Widespread use of digital imaging technologies since the 1990s has dramatically altered the status of the photograph, particularly in the news media. Digital imaging thus can be said to have partially eroded the public's trust in the truth-value of photography and the camera image as evidence. Yet, at the same time, the altered image may still appear to represent a photographic truth. The meaning of an image, and our expectations of it, is thus tied to the technology through which it is produced. We will discuss this further in Chapter 4.

Images and ideology

To explore the meaning of images is to recognize that they are produced within dynamics of social power and *ideology*. Ideologies are systems of belief that exist within all cultures. Images are an important means through which ideologies are produced and onto which ideologies are projected. When people think of ideologies, they often think in terms of *propaganda*—the crude process of using false representations to lure people into holding beliefs that may compromise their own interests. This understanding of ideology assumes that to act ideologically is to act out of ignorance. In this particular sense, the term "ideology" carries a pejorative cast. However, ideology is a much more pervasive, mundane process in which we all engage, whether we are aware of it or not. For our purposes, we define ideology as the broad but indispensable, shared set of values and beliefs through which individuals live out their complex relations to a range of social structures. Ideologies are widely varied and exist at all levels of all cultures. Our ideologies are diverse and ubiquitous; they inform our everyday lives in often subtle and barely noticeable forms. One could say that ideology is the means by which certain values, such as individual freedom, progress, and the importance of home, are made to seem like natural, inevitable aspects of everyday life. Ideology is manifested in widely shared social assumptions about not only the way things are but the way we all know things should be. Images and media representations are some of the forms through which we persuade others to share certain views or not, to hold certain values or not.

Practices of looking are intimately tied to ideology. The image culture in which we live is an arena of diverse and often conflicting ideologies. Images are elements of contemporary advertising and consumer culture through which assumptions about beauty, desire, glamour, and social value are both constructed and responded to. Film and television are media through which we see reinforced ideological constructions such as the value of romantic love, the norm of heterosexuality, nationalism, or traditional concepts of good and evil. The most important aspect of ideologies is that they appear to be natural or given, rather than part of a system of belief that a culture produces in order to function in a particular way. Ideologies are thus, like Barthes's concept of myth, connotations parading as denotations.

Visual culture is integral to ideologies and power relations. Ideologies are produced and affirmed through the social institutions in a given society, such as the family, education, medicine, the law, the government, and the entertainment industry, among others. Ideologies permeate the world of entertainment, and images are also used for regulation, categorization, identification, and evidence. Shortly after photography was developed in the early nineteenth century, private citizens began hiring photographers to make individual and family portraits. Portraits often marked important moments such as births, marriages, and even deaths (the funerary portrait was a popular convention). But photographs were also widely regarded as tools of science and of public surveillance. Astronomers spoke of using photographic film to mark the movements of the stars. Photographs were used in hospitals, mental institutions, and prisons to record, classify, and study populations. Indeed, in rapidly growing urban industrial centers, photographs quickly became an important way for police and public health officials to monitor urban populations perceived to be growing not only in numbers, but also in rates of crime and social deviance.

What is the legacy of this use of images as a means of controlling popula-

tions today? We live in a society in which portrait images are frequently used, like fingerprints, as personal identification—on passports, driver's licenses, credit cards, and identification cards for schools, the welfare system, and many other institutions. Photographs are a primary medium for evidence in the criminal justice system. We are accustomed to the fact that most stores and banks are outfitted with surveillance cameras and that our daily lives are tracked not only through our credit records, but through camera records. On a typical day of work, errands, and leisure, the activities of people in cities are recorded, often unbeknownst to them, by numerous cameras. Often these images stay within the realm of identification and surveillance, where they go unnoticed by most of us. But sometimes their venues change and they circulate in the public realm, where they acquire new meanings.

This happened in 1994, when the former football star O. J. Simpson was arrested as a suspect in a notorious murder case. Simpson's image had previously appeared only in sports media, advertising, and celebrity news media. He was rendered a different kind of public figure when his portrait, in the form of his police mug shot, was published on the covers of *Time* and *Newsweek* magazines. The mug shot is a common use of photography in the criminal justice system. Information about all arrested people, whether they are convicted or not, is entered into the system in the form of personal data, fingerprints, and photographs. The conventions of the mug shot were presumably familiar to most people who saw the covers of *Time* and *Newsweek*. Frontal and side views of suspects' unsmiling, unadorned faces are shot. These conventions of framing and composition alone connote to viewers a sense of the subject's deviance and guilt, regardless of who is thus framed; the image format has the power to suggest the photographic subject's guilt. O. J. Simpson's mug shot seemed to be no different from any other in this regard.

Whereas *Newsweek* used the mug shot as it was, *Time* heightened the contrast and darkened Simpson's skin tone in its use of this image on the magazine's cover, reputedly for "aesthetic" reasons. Interestingly, the magazine's publishers do not allow this cover to be reproduced. What ideological assumption might be said to underlie this concept of aesthetics? Critics charged that *Time* was following the historical convention of using darker skin tones to connote evil and to imply guilt. In motion pictures made during the first half of this century, when black and Latino performers appeared, they were most often cast in the roles of villains and evil characters. This convention tied into the lingering ideologies of nineteenth-century racial science, in which it was proposed that certain bodily forms and attributes, including darker shades of skin, indicated a predisposition toward social deviance. Though this view was contested in the twentieth century, darker skin tones nonetheless continued to be used as literary, theatrical, and cinematic symbols of evil. Thus, darkness came to connote negative qualities. Hollywood studios even developed special makeup to darken the skin tones of Anglo, European, and light-skinned black and Latino performers to emphasize a character's evil nature.

In this broader context, the darkening of Simpson's skin tone cannot be seen as a purely aesthetic choice but rather an ideological one. Although the magazine cover designers may not have intended to evoke this history of media representations, we live in a culture in which the association of dark tones with evil and the stereotype of black men as criminals still circulate. In addition, because of the codes of the mug shot, it could be said that by simply taking Simpson's image out of the context of the police file and placing it in the public eye, *Time* and *Newsweek* influenced the public to see Simpson as a criminal even before he had been placed on trial.

Like Simpson's mug shot, images often move across social arenas. Documentary images can appear in advertisements, amateur photographs and videotapes can become news images, and news images are sometimes incorporated into art works. Each change in context produces a change in meaning.

How we negotiate the meaning of images

The capacity of images to affect us as viewers and consumers is dependent on the larger cultural meanings they invoke and the social, political, and cultural contexts in which they are viewed. Their meanings lie not within their image elements alone, but are acquired when they are "consumed," viewed, and interpreted. The meanings of each image are multiple; they are created each time it is viewed.

We use many tools to interpret images and create meanings with them, and we often use these tools of looking automatically, without giving them much thought. Images are produced according to social and aesthetic conventions. Conventions are like road signs; we must learn their *codes* for them to make sense; the codes we learn become second nature. Just as we recognize the meaning of most road sign symbols almost immediately, we read, or *decode*, more complex images almost instantly, giving little thought to our process of decoding. For instance, when we see the graphic of a torch that represents the Olympic Games, we do not need to think through the process whereby we come to make that association.

But our associations with symbols and codes and their meanings are far from fixed. Some images demonstrate this process of change quite nicely by playing on accepted conventions of representation to make us aware of the

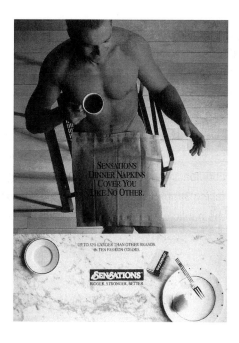

almost arbitrary connections we take for granted between codes and their meanings. The humor of the napkin advertisement on the previous page depends on the viewer's knowledge of the ways that women are typically posed in a state of undress in fashion advertisements. By putting a man in a pose coded as female, and making a joke about what a napkin "covers" on a man, the advertisement puts a humorous spin on the convention. This gender play might persuade potential consumers that the company advertised is not only aware of the gendered nature of advertisement codes and products such as napkins, it is hip enough to make a reflexive joke about it.

We decode images by interpreting clues to intended, unintended, and even merely suggested meanings. These clues may be formal elements such as color, shades of black and white, tone, contrast, composition, depth, perspective, and style of address to the viewer. As we saw in the case of the tonal rendering of O. J. Simpson's mug shot, seemingly neutral elements like tone and color can take on cultural meanings. We also interpret images according to their socio-historical contexts. For example, we may consider when and where the image was made and displayed or the social context in which it is presented. Just as Simpson's mug shot took on new meanings when taken out of police records and reproduced on the cover of popular magazines, so an image appearing as a work of art in a museum takes on quite a different meaning when it is reproduced in an advertisement. We are trained to read for cultural codes such as aspects of the image that signify gendered, racial, or class-specific meanings.

This advertisement by the clothing company Benetton has many layers of meaning. This image denotes a car on fire on a city street. From a formal perspective, it is visually arresting; the flames create a striking image against the dark background, setting an overall tone of danger and tension. Its impact comes in part from what it demonstrates about the power of documentary photography—the capacity of the camera to capture a fleeting moment in time and freeze it. But what does this image mean? Where and when was it taken? What kind of event does it depict? We are offered few clues about its socio-historical elements; there is no caption, no descriptive text through which the viewer might place this picture. Close examination reveals only that a sign in the background appears European and the make of the car may place it within a 1990s time frame.

However, the image's time frame and placement within an advertisement offers other clues. Prior to the 1970s, an image like this one would most likely

have signified civil unrest or urban street crime—issues of national or local concern. In the 1990s, it was more likely that the photograph connoted acts of terrorism as they occurred routinely throughout the world in the late twentieth century. Indeed, in the 1990s the connotation of terrorism was often automatically overlaid onto images of street violence because of widespread concerns, generated in part by the news media, about the apparently random and arbitrary nature of terrorist violence. When this image signifies terrorism, the specificity of its individual elements (which are not identified in the ad) lose their power—it no longer matters where and when the event took place. What matters is the larger symbolic meaning. In addition, the fact that this image is presented in an advertisement adds another level of connotation—the image is intended to transfer upon the name Benetton, and by extension the products offered by Benetton, a sense of social concern for the problems of the world, including terrorism. It could be argued that Benetton selected this generic image to invoke this contemporary issue, and to convey to viewers that Benetton, unlike most other companies, is concerned with current political issues. The ad constructs the idea that Benetton is a company with a political stance that sells clothes to people who care about the realities of contemporary politics on a global scale. We will discuss this sort of advertising strategy at more length in Chapter 7.

This process of interpretation is derived from *semiotics*. Every time we interpret an image around us (to understand what it *signifies*), whether consciously or not, we are using the tools of semiotics to understand its signification, or meaning. The principles of semiotics were formulated by American philosopher Charles Peirce in the nineteenth century and Swiss linguist Ferdinand de Saussure in the early twentieth century. Both proposed important theories. Saussure's writing, however, has had the most influence on the theories of *structuralism* that inform the ways of analyzing visual culture discussed in this book. Language, according to Saussure, is like a game of chess. It depends on conventions and codes for its meanings. At the same time, Saussure argued that the relationship between a word (or the sound of that word when spoken) and things in the world is arbitrary and relative, not fixed. For example, the words "dog" in English, "chien" in French, and "hund" in German all refer to the same kind of animal, hence the relationship between the words and the animal itself is dictated by the conventions of language rather than some natural connection. It was central to Saussure's theory that meanings change according to context and to the rules of language.

Charles Sanders Peirce introduced the idea of a science of signs a bit before Saussure developed his *Course in General Linguistics*. Peirce believed that language and thought are processes of sign interpretation. For Peirce, meaning resides not in the initial perception of a sign, but in the interpretation of the perception and subsequent action based on that perception. Every thought is a sign without meaning until a subsequent thought (what he called an *interpretant*) allows for its interpretation. For example, we perceive an octagonal red sign with the letters STOP inscribed. The meaning lies in the interpretation of the sign and subsequent action (we stop).

Saussure's ideas have since been explored by film scholars and theorists of images, including Roland Barthes, to understand visual systems of representation, and Peirce's concepts subsequently have been used for visual analysis. For instance, film scholars adapted Saussure's method to analyze the language-like systems underlying the meanings produced in films. As with language, films were understood to embody these systems not because their directors or producers intentionally used them, but because the language of film involved a set of rules or codes. There have been many revisions of the application of semiotics to images, but it nonetheless remains an important method of visual analysis. We choose to concentrate in this book on the model of semiotics introduced by Barthes and based on Saussure, since it offers a clear and direct way to understand how images create meaning.

In Barthes's model, in addition to the two levels of meaning of denotation and connotation, there is the *sign*, which is composed of the *signifier*, a sound, written word, or image, and the *signified,* which is the concept evoked by that word/image. In the Benetton ad, one interpretation could be that the burning car is the signifier, and terrorism is the signified. The image (or word) and its meaning together (the signifier and signified together) form the *sign*.

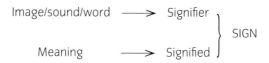

As in the Benetton advertisement, an image or word can have many meanings and constitute many signs. In certain contexts, this image might mean civil unrest, wartime violence, etc., each of which constitutes a different sign. Hence, the production of a sign is dependent on social, historical, and cultural context. It is also dependent on the context in which the image is presented (in a museum gallery or a magazine, for instance), and the viewers who interpret it. We live in a world of signs, and it is the labor of our interpretation that makes meaning of those signs. It is important to remember that we use semiotics all the time without labeling it as such or recognizing our interpretative acts.

Often the meaning of an image is predominantly derived from the objects within the frame. For instance, Marlboro advertisements are well known for their equation of Marlboro cigarettes with masculinity: Marlboro (signifier) + masculinity (signified) = Marlboro as masculinity (sign). The cowboy is featured on horseback or just relaxing with a smoke, surrounded by natural beauty evocative of the unspoiled American West. These advertisements connote rugged individualism and life on the American frontier, when men were "real" men. The Marlboro Man embodies a romanticized idea of freedom that stands in contrast to the more confined lives of most workers. It is testimony to the power of these ads to create the sign of Marlboro as masculinity (and the

Marlboro Man as connoting a lost ideal of masculinity) that many contemporary Marlboro ads dispense with the cowboy altogether and simply show the landscape, in which he exists by implication. This ad campaign also testifies to the ways that objects can become gendered through advertising. It is a little-known fact that Marlboro was marketed as a "feminine" cigarette (with lipstick-red-tipped filters) until the 1950s, when the Marlboro Man made his first appearance. In 1999, the well-known huge Marlboro Man billboard on Sunset Strip in Hollywood was taken down and replaced by an anti-smoking billboard that mocked this icon of masculinity. This remake effectively used the Marlboro Man to create a new sign, that of Marlboro Man = loss of virility, or smoking = impotence.

Our understanding of this image is dependent on our knowledge that cowboys are disappearing from the American landscape, that they are cultural symbols of a particular ideology of American expansionism and the frontier that began to fade with urban industrialization and modernization. We bring to this image cultural knowledge of the changing role of men and the recognition that it indicates a fading stereotype of virility. The Marlboro Man has recently been depicted on a motorcycle, but this updated figure nonetheless derives its meaning from the contrast it presents to the traditional masculine image. Contemporary advertisements of men driving 4 × 4 vehicles and pickup trucks through rough landscapes also reference the codes of the Marlboro Man to suggest an updated version of rugged male individualism. These vehicles, many of the advertisements suggest, provide a new high-tech way to meet the challenges of nature, allowing consumers to explore the wilderness without the physical hardships of being exposed to the elements. Clearly, our interpretation of images often depends upon historical context and the cultural knowledge we bring to them—the conventions they use or play off of, the other images they refer to, and the familiar figures and symbols they include.

We can see how Barthes's model can be useful in examining how images construct meanings. Moreover, the very fact that the sign is divided into a signifier and a signified can show us that a variety of images can convey many different meanings. As we noted, Barthes's model is not the only model of semiotics. For example, Charles Peirce worked with a somewhat different model in which the signifier (word/image) is distinguished not only from the signified (meaning) but also from the *referent*, or the object itself. In addition, Peirce defined categories of signs based on different kinds of relationships between signifiers and signifieds. For instance, Peirce made a distinction between *indexical, iconic,* and *symbolic signs*. These categories have been useful for the study of images, and we will discuss them in Chapter 4.

The value of images

The work of detecting social, cultural, and historical meanings in images often happens without our being aware of the process and is part of the pleasure of looking at images. Some of the information we bring to reading images has to do with what we perceive their value to be in a culture at large. This raises the question: What gives an image social value? Images do not have value in and of themselves, they are awarded different kinds of value—monetary, social, and political—in particular social contexts.

In the art market, the value of a work of art is determined by economic and

Vincent Van Gogh, *Irises*, 1889

cultural factors. The painting of irises on the previous page by Vincent Van Gogh achieved a new level of fame in 1991 when it was sold for an unprecedented price of $53.8 million to the Getty Museum in Los Angeles. The painting in itself does not reveal its worth, rather this is information we bring to an interpretation of it. Why is this painting worth so much? Beliefs about a work's *authenticity* and uniqueness, as well as about its aesthetic style, contribute to its value. The social mythology that surrounds a work of art or its artist can also contribute to its value. *Irises* is considered authentic because it has been proven that it is an original work by Van Gogh, not a copy. Van Gogh's work is valued because it is believed to be among the best examples of the innovative painting style of *modernism* in the late nineteenth century. The myths that surround Van Gogh's life and work also contribute to the value of his works. Most of us know that Van Gogh lived an unhappy and mentally unstable life, that he cut off his ear, and that he committed suicide. We may know more about his life than we know about the technical and aesthetic judgements made by art historians about his work. This information, while extraneous to the work, contributes to its value—partly insofar as it plays into the stereotype or myth of the creative artist as a sensitive figure whose artistic talent is not taught but rather is a "natural" form of creativity that can border on madness.

This painting thus gains its economic value through cultural determinations concerning what society judges to be important in assessing works of art. Many factors contribute to the value of this painting. It is one of relatively few works by the famous painter. It is regarded as authentic because it bears the artist's signature and has been verified by art historians. The artist has international fame and notoriety that go beyond the work itself to include his personality and life history. Finally, Van Gogh's technique is regarded as unique and superior among other works of the period. Part of our recognition of its value has to do simply with its stature within institutions such as museums, art history classes, and art auctions. One way that value is communicated is through the mechanisms of art display. We often know a work of art is important because it is encased in a gilded frame. This Häagen Dazs advertisement humorously comments on this convention by placing the product within such a frame to signify its status as the "masterpiece" of ice creams. We might assume that a work of art is valuable simply because it is on display in a prestigious museum or, as is the case with a certain number of very famous images, such as the *Mona Lisa* by Leonardo da Vinci, because it is displayed behind protective glass and surrounded by crowds of onlookers. In the 1910s, artist

Marcel Duchamp took a jab at this practice of venerating art objects in his "readymades," gallery and museum displays composed of mundane everyday objects such as a bicycle wheel. In April of 1917 Duchamp contributed a urinal, titled *The Fountain* and signed with the pseudonym R. Mutt, to a

The *Mona Lisa* in the Louvre

highly publicized painting exhibition he helped to organize. The exhibition's other organizers were offended by the piece and its clear message about art's value, taste, and the practices of display; they threw it out of the show. Duchamp subsequently became the cause célèbre of *Dada*, a movement that reflexively poked fun at the conventions of high art and museum display conventions.

While the fine art object often is valued because it is unique, it also is valued because it can be reproduced for popular consumption. For example, Van

Gogh's paintings have been reproduced endlessly on posters, postcards, coffee mugs, and T-shirts. Ordinary consumers can own a copy of the highly valued originals. Hence, the value of the original results not only from its uniqueness but from its being the source from which reproductions are made. The manufacturers who produce art reproductions (posters, T-shirts, greeting cards, etc.) and the consumers who purchase and display these items give value to the work of art by making it available to many people as an item of popular culture. We will discuss this aspect of image reproduction further in Chapter 4.

There are other kinds of values that adhere to images in our culture—for example, the value of an image to provide information and make distant events accessible to large audiences. As images are increasingly easy to generate and reproduce electronically, the values traditionally attributed to them have changed. In any given culture, we use different criteria to evaluate various media forms. Whereas we evaluate paintings according to the criteria of uniqueness, authenticity, and market values, we may award value to television news images, for instance, on the basis of their capacity to provide information and accessibility. The value of a television news image lies in its capacity to be transmitted quickly and widely to a vast number of geographically dispersed television screens.

Chinese student stopping tanks at Tiananmen Square, Beijing, 1989

The television news image on the previous page of the student protest at Tiananmen Square in Beijing in 1989 can be said to be a valuable image, although the criteria for its value have nothing to do with the art market or its monetary value. The value of this image is based in part on its specialness (it depicts a key moment in an event during which media coverage was restricted) and the speed with which it was transmitted around the world to provide information about that event. Its value is also derived from its powerful depiction of the courage of one student before the machinery of military power. Whereas its denotative meaning is simply a young man stopping a tank, its connotative meaning is commonly understood to be the importance of individual actions in the face of injustice. This image thus has value not as a singular image (once broadcast, it was not one image but millions of images on many different TV sets), but through its speed of transmission, informative value, and its political statement. We can say that it is culturally valuable because it makes a profound statement about human will, and has thus become an image *icon*.

Image icons

This image of the lone student at Tiananmen Square has value as an icon of world-wide struggles for democracy, precisely because many students lost their lives in the protests. An icon is an image that refers to something outside of its individual components, something (or someone) that has great symbolic meaning for many people. Icons are often perceived to represent universal concepts, emotions, and meanings. Thus, an image produced in a specific culture, time, and place might be interpreted as having universal meaning and the capacity to evoke similar responses across all cultures and in all viewers. For example, the image of mother and child is ubiquitous in Western art. It is widely believed to represent universal concepts of maternal emotion, the essential bond between a mother and her offspring, and the dependence of that child upon her. This image is perceived as an icon of motherhood and, by extension, the importance of motherhood throughout the world and in all human history. The sheer number of paintings created with a mother and child theme throughout the history of Western art attests not simply to the centrality of the Madonna figure in Christianity but also to the idea that the bond between mother and child represented

in images like this is universally understood to be natural, not culturally constructed.

What would it mean to question the assumptions underpinning these concepts of the universal? It would mean to look at the cultural, historical, and social meanings that are specific in these images. There is an increased understanding that these concepts of the universal were actually restricted to specific privileged groups. Icons do not represent individuals, but nor do they represent universal values. The mother and child motif present in these two paintings by Italian painter Raphael and Dutch painter Joos van Cleve can be read not as evidence of universal ideals of motherhood but as an indicator of specific cultural values of motherhood and the role of women in Western culture in the sixteenth century, particularly in Europe. Furthermore, these images situated these figures within particular cultural landscapes, Raphael's Madonna before an Italian landscape, and van Cleve's surrounded by symbols of Dutch culture.

It is in relationship to this tradition of Madonna and child paintings that more recent images of women and children gain meaning. For instance, the photograph on the next page by Dorothea Lange depicts a woman, who is also

Raphael, *The Small Cowper Madonna*, *c.*1505

Joos van Cleve, *Virgin and Child*, 1525

Dorothea Lange, *Migrant Mother, Nipomo, California*, 1936

apparently a mother, during the California migration of the 1930s. This photograph is regarded as an iconic image of the Great Depression in the United States. It is famous because it evokes both the despair and the perseverance of those who survived the hardships of that time. Yet the image gains much of its meaning from its implicit reference to the history of artistic depictions of women and their children, such as Madonna and child images, and its difference from them. This mother is hardly a nurturing figure. She is distracted. Her children cling to her and burden her thin frame. She looks not at her children but outward as if toward her future—one seemingly with little promise. This image derives its meaning largely from a viewer's knowledge of the historical moment it represents. At the same time, it makes a statement about the complex role of motherhood that is informed by its traditional representation. Like the earlier images, this photograph denotes a mother with children, but it casts this social relationship in terms of hunger, poverty, struggle, loss, and strength. Thus, it can be read in a number of ways.

Image icons can also evoke pleasure and desire. One could argue, for instance, that this image of Marilyn Monroe is an icon of glamour. Monroe embodies many of the stereotypical ingredients for twentieth-century American concepts of feminine beauty and sexuality—her wavy blond hair, open smile, and full figure. Concepts of glamour and sexiness form the basis of most advertising. What counts as glamorous or sexy, however, changes according to shifts in cultural ideas about beauty and visual pleasure. The cultural preference for full-figured women was replaced in the late twentieth century by an idealization of a thin or athletic body. As John Berger has written, glamour is the quality of being envied.[4] Monroe's glamour is derived in part through the combination of her apparent accessibility to the camera (and, by extension, to the viewer) through the medium of photography, and the unattainable, distant quality of her image. We want what she has precisely because it appears to be beyond our reach.

Artist Andy Warhol made works about the commodity culture that rendered women like Marilyn Monroe cultural icons whose images were familiar to virtually the entire nation. Warhol took an iconic, glamorous image of Marilyn Monroe and printed multiple versions of it into a colorful grid. His *Marilyn Diptych* (1962) on the next page comments not only upon the star's iconic status as a glamour figure, but also on the role of the star as media commodity—as a product of the entertainment industry that could be infinitely reproduced for mass consumption. Warhol's work emphasizes one of the most important aspects of contemporary images: the capacity to reproduce them in many different contexts, thereby changing their meaning and altering their value—and that of the objects or people they represent—as commodities. In this work, the multiple images of Monroe emphasize that cultural icons can and must be mass-distributed in order for them to have mass appeal. These copies do not refer back to the original so much as they indicate the endless reproducibility of Monroe as a mass-produced object to be consumed.

To call an image an icon raises the question of context. For whom is this image iconic and for whom is it not? These images of motherhood and glamour are specific to particular cultures

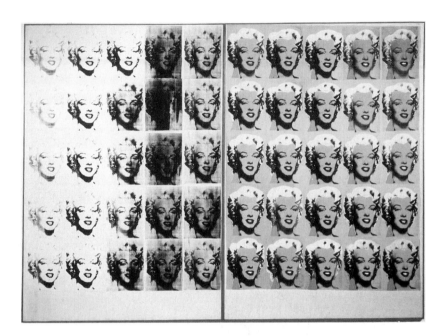

Andy Warhol, *Marilyn Diptych*, 1962

at particular moments in time. One could regard them as indicators of the cultural values attributed to women throughout history, and the restrictive roles women have often been allocated (mother or sex symbol, virgin or vamp). As we have noted, images have divergent meanings in different cultural and historical contexts.

When, for instance, Benetton produced this advertisement of a black woman nursing a white child, a range of interpretations were possible. This advertisement was published throughout Europe, but magazines in the United States refused to run it. The image can be understood in the history of images of mother and child, although its meaning is contingent on the viewer's assumption, on the basis of the contrast of their skin color, that this woman is not the child's biological mother but its caretaker. While in certain contexts, this image might connote racial harmony, in the United States it carried other connotations, most troubling the history of slavery in the United States and the use of black women slaves as "wet nurses" to breast-feed the white children of their owners. Thus, the intended meaning of this image as an icon of an idealized interracial mother-child relationship is not easily conveyed in a context where the image's meanings are *overdetermined* by historical factors. Similarly, the classical art history image of Madonna and child may not serve

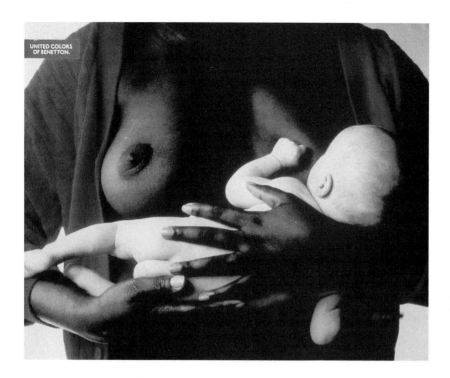

as an icon for motherhood in many other cultures, but rather as an example of specifically Western and particularly Christian beliefs about women's role as mothers.

When images acquire the status of icons, which are commonly understood, they also can become the object of humorous or ironic interpretations. For instance, pop star Madonna gained notoriety by playing off both Madonna and Marilyn Monroe. Madonna borrowed and reworked the elements of both these cultural icons. Not only did she use the name Madonna, early in her career she wore and used as props various symbols of Catholicism, such as crosses. Similarly, at one point she assumed Monroe's blond hair color and the look of her glamorous 1940s wardrobe. Through these acts of cultural *appropriation*, Madonna both acquired the power of these icons and reflected *ironically* on their meaning in the climate of the 1980s and 1990s. In contemporary culture, many cultural icons are thus reused, parodied, and ironically updated.

To interpret images is to examine the assumptions that we and others bring to them, and to decode the visual language that they "speak." All images

Madonna in one of her many identities

contain layers of meaning that include their formal aspects, their cultural and socio-historical references, the ways they make reference to the images that precede and surround them, and the contexts in which they are displayed. Reading and interpreting images is one way that we, as viewers, contribute to the process of assigning value to the culture in which we live. Practices of looking, then, are not passive acts of consumption. By looking at and engaging with images in the world, we influence the meanings and uses assigned to the images that fill our day-to-day lives. In the next chapter, we will examine the many ways that viewers create meaning when they engage in looking.

Notes

1. See Simon Schama, *The Embarrassment of Riches: An Interpretation of Dutch Culture in the Golden Age* (Berkeley and London: University of California Press, 1988), ch. 3.

2. See Michel Foucault, *This Is Not a Pipe*, with illustrations and letters by René Magritte, translated and edited by James Harkness (Berkeley and London: University of California Press, 1983).

3. Roland Barthes, "Rhetoric of the Image," from *Image Music Text*, translated by Stephen Heath (New York: Hill and Wang, 1977), 34.

4. John Berger, *Ways of Seeing* (New York and London: Penguin, 1972), 131.

Further Reading

Roland Barthes. *Mythologies*. Translated by Annette Lavers. New York: Hill and Wang, [1957] 1972.

——*Elements of Semiology*. Translated by Annette Lavers and Colin Smith. New York: Hill and Wang, 1967.

——"The Photographic Message" and "Rhetoric of the Image." In *Image Music Text*. Translated by Stephen Heath. New York: Hill and Wang, 1977.

——*Camera Lucida: Reflections on Photography*. Translated by Richard Howard. New York: Hill and Wang, 1981.

John Berger. *Ways of Seeing*. New York and London: Penguin, 1972.

Inguar Bergstrom. *Dutch Still-Life Painting in the Seventeenth Century*. London: Faber and Faber, 1956.

Norman Bryson. *Looking at the Overlooked: Four Essays on Still Life Painting*. Cambridge, Mass. and London: Harvard University Press, 1990.

Victor Burgin, ed. *Thinking Photography*. London: Macmillan, 1982.

Michel Foucault. *This Is Not a Pipe*. With illustrations and letters by René Magritte. Translated and edited by James Harkness. Berkeley and London: University of California Press, 1983.

Henry Giroux. "Consuming Social Change: The United Colors of Benetton." In *Disturbing Pleasures: Learning Popular Culture*. New York and London: Routledge, 1994.

Stuart Hall, ed. *Representation: Cultural Representations and Signifying Practices*. Thousand Oaks, Calif. and London: Sage, 1997.

Terence Hawkes. *Structuralism and Semiotics*. Berkeley and London: University of California Press, 1977.

Floyd Merrel. *Semiosis in the Postmodern Age*. Toronto: University of Toronto Press, 1995.

——*Peirce, Signs, and Meaning*. Toronto: University of Toronto Press, 1997.

Christian Metz. *Film Language: A Semiotics of the Cinema*. Translated by Michael Taylor. Chicago and London: University of Chicago Press, [1974] 1991.

Nicholas Mirzoeff. *An Introduction to Visual Culture*. New York and London: Routledge, 1999.

Richard Robin. *Annotated Catalog of the Papers of Charles Sanders Peirce*. Bloomington: Indiana University Press, 1998. On-line at: ⟨www.iupui.edu/%7Epeirce/web/index.htm⟩.

Ferdinand de Saussure. *Course in General Linguistics*. Contributor; Charles Bally. Translated by Roy Harris. Chicago: Open Court Publishing, [1915] 1988.

Simon Schama. *The Embarrassment of Riches: An Interpretation of Dutch Culture in the Golden Age*. Berkeley and London: University of California Press, 1988.

Thomas A. Sebeck. *Signs: An Introduction to Semiotics*. Toronto: University of Toronto Press, 1995.

Allan Sekula. "On the Invention of Photographic Meaning." In *Thinking Photography*. Edited by Victor Burgin. London: Macmillan, 1982, 84–109.

Kaja Silverman. *The Subject of Semiotics*. New York and Oxford: Oxford University Press, 1983.

Susan Sontag. *On Photography*. New York: Delta, 1977.

Mary Anne Staniszewski. *Believing is Seeing: Creating the Culture of Art*. New York and London: Penguin, 1995.

John Storey, ed. *Cultural Theory and Popular Culture: A Reader*. Athens: University of Georgia Press, 1998.

Peter Wollen. *Signs and Meaning in the Cinema*. London: British Film Institute, 1969.

Viewers Make Meaning 2

Images generate meanings. Yet, the meanings of a work of art or media image do not, strictly speaking, lie in the work itself where they were placed by the producer waiting for viewers to uncover them. Rather, meanings are produced through a complex social relationship that involves at least two elements besides the image itself and its producer: (1) how viewers interpret or experience the image and (2) the context in which an image is seen. Although images have what we call dominant or shared meanings, they can also be interpreted and used in ways that do not conform to these meanings.

It is important to recognize that works of art and media rarely "speak" to everyone universally. Rather, an image "speaks" to specific sets of viewers who happen to be tuned in to some aspect of the image, such as style, content, the world it constructs, or the issues it raises. When we say that an image speaks to us, we might also say that we recognize ourselves within the cultural group or audience imagined by the image. Just as viewers create meaning from images, images also construct audiences.

Producers' intended meanings

Most if not all images have a meaning that is preferred by their producers. Advertisers, for example, conduct audience research to try to ensure that the meanings they want to convey about a particular product are the ones viewers will interpret in the product's advertisements. Artists, graphic designers, filmmakers, and other image producers create advertisements and many other images with the intent that we read them in a certain way. Analyzing images according to the intentions of their producers, however, is rarely a completely useful strategy. We usually have no way of knowing for certain what a producer intended his or her image to mean. Furthermore, finding out a producer's intentions often does not tell us much about the image, since intentions may not match up with what viewers actually take away from an image or text. People often see an image differently from how it is intended to be seen, either because they bring experiences and associations to a particular image that were not anticipated by its producer, or because the meanings they derive are informed by the context (or setting) in which an image is seen. For example, we could say that the intentions of the producers of the many advertising images in an urban context such as this, may be seen by viewers in different ways. The visual clutter of the context alone may affect how viewers interpret these images, in addition to juxtapositions with other images. Many contemporary images, such as advertisements and television images, are viewed in a huge variety of contexts, each of which may affect their meaning. In addition, viewers themselves bring a particular set of cultural associations with them which will affect their individual interpretation of an image.

This does not mean that viewers wrongly interpret images, or that images are unsuccessful or fail to persuade viewers. Rather, meanings are created in part when, where, and by whom images are consumed, and not only when, where, and by whom they are produced. An artist or producer may make an image or media *text*, but he or she is not in full control of the meanings that

are subsequently seen in their work. Advertisers invest a lot of time and money in studying the impact of their advertisements on audiences precisely because they understand that they cannot have full control over the meanings their images will produce. Researching how different audiences interpret and use the images they encounter affords image producers a greater ability to anticipate received meanings; however, it will still not provide them with full control over the meaning of the image in various contexts and among different viewers.

Let us consider the following example. An episode of the syndicated hit television series *M*A*S*H* is watched by a working-class teenager in a suburb of Detroit in his family's basement recreation room in 1976, and then by a middle-aged shopkeeper watching on a battery-operated television outside her open-air shop along the Amazon River in a village in Brazil ten years later. We can assume that the meanings each viewer takes away from the show vary. Yet neither viewer's interpretation of the show is more or less accurate than the other's. In both cases, meanings are affected by the social orientation of the viewer and by the context of viewing. Some of the factors that impact meaning in these two examples include the age, class, gender, and regional and cultural identity of the respective viewers; the political and social events in their respective worlds when the show airs; and the respective locations and time periods of the viewings in relation to the time of the show's original production. Though it was set during the Korean War, *M*A*S*H* references events of the 1970s, in particular the Vietnam War, that would have a very different resonance for a US citizen during that same decade than for someone watching the show in Brazil a decade later.

As we discussed in Chapter 1, the interpretative work of *semiotics* shows us that the meaning of images changes according to different context, times, and viewers. Thus, we could say that the semiotic meaning of *M*A*S*H* will change in different viewing contexts, that elements of the program will create different *signs*. Through this shift in focus, we can also see the importance of the perceived or received meanings of the viewer over that of the intended meaning of the producer. An image creates meaning in the moment that it is received by a viewer, and interpreted. Hence, we can say that meanings are not inherent in images. Rather, meanings are the product of a complex social interaction among image, viewers, and context. Dominant meanings—the meanings that tend to predominate within a given culture—emerge out of this complex social interaction.

Aesthetics and taste

All images are subject to judgement about their qualities (such as beauty) and their capacity to have an impact on viewers. The criteria used to interpret and give value to images depend upon cultural *codes*, or shared concepts, of what makes an image pleasing or unpleasant, shocking or banal, interesting or boring. As we explained above, these qualities do not reside in the image, but depend upon the contexts in which it is viewed, the codes that prevail in a society, and the viewer who is making that judgement. All viewer interpretations involve two fundamental concepts of value— *aesthetics* and *taste*.

Aesthetics usually refers to philosophical notions about the perception of beauty and ugliness. Philosophers have debated for centuries the question of whether such qualities are within the object itself or exist solely within the mind of the viewer. For instance, the eighteenth-century philosopher Immanuel Kant wrote that beauty can be seen as a category separate from judgement or subjectivity. Kant believed that pure beauty could be found in nature and art, and that it is universal rather than specific to particular cultural or individual codes. In other words, he felt that certain things inevitably and objectively are beautiful.

Today, however, the idea of aesthetics has moved away from the belief that beauty resides within a particular object or image. We no longer think of beauty as a universally accepted set of qualities. Contemporary concepts of aesthetics emphasize the ways that the criteria for what is beautiful and what is not are based on taste, which is not innate but rather culturally specific. The phrase "beauty is in the eye of the beholder" refers to this idea that the quality of beauty is dependent on individual interpretation.

Taste, however, is not just a matter of individual interpretation. Rather, taste is informed by experiences relating to one's class, cultural background, education, and other aspects of identity. When we speak of taste, or say that someone "has taste," we are usually using culturally specific and class-based concepts. When we say people have good taste we often mean that they participate and are educated in middle-class or upper-class notions of what is tasteful, whether or not they actually inhabit these class positions. Taste thus can be a marker of education and an awareness of elite cultural values. "Bad taste" is often regarded as a product of ignorance of what is deemed "quality" or "tasteful" within a society. Taste, in this understanding, is something that can be learned through contact with cultural institutions (art museums or

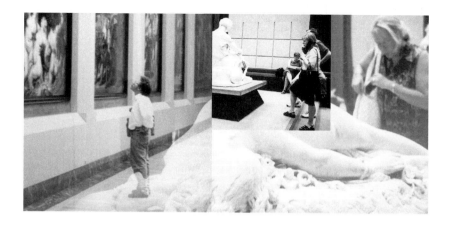

"tasteful" stores, for example) that instruct us in what is in good taste and what is not.

Notions of taste also provide the basis for the idea of *connoisseurship*. The image of a connoisseur evokes a "well-bred" person, most likely a "gentleman" who possesses "good taste" and knows the difference between a good work of art and a bad one. A connoisseur is considered to be an authority on beauty and aesthetics, who is more capable than others to pass judgement on the quality of cultural objects. This class-based notion of taste as a "discriminating" skill presents it as something that is natural to the connoisseur, rather than a skill learned through particular social and educational contexts. The idea of natural taste is a myth that masks the fact that taste is learned.

In the 1970s, French sociologist Pierre Bourdieu studied the responses of a range of French subjects to questions about taste. He concluded that taste is not inherent in particular people, but rather is learned through exposure to social and cultural institutions that promote certain class-based assumptions about correct taste. Institutions like museums function not only to educate people about the history of art, but to instill in them a sense of what is tasteful and what is not, what is "real" art and what is not. Through these institutions, working- and upper-class people alike learn to be "discriminating" viewers and consumers of images and objects. That is, they are able, regardless of their own class position, to rank images and objects according to a system of taste steeped in class-based values.

In Bourdieu's theory, taste is a gatekeeping structure that enforces class boundaries. Bourdieu's work has indicated ways in which all aspects of life are interconnected through social webs in a kind of *habitus*—that our taste in art is related to our taste in music, food, fashion, furniture, movies, sports, and leisure activities, and is in turn related to our profession, class status, and educational level. Taste may often work to the detriment of people of lower classes because it relegates objects and ways of seeing associated with their lifestyles as less worthy of attention and respect. What's more, the very things deemed tasteful—works of fine art, for example—are off limits to most consumers.

These distinctions between different kinds of culture have traditionally been understood as the difference between *high* and *low culture*. As we noted in the Introduction, the most common definition of culture throughout history was the idea of the best of a given culture. This definition was highly class-based, with those cultural pursuits of the ruling class seen as high culture, and the activities of the working class as low culture. Thus, high culture meant fine art, classical music, opera, and ballet. Low culture was a term used for comic strips, television, and at least initially, for the cinema. However, in recent years, this division of high and low has not only been heavily criticized as upper-class snobbery, but as cultural categories undergo constant change, it has become much more difficult to uphold. The distinction between fine art and popular culture has been consistently blurred in the art movements of the late twentieth century, from *Pop Art* to styles of *postmodernism*. (We will discuss this work in Chapters 6 and 7.) In addition, the collection of certain kinds of cultural artifacts, such as *kitsch*, which are valued precisely because they once evoked "bad" taste, blurs any distinction between high and low. Furthermore, analyses of B movies and other cultural products such as popular romance novels that were once regarded as low culture have emphasized the impact and value of contemporary popular culture among specific communities and individuals, who interpret these texts to strengthen their communities or to challenge oppression. We cannot understand a culture without analyzing its production and consumption of all forms of culture, from high to low.

Reading images as ideological subjects

Taste can be seen as a natural expression or logical extension of a culture's values and interests. We come to accept it unquestioningly. When something like taste is naturalized, it embodies the *ideologies* of its context and time. As we discussed in Chapter 1, any time that something within a social and cultural context is perceived to be "natural" in some way, it is an aspect of ideology, since ideology defines ideas about how life should be. Because our lives are steeped in ideologies, which are often in tension with each other, it is easy not to recognize them as such. This is because societies function by masking their ideologies as "natural" systems of value or belief. As a consequence, it is easier for us to recognize ideologies of other times and cultures than within our own.

Much of the way that ideology is conceived today originates with its formulation in the theories of Karl Marx. Marxism is a theory that analyzes both the role of economics in the progress of history and the ways that capitalism works in terms of class relations. According to Marx, who wrote in the nineteenth century during the rise of industrialism and *capitalism* in the Western world, those who own the *means of production* are also in control of the ideas and viewpoints produced and circulated in a society's media venues. Thus, in Marx's terms, the dominant social classes that own or control the newspapers, and, since Marx's time, the television networks and the film industry, are able to control the content generated by these media forms. We will discuss Marx's ideas in relationship to the mass media and mass culture in Chapter 5, and his theories of capitalism in relation to consumer culture in Chapter 6. Here, we look at how Marx's ideas, and the ideas that they inspired in subsequent theorists, can help us understand how we interpret images as ideological *subjects*. Marx thought of ideology as a kind of *false consciousness* that was spread by dominant powers among the masses, who are coerced by those in power to mindlessly buy into the belief systems that allow industrial capitalism to thrive. Marx's idea of false consciousness, which has since been rejected by many theorists, emphasized the ways that people who are oppressed by a particular economic system, such as capitalism, are encouraged to believe in it anyway. Many now view his concept of ideology as overly totalizing and too focused on a top-down notion of ideology.

There have been at least two significant challenges to the traditional Marxist definition of ideology which have shaped subsequent theories about media culture and looking practices. One challenge came from the French Marxist theorist Louis Althusser in the 1960s. He insisted that ideology cannot be dismissed as a simple distortion of the realities of capitalism. Rather, he argued, "ideology represents the imaginary relationship of individuals to their real conditions of existence."[1] Althusser moved the term "ideology" away from its association with false consciousness. For Althusser, ideology does not simply reflect the conditions of the world, whether falsely or not. Rather, it is the case that without ideology we would have no means of thinking about or experiencing that thing we call "reality." Ideology is the necessary representational means through which we come to experience and make sense of reality.

Althusser's modifications to the term "ideology" are crucial to visual studies because they emphasize the importance of *representation* (and hence images) to all aspects of social life, from the economic to the cultural. By the term "imaginary," Althusser does not mean false or mistaken. Rather, he draws from *psychoanalysis* to emphasize that ideology is a set of ideas and beliefs, shaped through the *unconscious*, in relationship to other social forces, such as the economy and institutions. By living in society, we live in ideology. Althusser's theories have been especially useful in film studies, where they helped theorists to analyze how media texts invite people to recognize themselves and identify with a position of authority or omniscience while watching films. In Chapter 3, we will discuss the importance of psychoanalysis to the study of image *spectators*.

Althusser stated that we are "hailed" or summoned by ideologies, which recruit us as their "authors" and their essential subject. By saying that ideologies speak to us and in the process recruit us as "authors," he refers to the way that we become/are the subject that we are addressed as. This is called *interpellation*, which refers to a process by which we are constructed by the ideologies that speak to us every day through language and images. In Althusser's terms, therefore, we are not so much unique individuals but rather we are "always already" subjects—spoken by the ideological discourses, into which we are born and are asked to find our place. In this light, images interpellate or hail us as viewers, and in so doing designate the kind of viewer they intend us to be. An overt example is this AT&T advertisement which asks its viewers, "Have you ever tucked your kid in from a phone booth? Have you ever paid a toll without slowing down? YOU WILL." In this ad, viewers are spoken to directly. We are told with certainty what our lives will look like, in a narrative that speaks with determination about all technological change being about progress. For instance, we could ask, is tucking in one's child from a phone booth a good thing?, but the advertisement does not. A particular kind of viewer is being constituted by this advertisement—someone who is a

Have you ever tucked your kid in from a phone booth?

YOU WILL

Have you ever paid a toll without slowing down?

AT&T

professional, on the move, who values work over time. This advertisement speaks to viewers as if they all have access to a broad range of communication technologies. In doing so, it hails or interpellates all viewers into this social category.

Althusser's concepts of ideology have been very influential, but they can be seen as very disempowering as well. If we are always already defined as subjects, and are interpellated to be who we are, then there is little hope for social change. In other words, the idea that we are already constructed as subjects does not allow us to feel that we have any *agency* in our lives. Another challenge to traditional concepts of ideology has emphasized that it is important for us to think in terms of ideologies in the plural. For example, the concept of a singular mass ideology makes it difficult to recognize how people in economically and socially disadvantaged positions really do challenge or resist dominant ideology. Long before Althusser, an Italian Marxist, Antonio Gramsci, had already introduced the concept of *hegemony* in place of the concept of domination in order to help us to think about this kind of *resistance*. Gramsci lived and wrote mostly during the 1920s and 1930s in Italy, but his ideas were taken up and became highly influential in the late twentieth century. There are two central aspects to Gramsci's definition of hegemony: that dominant ideologies are often presented as "common sense" and that dominant ideologies are in tension with other forces and constantly in flux.

The term "hegemony" emphasizes that power is not wielded by one class over another; rather, power is negotiated among all classes of people, who struggle with and against one another in the economic, social, political, and ideological arenas in which they live and work. Unlike domination, which is won by the ruling class through universal force, hegemony is constructed through the push and pull among all levels of a society over meanings, laws, and other aspects of a given society. No single class of people "has" hegemony; rather, hegemony is a state or condition of a culture arrived at through a negotiation or struggle over meanings, laws, and social relationships. Similarly, no one group of people ultimately "has" power; rather, power is a relationship within which classes struggle. One of the most important aspects of hegemony is that these relationships are constantly changing, hence dominant ideologies must constantly be reaffirmed in a culture precisely because the social existence of many people's daily lives can work against it. It also allows for *counter-hegemonic* forces, such as political movements or subversive cultural elements, to emerge and to question the status quo of how things are. The concept of hegemony and the related term "negotiation" allow us to acknowledge the role that people may play in challenging the status quo and effecting social change in ways that may not favor the interests of the marketplace. Within visual studies, Gramsci's concept of hegemony has been useful among critics who want to emphasize the role of image consumers in influencing the meanings and uses of popular culture in ways that do not benefit the interests of producers and the media industry.

How can Gramsci's concept of hegemony and counter-hegemony help us to understand how people create and make meaning of images? Artist Barbara Kruger specializes in taking "found" photographic images and using text to give them ironic meanings. In this work, created in 1981, she takes the well-known image of the atomic bomb and works to change its ideological meaning. The image of an atomic bomb indicates a broad set of ideologies, from the spectacle of high technology to anxiety about its tremendous capacity to destroy, which depend on the context in which the image is viewed. It could be argued that the bomb itself and images of it are indicative of a particular set of ideological assumptions that emerged from the Cold War about the rights of nations to build destructive weapons and the so-called "need" to create more and more destructive weapons in the name of protecting one's country. In the 1940s and 1950s, an image of the bomb was thus likely to uphold many ideas about the primacy of Western science and technology and the role of the United States and the USSR as superpowers. By the end of the twentieth century, however, it is most likely that this image would represent a cautionary reflection on the destructive weapons that exist throughout the world.

Kruger uses text in this image to comment upon these ideological assumptions about Western science. Who is the "you" of this image? We could say that Kruger is speaking to those with power, perhaps those who helped to create the atomic bomb and those who approved it. But she is also speaking in a larger sense to the "you" of Western science and philosophy, that allows a maniacal idea (bombing people) to acquire the validation of rational science. In this work, the image is awarded new meaning through the bold, accusatory statement spread across it. Here, the text dictates the meaning of the image, and provokes the viewer, in often oblique ways, to look at it differently. Kruger's work functions as a counter-hegemonic statement about the dominant ideology of science.

Barbara Kruger, *Untitled*, 1981

People use systems of representation to experience, interpret, and make sense of the conditions of their lives both as image-makers and as viewers. In essence, we construct ideological selves through a network of representations—many of them visual—that includes television, film, photography, popular magazines, art, and fashion. Media images and popular culture interpellate us as viewers, defining within their mode of address, style of presentation, and subject matter the ideological subjects to whom they speak, yet we also negotiate that process ourselves.

It is important, when thinking about ideologies and how they function, to keep in mind the complicated interactions of powerful systems of belief and the things that very different kinds of viewers bring to their experiences. If we give too much weight to the idea of a dominant ideology, we risk portraying viewers as cultural dupes who can be "force fed" ideas and values. At the same time, if we overemphasize the potential array of interpretations viewers can make of any given image, we can make it seem as if all viewers have the power to interpret images any way they want, and that these interpretations will be meaningful in their social world. In this perspective, we would lose any sense of dominant power and its attempt to organize our ways of looking. Meanings of images are created in a complex relationship among producer, viewer, image or text, and social context. Because meanings are produced out of this relationship, there are limits to the interpretive agency of any one member of this group.

Encoding and decoding

Images present to viewers clues about their dominant meaning. A dominant meaning can be the interpretation that an image's producers intended viewers to make. More often, though, it can be the meaning that most viewers within a given cultural setting will arrive at, regardless of the producers' intentions. All images are both *encoded* and *decoded*. An image or object is encoded with meaning in its creation or production; it is further encoded when it is placed in a given setting or context. It is then decoded by viewers when it is consumed by them. These processes work in tandem. So, for instance, a television show is encoded with meaning by the writers, producers, and the production apparatus that allows it to be made, and it is then decoded by television viewers according to their particular set of cultural assumptions and their viewing context.

Stuart Hall has written that there are three positions that viewers can take as decoders of cultural images and artifacts:

(1) *Dominant-hegemonic reading*. They can identify with the hegemonic position and receive the dominant message of an image or text (such as a television show) in an unquestioning manner.

(2) *Negotiated reading*. They can negotiate an interpretation from the image and its dominant meanings.

(3) *Oppositional reading*. Finally, they can take an oppositional position, either by completely disagreeing with the ideological position embodied in an image or rejecting it altogether (for example, by ignoring it).[2]

Viewers who take the dominant-hegemonic position can be said to decode images in a relatively passive manner. But it can be argued that few viewers actually consume images in this manner, because there is no mass culture that can satisfy all viewers' culturally specific experiences, memories, and desires. The second and third positions, negotiation and opposition, are more useful to us and deserve further explanation.

The term "negotiation" invokes the process of trade. We can think of it as a kind of bargaining over meaning that takes place among viewer, image, and context. We use the term "negotiation" in a metaphorical sense to say that we often "haggle" with the dominant meanings of an image when we interpret it. The process of deciphering an image always takes place at both the conscious and unconscious levels. It brings into play our own memories, knowledge, and cultural frameworks as well as the image itself and the dominant meanings that cling to it. Interpretation is thus a mental process of acceptance and rejection of the meanings and associations that adhere to a given image through the force of dominant ideologies. In this process, viewers actively struggle with dominant meanings, allowing culturally and personally specific meanings to transform and even override the meanings imposed by producers and broader social forces. The term "negotiation" allows us to see how cultural interpretation is a struggle in which consumers are active meaning-makers and not merely passive recipients in the process of decoding images.

Let us take, for example, the television show *Who Wants to Be a Millionaire*, which has versions in many countries and is based on the premise that any ordinary person can win large amounts of money with the proper amount of trivial knowledge and luck. The show stages a spectacle of both desire and greed, and is encoded by its producers with the meaning that we all desire large amounts of money. The show aims to create the fantasy for viewers that they too could win. A dominant hegemonic reading of the show would agree with its encoded values that money increases one's happiness and social status and that any viewer could potentially be on the show and win. However, the show has come under fire, even while it is immensely popular, for representing crass commercialism and the further debasement of mainstream popular culture. Many viewers have thus engaged in a negotiated reading of the show, so that even while they may enjoy watching it, they see it as an indicator of what's wrong with contemporary culture. Furthermore, the show has been criticized for equating knowledge with trivia. An oppositional reading might read the show critically as an example of how capitalism creates the impression that everyone has equal potential to succeed when in fact it is fundamental to the structure of capitalism that only some can accede to power and wealth. An oppositional reading might note, for instance, how the American version of the show has been criticized for having mostly white male contestants, thereby reflecting the structures of privilege in society.

To varying degrees, all cultures are in flux and constantly in the process of being reinvented through cultural representations. This is in part an effect of the economics and ideologies of the free market, which demand that participants negotiate not only to trade in goods, services, and capital, but to produce meaning and value in the objects and representations of cultural products. Hence conflicting ideologies coexist in tension. There is a constant reworking of hegemonic structures, which allows both for contradictory ideological messages and new, potentially subversive messages produced through culture products. At the same time, semiotics shows us that viewers create meaning from images, objects, and texts, and that meanings are not fixed within them. Most images we see are caught up in dominant ideologies, however, the value of negotiation as an analytic concept is that it allows space for the different subjectivities, identities, and pleasures of audiences.

Appropriation and oppositional readings

Of the three different modes of engagement with popular culture defined by Stuart Hall (dominant-hegemonic, negotiated, and oppositional), the category of oppositional readings raises perhaps the most complicated set of questions. What does it mean to read a television show in an oppositional way? Why does this matter? Does it make any difference that viewers may often read against the intended meaning of an image? The lone oppositional reading of a single viewer may mean nothing compared to the popularity of a particular cultural product. This consideration raises the important issue of power: Whose readings matter? Who ultimately controls the meanings of a given image or text? There are many ways that oppositional readings of popular culture demonstrate the complicated dance of power relations in contemporary societies, the tension of hegemonic and counter-hegemonic forces. The constant dynamic of culture comes in part from the ongoing exchange among dominant, negotiated, and oppositional practices.

While the advent of a broad array of computer technologies, the Internet, and home video cameras has meant that many more people have access to the technical equipment to produce images and cultural products, the fact remains that the vast amount of cultural production and image production is done through the entertainment and business industries. Hence, the primary engagement of the average citizen with everyday images is through viewership, not production. However, as we stated before, viewers are not simply passive recipients of the intended message of public images and cultural products such as films and television shows. They have a variety of means to engage with images and make meaning from them. This negotiation with popular culture is referred to as "the art of making do," a phrase that implies that while viewers may not be able to change the cultural products they observe, they can "make do" by interpreting, rejecting, or reconfiguring the cultural texts they see. As stated earlier, an oppositional reading can also take the form of dismissal or rejection—turning off the TV set, declaring boredom, or turning the page. But it can also take the form of making do with, or making a new use for, the objects and artifacts of a culture. This process is called *appropriation*. Appropriation can be a form of oppositional production and reading, although it is not always so. The term "appropriation" is traditionally defined as taking something for oneself without consent. To appropriate is, in essence, to steal. Cultural appropriation is the process of "borrowing" and changing the meaning of cultural products, slogans, images, or elements of fashion.

Cultural appropriation has been used quite effectively by artists seeking to make a statement that opposes the dominant ideology. A good example is the

READ MY LIPS

KISS IN

Friday, April 29:
9:00 pm   March from Christopher & West Sts.
10:00 pm   Rally at Sheridan Square
10:30 pm   Kiss In at 6th Avenue & 8th St.
11:30 pm   Tracks—ACT UP/ACT NOW Fundraiser

FIGHT HOMOPHOBIA: FIGHT AIDS

SPRING AIDS ACTION '88: Nine days of nationwide AIDS related actions & protests.

Gran Fury, *Read My Lips (girls)*, 1988

public art of Gran Fury, an art collective (named after the Plymouth car used by undercover police) that produced posters, performances, installations, and videos alerting people to facts about AIDS and HIV that public health officials refused to publicize. One of their posters advertised a 1988 demonstration, a "kiss in" intended to publicly dispel the myth that kissing transmits the AIDS virus. The phrase "read my lips," which refers to the poster's image of two women about to kiss, was appropriated from a much-discussed slogan in the presidential campaign of then President George Bush. Bush's slogan "read my lips, no new taxes" was in turn a reference to former President Ronald Reagan's appropriation of actor Clint Eastwood's famous phrase, "Make my day." In "lifting" the phrase "read my lips" and placing it with images about homosexual contact, Gran Fury suggested that the phrase had meanings that Bush and his campaign advisors clearly did not intend. Gran Fury's appropriation gives the poster a biting political humor, making it both a playful twist of words and an accusation against a president who was overtly homophobic and helped to lead a tragic political denial of the seriousness of the AIDS epidemic.

Strategies of appropriation, borrowing, and changing or reconfiguring images have proliferated in contemporary image-making processes. Barbara

Kruger's work, *Your Manias Become Science*, which we discussed earlier, is an example of such strategies, in which the original image of the atomic bomb is reconfigured by Kruger through her use of text. One could argue that Kruger is also appropriating the techniques of advertisers to make her statement, in effect using the technique of the slogan to create a new meaning. Such juxtapositions of text and image are often used in public service advertisements to create messages that work against viewer expectations. In this public service ad, for example, the viewer may come to the image with the expectation that it is an ad selling some baby products, only to learn, by reading the text in the image, that it is a statement about the omnipresence of racism. Thus, appropriating the techniques of a particular style of conventional images can create an oppositional statement.

Sometimes, appropriation can function as a means of reworking art history itself. One of the most well-known biblical motifs in the history of art is the story of Christ's last supper, a scene most famously painted by Leonardo da Vinci in 1484. Da Vinci's *The Last Supper* depicts Christ and his disciples sitting at a long table and is a universally recognized icon of Christian history and religion. This image was appropriated by pop artist Andy Warhol at the end of his career as the basis of a dozen monumental paintings. Warhol used tracings from projections of the da Vinci painting and silkscreen techniques to reproduce the image in fragmented, multiple, and vastly enlarged formats. Mural

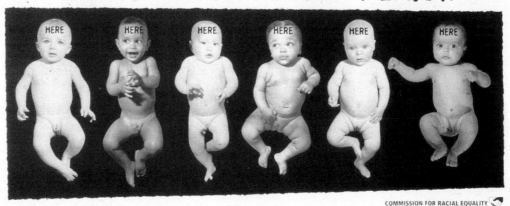

"...and to all those who died, scrubbed floors, wept and fought for us."

José Antonio Burciaga, *The Last Dinner of Chicano Heros*, 1986–89

artist José Antonio Burciaga also reworked *The Last Supper* in the late 1980s by replacing the disciples with Chicano heros, including Che Guevara, Emilio Zapata, Cesar Chavez, and Dolores Huerta. Using the religious symbols of the Virgin Guadalupe (draped with a banner that reads "America") and a Day of the Dead skeleton figure, both of which are very important icons in Chicano culture, Burciaga makes a statement about ethnic and political pride within the codes of traditional images. In appropriating a famous religious image, he endows his mural with a political statement about the importance of Chicano culture.

These examples show oppositional practices that involve cultural production. However, oppositional practices can also be about the consumption of images. As viewers, we can appropriate images and texts (films, television shows, news images, and advertisements), strategically altering their meanings to suit our purposes. As we explained earlier, however, meanings are determined through a complex negotiation among viewers, producers, texts, and contexts. Hence images themselves can be said to resist the oppositional readings that some viewers may wish to confer to them. In other words, meanings that oppose the dominant reading of an image may not "cling" to an image with the same tenacity as meanings that are more in line with dominant ideologies.

One example of oppositional looking is the technique of reading lesbian or gay subtexts in movies that feature *gender-bending* (bending the traditional codes of gender roles and sexual norms) performances or same-sex friendships. Films starring Greta Garbo, a well-known film star of the 1920s and 1930s, for example, have a cult following among lesbian viewers interested in appropriating Garbo's sometimes gender-bending performances for the under-considered history of lesbian and gay film culture. In the film *Blonde Venus* (1932), Garbo, who was an icon of glamour in her time, plays a nightclub performer who dresses in a man's tuxedo and kisses another woman. While this may have been understood as a theatrical gesture at the time, this film is now reread as a depiction of lesbian desire. Another example of oppositional viewing is the affirmation of qualities within genres previously regarded as exploitative or insulting to a group. The blaxploitation film genre, for example, has been widely noted for its negative representations of Black culture during the 1970s, with such stereotypes as the black male stud, gangster, and pimp. Yet, more recently, this genre has been reconsidered to emphasize the evidence these films provide of valuable aspects of Black culture and talent during the 1970s. We can say, then, that this genre has been appropriated, its meanings strategically transformed to create an alternative view of black culture.

These forms of appropriation for political empowerment can also be found at the level of language. Social movements often take terms that are considered to be derogatory and re-use them in empowering ways. This process is called *trans-coding*. In recent years, the term "queer," which was traditionally used to insult gays, has been trans-coded as a cultural identity to be embraced and proudly declared. Similarly, in the 1960s, the phrase "Black is beautiful" was used by the civil rights and black power movements as a means to reappropriate the term "black" and change its meaning from a negative to a positive one.

One of the terms used to describe tactics of appropriation is *bricolage*, which literally means "making do" or piecing together one's culture with whatever is at hand. The term was derived from the ideas of anthropologist Claude Lévi-Strauss by a number of cultural theorists, including Dick Hebdige.[3] The idea of consumers of popular culture "making do" with given elements of a culture seems inevitable, given that most consumers typically have relatively little influence on the production of art, media, and fashion. Hebdige has argued that bricolage can be seen as a deliberate tactic to appropriate commodities in the construction of youth style. For instance, many youth *subcultures* appropriate particular fashion styles and, through bricolage, change the meaning of particular articles of clothing or styles of dress. A subculture is a group that defines its distinction from mainstream culture through various aspects of its style—dress, music, lifestyle, etc. A baseball cap turned backwards, a pair of oversized Carhart jeans worn very low, a lace gothic dress worn with Doc Martens boots—these are all elements of styles assembled by participants in various youth subcultures which appropriate various elements and "found" items and alter their meanings. Doc Martens boots, for example, were originally created in the 1940s as orthopedic boots and sold in Britain in the 1960s as work boots, but were appropriated to become key

elements in various subcultures from the 1970s onwards, such as punk, AIDS activism, neopunk, and grunge. The Carhart brand of denim clothing, also originating as blue-collar work gear, became popular among youth favoring the hip-hop look during the 1990s. Cultural theorist Angela McRobbie has examined the ways that the "ragmarket" of used clothing allows young people to create new styles by mining styles of the past. McRobbie argues that women have played a central role as both entrepreneurial street sellers and as consumers in fostering complex styles of retro fashion, the appropriation of work clothes, and the use of men's clothing such as formal dress suits and long underwear (as leggings) to create styles that were then appropriated by mainstream fashion.

For participants in subcultures, the remaking of style through appropriation of historical objects and images can be a political statement about class and cultural identity. Many young people assert their defiance of mainstream culture specifically by developing styles that do not conform to the "good taste" of white mainstream culture. These styles can include dress, music, dance, and other cultural forms, often working together. Chicano low-riders, for instance, enact style with their cars, which are named and decorated with paintings of Mexican figures and history, remodeled to both rise up and drive slowly, and refashioned like living spaces. As cultural theorist George Lipsitz notes, the low-rider car defies utilitarianism, it is about cruising for display, codes of ethnic pride, and defying mainstream car culture. He writes, "Low riders are themselves masters of postmodern cultural manipulation. They juxtapose seemingly inappropriate realities—fast cars designed to go slowly, 'improvements' that flaunt their impracticality, like chandeliers instead of overhead lights. They encourage a bi-focal perspective—they are made to be watched but only after adjustments have been made to provide ironic and playful commentary on prevailing standard of automobile design."[4] We will discuss postmodern style at length in Chapter 7. Here, we would like to note the ways that low-riders change the meanings of automobiles so that they function as a cultural and political statement.

Subculture style, according to Hebdige, signals a defiance among youth against a homogeneous culture—that is, a culture that tries to unify its members, or make them conform to the stylistic norms of white, upper- and middle-class culture. As we explained at the beginning of this chapter, the concept of taste is tacitly based on a value system that valorizes the tastes of the middle and upper classes. What some members of society may perceive

Jorge and Rosa Salazar,
Azteca, low rider car

as being "in bad taste" may in fact be a strategic assault on the normative values inherent in "tasteful" fashions.

In relationship to cultural texts, such as literature, film, and television, bricolage can be seen as a reconfiguring of the meaning of the text. This strategy is called *textual poaching* by literary and cultural theorist Michel de Certeau. Textual poaching was defined by de Certeau as a process analogous to inhabiting a text "like a rented apartment."[5] In other words, viewers of popular culture can "inhabit" that text by negotiating meanings through it and creating new cultural products in response to it, making it their own. While the idea of textual poaching can be seen as allied with Stuart Hall's formulation of three readings (dominant, negotiated, and oppositional), it is a more fluid and less fixed process. De Certeau saw reading texts and images as a series of advances and retreats, of tactics and games. Readers can fragment and reassemble texts (with as simple a strategy as a television remote control) as a form of cultural bricolage.

De Certeau saw the relationship of readers/writers and producers/viewers as an ongoing struggle for possession of the text—a struggle over its meaning and potential meanings. This notion operates in opposition to the educational training that teaches readers to search for the author's intended meanings and to leave a text unmarked by their own fingerprints, so to speak. However, this is a process steeped in the unequal power relations that exist between those who produce dominant popular culture and those who consume it. De Certeau defined *strategies* as the means through which institutions exercise power and set up well-ordered systems that consumers must negotiate (the programming schedule of television, for instance), and *tactics* as the "hit and run" acts of random engagement by viewers/consumers to usurp these systems, which might include everything from using a remote control to change the "text" of television to creating a web site that analyzes a particular film or TV show.

De Certeau's ideas have been used to examine the ways that viewers engage in various negotiated and oppositional tactics with popular culture. Some of this work of textual poaching is at the level of interpretation, and some of it is about cultural production, actually producing new texts out of old, say, by re-editing films or writing stories that feature well-known television characters. Some contemporary theorists have looked at the cultural labor of fan cultures as an example of poaching.[6] Many fan cultures are active in discussions about certain television shows, engage in speculation about show scripts, post reviews, write their own scripts, and consider themselves more authoritative about the shows than the producers themselves.

The television show *The X-Files* inspired an active fan culture that writes magazines, speculates about the show's various plots, discusses the show on line, and reworks various episodes. Many fan cultures have emerged around television shows that are suggestive yet not explanatory about the larger world of their drama, such as the series *Star Trek*, which indicates many other civilizations that fans are then compelled to create themselves. Similarly, the plot of *The X-Files* is highly complex, involving many unexplained incidents and characters. This show is deliberately designed to suggest rather than explain many elements of its story, hence it is open to a variety of interpretations. Many of these plot elements require repeat (VCR) viewing, which is a serious fan activity. The show is thus a remarkably loose cultural text that allows for many levels of engagement, of which ritualistic weekly viewing is only one. Many fans interact with the series through the textual poaching activities of actively engaging in weekly critiques of episodes, participating in web site discussions about unresolved aspects of the plot, and rewriting episodes to their liking.

Re-appropriations and counter-bricolage

However, appropriation is not always an oppositional practice. Active viewer/reader engagement can also work in ways that are in sync with dominant culture. Television fans may sometimes be reading the show against the intended meaning of its producers, but as active and loyal fans, they also form a lucrative market for it. In the case of *The X-Files*, the producers regularly monitor fan activity and often put clues in episodes that are intended only for the fan viewer who is paying close attention.

In addition, the vintage thrift store clothing fashions originally associated with oppositional youth culture were, in turn, re-appropriated by the mainstream fashion industry, which capitalized on the market for inexpensive and widely available knock-offs of vintage fashions. Whereas Doc Martens work boots in the early 1990s might have signaled an association with AIDS activism or the values of neopunk culture, within a few years they had become respectable everyday shoes for a wide range of consumers, bearing no clear political significance beyond being somewhat fashionable.

The relationship of viewers of mainstream popular culture and the industries that produce them is a highly complex exchange. While cultural bricolage and fan tactics on the part of viewers might offer resistant practices to dominant hegemonic readings of cultural products, it can also be said that hegemonic forces in these industries re-appropriate the tactics of marginalized cultures into the mainstream—a form of *counter-bricolage*. We could think of this as the way in which advertisers and fashion designers have become highly skilled at designing and packaging the style of various subcultures and selling them back to the mainstream public. The mainstreaming of rap music is another example. Whereas rap began in defiance of the music industry and popular music, it soon became immensely popular and widely appropriated. As particular rap styles become part of the mainstream, new forms of music emerge at the margins in order to redefine its defiance. This means that culture industries are constantly establishing what is new style, and that subcultures on the margins are always reinventing themselves.

This is, in many ways, how hegemony works, with the dominant culture in constant flux as it works in tension with marginal cultures. It is also the case that since the 1960s, marketers have been actively working to associate the meaning of "cool" with their products.[7] Since marketers began to borrow the concepts of the counterculture of the 1960s to sell products as youthful and hip, there has been a constant mining of youth cultures and marginal subcultures for mainstream fashion and other products.

Cultural meaning is thus a highly fluid, ever-changing thing, the result of complex interactions among images, producers, cultural products, and readers/viewers/consumers. The meaning of images emerges through these processes of interpretation, engagement, and negotiation. Culture is a process, in a constant state of flux. Furthermore, the marketing of the qualities of hipness and cool means that the categories of high and low culture are not only inappropriate class-based distinctions, they are very difficult to discern. When the culture of youth on the street is marketed to middle- and upper-class consumers, and the culture of inner-city ethnic subcultures is marketed to white consumers with the promise of confering hipness, then we can see how mainstream culture, through the processes of hegemony and counter-hegemony, is constantly mining the margins of culture for meaning.

Notes

1. Louis Althusser, "Ideology and Ideological State Apparatuses," from *Lenin and Philosophy and Other Essays*, translated by Ben Brewster (New York and London: Monthly Review Press, 1971), 162.
2. Stuart Hall, "Encoding, Decoding," in *The Cultural Studies Reader*, edited by Simon During (New York and London: Routledge, 1993), 90–103.
3. Dick Hebdige, *Subculture: The Meaning of Style* (New York and London: Routledge, 1979), 102–04.
4. George Lipsitz, "Cruising around the Historical Bloc," in *The Subcultures Reader*, edited by Ken Gelder and Sarah Thornton (New York and London: Routledge, 1997), 358.
5. Michel de Certeau, *The Practice of Everyday Life*, translated by Steven Rendall (Berkeley and London: University of California Press, 1984), p. xxi.
6. See in particular work by Henry Jenkins and Constance Penley on the television series *Star Trek*: Henry Jenkins, *Textual Poachers: Television Fans and Participatory Culture* (New York and London: Routledge, 1992); and Constance Penley, *NASA/Trek: Popular Science and Sex in America* (New York and London: Verso, 1997).
7. See Thomas Frank, *The Conquest of Cool* (Chicago and London: University of Chicago Press, 1998).

Further Reading

Louis Althusser. "Ideology and Ideological State Apparatuses." In *Lenin and Philosophy and Other Essays*. Translated by Ben Brewster. New York and London: Monthly Review Press, 1971, 127–86.

Bad-Object Choices. *How Do I Look? Queer Film and Video*. Seattle: Bay Press, 1991.

Pierre Bourdieu. *Distinction: A Social Critique of the Judgement of Taste*. Translated by Richard Nice. Cambridge, Mass. and London: Harvard University Press, 1984.

Michel de Certeau. *The Practice of Everyday Life*. Translated by Steven Rendall. Berkeley and London: University of California Press, 1984.

Alexander Doty. *Making Things Perfectly Queer: Interpreting Mass Culture*. Minneapolis and London: University of Minnesota Press, 1993.

Terry Eagleton, ed. *Ideology*. New York and London: Longman Press, 1994.

John Fiske. *Reading Popular Culture*. New York and London: Routledge, 1989.

Thomas Frank. *The Conquest of Cool: Business Culture, Counterculture, and the Rise of Hip Consumerism*. Chicago and London: University of Chicago Press, 1998.

Antonio Gramsci. *Selections from the Prison Notebooks*. Translated by Quintin Hoare and Geoffrey Nowell-Smith. New York: International Publishers and London: Lawrence & Wishart, 1971.

Stuart Hall. "Encoding, Decoding," in *The Cultural Studies Reader*. Edited by Simon During. New York and London: Routledge, 1993, 90–103.

——"The Problem of Ideology: Marxism Without Guarantees." In *Stuart Hall: Critical Dialogues in Cultural Studies*. Edited by David Morley and Kuan-Hsing Chen. New York and London: Routledge, 1996, 25–46.

——"Gramsci's Relevance for the Study of Race and Ethnicity." In *Stuart Hall: Critical Dialogues in Cultural Studies*. Edited by David Morley and Kuan-Hsing Chen. New York and London: Routledge, 1996, 411–40.

Dick Hebdige. *Subculture: The Meaning of Style*. New York and London: Routledge, 1979.

Henry Jenkins. *Textual Poachers: Television Fans and Participatory Culture*. New York and London: Routledge, 1992.

George Lipsitz. "Cruising around the Historical Bloc: Postmodernism and Popular Music in East Los Angeles." In *The Subcultures Reader*. Edited by Ken Gelder and Sarah Thornton. New York and London: Routledge, 1997, 350–59.

Angela McRobbie. "Second-Hand Dresses and the Role of the Ragmarket." In *Postmodernism and Popular Culture*. New York and London: Routledge, 1994, 135–54.

Constance Penley. *NASA/TREK: Popular Science and Sex in America*. New York and London: Verso, 1997.

Sally Price. *Primitive Art in Civilized Places*. Chicago and London: University of Chicago, 1989.

Janice Radway. *Reading the Romance: Women, Patriarchy, and Popular Culture*. Revised Edition. Chapel Hill, NC and London: University of North Carolina Press, 1991.

3 Spectatorship, Power, and Knowledge

The world of images that we interact with on a daily basis is caught up in the power relations of the societies in which we live. We invest images with the power to incite emotions within us, and images are also elements within the power relations between human subjects, and between individuals and institutions. Just as images are both representations and producers of the ideologies of their time, they are also factors in relations of power. In Chapter 2, we examined the process of reception, in which actual viewers make meaning of images. In this chapter, we will look at the role of the spectator of the image, and the ways that the gaze—of images, *subjects*, and institutions—is a fundamental aspect of the practice of looking. This means shifting the focus from issues of reception to concepts of address. This distinction between address and reception is one between thinking about the ideal viewer of an image, and the potential real viewer who looks. Address refers to the way that an image constructs certain responses from an idealized viewer, whereas reception is about the ways in which actual viewers respond.[1] Both ways of examining images are incomplete in themselves, but can be seen to work together to understand what happens in the process of looking.

Psychoanalysis and the image spectator

Of all contemporary theories that can help us understand how viewers make meaning, *psychoanalytic theory* has addressed most directly the pleasure we derive from images, and the relationship between our desires and our visual world. We can have intense relationships with images precisely because of the power they have both to give us pleasure and to allow us to articulate our desires through looking. Since the 1970s, film scholars have introduced a number of approaches to help us consider this process. One concept that has provided a particularly useful way to examine practices of looking is that of the *spectator*. Spectatorship theory emphasizes the role of the psyche—particularly the *unconscious*, desire, and fantasy—in the practice of looking. In this theory, the term "spectator" does not refer to a flesh-and-blood individual viewer or a member of a particular viewing audience, as we discussed in Chapter 2. Rather, when psychoanalytic theory talks of the spectator, it treats it as an "ideal subject." In using this term, psychoanalytic theory abstracts from real audience members and the experience of a particular film to refer instead to a construction. Independent of individual identity, the spectator is socially constructed by the *cinematic apparatus* (the traditional social space of the cinema that includes a darkened theater, projector, film, sound) and by the *ideologies* that are a part of a given viewing situation. It can be said that particular films, targeted toward specific categories of viewers during particular periods (the genre of women's films of the 1940s, for example) create and offer to their viewers an ideal *subject position*. For instance, there is an ideal spectator for the woman's film regardless of how any particular viewer might make personal meaning of the film. Theories of spectatorship often give us the means to analyze the subject position constructed for and offered to viewers by a given film or set of media texts.

Althusser's concept of *interpellation*, which we discussed in Chapter 2, helps to show us how viewers are made to recognize themselves and identify with the ideal subject offered by images. In addition, *semiotics*, which we discussed in Chapter 1, allows us to see the ways in which images can be understood as a language with *codes* and conventions that can be subject to textual analysis. Christian Metz and other French theorists who wrote about film in the 1970s generally described the process of spectatorship as follows: the viewer suspends disbelief in the fictional world of the film, identifies not only with specific characters in the film but more importantly with the film's overall ideology through identification with the film's narrative structure and visual point of view, and puts into play fantasy structures (such as an imagined ideal family) that derive from the viewer's unconscious.

The concept of the unconscious is crucial to these theories. One of the fundamental elements of psychoanalysis lies in its demonstration of the existence and mode of operation of unconscious mental processes. According to psychoanalytic theory, in order to function in our lives, we actively repress various desires, fears, memories, and fantasies. Hence, beneath our conscious, daily social interaction there exists a dynamic, active realm of forces of desire that is inaccessible to our rational and logical selves. The unconscious often motivates us in ways which we are unaware of, and, according to psychoanalysis, is active in our dreams.

Early theories of spectatorship were based on the psychoanalytic theories of Sigmund Freud, who is considered to be the founder of psychoanalysis and who worked in the late nineteenth and early twentieth century in Vienna, and Jacques Lacan, a well-known French psychoanalyst who revised many of Freud's ideas in the mid to late twentieth century. Practices of looking are particularly central to Lacan's thinking about how humans come to develop as subjects. Lacan used the term "subject" rather than individual or human being to describe his object of inquiry. The subject of Lacan's study was not so much the individual but rather an entity he thought of as being constructed through the mechanisms of the unconscious, language, and desire. He was most concerned with how human beings come to imagine themselves as unique individuals even as they are given identity within the social structures of Western capitalism. The term "subject," then, carries within it the implication that individuality is a construction that takes place through ideology, language, and representation.

Film theorists used the work of Lacan, which emphasizes the role of desire in creating subjects, to explain the powerful lure of film images in our culture. For example, the well-known film theorists Jean-Louis Baudry and Christian Metz drew an analogy between the early process of a child's ego construction and the experience of film viewing, using Lacan's concept of the *mirror phase* of childhood development. According to Lacan, children go through a developmental stage at about 18 months that establishes fundamental aspects of their notion of selfhood and separateness from other human beings (primarily their mothers, on whom they are dependent for their needs). In the mirror phase, Lacan proposed, infants begin to establish their egos through the process of looking at a mirror body-image, which may be their own mirror image, their mother, or another figure. The infants recognize the mirror image to be both their selves and different. Although infants have no physical ability to grasp or control this mirror-image, it is thought that they fantasize having control and mastery over it. Looking and the ability to fantasize based on what they see is crucial to infants' sense of control and mastery (of the body in the image) in this scenario. The mirror phase, as described by Lacan, is an important step in infants' recognition of themselves as autonomous beings with the potential ability to control their worlds.

This recognition of self and other comes at a stage of growth when the infant's intellectual growth outpaces its motor skills—the infant can imagine control over the body in the image, but cannot actually physically exert that control. The mirror phase thus provides infants with a sense of their existence as a separate body in relationship to another body, but it also provides a basis for *alienation*, since the process of image recognition involves a splitting between what they are physically capable of and what they see and imagine themselves to be (powerful, in control). There are two contradictory relationships here to the image—infants see that they and the image are the same, yet at the same time they see the image as an ideal (not the same). Hence, the mirror phase is also about recognition and misrecognition. While this concept may seem highly abstract if not far-fetched to some readers, who might want to argue that it has little to do with adult subjects watching films, it is important to see how it helps us to understand the very question of how we become subjects. It can provide a useful framework to understand the investment of tremendous power that viewers place in images, and the reasons why we can so easily read images as a kind of ideal.

Part of the fascination with cinema, according to Baudry, is that the darkened theater and the conditions of watching a mirror-like screen invite the viewer to regress to a childlike state. The viewer undergoes a temporary loss of ego as he or she identifies with the powerful position of apprehending the world on the screen, much as the infant apprehended the mirror image. The spectators' egos are built up through their illusory sense of owning the body on the film screen. It is important to emphasize that it is not the specific image of bodies on screen with which the viewer is thought to identify most significantly, but with the cinematic apparatus. The idea that the viewer is in a regressive mode is the aspect of psychoanalytic theory that has come under the most criticism, because it presents a definition of the spectator as existing in an infantile state, one that stands in contrast to the engaged viewer practices we discussed in Chapter 2.

In the late 1970s and 1980s, many feminist film theorists interested in the power of film images over viewers took up these theories and engaged in productive criticism of them in order to emphasize that the film viewer is not a singular, undifferentiated subject, but is already enculturated as either male or female. Hence, we cannot speak of a singular universal spectator because viewing circumstances are influenced by the psychic structures that inform our formation as gendered subjects. This intervention in questions of desire and the image led to a focus on the *gaze*.

The gaze

Earlier we noted that Lacan considered practices of looking to be important processes in the formation of the subject. One of the terms he used to describe looking relations is the gaze (in French, *le regard*). In common parlance, to gaze is to look or stare, often with eagerness or desire. In much psychoanalytic film criticism, the gaze is not the act of looking itself, but the viewing relationship characteristic of a particular set of social circumstances. The concept of the gaze has been the focus of inquiry in both art history and film studies, with different emphases.

Throughout the history of art, and in the contemporary world of film and advertising, images of women often have been presented in ways that emphasize their status as sexual beings or maternal figures. In 1975 filmmaker and writer Laura Mulvey published a groundbreaking essay about images of women in classical Hollywood cinema. This essay, "Visual Pleasure and Narrative Cinema," used psychoanalysis to propose that the conventions of popular narrative cinema are structured by a patriarchal unconscious, positioning women represented in films as objects of a "male gaze." In other words, Mulvey argued that Hollywood cinema offered images geared toward male viewing pleasure, which she read within certain psychoanalytic paradigms including *scopophilia* and *voyeurism*. The concept of the gaze is fundamentally about the relationship of pleasure and images. In psychoanalysis, the term "scopophilia" refers to pleasure in looking, and *exhibitionism* in the pleasure of being looked at. Both of these terms acknowledge the ways in which reciprocal relationships of looking can be sources of pleasure. Voyeurism is the pleasure in looking while not being seen, and carries a more negative connotation of a powerful, if not sadistic, position. The idea of the camera as a mechanism for voyeurism has been often discussed, since, for instance, the position of viewers of cinema can be seen as voyeuristic—they sit in a darkened room, where they cannot be seen, in order to watch the film. In Mulvey's theory, the camera is used as a tool of voyeurism and sadism, disempowering those before its gaze. She and other theorists who pursued this line of thinking examined certain films of classic Hollywood cinema to demonstrate the power of the male gaze.

Alfred Hitchcock's *Rear Window* (1954) is a popular example of a film that is explicitly about gendered looking. The film's main protagonist is Jeffries (Jimmy Stewart), a photographer who has broken his leg and is temporarily confined to a wheelchair in his New York City apartment. Jeffries spends much of his time seated at a window that affords him a perfect view into the windows of the various people who live in the building across the way, where he believes he has witnessed evidence of a murder. *Rear Window* has been read by film theorists (including Mulvey) as a metaphor of the act of film viewing itself, with Jeffries standing in for the cinematic audience. Confined to a fixed position like the film viewer, his gaze is similarly voyeuristic in that he freely looks but is not

Alfred Hitchcock, *Rear Window*,1954

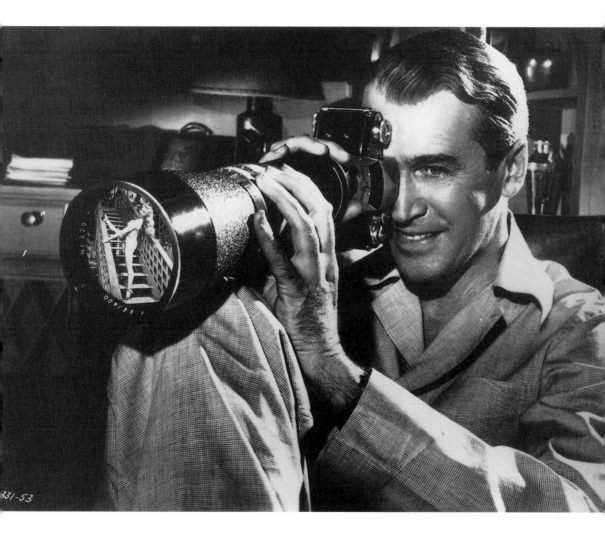

seen by the objects of his gaze. Like characters in a movie, his neighbors are apparently unaware that this audience of one exists, much less that he has seen them up close in the intimate setting of their homes. The windows frame their actions just as the camera frames narrative action in a film, both determining and restricting what Jeffries can know about their lives, and generating in him a desire to see and know more. The studio advertising still pictured on the previous page shows us one of the objects of his interest, a dancer, captured in his lens. In the film, we see through his point of view as he observes his neighbors and tracks the movements of his girlfriend Lisa (Grace Kelly) as she becomes his mobile surrogate, his "private eye." Lisa steals up the fire escape across the way to search for murder clues in the off-screen space beyond the window frame that is off-limits to Jeffries and us, the film viewers.

Rear Window is a quintessential example of the male gaze in relationship to female objects of visual pleasure. Yet, as the example of Lisa's investigation suggests, the male gaze is not as controlling and powerful as some theorists have suggested. Jeffries gains power by looking, but he is emasculated by his confined state, and must rely on the eyes and legs of a woman to gain access to knowledge. The cinematic viewer, like Jeffries, is confined to a fixed seat and the field of vision offered by this position and the restricted framing of the scene. The gendered relations of power of the cinematic gaze are clearly quite complex. Indeed, not only is Jeffries frustrated in his attempts to know more, he is also punished for looking. Once Jeffries gets caught looking, he becomes vulnerable and trapped; the murderer comes looking for him. Clearly, male looking is not without its limitations and its consequences.

There are other examples in popular culture of more extreme and literal portrayals of the camera's gaze as a kind of violence. The cult film *Peeping Tom* (1960) makes literal the idea of the camera as a weapon of a voyeuristic male gaze. Director Michael Powell depicts a protagonist who turns his camera into an elaborate device that can kill women while filming them before a mirror, so that they witness their own terror. *Peeping Tom* renders explicit the idea that the gaze can be implicated in sadism, and is an example, albeit an extreme one, of the ways that cameras have been seen as weapons of *phallic* power. Powell's film is an extreme dramatization of another sort of fantasy about the power of vision, a fantasy in which the camera is imagined to grant direct sexualized power over life and death.

Whereas analysis of the gaze in cinema takes into account the context of

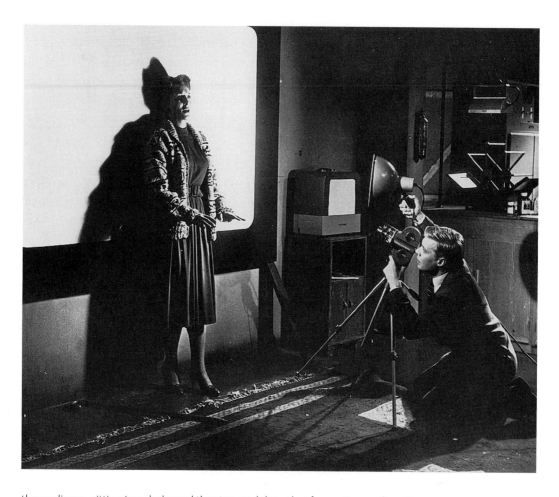

the audience sitting in a darkened theater, and the role of narrative and motion in viewer identification with the cinematic apparatus, concepts of the gaze in still images have concentrated more specifically on the different kinds of looks that an image can imply. In the history of art, the fact that paintings were geared toward male viewers had as much to do with the commerce of art as it did with the social roles and sexual stereotypes of men and women. Until quite recently, most collectors of art were men and the primary viewing audience of art was men. Since the owner of a painting was understood to be male, its spectator was also defined as such. In a typical depiction of a female nude, for instance, a woman is posed so that her body is on display for the viewer, who is implied to be male by the codes of the image. The female body is thus understood here in terms of form and allure, as an object before the viewer's gaze. There is a long tradition in art of defining the female nude as the project

Michael Powell, *Peeping Tom*, 1960

and possession of the male artist. In these paintings, the men gaze upon the female figures as possessions. The women are the objects of the male gaze, and their returning looks are accorded no power in the image.

The image convention of depicting women as objects of the gaze and men

Jean-Désiré-Gustave Courbet, *Woman with a Parrot*, 1866

Jean-Léon Gérôme, *Pygmalion and Galatea*, late 1800s

as lookers continues to exist today, although in an image context that is considerably more complex. This convention has many cultural and social implications. In the classic Western tradition of images, which was dominant throughout the history of painting, men were depicted in action and women as objects to be looked at. John Berger wrote that in this history of images, "men act, women appear."[2] Berger noted that the tradition of the nude in painting was almost exclusively about images of nude women who were presented for male viewers. Indeed, the women in these paintings were often turned away from the men depicted within the pictures toward the spectator. This way of viewing women thus defined them by their appearance, in essence their ability to be pleasing to look at, and this carries important weight in the context of contemporary image culture. The implication of a male gaze was often depicted quite literally in the history of painting with a woman whose body is turned toward the (presumably male) viewer, but whose head is turned to gaze into a mirror. This image convention has also been used extensively by advertisers.

One of the primary elements of the concept of the gaze is a kind of split that viewers experience in looking at images. This is related to Lacan's notion of the alienation that results from the split between seeing the image as oneself and also as an ideal—as both the same and not the same as oneself. This can also be understood as the split that results from being simultaneously the surveyor and the surveyed, in looking at oneself through the implied gaze of others. The split self of the viewer is always connected to the idea that the gaze is omnipresent.

Lorenzo Lotto, *Venus and Cupid*, early 1500s

Titian, *Venus with a Mirror*, c.1555

Changing concepts of the gaze

Today, we are surrounded on a daily basis by images of fashion models whose looks conform to a rigid set of normative codes about beauty. The cultural practices of cosmetics, plastic surgery, dieting, fitness programs, and image management go hand in hand with an image culture that incites women, and increasingly men, to see themselves and their appearance as inadequate in some way and in need of improvement. Berger's dictum, "men act and women appear," still applies to

images today. However, in Euro-American cultures, the traditional roles of men and women are in upheaval, and women are increasingly socially defined by their work in addition to their appearance. In addition, men are increasingly subject to many of the codes of appearance management that were once considered to be exclusively female. While men have been portrayed through twentieth-century advertising images as men in action, whose rigid muscular frames and active poses counter their role as objects of the gaze, today they are increasingly shown in an array of poses that were previously understood as specifically feminine.

Image conventions have changed, and so have the ways of understanding traditional images. The theoretical concept of the male gaze has been rethought, in particular because of the ways in which it could not account for the pleasures of female viewers (except by seeing them as masochistic or as viewing "as men") or for the male figure as the object of the gaze. Mulvey's essay launched more than a decade of writing about modes of spectatorship. Mulvey herself revised her thinking about visual pleasure in an essay of 1981. Meanwhile, feminist critics have continued to mine the theories of sexual difference put forth by Freud and Lacan.[3]

Mary Ann Doane used psychoanalysis to theorize female spectators of films made specifically for women viewers, such as the genre of the woman's film of the 1940s (also known as "weepies"). Some theorists responded that gendered viewing relations are not fixed; viewers readily deploy fantasy to occupy the "wrong" gender position in their spectatorial relationships to films. For example, women can identify with the male position of mastery or exercise voyeuristic tendencies, and men can be looked upon with pleasure and desire. In the studio still on the next page, from the 1953 film *Gentlemen Prefer Blondes*, actress Jane Russell is the object of both the camera's gaze and that of the adoring male athletes (of the US Olympic team). Yet, the men are also on display and subject to the gaze of viewers. One could posit an array of viewer pleasures and analyses across gender and sexuality in looking at this image. Many contemporary films aim precisely to defy the conventions of looking in film, and present women's gazes with agency. For example, the 1991 film *Thelma & Louise* defies traditional formulas of the gaze, and shows the complexity of the power relations of looking. The film begins with a scene, shown on the next page, in which the two women take a photograph of themselves. Here, the women control the camera, belying the dominant view that women are objects not subjects of the gaze.

Howard Hawks,
*Gentlemen Prefer
Blondes*, 1953

Ridley Scott, *Thelma &
Louise*, 1991

Yet another set of writers forwarded the view that we need to take into account the social and historical conditions of spectatorship. In the late 1980s and 1990s, film historians raised the question of how modes of spectatorship have been particular to historical and cultural contexts and audiences, and how the cinematic gaze intersects with the gaze that functions in other aspects of mass culture.[4] Some film scholars turned to the techniques of social science to emphasize that we need to recognize that spectators are real people, and that audiences need to be studied to learn how they actually respond to film texts.[5] Some authors launched inquiries into viewing pleasure and responses among particular audiences, such as black women viewers, to suggest that we cannot just assume that a gender binary determines the gaze on its own.[6] The late 1980s and early 1990s saw the proposition put forth that we cannot assume male spectatorial positions are available only to men; men are not the only ones who can assume the position of a "male gaze" offered in a given film.[7] Dominant viewing positions offered in film texts can be resisted by spectators who use texts to different ends, as in the case of black viewers who resist identification with the positions offered to black characters in so many films.[8] The concept of appropriating the male gaze for transgressive female looking, or for lesbian pleasure, was also launched during this period.[9] Judith Mayne emphasized the role of women directors in offering a different perspective than the male-directed films that dominated the studio era. Christine Holmlund and Patricia White have taken this focus on the director's role in shifting the gaze a step further. They suggest that we find a critique of the gaze of dominant cinema in films produced by lesbian directors who appropriate images of women and "re-stitch" them together in films that function as analyses of representations of women and sexuality.

One work that has become a classic of this genre is *Meeting of Two Queens*, a 1991 tape by Spanish video artist Cecilia Barriga. Barriga intercuts footage from films starring Greta Garbo and Marlene Dietrich, two stars whose representations were the subject of many written feminist analyses of the female image and the male gaze in the previous decades. The soundtrack is stripped from footage of these stars in their respective roles as queens (Garbo in *Queen Christina*, directed by Rouben Mamoulian in 1933, and Dietrich in *The Scarlet Empress*, directed by Josef von Sternberg in 1934) to construct new narrative scenarios in which the stars become the objects of one another's lesbian desires. Barriga's video realizes arguments put forth by some feminist film theorists about how viewers can enact lesbian desire through fantasies that construct what they see on the screen in ways that do not conform to the dominant readings of films. As Patricia White notes, this film invites its viewers to weave these images into a fantasy narrative that runs counter to the preferred reading of the original films.

A video that takes further the idea of a media text functioning as critique and analysis of the gaze is *Badass Supermama* (1996) by Etang Inyang. Analyzed by film scholar Kelly Hankin, this tape offers a theoretical perspective on lesbian and black spectatorship by performing "celluloid surgery" on two classics of the blaxploitation genre of the 1970s, *Sheba, Baby* (William Girdler, 1975) and *Foxy Brown* (Jack Hill, 1974). Both films feature star Pam Grier, who experienced a rekindling of star status in the late 1990s with her starring role in Quentin Tarantino's film *Jackie Brown* (1997). Inyang intercuts footage from these two 1970s feature hits with personal voiceover and superimposed footage of her own image. She comments, through voiceover and image, on her own involvement in fantasies and desires centering on the Pam Grier characters and the lesbian bar scenes in *Foxy Brown*. As Hankin explains, this film takes us through a critical analysis of the politics of the blaxploitation genre as it engages in issues of sexuality relative to race while also articulating these films through a reading position of black lesbian desire. This kind of resistant reading is enacted not just in critical writing or the voiceover, but through the images themselves.

Laura Mulvey's essay and the subsequent debates were concurrent with a period during which feminism was fraught with debate about sexual depictions of women and pornography in particular. In 1983, Barnard College in New York hosted a conference on pornography that became a watershed in the debates about pornography. The conference featured women from two sides of an emerging divide: those feminists, represented in Woman Against Pornography, who were interested in banning what they regarded as demeaning representations of women; and those feminists who argued that this move would only result in the repression of sexual representation, including representations of resistant and alternative sexualities (such as lesbian-affirmative images and images of sadomasochism). The latter argument, which also fell within the realm of feminism, was that repression or censorship of any sexual images would always be turned against those putting forth alternative sexual identities through visual and textual media. Originally, these arguments rarely brought into play psychoanalytic theory. However, in 1989 film scholar Linda Williams published a groundbreaking book, *Hard Core*, that analyzed pornography in a psychoanalytic mode in order to examine a variety of desires and *subject positions*. This work opened the way for feminist film scholars to engage in the broader feminist politics of pornography, and to offer more nuanced theories of the function of pornography in conjunction with readings of the perils of repressive mandates against "negative" images.

These changing views of scholarship, and the idea of what kinds of images were important objects of intellectual inquiry, have been paralleled by trends in image-making that reflect new concepts of gender and aesthetic conventions. Contemporary visual culture involves not only a highly complex array of images and spectators but also of gazes. There are in contemporary images, be they art, news, advertising, television, or film images, a broad array of gazes and implied viewers. Some may be voyeuristic, sadistic, or assaultive, others loving or passionate. Some gazes can be seen as policing, normalizing, or inspecting. Some images, such as the ad below, may subject both men and women to the gaze. Yet, it is also possible to see images that deflect a possessive gaze and gazes that are respectful and non-objectifying. It is thus central to the ways that the concept of the gaze has been rethought that we can think of many different kinds of gazes, each with a different relationship to power, and that these gazes are not seen strictly along the lines of male and female.

The desires that spectators have in looking and being looked at are caught

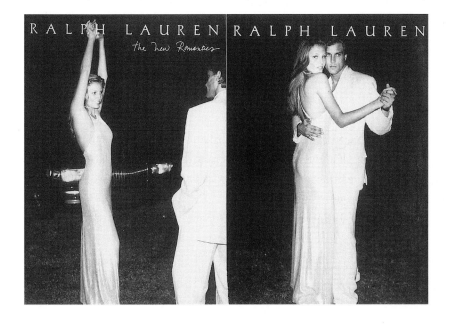

up in relationships of power. Traditionally, this meant that the spectator was always perceived to have more power than the object of the gaze (or person looked at), but the contemporary landscape of images shows that this is not always the case. In contemporary advertising, for instance, the idea of a powerful or disempowering gaze is often the source of a joke or counter gaze. In a much-discussed diet Coke television ad, a group of women office workers meet every day at 11:30 to gaze longingly on a muscled construction worker who takes a morning break by drinking a diet Coke. A humorous reversal of the stereotype of male construction workers ogling women on the street, the ad prompted a public discussion about what it means when women look at men with desire.

A potentially objectifying gaze can be deflected in an image, if the subject refuses to acknowledge it. For instance, in the diet Coke ad, the power of the women to gaze is thwarted by the man's refusal to acknowledge their presence. Part of the tradition of imaging men as objects of desire has involved particular codes of resisting the power of the gaze upon them. For instance, men have been traditionally depicted in action (such as this Range Rover ad), which negates attempts to objectify them because they are shown as powerfully within the frame. Hyper-muscled bodies, even if they are stationary, have the effect of connoting action and hence also work to give more power to the subject. In addition, men are often shown as either confronting the gaze or turning away from it. In this ad for Jockey underwear, five male fire fighters posed in Jockey underwear in a strategy of role reversal. The men, however, retain many of the image codes of the traditional male figure in their defiant stances and stares at the camera. These authoritative poses create a comic tension with the fact that they are standing in their underwear.

Sometimes you have to get out and push a Range Rover.

There are, we admit, things in this world that can quite capably stop a Range Rover in its tracks.

Active tar pits. Brick walls. And yes, ten feet of water.

Beyond these, however, a Range Rover's spirited 3.9 liter V8 engine, fully articulated suspension system and permanent four wheel drive are designed to steer you through equally unpleasant, if far less far-fetched, driving conditions.

From sleet and freezing rain, to the occasional blizzard and monsoon.

In short, anything short of the impossible.

So why not call 1-800-FINE-4WD today for the dealer nearest you?

After all, for just under $39,000, you too could be driving off in a Range Rover.

And considering all that it has to offer, would you really want to be up the creek in anything less?

RANGE ROVER

THE PERFECT MACHINE FOR THE PERFECT MACHINE.

INTERPLAK

Nothing works quite like the human body. But there's one device that works quite well with it. The INTERPLAK® Home Plaque Removal Instrument. It was created for one simple reason — to power away plaque that can cause gingivitis and destroy perfectly healthy teeth and gums. In fact it's engineered to clean your teeth nearly plaque free, with gentle bristles that conform to the individual contours of your teeth and gums, rotating 4200 times a minute and reversing direction 46 times a second. No other toothbrush works quite like it. That's why INTERPLAK is the brand dental professionals recommend most. So if you're looking for a better way to care for your teeth, the answer should be perfectly obvious. For more information call Bausch & Lomb at 1-800-334-4031.

BAUSCH & LOMB

INTERPLAK is the registered trademark of Bausch & Lomb Oral Care Division ©1992 Bausch & Lomb Oral Care Division.

Five Alarm Jockey

Let 'em know you're
JOCKEY POUCH®

Firefighters
Dallas, TX
November 20, 1998

While many contemporary advertisements continue to sell products through traditional gender codes, by portraying women in demure, seductive poses for a possessive male gaze (such as this Guess? ad), other ads play off these traditions by reversing them and showing both the pleasure of looking at men as objects and the power of women in action. In this cologne ad, the male figure is posed in a state that is classically associated with female figures. He reclines with his body turned toward the camera, and we can see him as

an object of beauty. Is he objectified by the camera's gaze? What kind of gaze does this image invoke? Can we say that it is a female gaze, one that defines men as looked upon by women? Or that the male figure continues to retain power before the gaze simply because of the conventions of the image with which we are familiar? Certainly it could be argued that this ad is selling an image of the sensitive, new man, who is confident enough in his masculinity to be the object of a desiring gaze.

At the same time, there are ads for female consumers that attempt to usurp the traditions of the male gaze. This ad replaces the female figure with an abstract cut-out, one evocative of the work of modern artist Henri Matisse. This abstraction does not allow a conventional gaze upon a woman as object. Rather, it shifts the focus from the figure to the clothing and the pose. In the Reebok ad on the next page, we see a woman in action, exercising in her apartment, oblivious to our gaze, and determined in her body movements. This ad wants its target audience (women who exercise and wear sport shoes) to identify with particular codes of self-empowerment (exercise, control of one's body, determination) and it uses text to back this up ("I believe that happy hour

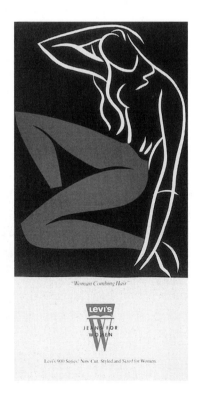

"Woman Combing Hair"

Levi's 900 Series.' New Cut. Styled and Sized for Women.

is at 6 a.m. . . . I believe that a man who wants something soft and cuddly to hold should buy a teddy bear."). Certainly, it is possible to see the ways in which the gaze still operates in this image, in that we are invited to assess this woman's appearance in looking upon her. In addition, the ad's emphasis on controlling one's body and determining one's life through the shaping of one's body (here, replacing cosmetics with exercise to shape the body) replicates many of the traditional ideas of women's worth being determined by their bodies. Yet, at the same time, this woman's active stance and defiant words are resistant to the traditional power dynamic of the gaze.

These different ways of reading the gaze are related to contemporary theories of identity and subjectivity. The feminist theories of female spectatorship which we discussed opened up the way for a consideration of other identity categories to describe relationships to the image. As we have noted, the late 1980s and 1990s saw the development of a broad literature about black spectatorship and lesbian spectatorship. This work made a fundamental challenge to earlier film theory by questioning the usefulness of psychoanalytic theory.

Freud and Lacan's psychoanalytic theory took the binary categories of male and female as core elements in their theories of how subjects are formed. While critics writing about black spectatorship raised the point that this model did not account for the specificity of racial experience and identity formation, those writing about lesbian and gay spectatorship emphasized that Freud and Lacan's theories of subject formation could not adequately account for the specificity of gay, lesbian, and transgendered identities.

From feminist theories of female spectatorship forward, the idea of the subject as ideal rather than as a historically or socially specific being has come under serious scrutiny. One of the central tensions between older and current theories of film and media spectatorship is that between the construction of the ideal spectator and the recognition of the multiple subject positions and social contexts from which we view films. The concept of regressive cinematic viewers, who are encouraged to repress their identities and to identify with the screen has been replaced by a broader set of models about the multiplicity of gazes and looks that mediate power between viewers and objects of the gaze.

Discourse, the gaze, and the other

The concept of the gaze is not restricted to questions of subjectivity and spectators. There are also ways of thinking about institutional gazes, which have the capacity to establish relationships of power and to affect individuals within them. The work of French philosopher Michel Foucault is helpful in explaining both the institutional gaze and the relationship of images to power. Foucault wrote about an inspecting gaze and a normalizing gaze, both of which are enacted in social and institutional contexts through frameworks of power.

It is important to note the ways that images are not only factors in interpersonal power relationships, such as the relation between those who look and those who are gazed upon, but are also elements in the functioning of institutional power. Images can both exert power and act as instruments of power. Here, Foucault's concept of *discourse* is helpful to understand how such power systems work to define how things are understood and spoken about (and, by implication, represented in images) in a given society. The term "discourse" is usually used to describe passages of writing or speech, the act of talking about something. Foucault used the term more specifically. He was interested in the rules and practices that produce meaningful statements and regulate what can be spoken in different historical periods. By discourse he meant a group of statements which provide a means for talking about (and a way of representing knowledge about) a particular topic at a particular historical moment. Hence, for Foucault, discourse is a body of knowledge that both defines and limits what can be said about something. In Foucault's terms, one could talk about the discourses of law, medicine, criminality, sexuality, technology, etc., in other words, broad social domains that define particular forms of knowledge and that change from any given time period and social context to another.

One of Foucault's topics of study was the concept of madness, and the modern institutionalization of the idea of insanity. In the nineteenth century, psychiatry emerged as a science, medical definitions of madness were produced, and the insane asylum came into being. By comparison, during the Renaissance, madness was not considered to be a disease or an illness, and the mad were not excluded from the rest of society, but rather were integrated into the fabric of small villages. They were considered to be under the influence of "folly"—a benign way of thinking—and sometimes seen as wise or revelatory, such as the idiot savant.

With the emergence of *modernity* in the eighteenth and nineteenth century, as people moved increasingly into urban centers and the modern political state emerged, madness became medicalized, pathologized, and seen as a polluting factor that had to be removed from society. According to Foucault, the discourse about madness is defined through the varying discourses of medicine, the law, education, etc., and includes: statements about madness which give us a certain kind of knowledge about it; the rules that govern what can be said and thought about insanity at a particular moment; subjects who in some ways personify the discourse of madness—the paranoid schizophrenic, the criminally insane, the psychiatric patient, the therapist, the doctor; how the knowledge about madness acquires authority and is produced with a sense of the truth; the practices within institutions for dealing with these subjects, such as medical treatment for the insane; and the acknowledgement that a different discourse will arise at a later historical moment, supplanting the existing one, producing in turn a new concept of madness and new truths about it. This can be seen in the fact that certain concepts about the discourse of madness did not exist (and hence could not be spoken or represented) before they emerged in the discourse (the concept of the paranoid schizophrenic emerged in the mid-twentieth century, the idea of the criminally insane person first existed at the end of the nineteenth century but is now highly debated). Hence, in this example, mental illness is not an objective fact, which remains the same in different historical periods and in different cultures. It is only within a particular discourse that it is made a meaningful and intelligible construct. It is fundamental to Foucault's theory that discourses produce certain kinds of subjects and knowledge, and that we occupy to varying degrees the subject positions defined within a broad array of discourses.

Photography has often been a central factor in the functioning of discourses since the nineteenth century. When photography was invented in the early nineteenth century, its development coincided with the rise of the modern political state. Photography thus became an integral part of both scientific professions and the regulation of social behavior by bureaucratic institutions of the state. It is used in the law to designate evidence and criminality, in medicine to document pathologies and define a visual difference between the "normal" and "abnormal," and in the social sciences, such as anthropology and sociology, to enable the creation of the subject positions of the researcher (anthropologist) and the object of study (in many cases, defined as the "native"). The versatility of the photographic image thus spawned a broad array of image-making activities for the purpose of *surveillance*, regulation, and categorization. Photographs thus often function to establish difference, through which that which is defined as *other* is posited as that which is not the norm or the primary subject.

Photographs were thus deployed as a means of categorization in order to distinguish, for instance, the normal and the abnormal according to the discourses of a particular time. In nineteenth-century France, Alphonse Bertillon created a system of measurement to identify the body types of criminals. Bertillon used photographs of subjects from the side and front as a means to identify what he saw as criminal characteristics, thus creating the first modern-day mug shots.[10] The image of an epileptic boy shown on the next page, taken in 1911, was used in a project of criminal anthropology by the Italian Cesare Lombroso. Lombroso was convinced, like Bertillon, that criminality was biologically rooted, and that epileptics were predisposed to criminality. Lombroso used photographs to establish what he felt were the identifiable physical traits of the criminal. In Chapter 8, we will discuss in more depth the use of photographs in medicine and nineteenth-century scientific practices that

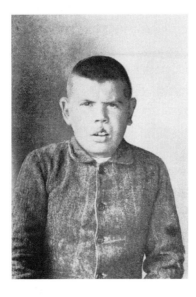

Gina Lombroso-Ferrero, *An Epileptic Boy, Figure 14*
from the book *Criminal Man: According to the
Classification of Cesare Lombroso*, 1911

attempted to create racial categories. As Foucault noted, the practices of social institutions such as prisons and hospitals tend to bear similarities. There are similar styles in images of criminals and medical patients throughout history.

Power/knowledge and panopticism

We can thus begin to see the complexity of the ways that images are integral to systems of power and ideas about knowledge. Three central concepts introduced by Foucault are useful for thinking about the relation of images and power: *power/knowledge*, *biopower*, and *panopticism*. Foucault wrote about how modern societies are structured on a basic relationship of power/knowledge. Whereas monarchies and totalitarian political systems function through the overt exercise and display of punishment for the violation of laws, such as public execution, in modern societies power relations are structured to produce citizens who will actively participate in self-regulating behavior. Hence the functioning of power in modern political states is less visible. This means that citizens willingly obey laws, participate in social norms, and adhere to dominant social values. Modern societies function, Foucault argued, not through coercion but through cooperation. Foucault saw modern power not as a conspiracy or as authoritarian, but as capable of normalizing bodies in order to maintain relations of dominance and subordination. Power relations, he argued, establish the criteria for what gets to count as knowledge in a given society, and knowledge systems in turn produce power relations.

For instance, there are many ways in which certain kinds of "knowledges" are validated in our society through social institutions such as the press, the medical profession, and education, and other knowledges are discredited. This means that the word of a journalist is taken over that of the witness, the doctor over the patient, the anthropologist over the people they are studying, the police officer over the suspect, or the teacher over the student. While certainly one could argue that expertise may give more credence to those in the first category over the second, Foucault's work demonstrates that the idea of expertise (and who has it) is a fundamental aspect of power relations. In Foucault's terms, we can see how the structure of a classroom itself sets up a particular power dynamic between teacher and students, getting students to internalize the oversight of the teacher so that discipline is enacted in a passive and self-regulating manner.

For Foucault, modern power is not something that negates and represses so much as it is a force that produces—it produces knowledge, and it produces particular kinds of citizens and subjects. Many of the relationships of power in the modern political state are exercised indirectly upon the body, and this is what Foucault termed biopower. He wrote that "the body is also directly involved in a political field; power relations have an immediate hold upon it; they invest it, mark it, train it, torture it, force it to carry out tasks, to perform ceremonies, to emit signs."[11] This means that the modern state has a vested interest in the maintenance and regulation of its citizens; in order to function properly it needs citizens who are willing to work, to fight in wars, and to reproduce, and to have healthy and capable bodies to do so. Therefore the state actively manages, orders, and catalogues the properties of the body through social hygiene, public health, education, demography, census-taking, and regulating reproductive practices. Foucault argued that these institutional practices create knowledge of the body. They force the body to "emit signs," that is, to signify its relation to social norms. The body that is trained, exercised, and regulated was also captured in photographs. Importantly, the emergence of an array of social institutions in the nineteenth century that regulated the bodies of the citizens through public health, a burgeoning mental health field, and changing concepts of normalcy and deviance was simultaneous with the emergence of photography.

Biopower in action

Photographic images have been instrumental in the production of what Foucault called the *docile bodies* of the modern state—citizens who participate in the ideologies of the society through cooperation and a desire to fit in and conform. This happens in the vast array of media images that produce homogeneous images for us of the perfect look, the perfect body, and the perfect pose. Because we as viewers of advertising images do not often think of the ways in which they are operating as ideological texts, these images often have the power to affect our self-images. This means that the norms of beauty and aesthetics which they present, in standards that establish white and Anglo features as the desired look and thinness as the essential body type, can become part of the normalizing gaze that viewers deploy upon themselves.

A central aspect of Foucault's theory is that systems are in place that encourage us to self-regulate without any active threat of punishment. We internalize a managerial gaze that watches over us, and this imagined gaze makes us behave and conform. This is a crucial aspect of Foucault's rethinking of the idea of panopticism. The panopticon is an architectural model, originally for a prison, that can be seen as a metaphor for the way in which power works. In the panopticon model, a central guard tower looks out on a circular set of prison cells, with the activities of each cell in full view of the tower. In this model, the building design produces regulatory behavior, because whether or not there are actually guards in the tower (this cannot be seen by prisoners), the prisoners will feel that gaze upon them and regulate their

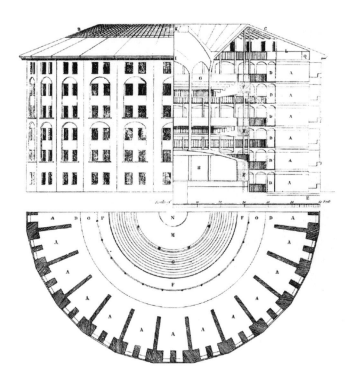

The Penitentiary
Panopticon

behavior accordingly. Power thus is most effective when it is invisible and unverifiable (when the prisoner is unable to verify if the tower guard is watching or not). The point of the panopticon is thus not that active surveillance can affect behavior, but more importantly that the structure of surveillance, whether it is active or not, produces conforming behavior. It thus acts as a powerful metaphor for the way that the circulation of power produces particular kinds of behavior.

There are many ways in which camera surveillance is a part of our everyday experience, in stores, on elevators, in parking garages, etc. We could easily say that the camera is used here as a form of intrusion and policing of our behavior. However, if we use Foucault's concept of the panopticon, we would also have to recognize that the camera is often simply a visible presence of the inspecting gaze that we imagine, whether it is there or not, visible to us or not. In other words, the camera does not need to be turned on or even in place for the inspecting gaze to exist, merely its potential to exist will have this effect. At the same time, the idea of photographic identification, in the criminal justice system, the legal system, and the bureaucracy of everyday life, is prevalent. We have grown accustomed to using a photographic ID for almost

Walker Evans, *License Photo Studio, New York*, 1934

all monetary transactions. In this image, American photographer Walker Evans, who took many photographs of Depression-era people and communities, shows a straightforward view of a license photo studio, where consumers can have their pictures taken for five cents for licenses and other public uses. Evans's image demonstrates the extent to which the photograph is integrated into institutional life. Like all camera images, these photographs are intricately tied up in questions of power.

The gaze and the exotic

The photographic gaze thus helps to establish relationships of power. The person with the camera looks at a person, event, place, or object. The act of looking is commonly thought of as awarding more power to the person who is looking than to the person who is the object of the look. The tradition of institutional photography, in which prisoners, mental patients, and people of various ethnicities were photographed and catalogued, can be related to the traditions of visual anthropology and travel photography as well as to the tradition of painting peoples of so-called exotic locales. All function to varying degrees to represent codes of dominance and subjugation, difference and otherness.

French painter Paul Gauguin spent much of his career in the late nineteenth century painting the people of Tahiti and other French colonies. One can look at these works in terms of their use of bold color, that is, in terms of their aesthetic style. They are now considered to be an important part of the canon of modern art, displayed in museums throughout the world. Yet, these paintings

Paul Gauguin, *Two Tahitian Women*, 1899

also produce meanings of discourses of race, gender, and colonialism. The women in Gauguin's paintings are specifically coded as other, in particular as the exotic other who represent a world supposedly unspoiled by modern civilization, a paradise. In these paintings, the race of the women is marked. In fact, when Gauguin arrived in Tahiti, the influences of French colonialism had already dramatically changed the island, hence Gauguin's depiction of it was highly idealized. Yet, he can be understood within a larger tradition of white men who traveled to "faraway" places (that is, far from Europe, in this case) to supposedly "find" themselves through their encounters with native women. These images operate within the *binary oppositions* of civilization/nature, white/other, and male/female, establishing the women in them as exotic, different, and other to both the painter and the viewer.

The gaze of the camera of the anthropologist, of travel magazines or of magazines that represent non-Western places, such as *National Geographic*, are also forms through which categories of the normal and the exotic are

Two Aiome women of Papua New Guinea, "measured" by Lord Moyne (right) and colleague.

established. Photography has been used to document foreign cultures since its beginnings, and hence to provide visual codes of difference between the anthropologists and their subjects. The codes of the 1935 photograph from Papua New Guinea on the previous page presume the viewer to be white and establish the anthropologists within the dominant category of whiteness in relation to the natives as other. Even the pose of the men, with their arms draped above the smaller islanders, signals a relationship of power. The photograph thus sets up binary oppositions of white/dark, European/native, civilized/primitive through its very conventions. Commercial images of natives in ceremonial dress, which were produced throughout the nineteenth century, clearly have different meanings in different contexts. The image below would mean something very different in the context of this boy's family or village than in the photographic album of a Western traveler. The subjects of these photographs are not named as individuals, rather they are identified as a particular category of people, established as other. They cannot speak in this context, nor do they have any control over the way in which they are represented.

The photograph is thus a central tool in establishing difference. In systems of representation, meaning is established through difference. Hence,

Young man described as "Manaia (buck of village)," Papua New Guinea

throughout the history of representation and language, binary oppositions, such as man/woman, masculine/feminine, culture/nature, or white/black, have been used to organize meaning. We believe we know what culture is because we can identify its opposite (nature), thus difference is essential to its meaning. However, binary oppositions are reductive ways of viewing the complexity of difference and, as philosopher Jacques Derrida has argued, all binary oppositions are encoded with values and concepts of power, superiority, and worth. Hence, the category of the norm is always set up in opposition to that which is deemed abnormal or aberrant in some way, hence other. Thus, binary oppositions designate the first category as *unmarked* (the "norm") and the second as *marked*, or other. The category of femininity is marked, and commonly understood as that which is not masculine (unmarked, most obviously in the way that the term "man" stands in for all humans), while in reality these distinctions are often blurred and people can be understood to have aspects of both. The category of white is understood in Western terms of representation to be the primary category, while black (or brown, etc.) is understood as other to that category—what white is not. Hence, the work of understanding how racism and sexism function, and how to understand difference in terms that do not replicate concepts of dominance and superiority, must take place at the level of linguistic meaning as well as social and cultural meaning.

Photographs and other forms of representation can thus be seen as central elements in the production of *Orientalism*, or the ways in which Western cultures attribute to Eastern and Middle-Eastern cultures qualities of exoticism and barbarism, and hence establish those cultures as other. Cultural theorist Edward Said has written that Orientalism is about "the Orient's special place in European Western experience. The Orient is not only adjacent to Europe; it is also the place of Europe's greatest and richest and oldest colonies, the source of its civilizations and languages, it cultural contestant, and one of its deepest and most recurring images of the Other."[12] Said argues that the concept of the Orient defines in turn Europe and the West. Orientalism is thus used to set up a binary opposition between the West (the Occident) and the East (the Orient) in which negative qualities are attributed to the latter. Orientalism can be found not only in political policy but also in cultural representations, such as contemporary popular culture in which, for instance, films depict all Arab men as terrorists and Asian women as highly sexualized.

The capacity of the photograph to establish exoticism and enact Oriental-ism can also be seen in contemporary advertising, where products are often sold through ads that attach notions of exoticism to their products through images of places that are coded as distant and elsewhere. In some ads, such as the one below, the implied locale of a rice paddy or the use of a model of Asian ethnicity is used to give products as ordinary as women's clothing an exotic quality, intended to draw on stereotypes of Asian women as sexy and different. Sometimes in an advertisement, such as the Safari ad on the next page, the quality of exoticism is attached to a place. In this ad, the nostalgic sense of an earlier era and a colonial context pervades the images, conjuring the traveler as a person who moves through distant, exotic terrains. The ad invites the viewer/consumer to desire the role of the liberated traveler through an unidentified, exotic locale. As we will discuss at more length in Chapter 7, the selling of difference is a central aspect of today's marketing. The consumer is *interpellated* in these ads as a white person who can buy an "authentic" exotic experience. While these ads do not go so far as to sell the idea that the

experience being sold will actually impute the culture to the consumer, they do encode products and salable experiences with the *aura* of the exotic. The consumer is promised a virtually authentic experience as tourist.

Images thus provide a complex field in which power relations are exercised and looks are exchanged. As both spectators and subjects of images, we engage in and are subject to complex practices of looking and being looked at. Increasingly, both the implied gazes of contemporary images and the ways of theorizing them have become highly varied. By examining the power that underlies these exchanges of looks, we can better understand the ways they affect cultural norms about gender, race, sexuality, and ethnicity, and the ways they may impact our lives. In this chapter, we have examined how the media of photography and film are implicated in particular ways in the systems of power and knowledge of the modern state. In both Chapters 2 and 3 we have focused on the role of the viewer in making meaning of the image, and theories about the viewer as subject. In the next chapter, we will trace the history of how visual technologies have affected both concepts of realism and ideas about the political.

Notes

1. Judith Mayne, "Paradoxes of Spectatorship," in *Viewing Positions: Ways of Seeing Film*, edited by Linda Williams (New Brunswick, NJ: Rutgers University Press, 1995), 157.

2. John Berger, *Ways of Seeing* (New York and London: Penguin, 1972), 47.

3. Mary Ann Doane, *The Desire to Desire: The Woman's Film of the 1940s* (Bloomington: Indiana University Press, 1987).

4. Miriam Hansen, *Babel and Babylon: Spectatorship in American Silent Film* (Cambridge, Mass. and London: Harvard University Press, 1991).

5. See Jackie Stacey, *Star Gazing: Hollywood Cinema and Female Spectatorship* (New York and London: Routledge, 1994); and Jacqueline Bobo, *Black Women as Cultural Readers* (New York: Columbia University Press, 1995).

6. Bobo, *Black Women as Cultural Readers* (as above).

7. David Rodowick, *The Difficulty of Difference: Psychoanalysis, Sexual Difference, and Film Theory* (New York and London: Routledge, 1991).

8. See Manthia Diawara, "Black Spectatorship: Problems of Identification and Resistance," *Screen*, 29 (4) (Autumn 1988), 66–79; and bell hooks, "The Oppositional Gaze," in *Black Looks: Race and Representation* (Boston: South End Press, 1993), 115–32.

9. See Judith Mayne, *Framed: Lesbians, Feminists, and Media Culture* (Minneapolis and London: University of Minnesota Press, 2000); Chris Straayer, *Deviant Eyes, Deviant Bodies: Sexual Re-Orientation in Film and Video* (New York: Columbia University Press, 1996); and Patricia White, *Uninvited: Classical Hollywood Cinema and Lesbian Representability* (Bloomington: Indiana University Press, 1999).

10. Sandra S. Phillips, "Identifying the Criminal," in *Police Pictures: The Photograph as Evidence*, edited by Sandra S. Phillips (San Francisco: San Francisco Museum of Modern Art/Chronicle Books, 1997), 20.

11. Michel Foucault, *Discipline and Punish: The Birth of the Prison*, translated by Alan Sheridan (New York: Vintage, 1979), 25.

12. Edward Said, *Orientalism* (New York: Vintage, 1979), 1.

Further Reading

Lucy Arbuthnot and Gail Seneca. "Pre-text and Text in *Gentlemen Prefer Blondes*." In *Issues in Feminist Film Criticism*. Edited by Patricia Erens. Bloomington: Indiana University Press, 1991, 112–25.

Jean-Louis Baudry. "The Apparatus: Metapsychological Approaches to the Impression of Reality in the Cinema." In *Narrative, Apparatus, Ideology: A Film Theory Reader*. Edited by Philip Rosen. New York: Columbia University Press, [1975] 1986, 299–318.

——"Ideological Effects of the Basic Cinematographic Apparatus." In *Narrative, Apparatus, Ideology: A Film Theory Reader*. Edited by Philip Rosen. New York: Columbia University Press, [1970] 1986, 286–89.

Jacqueline Bobo. *Black Women as Cultural Readers*. New York: Columbia University Press, 1995.

Elizabeth Cowie. *Representing the Woman: Cinema and Psychoanalysis*. Minneapolis and London: University of Minnesota Press, 1997.

Manthia Diawara. "Black Spectatorship: Problems of Identification and Resistance." *Screen*, 29 (4) (Autumn 1988), 66–79.

Mary Ann Doane. *The Desire to Desire: The Woman's Film of the 1940s*. Bloomington: Indiana University Press, 1987.

——*Femmes Fatales: Feminism, Film Theory, Psychoanalysis*. New York and London: Routledge, 1991.

Elizabeth Edwards, ed. *Anthropology & Photography 1860–1920*. New Haven and London: Yale University Press, 1992.

Michel Foucault. *Madness and Civilization*. Translated by Richard Howard. New York: Random House, 1965.

——*Discipline and Punish: The Birth of the Prison*. Translated by Alan Sheridan. New York: Vintage, 1979.

——*Power/Knowledge: Selected Interviews and Other Writings 1972–77*. Edited by Colin Gordon. Translated by Colin Gordon, Leo Marshall, John Mepham, and Kate Soper. New York: Pantheon, 1980.

David Green. "Classified Subjects: Photography and Anthropology: The Technology of Power." *Ten.8*, 14 (1984), 30–37.

Kelly Hankin. "The Girls in the Back Room: The Lesbian Bar in Film, Television, and Video." Ph.D. thesis, University of Rochester, 2000.

Miriam Hansen. *Babel and Babylon: Spectatorship in American Silent Film*. Cambridge, Mass. and London: Harvard University Press, 1991.

Chris Holmlund. "When is a Lesbian Not a Lesbian? The Lesbian Continuum and the Mainstream Femme Film." *Camera Obscura*, 25–26 (May 1991), 145–78.

bell hooks. "The Oppositional Gaze." In *Black Looks: Race and Representation*. Boston: South End Press, 1993, 115–32.

E. Ann Kaplan, ed. *Feminism and Film*. New York and Oxford: Oxford University Press, 2000.

Catherine A. Lutz and Jane L. Collins. *Reading National Geographic*. Chicago and London: University of Chicago Press, 1993.

Judith Mayne. *Cinema and Spectatorship*. New York and London: Routledge, 1993.

——*Framed: Lesbians, Feminists, and Media Culture*. Minneapolis and London: University of Minnesota Press, 2000.

Christian Metz. *Film Language: A Semiotics of Cinema*. Translated by Michael Taylor. New York and Oxford: Oxford University Press, 1974.

Laura Mulvey. "Visual Pleasure and Narrative Cinema," and "Afterthoughts on Visual Pleasure and Narrative Cinema." In *Visual and Other Pleasures*. Bloomington: Indiana University Press, 1989.

Bill Nichols, ed. *Movies and Methods*. Berkeley and London: University of California Press, 1976.

Constance Penley, ed. *Feminism and Film Theory*. New York and London: Routledge, 1988.

Sandra S. Phillips, ed. *Police Pictures: The Photograph as Evidence*. San Francisco: San Francisco Museum of Modern Art/Chronicle Books, 1997.

David Rodowick. *The Difficulty of Difference*: Psychoanalysis, Sexual Difference, and Film Theory. New York and London: Routledge, 1991.

Vito Russo. *The Celluloid Closet: Homosexuality in the Movies*. New York: HarperCollins, 1987.

Edward Said. *Orientalism*. New York: Vintage, 1979.

Kaja Silverman. *Male Subjectivity at the Margins*. New York and London: Routledge, 1992.

——*Threshold of the Visible World*. New York and London: Routledge, 1996.

Jackie Stacey. *Star Gazing: Hollywood Cinema and Female Spectatorship*. New York and London: Routledge, 1994.

Chris Straayer. *Deviant Eyes, Deviant Bodies: Sexual Re-Orientation in Film and Video*. New York: Columbia University Press, 1996.

Andrea Weiss. "'A Queer Feeling When I Look at You': Female Stars and Lesbian Spectatorship." In *Stardom: Industry of Desire*. Edited by Christine Gledhill. New York and London: Routledge, 1991, 283–99.

Patricia White. *Uninvited: Classical Hollywood Cinema and Lesbian Representability*. Bloomington: Indiana University Press, 1999.

Linda Williams. *Hard Core: Power, Pleasure, and the Frenzy of the Visible*. Berkeley and London: University of California Press, 1989.

——ed. *Viewing Positions: Ways of Seeing Film*. New Brunswick, NJ: Rutgers University Press, 1995.

Judith Williamson. "Woman Is an Island: Femininity and Colonialism." In *Studies in Entertainment*. Edited by Tania Modleski. Bloomington: Indiana University Press, 1986.

Reproduction and Visual Technologies 4

Throughout history, the social roles played by images have changed dramatically. For example, art's origins as an expression of religious tenets evolved over time to its role as an object of value restricted to the wealthy classes, and eventually to the context of art commodification today, in which consumers can purchase art in the form of reproductions. Similarly, the photograph has played many different social roles since it was developed in the early nineteenth century, including those of art, science, marketing, the law, and personal memory. The emergence of electronic imaging in the late twentieth century, with *digital* imaging, the *Internet*, and the *World Wide Web*, has radically altered the distribution and social meaning of images. Hence, both the conventions of imaging and the concepts of the visual have changed throughout history.

We look at images of the past differently today than they were viewed during the time in which they were created. A viewer may make assumptions about the historical status of an image from its style, medium, and formal qualities. For instance, we might assume that a painting composed in a classical style was made prior to the *modernist* art period of the late nineteenth to early twentieth century, or that a brown sepia-toned, black-and-white photograph, or a faded color image, is a historical image.

There are many aspects of the photograph on the next page, for instance, that indicate its historical status. As viewers, we can make certain assumptions about when it was made, even if we know nothing about its origins. Its original tone is a soft brown sepia color, which was a convention of nineteenth-century photography and hence signifies an aged image. The woman in the portrait is dressed in a style of a different era, and the soft focus on the edges

Julia Margaret Cameron, *Alice Liddell*, 1872

of the frame give a faded sense of time. She is framed by branches of a tree, and stares boldly at the camera. This image is, in fact, photographer Julia Margaret Cameron's 1872 portrait of Alice Liddell, the inspiration for *Alice in Wonderland*. It is possible for this image to have been made today, using older imaging techniques and nineteenth-century clothing styles. Yet, its meaning would then be different. It would then signify, among other things, a reference to a historical style rather than a simple portrait.

Advertisers have often used the codes of classical style to attach to their products both a sense of history and a nostalgia for previous times. This is intended to add concepts of value and class to that product, so that it will evoke both tradition and *taste*. In the ad above, for instance, the classical pose of the model evokes the history of painting of female nudes, and thus attaches to the product—a designer shawl—the qualities of art and upper-class taste. The old lantern, wooden bench, and 1920s hairstyle are *signifiers* of the past and tradition. The phrase, "art becomes you," thus suggests to consumers that they can themselves acquire the attributes of classical art through the purchase of the shawl. As we shall discuss in Chapters 6 and 7, the signification of history in visual images now exists in a broad array of remakes, *paro-dies*, and images of nostalgia.

Realism and the history of perspective

One way to understand how the meaning of images has changed throughout history is to examine the role of realism in art. Changes in the *aesthetic* style of images do more than simply chart the history of art and visual culture, they can also indicate the development of different kinds of world views. By examining the stylistic changes of the history of Euro-American visual culture, we can see how images indicate changing ways of seeing the world.

Realism has been a fundamental goal of many styles of art, because art has often functioned to reflect society and nature back to its spectators. While the history of religious art has been concerned with depicting not the real world but the metaphysical world of myth and religious figures and events, painting has had a very long tradition of representing the human figure and the world in which we live. The desire to have images represent either the real world or an imagined world has changed dramatically throughout different moments of history. Similarly, the concept of what makes an image realistic has changed throughout history and varies between cultures.

One of the fundamental shifts of the depiction of reality in the history of Western art took place with the development of *perspective* as a convention of European art. The invention of perspective in the mid-fifteenth century was the result of a *Renaissance* interest in the fusion of art and science. It is a mechanically inspired technique to make paintings appear more realistic in their translation of three-dimensional space to a two-dimensional image. To use linear perspective to create an image, the painter has to designate at least one vanishing point and design the objects within the image to recede in size toward that point. Techniques of perspective demand that the objects and people depicted in the background of images be painted smaller and along receding planes. In the 1448 depiction of the annunciation on the next page, a motif in Christian art by Fra Carnevale, the buildings and landscape are scaled to be increasingly small as they recede toward a central vanishing point. This has the effect of drawing the viewer's eye toward this central point, and in giving the image a depth which, in this case, foregrounds the figures.

The technique of perspective appears to us to be realistic precisely because

Fra Carnevale, *The Annunciation*, c.1448

Funerary Papyrus of the Princess Entiu-ny, 1025 BC

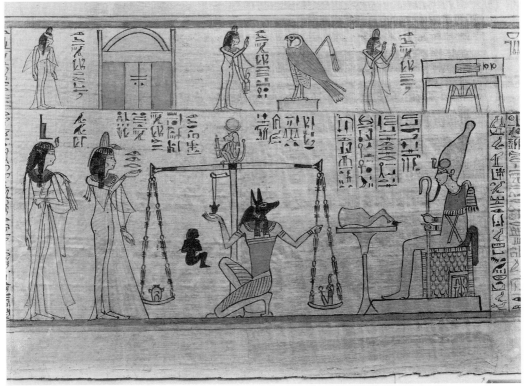

it is a stylistic convention that dominates in Western images to this day. Prior image conventions, for instance, used flat space with little sense of depth, and some ancient styles, such as ancient Egyptian art, depicted the size of an object or person according to its social importance rather than its distance from the viewer. In this Egyptian drawing on papyrus, the figures are flattened in space and there is little sense of depth. The figures exist within an abstract space, and tell a narrative in relation to each other and the written text. Yet, this work would have been understood in ancient Egypt to represent the real world.

Perspective redefined painting styles from the fifteenth century on. It is not simply a visual technique but a way of seeing, one that indicates a change in the world view of Renaissance Europe at the time that it became an aesthetic convention. The Renaissance, which began in Italy in the early fourteenth century and reached its height throughout Europe in the early sixteenth century, has been defined as a time of intellectual and artistic resurgence that was fueled by a renewed interest in *Classical* art and literature. The Renaissance represented a conscious embrace of culture, science, art, and politics. One of the primary aspects of Renaissance perspective is its designation of a single spectator in space. Perspective emphasizes a scientific and mechanical view toward ordering and depicting nature, and focuses a work of art toward a perceived viewer. The spectator defines the center of the image. Whereas, for instance, Medieval imaging conventions assumed that there could be many vantage points from which a scene could be depicted, perspective demanded that one, unique point be established. Thus, it has been said that the technique of perspective turns the viewer into a "god," whose view is the defining position from which to look at a scene. As art critic John Berger has written, "Every drawing or painting that used perspective proposed to the spectator that he was the unique centre of the world."[1]

In addition, perspective took hold in Europe in the same era as the emergence of new ideas in astronomy, such as Copernicus's concept of the earth rotating around the sun rather than being the center of the universe, ideas which radically challenged the Church's view of a god-centered universe. As perspective gained prominence in fifteenth-century painting, it formed part of a larger set of social changes, including the embrace of science in the emerging *Scientific Revolution*. One of its primary early proponents was Leonardo da Vinci, whose work is famous in the history of art for its integration of principles of science and art. The emphasis on a single spectator in perspective thus can be seen in the context of changing notions about religious definitions of the world and the beginning of a shift in social values from religion to science. Whereas previous cultures, such as Classical Greece, had philosophical debates about realism in art, and rejected the use of techniques such as perspective as a form of trickery, the Renaissance era embraced the idea that it was art's social function to represent the real as closely as possible. Indeed, da Vinci wrote in his diaries, "In art we may be said to be grandsons to God. . . . Have we not seen pictures which bear so close a resemblance to the actual thing that they have deceived both men and beasts?"

The artists who first began working with the technique of perspective in the fifteenth century were enthusiastic about its results. Here, they felt, was a scientific approach that helped them to create objective images of reality. Hence, perspective reveals the desire for art to be an *objective*, as opposed to *subjective*, depiction of reality. Yet, though it may seem to be a realistic depiction of the world, perspective is a highly reductive, abstract form of representation. It is a convention that makes images that use perspective seem like reality. Among other things, perspective reduces the relationship between eye and object to a single exchange in space. The spectator is situated in perspective as having a view from one specific place. It has been argued by many art historians and others that human vision is infinitely more complex than this notion of a stationary viewer. When we look, our eyes are in constant motion, and any sight we have is the composite of many different views and glances. In addition, much contemporary philosophy has emphasized that the view of the spectator affects the thing looked upon. As we noted in Chapters 2 and 3, a central part of looking is about the particular relationship of a spectator to a specific image at a specific moment in time and place. The world of perspective indicates the desire for vision to be stable and unchanging and for the meaning of images to be fixed, when the act of looking is in fact highly changeable and contextual.

The technique of perspective also shifted the role of space in images, allowing space to dominate over the figures in the frame.[2] As we can see in the painting of *The Annunciation*, the architectural forms and space dominate in the image, almost at the expense of the human figures in the foreground. Space is organized in perspective as linear and uniform rather than symbolic. This scientifically defined sense of space related to a broader set of philosophical developments. French philosopher René Descartes, who lived in the seventeenth century, is responsible for many contemporary concepts of space which can be related to his privileging of the visual. Descartes's concept of space, known as *Cartesian space*, is defined as that which can be mathematically mapped and measured. A Cartesian grid refers to the organization of space through three axes, each intersecting the others at 90 degrees to produce three-dimensional space. Cartesian space is derived from Descartes's theories about rational ways of viewing the world and is contingent on the idea of an all-knowing, all-seeing human subject. Descartes was very influential in the legitimation of ideas about visual observation forming the basis for evidence, which is one of the foundations of *empiricism*. He famously wrote: "All the management of our lives depends on the senses, and since that of sight is the most comprehensive and noblest of these, there is no doubt that the inventions which serve to augment its power are among the most useful that there can be."[3] Thus through the development of perspective and the subsequent philosophical turn toward the visual, the relationship of science/technology and vision is firmly established in Western philosophy. In Chapter 8, we will discuss in more detail the implications of the relationship between the visual and scientific or legal evidence.

Realism and visual technologies

As we can see with the fusion of science and art in the technique of perspective, changing historical understandings of images have been directly influenced by imaging technologies. The privileging of both science and the visual in Western philosophy emerged after the Scientific Revolution that took place from the mid-fifteenth through the seventeenth century. During this time period, developments in science, in fields such as navigation, astronomy, and biology, prompted radical changes in the world view, changes that eroded the dominant role of the Church. Many new scientific ideas, such as Galileo's theories about planetary movement, were seen as a threat to the Church, and were the source of difficult struggle (Galileo was tried, for instance, for heresy for his scientific ideas). However, by the eighteenth century, science had emerged as a dominant social force. In the *Enlightenment*, an eighteenth-century intellectual movement, there was an embrace of the importance of science, and the concepts of rationalism and progress. The Enlightenment promised that the power of human reason would overcome superstition, end ignorance through the development of scientific knowledge, bring prosperity through the technical mastery of nature, and introduce justice and order to human affairs. The rationalism and elevation of science and technology that we saw with Descartes was thus firmly established in this time period, and would lay the foundations for *modernity*.

The history of visual images can be seen in light of the development of science and technology. It is a history of visual technologies as well, from the invention of perspective to photography, film, television, and, more recently, digital imaging. Seen through this framework of image technology, the history of image production in Western culture can be viewed in four general periods: (1) ancient art produced prior to the development of perspective in 1425; (2) the age of perspective until the era of the mechanical, including the Renaissance, Baroque, Rococo, and Romantic periods (roughly the mid-fifteenth century until the eighteenth-century), a time period that includes the Scientific Revolution and the Enlightenment; (3) the modern era of technical developments with the rise of mechanization and the Industrial Revolution, including the development of photography in the 1830s, that made image *reproduction* and *mass media* possible (the mid-eighteenth century until the late twentieth century); (4) and the *postmodern* era of electronic technology, computer and digital imaging, and *virtual* space (overlapping with the mechanical, approximately from the 1960s until the present). The rest of this chapter will concentrate on these last two time periods and the social and cultural views they represent.

Technologies of imaging, such as perspective or photography, are not simply sitting out there in the world, waiting to be invented. To say that a given technology dictates its invention is to engage in *technological determinism*. Technological determinism is the belief that technology determines social effect and change, and that it is autonomous and hence separate from social effects. In this book, we argue against technological determinism. Instead, we look at technologies (specifically visual technologies) as the products of particular social and historical contexts. They emerge from collective cultural and social desires. In other words, it can be argued that technologies have important and influential effects on society, but they are also themselves the product of their societies and times, and the ideologies that exist within them.

For instance, the scientific elements of the technique of perspective existed prior to its "invention." As we mentioned before, the Greeks understood the basics of perspective, yet they rejected it as a technique because it was in contrast to certain fundamental philosophical ideas that were prevalent in Greek culture—that one should not paint a painting that might "trick" a viewer into thinking it was real, for instance. The development of perspective as a technique was the outcome of the social views of European culture in the early fifteenth century, including an emergent interest in scientific process. Similarly, many of the chemical and mechanical elements necessary to produce photographic images existed prior to when photography was invented simultaneously by several people working in different countries in the 1830s. Indeed, some art historians have argued that photography could not have emerged as a visual technology until Western artists had begun to paint in the language of photography—not rigidly composed realist works but paintings that were like snapshots, seemingly life-like and spontaneous. In addition, the early uses of photography, which was instantly popular, were both institutional (for medical, legal, and scientific uses) and personal (an early widespread use of photography was for portraits). These uses influenced the ways that photographic technology developed.

It could thus be said that photography emerged as a visual technology because it fit certain emerging social concepts and needs of the time—modern ideas about the individual in the context of growing urban centers, modern concepts of technological progress and mechanization, and the rise of bureaucratic institutions in the modern state. In combining scientific technique with art, like the technique of perspective, yet also deploying a mechanical device, photography is in many ways the visual technology that helped to usher in the age of modernity. It could thus be said, in the terms of Michel Foucault that we discussed in Chapter 3, that photography emerged as a medium when certain *discourses* of science, law, technology, and modernity made its social roles possible.

The historical moment when photography was developed and became popular, from the early nineteenth century until the mid-twentieth century, when the question of reproduction became crucial to the meaning of images, is considered to be the height of modernity. Modernity is a term that refers both to a specific period of time (dating approximately from the sixteenth century until the mid-twentieth century, with its height in the nineteenth century) and to a particular era of social development in Euro-American culture and modernism to a style of Western art (dating approximately from the turn of the century to the late twentieth century). The modern era is characterized by a sense of both upheaval and possibility that accompanied the increased urbanization of the eighteenth and nineteenth centuries, as large numbers of people moved from agrarian, rural lifestyles into growing cities. It is defined by industrialization and mechanization, the rise of the modern political state, and the increased bureaucratization of daily life. These social factors contributed to a breakdown of traditions and a sense of collective *alienation*, yet also to an embrace of the future with both anxiety and utopian optimism. (We will discuss modernism and postmodernism at more length in Chapter 7.)

Photography is in many ways the mechanical realization of perspective, and its effect on painting was profound. With the development of a camera device that could produce realistic images of the world, the social role of painting changed dramatically. Whereas painting had functioned throughout most of Western history as a means to produce an idealized view of the world, specifically through the world view of the Church, it had become increasingly a tool of realism after the invention of perspective. The invention of photography was greeted by such proclamations of its verisimilitude, that some even suggested it had redefined human vision altogether. French writer Emile Zola even wrote at the time, "We cannot claim to have really seen anything before having photographed it."[4] Many thus felt that the camera could do a "better" job of producing realistic images of the world than a painting, and this allowed painters to think of painting in new ways not always tied to realism or to the *ideology* of fixed perspective.

As a consequence, many styles of modern art that followed the invention of photography defied the tradition of perspective. *Impressionism*, for instance, was an art movement of the late nineteenth century that featured works that used visible brushstrokes and impressionistic depictions of light to capture a sense of human vision. The style of Impressionism shifted its focus to light and color and aimed for a visual spontaneity. The Impressionist work is not a moment captured in time, like a photograph, but an image that evokes the ongoing play of light and color in the experience of looking. Impressionism was greeted, as many changes in representational style are, as a disturbing way of looking (prompting French cartoonists to predict that the images would cause women to miscarry). It remains an extremely popular style of art today.

One of the primary figures of Impressionism was Claude Monet, whose works have a particular emphasis on the play of light and water. Monet examined the process of looking by painting many different works of the same scene. He made some twenty paintings, for instance of the cathedral in Rouen, each a portrait of different light and color. In works such as these, Monet demonstrated the complexity of vision and also established it as a fluid process. The Rouen Cathedral never looks the same; it is not simply one set

Claude Monet, *Rouen Cathedral: The Portal (in Sun)*, 1894

view, but many impressions. The act of seeing is thus established in these works as active, changing, never fixed, a process of thought. In later years, Monet would paint many versions of his now famous garden in Giverny.

New ways of looking were a primary focus of the French *avant-garde* in the late nineteenth and early twentieth centuries. What it means to look was thus a central concern of modern art at a time of rapid social change that included the increased social role of photography and a sense of upheaval. One of the central movements of the avant-garde at the turn of the century was *Cubism*, a style that was associated initially with Pablo Picasso and Georges Braque. The painters who worked in Cubism were interested in depicting objects from several different points of view simultaneously. Cubism was thus a style resistant to the dominant model of perspective; it proclaimed that the human eye is never at rest upon a single point but is always in motion. The Cubists painted objects as if they were being viewed from several different angles simultaneously, and focused on the visual relationship between objects. In the painting by Georges Braque on the next page, a rendering of realistic space and light has been discarded for a kinetic view of a guitar player through different angles and fragments. The painting is intended to show a view of a man with a guitar composed as a series of simultaneous glances. This was, according to the Cubists, a means of depicting the restless and complicated process of human

Georges Braque, *The Portuguese*, 1911

vision. We could compare this image to another still life, the seventeenth-century Dutch still life by Pieter Claesz, which we discussed in Chapter 1. Both images are still lifes, but Braque's vision defies the singular perspective of Claesz's realist image. Although each painting presents itself as a representation of how we really see, the Claesz painting posits a singular spectator looking toward the image and the Braque offers the restless view of a spectator in constant motion. It is important to note that the Cubists were interested in depicting reality, in creating a new way of looking at the real. John Berger has written, "Cubism changed the nature of the relationship between the painted image and reality, and by so doing it expressed a new relationship between man and reality."[5]

Modernist styles such as Impressionism, Cubism, and, later, *Abstract Expressionism* were all, among other things, responses to the dominance of perspective in Western art for centuries; each declared vision to be infinitely more subjective and complex. What realism is in images has thus changed dramatically throughout history, and continues to change. The idea that a perspective-based realistic view is actually no more than one of the many ways of representing human vision has been taken further by many contemporary artists. For instance, in this photo collage, David Hockney composes an image of a desert intersection through many snapshots taken from different posi-

David Hockney,
Pearblossom Hwy.,
11–18th April 1986, #2,
1986

tions. Where is the "real" image here? At what "moment" was this image taken? Where is the spectator of this image positioned? Hockney's work suggests that this mundane roadside is never one view but many views from many perspectives over time. His image is a portrait of the vibrancy of everyday vision.

The reproduction of images

One of the primary aspects of the relationship of technology to the history of imaging is that of image reproduction. In the context of modernism, with the rise of photography in the early nineteenth century and the invention of film in the 1890s, image conventions changed in significant ways. Hence, of the four eras we defined earlier through which the relationship of technology and images can be charted, the third era of modernism is defined in many ways by the new capacities of image reproduction and the development of the mass media. Photographic, cinematic, and television images are infinitely reproducible, and that fact has radically changed the role of images in society. In Chapter 5, we will discuss the rise of mass media. In this chapter, we will focus on the effect of image reproduction on the social role of images in the nineteenth and twentieth centuries.

Prior to the development of technologies that could reproduce images, a work of art was considered to be unique and original, its meaning tied to the

place where it resided (which was often a church or palace). These works of art were always potentially reproducible, indeed the practice of creating *replicas* of famous works of art has always been quite common. However, the mechanical reproduction of art is quite different from the more inexact creation of replicas. Mechanical reproduction changes the meaning and value of an image and, ultimately, the role images play in society. Walter Benjamin, a German critic of the early twentieth century, wrote a famous essay in 1936 about this cultural shift, entitled "The Work of Art in the Age of Mechanical Reproduction." Benjamin was an early member of the *Frankfurt School*, which we will discuss in Chapter 5. His essay, like many of his writings, is still highly influential today, precisely because it explains and predicts the changing visual culture of the twentieth century.

There are many technologies of imaging that can produce multiple similar images. Printmaking techniques such as engraving, etching, and woodcuts were developed in the fifteenth and sixteenth centuries, and lithography in the early nineteenth century. It has been argued, most notably by art historian William Ivins, that while great emphasis has always been placed on the social impact of the invention of the printing press in the mid-fifteenth century by Johann Gutenberg, the slightly earlier discovery of how to print pictures and diagrams was tremendously important to the emergence of modern life and thought. Without prints, Ivins states, "we should have very few of our modern sciences, technologies, archaeologies, or ethnologies—for all of these are dependent, first or last, upon information conveyed by exactly repeatable visual or pictorial statements."[6]

The importance of the "exactly repeatable visual or pictorial statement" was central to the dissemination of knowledge. However, the medium of photography changed the status of the image further by making it possible to reproduce pre-existing works of art, such as paintings and frescoes, which were previously unique. Benjamin wrote that this technological change had a profound influence on the meaning of art in society. For instance, the invention of photography coincided with a cult of originality. Artists would often in the past produce several versions of the same painting, and there were traditions of making replicas of works, usually by the artist or under his/her supervision, in the same medium. However, with the rise of reproduction, these practices disappeared. Instead, a reaffirmation of the unique image, one that had more value, took place precisely at the time when that original image could be reproduced into copies by the mechanical photographic camera.

Benjamin argued that the one-of-a-kind art work has a particular *aura* to it. Its value is derived from its uniqueness and its role in ritual, meaning that it may carry a kind of sacred value, whether religious or not. Indeed, it is because of the fact that it is one of a kind that it retains a sacred status. He wrote, "Even the most perfect reproduction of a work of art is lacking in one element: its presence in time and space, its unique existence at the place where it happens to be."[7] It is precisely this "presence in time and space" that Benjamin refers to as the aura of the image, a quality that makes it seem authentic.

The concept of *authenticity* is crucial to the way in which images are perceived to have value. Benjamin points out that the original of a reproduction is understood to be more authentic than the copies made from it. In other words, in Benjamin's terms, authenticity cannot be reproduced. Traditionally, authenticity has meant "genuine, reliable, not false or copied," indeed, the idea that something is more "real." Yet, the concept of authenticity is used in many different ways today. For instance, an advertisement might claim that its product is "authentic" in order to sell it. In the ad on the next page, authenticity is defined as "something new that's been there all along," in an attempt to sell both tradition and newness simultaneously. The idea of authenticity is something that advertisers often attempt to attach to consumer products through codes of realism. Jerky "amateur" camera work and "natural" sound and lighting are used to create a realist effect, selling the idea that nothing in the ad has been orchestrated or faked, and references to tradition are used to

sell identities that cannot be acquired simply by purchasing a product. For instance, Ralph Lauren's western wear acquires the code of authenticity by appearing to be just like the clothes of cowboys on the ranch; Reebok and Nike use images of inner-city basketball courts (presumably the most "authentic" place where basketball is played) to attach the quality of authenticity to high-priced sneakers. It could be argued that authenticity is about being genuine and original. Paradoxically, we live in a world in which the concept of authenticity is routinely reproduced, packaged, sold, and bought.

We live in a society that is also permeated with mass-produced images. The idea that only a one-of-a-kind image can be authentic holds little currency in our world. Many copies can exist of a photographic image, each of equal value, and cinematic, television, and computer images consist of many simultaneous images all at once. Their value lies not in their uniqueness but in their aesthetic, cultural, and social worth. As we discussed in Chapter 1, a television news image can be considered valuable because it can be seen simultaneously on many screens at the same time. However, Benjamin's central point is about the effect of reproduction upon the image, and how the meaning of an original image changes when it is reproduced.

Many famous paintings have been reproduced in art books and on posters, postcards, and T-shirts. What effect does this have on the quality of the origi-

T-shirt with reproduction of Andy Warhol's signature, portrait, and artwork

nal? The original is more valuable, in both financial and social terms, than the copies. However, Benjamin wrote that this value has changed, since it comes not from the uniqueness of the image as one of a kind, but rather from it being the original of many copies.

Mechanical reproduction means that famous works of art are more accessible to people, because they can view these images in books and even own copies of them to put on their own walls in the form of posters. One could say that this demystifies these works of art and makes them seem less untouchable and magical than they may appear in the original. One of the most fundamental consequences of reproduction is that an image that before had existed within a single place can now be seen in many different contexts: an art history book, a bulletin board, an advertisement. The painting, *The Scream*, shown on the next page, was painted by Edvard Munch in 1893. Munch was adept at depicting the angst of modern life, and his painting has become an icon for neurosis and fear. In the original, the red sky creates an ominous feel and the figure, more a homunculus than a man, is a ghostlike embodiment of anxiety. Like other famous paintings, *The Scream* has been reproduced as a postcard and poster, but because of its iconic value, it has also proliferated as a kind of *kitsch* object—an inflatable figure, a birthday card, a key chain, a refrigerator magnet. It was also used as a reference in the 1996 film *Scream*, in which the killer wears a *Scream*-inspired mask. Importantly, the meaning of the image changes with

Edvard Munch,
The Scream, 1893

each context. For instance, when *The Scream* is an inflatable figure, it is almost impossible to invest the image with the deep seriousness of its original terror. Rather, it is intended to make us laugh about the stress of everyday life, in effect to laugh at modern angst. Similarly, when *The Scream* appears on a 40th birthday card, it is used for humorous effect. One could say, then, that this image has the opposite effect from its original when it is reproduced as a kitsch object of questionable taste.

The changes in visual culture that have taken place with the emergence of digital imaging have also changed the contexts in which famous works of art have been reproduced. The impact of computers and digital media on Western visual culture has often been compared to the impact of perspective during the Renaissance. Hence, there are many references in digital culture to the Renaissance and in particular to Leonardo da Vinci as an icon of that era's merging of science of art. For instance, one of the computer art field's publications, *Leonardo*, uses his name to signify the powerful impact of the computer in changing paradigms in art. Leonardo's painting, the *Mona Lisa*,

painted in 1503, has also been used to imply the computer's value as a high art form and not just a commercial technique, precisely because, as we noted in Chapter 1, it is known as one of the most famous paintings in the world. A reproduction of the *Mona Lisa* was one of the first images to be scanned and digitally reproduced on a computer in 1965, along with a portrait of computer scientist Norbert Wiener (who coined the term "cybernetics"). Copies of this "digital masterpiece" are sold on the World Wide Web, where the image is described as "unique." In this case, unique means not one of a kind, but unusual. One such "unique" copy of the digital Mona Lisa hangs in the Computer Museum in Boston. One might ask the question, who is the "artist" behind this "masterpiece" reproduction, Leonardo da Vinci (who had no say in its digitization), the computer scientist who was in charge of its production process, or the workers at the laboratory that made the reproduction technology possible?

The questions of authorship and artistic ownership become even more complex in contexts where consumers are invited to reproduce art masterpieces as their own. For instance, the cross-stitch company Charles Craft sells a fabric reproduction of the *Mona Lisa* in a gold frame, which cross-stitchers are then invited to sew as their own masterpiece. The advertisement suggests that the consumer can not only "own" this priceless masterpiece, he or she can also create it by hand and, what's more, wear the famous Mona Lisa smile as well. It is also possible to "wear" the Mona Lisa in the form of jewelry and clothing, in necklace pendants, pins, and ties imprinted with its image, sold in

Andrew Patros, close-ups of early digital reproduction of the *Mona Lisa*, 1965

Ralph Marlin, Mona Lisa tie

novelty stores, museum shops, and on the Web. To whom then does the image belong, and who is its artist? The question of artistic ownership becomes increasingly complex in digital media, which make accessible to the average consumer many of the processes of reproduction.

Another way that famous works of art change meaning through reproduction is through both art references and the constant reworking and remaking of popular culture. We will discuss many aspects of this recycling in Chapter 7. Here, we would like to emphasize how this operates in the context of remaking famous, original images. The *Mona Lisa* was "remade" by several modern artists. For instance, in 1919 Marcel Duchamp drew a moustache and goatee on the famous portrait in a kind of satirical irreverence that was characteristic of *Dada* art, naming it *L.H.O.O.Q.*, which when spoken in French means "she has a hot ass", and later *Surrealist* painter Salvador Dali redid the *Mona Lisa* with his own famous swirling moustache, referring back to Duchamp.

Hence, the *Mona Lisa* carries a range of culture references. In the cover on the next page from *The New Yorker*, a popular magazine about culture and politics, the *Mona Lisa* is evoked in an image of Monica Lewinsky, who became briefly famous in the late 1990s for allegedly having an affair with US President Bill Clinton. There are many interesting visual puns and plays on meaning that give this image its wry humor. Both figures share dark hair and round faces, the initials ML, and names beginning with M-o-n. Both are female icons who command instant face recognition in contemporary Western culture. The

model for da Vinci's *Mona Lisa* has remained anonymous despite endless speculation about her identity. Her appeal is attributed in part to her mystery, represented in her ambiguous smile, sometimes referred to as the most famous smile in the world. Like the *Mona Lisa*'s model, Monica Lewinsky was (before the White House scandal) an anonymous and relatively unremarkable woman. She then became, at least briefly, as famous as the *Mona Lisa*, though certainly without the enigma of the woman of the original painting, whose mystery is based in part on the fact that she, unlike Lewinsky, does not speak. Ironically, Lewinsky's image, like the *Mona Lisa* in relationship to the Renaissance, may be more visually symbolic of this era in history (and its intense media focus on the private lives of public figures) than the image of the powerful man through whom she achieved fame. The remaking of this famous original thus allows this image to convey a broad set of meanings in a compact form.

Reproduced images as politics

Walter Benjamin wrote that the result of mechanical reproduction was a profound change in the function of art. He stated, "Instead of being based on ritual, [art] begins to be based on another practice—politics."[8] What did he mean by this? Benjamin wrote this essay in Germany in the 1930s, as the rise of Fascism and the Nazi Party was orchestrated in part by an elaborate *propaganda* machine of images. Germany's

Third Reich anticipated much of the contemporary use of images in politics to groom the image of political leaders and the cult value that images can produce. Its images of grandeur, monumentality, and massive regimentation are now *icons* for both a Fascist aesthetic and the practice of propaganda.

We often think of propaganda as a practice used exclusively by totalitarian and authoritarian governments, an obvious campaign to "sway the masses," and we will discuss this concept of propaganda at length in Chapter 5. But, the term "propaganda" can refer to any attempt to use words and images to promote particular ideas and persuade people to believe certain concepts. This definition could also fit advertising images and any image with an intention to convey a political message or persuade. It is, in fact, what we mean by the use of images as politics.

Mechanically or electronically reproduced images can be in many places simultaneously and can be combined or put with text. These capabilities have greatly increased the ability of images to captivate and persuade. In the 1930s, German artist John Heartfield produced photo collages against the Nazis that had a biting political edge. The powerful effect of Heartfield's images is derived in part from his use of "found" photographic images to make political statements. In this image, he portrays Hitler swallowing gold coins and taking the money of the German people. The photo-collage form allows Heartfield to make a statement. We do not read his image as realistic, but rather as a metaphor for political themes. Heartfield borrowed from the style of

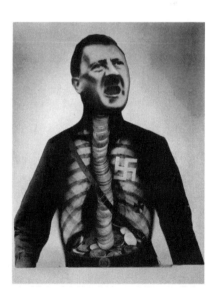

John Heartfield, *Adolf as Superman: "He Swallows Gold and Spits Out Tin-Plate,"* 1932

propaganda images at the time to make his political art, using the images of the Nazis against them.

The tradition of political and protest art, which expanded in significant ways in the era of mechanical reproduction, often stands in opposition to the concept that images should be unique, sacred, and have monetary value. For instance, AIDS activists have produced images for the purpose of distributing as many symbols and messages as possible on the street, in posters, buttons, stickers, and T-shirts. These images were disseminated in the 1980s and 1990s in cities like New York as a means of using the street as a forum for protest art. The *Silence = Death* image (which has an inverted pink triangle in its center) has been distributed in many forms and even spray-painted onto sidewalks in certain cities. The value of this image comes not from its reference to any orig- inal, but from its ubiquity. It is intended to make people recognize and re- consider their passivity precisely because it is an omnipresent symbol. The triangle refers to the pink triangle that homosexuals were forced to wear in Nazi Germany, just as Jews were forced to wear yellow stars. As such it is intended to refer to the tragic consequences of ignoring a crisis at hand. With the triangle placed upside down, this image appropriates a homophobic symbol of the past in order to create new meanings. This act of *appropriation* and *trans-coding*, or changing the meaning of the original symbol, has impor- tant political meaning precisely because it empties the original symbol, here the pink triangle, of its power. The effectiveness of the *Silence = Death* image

ACT UP, *Silence = Death*, 1986

to convey a message is directly related to its capacity to be multiply reproduced and to exist in many different places at the same time. The more it proliferates, the more powerful its message. Importantly, it is not a copyrighted image, but an image made to be copied and passed around—an image that is free of charge and not owned by anyone.

The proliferation of images through reproduction also means that they can be accompanied by different kinds of text, which can dramatically change the signification of the image. Text can ask us to look at an image differently. Words can direct our eyes to particular aspects of the image, indeed they can tell us what to see in a picture. This is often the case in advertising, where the text directs the viewer to read an image in a particular way. We can see that the text that accompanies the Heartfield photo collage, "He swallows gold and spits out tin-plate," explains the image to us, and makes clear its political meaning. It strongly condemns Hitler as a leader who is robbing the German people and selling them a fake message. The words "Silence = Death" give a particular meaning to the transformed pink triangle, encoding it with a complex set of meanings. Often text is combined with images as a means to jolt the viewer into reading the image differently. This effect has been widely used for public service ads, which act as advertisements for public policies. A widespread antismoking advertisement campaign in the USA has, among other tactics, appropriated some of the most iconic images of tobacco ads. In this image, the familiar photograph of the cowboy that signifies both cigarette smoking and masculinity, an association that Marlboro has produced through years of advertising, is given new meaning through its text. Indeed, the text here functions to produce a new sign with the image (cigarette-smoking cowboy = lung disease) specifically because of its previously established sign

I miss my lung, Bob.

California Department Of Health Services.
Funded By The Tobacco Tax Initiative

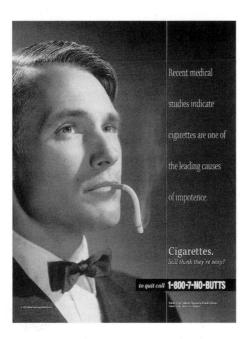

Recent medical studies indicate cigarettes are one of the leading causes of impotence.

Cigarettes.
Still think they're sexy?

to quit call **1-800-7-NO-BUTTS**

(cigarette-smoking cowboy = masculinity). In this ad, like the remake of the Marlboro Man that we discussed in Chapter 1, the equation of cigarette smoking with sexuality and virility is reversed to connote impotence. The words serve to give these images the opposite meaning. This appropriation depends, however, on the viewer being familiar with the original meaning.

Visual technologies and phenomenology

The photographic image was primary in the rise of mechanical reproduction and the changing role of images in modernity. Subsequently, the role of images has been transformed again with the invention of cinema in the 1890s, the development of the electronic image of television in the 1940s and 1950s, and, more recently, with the World Wide Web and digital imaging. Each medium has built upon and recoded the media that existed prior to it. One way of considering the difference between these media is to examine the phenomenological aspects of each.

In the most general sense, *phenomenology* is the belief that all knowledge and truth derives from subjective human experience and not solely from things themselves. Philosopher Edmund Husserl, who is considered the founder of the philosophy of phenomenology, rebelled against the rational age of scientific inquiry by insisting that experience cannot be known in an objective sense. He proposed, in his writings of the 1910s and 1920s, a science of experience of the ways we react bodily and emotionally as well as intellectually to the world around us. Philosopher Maurice Merleau-Ponty, who wrote his most influential works in the 1950s and 1960s, emphasized the importance of recognizing bodies as the entity through which we experience the world and emerge as individual subjects. He challenged the idea of mind-body dualism, that the mind and body are separate, which was central to Greek philosophy and expanded by Descartes, and he asserted instead that perception is the most important sensory register through which we can know of our embodied experiences. This in turn has particular importance for the study of practices of looking as embodied and perceptual in nature. A phenomenological understanding of images would, for instance, work against the erasure of the painter's body that takes place in the science of perspective.

The phenomenological approach has traditionally gotten short shrift in theories of film and media, where the theories of *Marxism*, *structuralism*, and *psychoanalysis* have clashed with certain tenets of phenomenology. Marxism places its emphasis on the collective body and material relations, not individual experience. Structural linguistics, with its focus on language and meaning, has not accounted for the physicality of voice and motor aspects of language. Psychoanalysis has not fully accounted for physiological and biological aspects of behavior, hence its understanding of the body is limited.

Perception, memory, and imagination are key concerns of phenomenological approaches to cultural analysis.[9] In using phenomenology to examine visual media, we focus on the specific capacities of each medium that distinguish its properties, and the effect of these properties on our experience of the images produced in each. For instance, the phenomenology of photography consists of those properties that affect the viewer's experience of it—it is usually a paper object that we can hold in our hand or see in a book, it is created with a camera and light, and it is static as opposed to time-based. We might want to ask, then, how looking at a photograph is phenomenologically different from, say, looking at a film. The traditional context of experiencing film involves looking at a projected image on a large screen, sitting in a dark room, and having no control over the timing of the work. A film is not, like a photograph, an object we can hold in our hands. Hence, phenomenology offers a means to examine the distinct materialities of these media in terms of how each affects the viewer's experience of it, and its impact on the lived body of the viewer. Given the necessity of grounding this material difference in specific historical and political contexts, phenomenology is most useful when used in conjunction with socio-historical and cultural analyses.

Just as the invention of photography in the early 1800s signaled a broad set of social needs and desires at the time, which were related to the rise of modernism, the invention of cinema corresponded with an increased desire to visualize movement. Indeed, the invention of cinema was preceded by an interest in paintings and photographs that could visualize movement. Most notable among photographers was Eadweard Muybridge, who in the late nineteenth century produced a study of animal and human locomotion. Muybridge used an elaborate system of cameras and trip wires to take a series of images that depict the complexity of human and animal form when in motion. We will discuss his images further in Chapter 8. Photographic images of movement set the stage for the development of cinema, which necessitated both the invention of a moving picture camera and projector and a flexible form of film (celluloid) that would not break when wound on reels. Hence, the primary phenomenological differences between photography and cinema are temporality, sound, and movement. These differences allowed cinema to become a primary means of storytelling. The development of cinematic conventions of framing, camera movement, and editing has tended to facilitate the construction of narratives. Cinematic meaning is derived through the combination of images rather than from a single frame. The juxtaposition of two images to create a third meaning is a central concept of film. While in conventional films, the combination of two shots is often intended to have a seamless effect that is unnoticed by the viewer, there is also a tradition in experimental cinema of juxtaposing images to create meaning through contrast. In *Ashputtle* (1982), artist John Baldessari references this aspect of cinema. Juxtaposing a series of found still images, many presumably from films, Baldessari creates an enigmatic set of meanings. Each individual image is a glimpse of a larger unexplained narrative, and the combination of these disparate frames creates a new set of stories. In addition, each image indicates a possible set of stories about what is happening outside of its frame, referring to that which is "off screen." In this sense, the image collage creates a multi-layered space and many potential narratives.

While the media of photography and film share many properties, in particular the mechanical process of photography (which necessitates, among other things, the development of film), the television image is phenomenologically quite different from each. It is true that for many viewers, distinctions between

John Baldessari, *Ashputtle*,
1982

the television image and the film image are increasingly difficult to make, as
we watch films on VCRs and television images are incorporated into film. As
both become digital, these differences will lessen. Yet, by nature of the fact
that it is composed electronically, the television image has a set of properties
distinct from film. In the television image, the audio and video are derived from
the same electronic signal. They do not require chemical developing, hence
they can be seen instantly. Television images are transmitted to many different television sets at the same time. They can be seen live, and in today's world
of satellite technology, can be broadcast live around the world. They gain their
value not through their aesthetic range, as is the case for many photographs
and films, but through their immediacy, speed, and transmission.

The criteria that assigns more value to an original image and less to a copy,
as outlined by Walter Benjamin, makes no sense when applied to television
transmission. Indeed, the concept of image transmission forces us to think in
different ways about the reproduction of an image, since the television image
is in fact many simultaneous images in different places. However, Benjamin's
argument that images that are reproduced can acquire political meaning does
make sense in relation to television. As a mass medium, television is a

powerful tool in the dissemination of ideas and ideologies. What gives value to a television image? In the case of news images, we could say it is its immediacy and the depiction of important events; in the case of popular culture, it is its entertainment value and widespread transmission to many TV sets at once. When we watch television we may think of ourselves as watching with a broader audience. This imagined audience may be global or national, as in the case of viewing important news events, or a group of fans, as in the case of watching TV dramas and sitcoms. We can thus say that the phenomenological properties of television affect the kinds of experiences that audiences derive from television programs.

Similarly, we can say that our experience of computer images in the context of the Internet and the World Wide Web presents us with yet another phenomenological difference. When it emerged in the early 1990s, the World Wide Web allowed for a broad range of images and graphics to become available to computer users through the Internet. We will discuss the history of the Internet at more length in Chapter 9, but here we would like to note the important visual aspects of the Web. The World Wide Web became popular very quickly because of its emphasis on visual images, at a time when the idea of a *graphical user interface* took hold in computers. This means that computer users are now accustomed to navigating software and information on data bases through graphics and images (using a computer mouse) rather than simply through entering commands as text. Phenomenologically, however, it is important to note that the computer user's relationship to images on the computer screen is interactive. Users make choices, browse, and move to new screens and images through *hypertext* links. Because the images that we access this way are digital, they can be easily downloaded onto our computers, and used in different contexts. The age of the computer, electronic imaging, and the digital thus presents a profound shift in the status of the image.

The digital image

In the 1980s and 1990s, the development of digital images began to radically transform the meaning of images in Western culture. Digital images differ from photographic images in that they are computer generated (or, at least, computer enhanced). *Analog* images bear a physical correspondence with their material *referents*. Analog computers used physical quantities (such as length) to represent numbers. Whereas analog images, such as photographs and most video images, are defined by properties that express value along a continuous scale, such as gradations of tone (or changes in intensity through increasing or decreasing voltage in video), digital images are *encoded* as information. Digital computers make calculations with data represented by digits. The pixel, the smallest unit of the visual field that makes up the digital image, is one such digit. John Berger, in his classic essay "Understanding a Photograph," claims that photographs are simply "records of things seen" and are "no closer to works of art than cardiograms."[10] He is referring to the analog process of correspondence between a referent and its representation. As a set of encoded *bits*, a digital image can be easily stored, manipulated, and reproduced. Here we can see again how the concept of reproduction changes with electronic images. In digital images, the idea of the difference between a copy and an original is nonexistent. Indeed, a "copy" of a digital image is exactly like the "original." The value of a digital image is derived in part by its role as information, and its capacity to be easily accessed, manipulated, stored in a computer or on a web site, downloaded, etc. The idea of an image being unique makes no sense with digital images.

We can see, in retrospect, how each of the different time eras of image technology outlined earlier in this chapter (ancient art, the age of perspective, the modern era of mechanical reproduction, and the postmodern era of electronic and computer imaging) entails a different set of criteria by which images are valued and perceived. The premechanical image, such as the painting that was situated within a specific place, gained its cultural value from being unique. It had a role in ritual and a cult value precisely because it was one of a kind. The mechanically reproduced image gains its value through its reproducibility, potential distribution, and role in the mass media. It can disseminate ideas, persuade viewers, and circulate political ideas. The digital and virtual image gains its value from its accessibility, malleability, and information status. All of these images with their different meanings coexist in our societies today.

The increased versatility of digital images raises important questions about the cultural concept of *photographic truth*. As we noted in Chapter 1, it has always been possible to "fake" realism in photographs. Digital techniques have made it possible to build on this ability to artificially construct realism. For example, digital images that look like photographs can be produced without a camera. In *semiotic* terms, this means that the photographic image is produced without a referent, or a real-life component, in the real. As we noted in Chapter 1, semiotician Charles Peirce used a three-part system to identify *signs*, with the referent referring to the object itself, rather than its representation in an image or word. The meaning of a photograph is thus derived from the belief that it has a referent in the real.

Peirce's work has been important for looking at images because of the distinctions that he makes between different kinds of signs and their relationship to the real. Peirce defined three kinds of signs: *iconic*, *indexical*, and *symbolic*. As conventions, signs are often a kind of short-hand language for viewers of images, and we are often incited to feel that the relationship between a *signifier* and *signified* is "natural." For instance, we are so accustomed to identifying the American flag with the United States, a rose with the concept of romantic love, and a dove with peace that it is difficult to recognize that their relationship is constructed rather than natural.

- Peirce's definition of iconic is different from the general meaning of icons that we discussed in Chapter 1. Iconic signs resemble their object in some way. Hence forms of visual representation such as paintings and graphs are iconic, as are photographs and film and television images.

- Symbolic signs, unlike icons which resemble their objects, bear no obvious relationship to their objects. Symbols are created through an arbitrary (one could say "unnatural") alliance of a particular object and a particular meaning. For example, languages are symbolic systems which use conventions to establish meaning. There is no natural link between the word "cat" and an actual cat; the convention in the English language gives the word its signification. Symbolic signs are inevitably more restricted in their capacity to convey meaning in that they refer to learned systems. Someone who does not speak English can probably recognize an image of a cat (an iconic sign), whereas the word "cat" (a symbolic sign) will have no meaning to them.

- Indexical signs as defined by Peirce involve an "existential" relationship between the signifier and the signified. This means that they have co-existed in the same place at some time. Peirce uses as examples the symptom of a disease, a pointing hand, and a weathervane. Fingerprints are indexical signs of a person, and photographs are also indexical signs that testify to the moment that the camera was in the presence of its subject. Indeed, while photographs are both iconic and indexical, their cultural meaning is derived in large part from their indexical meaning as a trace of the real.

Importantly, though, most digital images and *simulations* are not indexical, since they cannot be said to have been in the presence of the real world that they depict. For instance, an image that inserts people digitally into a landscape where they have never been does not refer to an actual moment in time. This raises the question, what happens to the idea of photographic truth when an image that looks like a photograph is created on a computer with no camera at all? In Peirce's terms, this marks a fundamental shift in meaning from the photograph to the digital image. Here, index gives way to icon, since we take these computer-generated images to resemble real-life subjects.

Of course most of the images that we see on a daily basis have been modified in some way. Most advertising images are produced with a significant amount of airbrushing and modification. This means that the so-called "natural" images of fashion models have all been highly doctored and manipulated, with wrinkles and blemishes erased, lips enhanced, features moved, and colors changed. The advertising images that entice consumers to try to look like certain models thus offer up an ideal that, in fact, has no basis in reality. This construction of the idea of a perfect face or body is intended of course to produce feelings of inadequacy in viewers, so that they will feel impelled to purchase more consumer products. Hence, as we will discuss further in Chapter 6, the photographic "truth" in advertising has always been highly questionable.

A different set of questions is raised when we consider the impact of digital imaging on news and historical images. It is now a common practice to have personal photographs digitally reconfigured, to take now out-of-favor relatives out of wedding pictures, for instance, or to erase ex-boyfriends from treasured images. In most cases, this kind of toying with the historical record is relatively harmless. Yet, we can also imagine a context in which all historical images are up for grabs. There has been a long tradition in certain countries of rearranging photographs to retell history, such as the tradition of erasing deposed politicians from official historical images in the former Soviet Union; these technical procedures are now vastly improved and widely accessible with digital technology.

There are very important stakes in the news industry—for instance, in certain ethical codes of truth-telling—which include, among other tenets, the idea that photographic news images are realistic and unmanipulated. In other words, we assume that the photographs we see in mainstream newspapers and news journals are unaltered (whereas we often assume that the images

we see in certain tabloids are fake). Often the discovery that a news organization has altered an image has sparked scandal and debate, such as the debate over *Time* magazine's cover image of O. J. Simpson that we discussed in Chapter 1. Yet, in the context of digital imaging, with its increased capacity to change images in seamless and realistic ways, can the idea of photographs as unmanipulated survive? One recent case in point: *National Geographic* magazine digitally moved the Egyptian pyramids closer together in order to fit them on its cover. This manipulation of the image was done for ostensible aesthetic reasons, yet it caused an uproar because it was seen as tainting *National Geographic*'s reputation for publishing documentary, read "truthful," images of the world. In other words, the magazine's reputation was based on a modern notion of photographic truth that clashed with the digital possibilities for image manipulation.

In the contemporary world of visual images, digital and analog forms of image manipulation are creating a broad array of images that defy traditional notions of time. The images of deceased celebrities have been digitally enhanced to have them say words they never spoke or to interact in scenes they never performed (such as an advertisement in which the late Fred Astaire dances with a vacuum cleaner). There is discussion of the potential to create entire new films with virtual versions of now-dead film stars. How will popular culture recycle images of the past? Artist Deborah Bright uses this image context to comment ironically on the representation of compulsive hetero-sexuality in classic Hollywood films. Here, she sits in boredom as film stars Spencer Tracy and Katherine Hepburn embrace in "her" car. Image manipula-tion thus allows Bright to re-code the film image, to insert herself into its space of signification so that its meaning is irrevocably changed. Rather than a nos-talgic image of Hollywood romance, it becomes a commentary on the ideol-ogy of compulsive heterosexuality.

The vast array of photographic, electronic, and digital images in contempo-rary visual culture has also had the effect of changing certain painting styles. From its very beginning, photography changed the social role of painting as a mode of representation. Many critics feel that the emergence of photography helped free painting styles to move away from realism and into abstraction. Yet, in the late twentieth century, the style of photorealism emerged among painters who self-consciously deployed a "photographic" style. For instance, artist Chuck Close creates very large paintings that reflect the tonal precision

Deborah Bright, *Untitled*, from *Dream Girls* series, 1989–90

Chuck Close, *Roy II*, 1994

of photographs. Close photographs his subjects, draws a grid over the photograph and a much larger canvas, and then paints the image one square at a time. The result, as seen in this portrait of artist Roy Lichtenstein, is an abstract rendering of the effect of the photographic and the digital. This image evokes both the grainy form of a photograph and the grid structure of a digital image, with its multiple squares (pixels) that merge to form a likeness. If one moves too close to the image, it becomes an abstract grid of shapes and colors, but at a distance the face emerges. The image thus changes substantially according to the position of the viewer in relation to it.

Virtual space and interactive images

A common misconception about the term *virtual* is that it means not real, or that it refers to something that exists in our imaginations only. There is also a misconception that whereas actual or representational images are produced through analog technologies, virtual images are produced through digital technologies and are specific to their era. In fact, virtual images are both analog and digital. Virtual images break with the convention of representing what is seen. They are simulations that represent ideal or constructed rather than actual conditions. A virtual image of a human body may represent no actual body in particular, but may be based on a composite or simulation of human bodies drawn from various sources. Its realism stems from its embodiment of ideal or composite conditions of human bodies, not on its correspondence with an actual body referent.

Digital imaging makes possible the un-sticking of the referent from the image. But virtual images can also be produced through analog technologies like photography. As we discussed earlier, photographs have been manipulated since their invention, and these can be thought of as virtual images—with no referent in the real. William J. Mitchell, in his important study of visual truth in the photographic era, *The Reconfigured Eye*, describes an array of examples dating back to the origins of photography where the relationship of the image to its presumed referent is under question. He mentions Alexander Gardner's famous photograph of July 1863, "Slain Rebel Sharpshooter" at the battle of Gettysburg. This image, he notes, has been revealed to contain the same body as the one in an earlier photograph of a fallen Union sharpshooter. The body was apparently dragged and staged in a still life and photographed as if it were a recording of a scene that had occurred.[11] It can be said that this is an early example of the production of a virtual image insofar as the image does not exactly lie; rather, it is a virtual construction of a reality of war with no actual, particular referent. Virtual images are also central to the use of special effects in cinema. Steven Spielberg's film *Jurassic Park* mixed analog images of real actors with digital, computer-generated images of dinosaurs. These were not films or animations of dinosaur models, but objects that existed as virtual images only, simulated on the screen. The actors never experienced physical proximity with them. The world of the film, even as experienced by the actors themselves, was thus very much a virtual world insofar as no film set ever contained it.

Virtual reality (VR) is a term that was coined by computer simulation virtuoso Jaron Lanier to describe the way that users experience the computer worlds generated in science and popular computer games of the late 1980s and 1990s. Virtual reality systems incorporate computer imaging, sound, and sensory systems to put the user's body in a direct feedback loop with the technology itself and the world it simulates. Subjectivity is experienced in and through the technology. Rather than offering a world to simply view and hear, as the cinema does, virtual reality systems attempt to create an experience in which the user feels as if he or she is physically incorporated into the world represented on all sensory levels. Likewise the technology of the VR system is linked with the body of the user through prosthetic extensions of sensory systems. Virtual reality systems are particular to the technologies of late capitalist society that at once extend into our bodies and offer experiences of simulated worlds that are indistinguishable from what we know as the real world. Virtual technologies include the mundane and real-world augmentations of reality like pacemakers and hearing aids. They also include simulations that aim to exist parallel to what we think of as the real world, such as flight simulation training systems and game systems that invite us to enter their imagined world on multiple sensory levels.

One of the unique qualities of virtual reality systems is that they unleash the spectator from his or her bodily position in space, allowing for a more free-floating experience of perception. In a virtual system, one might choose to occupy various positions within the virtual world, positions not possible within actual space. For example, in this virtual simulation inside a colon by bio-physicist Richard Robb, created with the Virtual Reality Assisted Surgery Program (designed by Robb and Bruce Cameron), the human body (represented in the avatar figure) can assume any perspective he or she wishes to by selecting different views through the computer program. This system allows users to take a virtual fly-through tour of the human colon along the lines imagined in the 1966 Cold War film classic, *Fantastic Voyage*. In the film, a team of military scientists and technicians are shrunk down small enough to be injected through a hypodermic needle into the body of a scientist who has

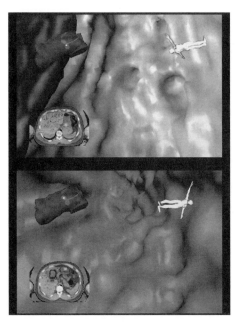

Richard Robb, virtual (computed) endoscopy

defected to the USA with crucial knowledge about a miniaturization program that will revolutionize warfare techniques. His own technique becomes the means of saving him as this team is injected into his body to perform surgery from within on a life-threatening brain tumor. Thirty years later, this fantasy of physically entering the human body through virtual surgery has come closer to reality as medical experts devise the means to play with scale and generate virtual worlds where the surgeon may enter the human body to see things never before seen (because they are too small, too remote) and operate at a scale never before possible (at the level of cells, for example). This is an example of science fiction preceding science in imagining the potential of visualization in changing the experiences and conditions of real bodies and real life. Artist Mona Hatoum's *Corps étranger*, which we will discuss in Chapter 8, is an installation that allows the viewer physically to enter the artist's body virtually by borrowing some of the imagery from an endoscopic video. Her work is one example of artists' commentary on and appropriations of the virtual worlds of science and medicine.

The significant cultural changes that have resulted from the digitizing of images and the increased role of the virtual image have also gone hand in hand with changes in thinking about space and authorship. For instance, when a computer user is downloading images off the Internet to use in his/her own home page or in a paper, how can traditional notions of authorship (and contemporary concepts of copyright ownership) remain in place? In addition, the realm of the Internet, the World Wide Web, and technologies of imaging such as virtual reality and computer games, is one of virtual rather than physical space. This realm entails a dramatic shift in the concept of space, one that has broad cultural implications. Traditionally, space has been defined as material and physical according to the tradition of Cartesian mathematics. As we mentioned before, Cartesian space, as defined by René Descartes, is a physical, three-dimensional space that can be mathematically measured.

However, virtual space, or the space created by electronic and digital technologies, cannot be mathematically measured and mapped. The term "virtual space" thus refers to spaces that appear to be like physical space as we understand it, but which are not physical. It has been used broadly to refer to those spaces that are electronically constituted, such as the space defined by the computer, but that do not conform to the laws of physical, material, or Cartesian space. Many aspects of computer programs encourage us to think of these spaces as akin to the physical spaces that we encounter in the real world (when they are referred to as "chat rooms" or "sites" for instance); however, virtual space exists in opposition to the rules of traditional physical space. We could say that it is a "space" in traditional terms only conceptually. In addition, systems of virtual reality, in which users wear various headgear and gloves to have an experience of a virtual space through both sight and touch, operate on a different concept of space than Cartesian space or the space defined by systems of two-dimensional representation. The virtual can thus be seen as a dramatic change in the forms of representation, space, and images as we have known them.

Contemporary visual images circulate in virtual space not only on the Web but also as elements of video games, CD-Roms, and DVDs. These images are primary elements in interactive narratives, in which users can navigate a game or CD-Rom to create their own individual pathway through its story. This is not only a central aspect of video games, it has also become a means through which art institutions such as museums are expanding their venues. Many contemporary museums now market CDs that are virtual galleries, through which viewers can move through the images displayed in the museum on their computer. These digital image reproductions have the added dimension of virtual space that encourages viewers to experience themselves as moving through actual museum space. Many artists are now producing works on CDs that provide a different image experience (in both phenomenological and narrative terms) for viewers. The interactivity of these works demands that viewers make choices about how to navigate an art work, thus making it possible for each individual to have a unique experience of the work. This kind of interactive image experience is dramatically different from the experience of an original, stationary painting prior to the emergence of mechanical reproduction described by Benjamin.

With the range of reproduced and multiple images in contemporary visual culture, concepts of authenticity, originality, and space gain new meaning. The art of the past has been transformed in this contemporary image world. The work has lost its uniqueness and become many images in many different contexts, each open to new forms of interpretation. Yet, it is not the case that the images of the past have less value in our culture. Rather, they are more prone to the circulation, changed contexts, and remaking that are central aspects of contemporary media culture. The extent to which the digital will change image culture remains to be seen, but it is already clear that it entails a fundamental shift not only in the technology and circulation of images but also of their semiotic and social meanings. The meaning of the image in the age of electronic reproduction is thus a radical change from the meaning of the image described in Walter Benjamin's treatise on mechanical reproduction.

Notes

1. John Berger, *Ways of Seeing* (New York and London: Penguin, 1972), 18.
2. See Martin Jay, *Downcast Eyes* (Berkeley and London: University of California Press, 1993), 52.
3. René Descartes, *Discourse on Method, Optics, Geometry and Meteorology*, translated by Paul J. Olscamp (New York: Bobbs-Merrill, 1965), 65. See also Jay, *Downcast Eyes*, 69–72.
4. Georges Didi-Huberman, "Photography—Scientific and Pseudo-scientific," in *A History of Photography: Social and Cultural Perspectives*, edited by Jean-Claude Lemagny and André Rouille, translated by Janet Lloyd (New York and Cambridge: Cambridge University Press, 1987), 71.
5. John Berger, "The Moment of Cubism," in *The Sense of Sight* (New York: Pantheon, 1985), 171.
6. William M. Ivins, Jr., *Prints and Visual Communication* (Cambridge, Mass. and London: MIT Press, 1969), 3.
7. Walter Benjamin, "The Work of Art in the Age of Mechanical Reproduction," in *Illuminations*, translated by Harry Zohn (New York: Schocken Books, 1969), 220.
8. Benjamin, "The Work of Art in the Age of Mechanical Reproduction," 224.
9. For an in-depth analysis of the phenomenological approach to film, see Vivian Sobchack, *The Address of the Eye* (Princeton: Princeton University Press, 1992).
10. John Berger, "Understanding a Photograph," in *Classic Essays on Photography*, edited by Alan Trachtenberg (New Haven: Leetes's Island Books, 1980), 291–92.
11. William J. Mitchell, *The Reconfigured Eye: Visual Truth in the Post-Photographic Era* (Cambridge, Mass. and London: MIT Press, 1992), 43–44.

Further Reading

Geoffrey Batchen. *Burning with Desire: The Conception of Photography*. Cambridge, Mass. and London: MIT Press, 1997.

Walter Benjamin. "The Work of Art in the Age of Mechanical Reproduction." In *Illuminations*. Translated by Harry Zohn. New York: Schocken Books, 1969, 217–51.

John Berger. *Ways of Seeing*. New York and London: Penguin, 1972.

——"Understanding a Photograph." In *Classic Essays on Photography*. Edited by Alan Trachtenberg. New Haven: Leetes's Island Books, 1980, 291–94.

——*The Sense of Sight*. New York: Pantheon, 1985.

J. D. Bernal. *Science in History, ii. The Scientific and Industrial Revolutions*. Cambridge, Mass. and London: MIT Press, 1954.

René Descartes. *Discourse on Method, Optics, Geometry, and Meteorology*. Translated by Paul J. Olscamp. New York: Bobbs-Merrill, 1965.

Timothy Druckrey, ed. *Electronic Culture: Technology and Visual Representation*. New York: Aperture, 1996.

E. H. Gombrich. *Art and Illusion: A Study in the Psychology of Pictorial Representation*. Princeton: Princeton University Press, 1960.

Terence Hawkes. *Structuralism and Semiotics*. Berkeley and London: University of California Press, 1977.

James Hoopes, ed. *Peirce on Signs*. Chapel Hill and London: University of North Carolina Press, 1991.

Robert Hughes. *The Shock of the New*. Revised Edition. New York: Alfred Knopf, 1995.

William M. Ivins, Jr. *Prints and Visual Communication*. Cambridge, Mass. and London: MIT Press, 1969.

H. W. Janson and Anthony F. Janson. *A Basic History of Art*. Englewood Cliffs, NJ: Prentice-Hall, 1992.

Martin Jay. *Downcast Eyes: The Denigration of Vision in Twentieth-Century French Thought*. Berkeley and London: University of California Press, 1993.

Sarah Kember. *Virtual Anxiety: Photography, New Technology, and Subjectivity*. Manchester: Manchester University Press, 1998.

Martin Kemp. *The Science of Art*. New Haven and London: Yale University Press, 1990.

James Jakób Liszka. *A General Introduction to the Semiotics of Charles Sanders Peirce*. Bloomington: Indiana University Press, 1996.

Jean-François Lyotard. *Phenomenology*. Translated by Brian Beakley. Albany: SUNY Press, 1991.

Floyd Merrel. *Peirce, Signs, and Meaning*. Toronto: University of Toronto Press, 1997.

William J. Mitchell. *The Reconfigured Eye: Visual Truth in the Post-Photographic Era*. Cambridge, Mass. and London: MIT Press, 1992.

Bill Nichols. "The Work of Culture in the Age of Cybernetic Systems." In *Electronic Culture: Technology and Visual Representation*. Edited by Timothy Druckrey. New York: Aperture, 1996, 121–43.

Richard Robin. *Annotated Catalog of the Papers of Charles Sanders Peirce*. Bloomington: Indiana University Press, 1998. On-line at: ⟨www.iupui.edu/%7Epeirce/web/index.htm⟩.

Vivian Sobchack. *The Address of the Eye: A Phenomenology of Film Experience*. Princeton: Princeton University Press, 1992.

Robert Sokolowski. *Introduction to Phenomenology*. New York and Cambridge: Cambridge University Press, 2000.

Shearer West, ed. *The Bulfinch Guide to Art History*. New York and London: Little, Brown, 1996.

The Mass Media and the Public Sphere 5

Those of us in Western industrialized cultures live in a multimedia environment in which mechanical and electronic images, text, and sound are an almost constant presence. The media are pervasive in most of our lives, yet we tend to take them for granted. In the course of a day, we may encounter many different kinds of images, texts, and sounds produced in many different media, from our first waking moments on. Take this hypothetical day: having been awakened by a broadcast on your clock radio, the first thing you look at is the digital time display. Over coffee, you read a newspaper or watch a television news program. Maybe you check your e-mail before leaving for school or work. If you are driving, you absent-mindedly surf the car radio stations during the commute, barely noticing the billboard advertisements you pass as you talk on your cell phone. Or, if you commute by train, you pop your favorite new CD into a Sony Discman and look absently up at the advertisements. You gaze into a computer screen for part of the morning, working with programs designed for your field of work or study, taking a break to play a computer game or peek in on a few web sites. At lunch, you subconsciously take in the logos on the products you consume, or you flip through a magazine, check your e-mail, or take in a soap opera or talk show in the cafeteria or while working out on exercise machines at the gym. You probably talk on the phone, leave messages on voice mail, and listen to an answering machine. After work or school, you might watch the news and sitcoms on television, take in a film on the VCR, or go to see a movie in a theater. Or, you might surf the Web, consult a course web site for assignments, or engage in some late-night on-line discussion.

Although we perform some of these activities alone, some involve participation with, or simply the presence of, other people (as audience members in a movie theater, for instance). Many of these experiences incorporate visual media. In most of these contexts, we are the recipients as well as the authors, to varying degrees, of media messages that are conveyed through a variety and mix of media. Some of these media are simultaneously present and even work in conjunction with one another, as in the case of the digital alarm clock radio or the movie on video. As vehicles of images and the messages they convey, these media are central to visual culture. As this image, taken in the 1950s by photographer Robert Frank, suggests, we tend to experience the mass media as a system that operates whether or not we are watching.

The term *mass media* has been used to define those media designed to reach large audiences perceived to have shared interests. The mass media refers to forms and texts that work in unison to generate specific dominant or popular representations of events, people, and places, whether these events are fictional, actual, or somewhere in between. It is a term that often refers to the ways that audiences receive news information about the events of the world on a daily basis. The primary mass media forms are radio, television, the cinema, and the press (including newspapers and magazines), hence visual images are primary though not sole elements of mass media. Computer-mediated forms, such as the *Internet*, the *World Wide Web*, and *digital* multi-media, are relatively new additions to the list, but are quickly becoming as pervasive as television. Radio is an underconsidered aspect of the mass media

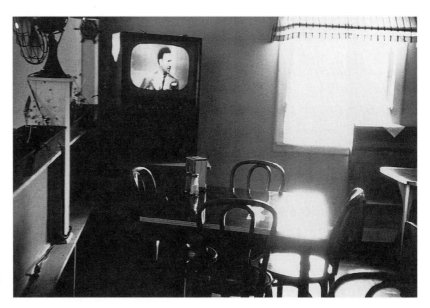

Robert Frank,
*Restaurant, U.S. 1
leaving Columbia, South
Carolina*, 1955

that experienced something of a resurgence of attention in the late 1990s. It is useful to consider the practices of looking and modes of attention we engage in when we listen to the radio, for practices of looking are not put on hold when we listen.

It is important to note the social impact of the expansion of the mass media beyond the printed word into images and sound. Before radio, literacy was essential to the flow of information in society. Since only the educated minority could read and write, this portion of the society was largely in control of the exchange of information beyond word of mouth. Some critics of the media have argued that radio and television furthered this control by restricting authorship of information to those with access to the means of media production, creating a society of producers (who represent the ruling classes) separate from consumers (who are duped by mass media messages). Other scholars, such as John Fiske, argue that the two primary mass media forms, radio and television, changed the dynamics of the flow of information by making more information directly available to non-literate people, thus making possible a more democratic flow. In the late 1910s and 1920s, immediately following the 1917 Russian Revolution, Soviet filmmakers relied on the theory that the visual medium of film could be an important means of building a new revolutionary Soviet consciousness among illiterate Russian proletarians and peasants. In the 1950s, European filmmakers in African colonies used films as a mode of visual instruction to teach Western ways to colonized peoples. This strategy of using film as a pedagogical medium was *appropriated* by African filmmakers in the *postcolonial* period as they generated autonomous African national cinemas. In these examples, visual images expanded the cultural and class limits of media audiences in a process that some have called visual literacy or media literacy.

To understand the place of the visual media in our culture today we need to know what is meant by the term "the mass media." What do we mean by "mass"? What does the term "media" really mean? Media is, quite simply, the plural form of the term *medium*. The familiar definition of a medium is a means of mediation or communication—a neutral or intermediary form through which messages pass. In this sense, it refers to the group of communications industries and technologies that together produce and spread public news, entertainment, and information. The term "medium" also refers to the specific technologies through which messages are transmitted. Radio is a medium, television is a medium, a megaphone is a medium, your voice is a medium. A medium does not necessarily require technology, though we most often refer to media as those forms that do involve some degree of machinery or hardware.

We often think of the mass media as inundating us with images. In this 1964 photographic collage, artist Robert Rauschenberg creates a tension between news images and painting techniques to give a sense of the ways that news images penetrate our lives. Rauschenberg appropriated "found" images from the news of the time and put them together to comment on the rush of daily modern life, the complexity of media culture, and the iconic status of John F. Kennedy after his death. If Rauschenberg had simply drawn these pictures, they would not have had the same impact as these found images. The collage gives this work a sense of urgency and media overload. Kennedy's powerful and charismatic media image is deployed here by the artist to establish him as a martyred public figure. Rauschenberg's borrowing, stealing, and reusing of these images gives his work an overall sense of the rush of information culture.

It is widely agreed among those who study the media that a medium is not a neutral technology through which meanings, messages, and information are

Robert Rauschenberg, *Retroactive I*, 1964

channeled unmodified. Even the medium of your voice, through conventions such as accent, loudness, pitch, tone, inflection, and modulation, encodes messages with meanings that are not inherent in the content of the message. The medium itself, whether that medium is a voice or a technology like television, has a major impact on the meaning it conveys.

There is no such thing as a message without a medium: this point has been driven home in media theory since the 1960s. In other words, it is impossible to separate messages, information, or meanings from the media technologies that convey them. First of all, as we discussed in Chapter 4, there are *phenomenological* differences among media—that is, there are differences in the way we experience media that are particular to their material qualities. When we listen to television news, for example, our experience of information or content is shaped by the form and conventions of the medium. When we watch a movie in a theater, as we discussed in Chapter 3, our experience is affected by the *cinematic apparatus*—the dark room, the projection of film on the screen, the sound system, the sense, muted or otherwise, of fellow audience members. Watching the same movie on video at home, or on a drive-in movie screen, changes the experience. For instance, when Robert Frank took this image of a drive-in movie theater in his well-known photographic essay *The Americans*, it symbolized many aspects of 1950s American culture, in particular the importance of the automobile in postwar culture. In another

Robert Frank, *Drive-in Movie–Detroit*, 1955

context, when we read a newspaper, we hold it in our hands, fold over its pages, and maybe finish a story later in the day. Television is an ongoing electronic presence that is set to a timetable and continuously transmitted. Watching television is a social activity even when done alone, in that we are likely to be aware of ourselves as part of a broader public tuned in to the same broadcast. Watching is sometimes performed in a collective social space such as the living room, where people talk during programs, move in and out of the space, or simultaneously perform other activities such as eating or doing homework. Our attention is divided and distracted, as we tune in and out. Cultural theorist Raymond Williams wrote about *television flow*, the concept that viewers' experience of television involves an ongoing rhythm that incorporates interruption (such as changes between programs and TV commercials). Television, insofar as it is time-based and establishes narrative flow over days, months, and even years (as, for example, in the case of ongoing soap operas), has a particular kind of continuity that weaves into and establishes patterns of daily experience in our lives. It provides a different phenomenological experience from that of the computer. When we engage in on-line chat groups, we sit alone before a computer screen and type on a keyboard, but we nonetheless participate in a social "space"—the *virtual* space that can span a vast geographical area in which our on-line communication takes place.

There are also important political and cultural differences in how we understand and judge the media messages of our daily lives. We may, for instance, consciously or unconsciously rank modes of news media in terms of importance or credibility—considering newspapers to be more reliable than television news, for instance, or seeing news on Internet or World Wide Web sources as less truthful than other sources. The way we rank media is based on where that medium stands in relation to older and newer media, and on cultural assumptions about the importance of various media and whether they are primarily oriented toward entertainment, news, or information. We may think of Internet news as being more "up to the minute" than televised news broadcasts, because the Internet has come to be associated with speed of transmission, a global scope, and instantaneous border-crossing. The advent of the Internet thus has profound consequences for our understanding of other media forms (we will discuss this further in Chapter 9). Yet, we may find it easy to blur the categories of news and fictional drama, such that we may think that certain popular films, such as Oliver Stone's *JFK* (1991), tell the "real story" of an event. This is partly because films like *JFK* incorporate media forms that we associate with documentary truth—television news footage, or film footage staged and shot to look like vintage news footage, for example—to convince the viewer of their accuracy. In addition, our perception of the news stories we see is shaped by elements including the cultural status of the newscaster (his or her gender, cultural identity, clothing and appearance, and accent and tone of voice), as well as by how he or she is framed and edited. All of these aspects—casting, costume, make-up and hair style, composition and editing of image and sound—work within certain conventions of news media to confer meaning to what we tend to think of as the "content" of the story covered. Media, then, are not neutral means of conveying messages and, moreover, they never operate wholly apart from other media forms. Media not only inform messages, they implicitly refer to and comment upon other media forms.

The idea of a mass medium refers to the term "masses," which emerged in the nineteenth and twentieth centuries to describe shifts in the way people live in Western industrialized countries. The masses is a term that was adopted by political economists including Karl Marx to describe social formations during the rise of industrial *capitalism*. The term can have negative connotations in media theory. In this sense, it implies an undifferentiated group of people with little individuality and a vast audience for the media made up of individuals who are passively accepting and uncritical of media practices and messages. The term "mass media" came into common use in the post–World War II era, a period marked by the dissemination of television throughout the United States, England, and much of Europe.

The rise of the mass media occurred during *modernity*, a period discussed in Chapter 4. *Mass society* describes social formations in Europe and the United States that began during the early period of industrialization and culminated after World War II. The rise of mass culture is usually characterized much like modernity: with the increased industrialization and mechanization of modern society, populations were more firmly consolidated in urban settings and the corporation replaced the local workplace. After the war, urban populations lost their sense of community and political belonging. Interpersonal life and group activity slacked off under the pressures of crowding in the home, workplace, and in the streets, and under the anonymity of corporate workplaces and other forces related to industrial growth and the rise of the city. People became more disaffected or alienated with these pressures, and family and community life eroded as the large urban metropolis and then dispersed suburban enclaves replaced tight-knit rural communities.

To speak of people as members of a mass society is to suggest that they receive their messages through centralized forms of national and international media. The term implies that they receive the majority of their opinions and information through the one-way *broadcast* model, and not through local channels of back-and-forth or networked exchange (members of the immediate community or family passing or sharing messages, for example). The idea of a monolithic mass or public culture is linked to a particular historical period—the period of modernity and industrialization when the television broadcast model dominated. In the 1980s and 1990s, with the rise of *narrowcast* cable and the network model of the Internet, it can be argued that the term "mass media" is no longer entirely applicable. As more diverse media forms emerge, more fragmented audiences form to replace the undifferentiated mass, and multidirectional experiences of media become available in place of the broadcast model, the mass media are less pervasive.

The concept of a public culture is essential to the definition of the media as a singular rather than plural entity. Some media forms are commonly regarded as a means of escape from public life. For example, entertainment television and popular cinema are often seen as media through which viewers can escape from reality. Other forms of media are regarded primarily as strengthening the viewer's or reader's connection to public life. Television news and the daily newspapers are means of inserting oneself into ongoing narratives about public culture and civic responsibility. When viewers use these forms of media, they can see themselves as members of a community, citizens of a nation, and agents in a global world of politics. The term "the media," as a singular entity, can be used to describe the effect of media forms as a whole upon the formation of a mass or public culture.

All media, including fictional television and the cinema, enmesh viewers in debates within different spheres of public action and debate. In the media landscape of the late twentieth century, the boundaries between news and fiction and between entertainment and information were increasingly blurred. This was strikingly obvious in 1992 when the popular television series *Murphy Brown* became part of the news headlines. The character Murphy Brown was a successful single, middle-aged professional who served as a popular role model for many women of the baby boomer generation during the early 1990s. When Brown bore a child out of wedlock during the election year of

1992, then-Vice President Dan Quayle publicly attacked the series for maligning "proper" family values. The episode, and Quayle's public pronouncement, became the subject of a heated debate in the USA about single mothers and television's influence on its public's social choices and views about issues such as parenting. This debate was fueled by the prevalence during the early 1990s of news stories about single motherhood, family values, and reproductive rights, and the rise of a growing religious right media presence that took family values as its chief platform. Eventually, the character of Murphy Brown responded within the fictional series to the real-life attacks of the Vice President as if Quayle were a part of the fictional world of the show.

One of the most important roles of the media in contemporary culture is to facilitate social spheres for public debate and action. How citizen-viewers participate in media debates depends in part on each viewer's relationship to particular media forms. Some media forms, like radio and television, developed on the model of one-way broadcasting. In this model, centralized networks and producers transmit media texts to vast numbers of listeners or viewers over a broad geographical region. These audiences are not given the chance to produce or alter the programs they receive in the first instance. As we discussed in Chapter 2, though viewers can change the channel or tape programs and re-evaluate or even edit them later, they have limited control over the initial content of these programs. While the industry may solicit ratings and

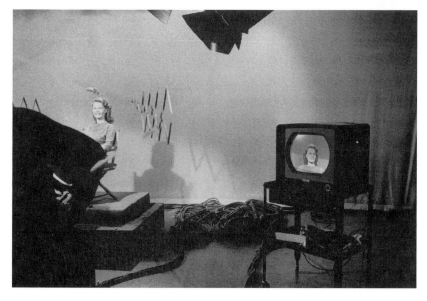

Robert Frank, *Television Studio–Burbank, California*, 1955/56

marketing surveys designed to get viewer feedback, studies have shown that viewer input is minimal. Television scholar Eileen R. Meehan has pointed out that the viewers who "count" in the most influential ratings systems (like the Nielsen ratings) belong to those classes who are identified as having the most consumer potential. This is because the industry is most interested in appealing to viewers with buying power, and not in a representative sampling of the population. Thus, in broadcast media, viewer agency is enacted primarily at the level of personal or localized consumption, interpretation, and use, through modes of appropriation and cultural translation. In other words, we most fully influence broadcast media in the ways we use it, not at the levels of its production or distribution.

Other media facilitate two-way or *multidirectional communication*. The Internet, for example, allows information to be exchanged and modified among a broad range of participants. The Web seems to offer a means of increased access to media production, and not just consumption, for those with access to the medium. It would be unlikely for a high school student to have access to the means to produce a television program for national broadcast. But he or she could easily produce and mount a globally accessible web page. The rise of international *subcultures* and special interest groups through web sites and listservers indicates the extent of this networked participatory model. The phenomenon of the personal page on the World Wide Web recalls pop artist Andy Warhol's wry prediction, voiced in the 1960s, that in the future everyone would have their fifteen minutes of media stardom. Computer authoring tools, desktop publishing, and the rise of photocopied hand- and computer-rendered magazines (called zines) by subcultural groups and individuals together suggest that in the 1990s, anyone could become an author or producer.

A second and related distinction among media forms is that between broadcast media and narrowcast media. In television's early years, the medium's range of transmission was limited in geographical distance to local communities, and programming often was produced by people living in the region, reflecting the particular cultural interests of their community. Local religious, entertainment, and issues-oriented programming was inflected by local opinion, labor, and cultural values. As distance transmission was facilitated through cables, and much later enhanced with satellite transmission, long-distance broadcasting networks became a reality. The broadcasting model replaced early narrowcast or community-based television, with satellite transmission making global communications a real possibility. With this expansion of regions and increase in potential markets, networks produced programs that appealed to more universal or "mass" cultural interests, replacing the earlier community television model. As media producer Marlon Riggs shows us in his documentary *Color Adjustment*, programs in the pre-cable era targeted to "minority" audiences (such as *Frank's Place*, a 1970s US television series that featured black characters) were relatively short-lived. By the late 1970s, the emergence of cable in the USA reintroduced the narrowcast model, allowing for the development of community-based programming again after twenty years of its near absence, and the rise of "minority" networks. The US-based Black Entertainment Television and the more global Telemundo, a network catering to the Spanish-speaking global *diaspora*, are two examples of cable network narrowcasting.

We can see from this discussion that in the 1980s and 1990s consumers became more active users and producers in an array of media forms including home video, narrowcast cable television, and Internet communications. This suggests that the concept of the broadcast model may not be as dominant in the media industries of the twenty-first century. We can also see that a singular mass audience is no longer a reality (and one could argue it never was). Indeed, some authors bemoan the fragmentation of society into special interest groups through narrowcasting. Their fear is that increased media choices and narrowcasting are tools of further *alienation*, confining people to their on-line and screen worlds where they engage in confined spheres of dialogue with like-minded people. While there are still persuasive arguments for the validity of the singular concept of the media, it is clear that media cultures in the plural best describes the visual culture of the twenty-first century.

Critiques of the mass media

The capacity of the mass media to reach so many viewers both nationally and globally gives it a significant amount of power. Perspectives in response to the mass media's powerful scope have ranged from utopian optimism about global connectivity to more dystopian (or anti-utopian) warnings about the potential for world domination through media. The coincidence of the rise of the mass media with the increased industrialization and movements of populations away from rural communities has prompted many theorists to see the mass media as contributing to the erosion of interpersonal and group life and fostering increasingly centralized models of communication and identity. The historical argument states that TV and radio provided a centralized means for mobilizing the new mass culture or mass society around a unified set of issues and ideas. The idea was that mass broadcasting, with its ability to reach large numbers of people with the same messages, fostered conformity to dominant ideas about politics and culture. Current critics of the mass media argue that new electronic technologies are powerful new tools for *propaganda* or mass persuasion, especially useful for political oppression and control. This view emphasizes the top-down unifying potential of various communications technologies together as the media singular. It sees the media as all-powerful and persuasive and, unlike many of the theories of viewership strategies that we discussed in Chapter 2, sees viewers as passive if not gullible recipients of media messages.

One critical perspective understands the mass media inherently to be forms of propaganda, imbuing audience members with false if not dangerous ideas. This view sees the mass media as tremendously powerful and persuasive; it often uses the German Third Reich, with its use of media images to produce a national *ideology* of Nazism, as its primary example. The films of Leni Riefenstahl, a German director who worked with the Nazi Party to produce propaganda for the German masses, have been discussed as an example of the ways that the media were used to instill ideologies of nationalism and racism among a vast populace. Her 1935 film, *Triumph of the Will*, documents a Nazi rally in Nuremberg in 1934. It is considered by many to be one of the most powerful examples of the use of visual images to instill and affirm political beliefs in its audience. The 1934 rally was planned and constructed as a mass visual spectacle with the film process well in mind. Hitler choreographed the rally and the film to give the impression that the whole nation was united behind him at a moment when his party and leadership had just weathered a major challenge from the National Socialist Party. Special equipment was constructed to provide optimal access to the events for more than thirty cameras and their vast crew, led by Riefenstahl. The film is composed of strikingly dramatic compositions in which Hitler is featured as both the master eye that takes in all of the populace assembled and the full scope of the city, and the single object that rivets the gaze of the vast crowds assembled before him.

The film opens with grand aerial tracking footage of Hitler's plane swooping in over the city, intercut with shots of the city from the plane's eye view as Hitler presumably scopes out his domain. We later see many shots of Hitler in

Leni Reifenstahl,
Triumph of the Will,
1935

the crowds, taken from a low camera angle to emphasize his might, and placing him at the focal point of cheering crowds who search out the chance to see him and gaze raptly upon him when he is finally in their view. *Triumph of the Will* is a perfect example of the way that practices of looking can work in the service of overt nationalism and idolatry.

Of course, we cannot equate all overt propaganda with Nazism or "bad" ways of generating ideological positions. As we noted in Chapter 4, images can be used for many political purposes, and media serve different social purposes in different cultures. For instance, Walter Benjamin called for the use of the presses by revolutionary student and worker groups, rather than governments. Whereas in the United States and many other countries, televisions were introduced as home appliances that took center stage in the relative domestic privacy of the family home, in Germany television was at first more frequently viewed collectively in public spaces. Television emerged during the era of Nazism as a nationalized industry that was used to forge a strong collective ideology. As such, it was a tool of mass persuasion not unlike mass rallies, where people physically gathered to express their support for the party. In this sense, the practice of looking collectively in a public space at the same spectacle was an important experience in the forging of a mass ideology. This is true whether we are talking about crowds of people looking upon Hitler himself in a rally, or rooms full of people gazing at a television program that supported Nazism.

One well-known analysis of collective practices of looking and the media that was influential in the 1960s is Guy Debord's 1967 *Society of the Spectacle*. Debord was a founding member of Situationist International, a group of social theorists with links to the older art movements of *Futurism*, *Dada*, and *Surrealism*. They sought to blur the distinction between art and life, and called for a constant transformation of lived experience. *Society of the Spectacle* describes how the social order of the late twentieth-century global economy exerts its influence through *representations*. Debord put forth the idea of the *spectacle* as both an "instrument of unification" and a world vision that forged a social relationship among people in which images and practices of gazing were central. All that was once directly lived, he argued, had become mere representation.[1]

Triumph of the Will can be seen as an illustration of this point about representation and the all-consuming power of the spectacle, given the power that its images had in establishing collective ideology. Yet Debord was not speaking about the extreme example of Nazism, but of industrialized Western cultures in which the conditions of production and reproduction have reduced experience to representation. His idea reached its fullest articulation two decades later in the writing of Jean Baudrillard, who made the case that the experience of *simulation* in realms like *cyberspace* transcends that of the real. Simulacra are copies without originals. This term is crucial to an understanding of the *postmodern*, which we will discuss in Chapter 7. Debord later wrote about the concept of integrated spectacle, which exerts greater control than the spectacle. The integrated spectacle, like the simulacra, pervades and overtakes all of reality, making every relationship without recourse to a real. The virtual worlds of Disneyland, computer worlds, simulated life, and the Internet are all examples of integrated spectacles behind which there is no "there" there.

Other critics of the mass media, writing before Baudrillard's work on simulation, have addressed more subtle forms of image persuasion with reference to the real of political experience. The idea of the hypodermic effect of the mass media refers to an increased passivity in viewers "drugged" by media texts with less explicitly political messages than the overtly propagandistic media text. The concept of a narcotic effect refers to the way that time spent with the media (viewing television, for instance) replaces actual participation in organized action. The mass media, in this concept, is understood as convincing people that being informed about a social issue by seeing it covered in the media is the same as doing something about it. In this view, television came to be regarded by some as the ideal medium of the masses. This is precisely because of its capacity to reach millions of viewers simultaneously, its instant transmission and, hence, its capacity to convey a sense of immediacy, and its "narcotic" effect. It was thus regarded as a unique medium that worked better than films to unify and consolidate the masses under a singular political belief. This view holds that the increasing dependency of the mass population on television for political news fosters the growth of political malaise. Hence, people who are socially isolated, either because they spend so much time in their homes with the media, or because they live in rural places where the media are their only outside contact, are more likely to be persuaded and to buy into extreme political views.

A critique of the mass media that has had a powerful influence over media criticism in the late twentieth century comes from a group of cultural critics that came to be known as the *Frankfurt School*. This group, which included Max Horkheimer, Theodor Adorno, Walter Benjamin, and Herbert Marcuse, among others, published a series of essays criticizing the capitalist and consumerist orientation of postwar entertainment and popular media forms including popular movies, television, and advertising. They studied mass culture because, in their view, "the whole world is made to pass through the filter of the culture industry." According to the Frankfurt School theorists, the *culture industry* is an entity that both creates and caters to a mass public that, tragically, can no longer see the difference between the real world and the illusory world that these popular media forms collectively generate. In their classic essay on the culture industry, Theodor Adorno and Max Horkheimer set up a contrast between mass entertainment and fine art. In this distinction of *high and low culture*, they criticize the culture industry for generating images that are nothing more than style and propaganda for industrial capitalism, reproducing the status quo and obeying the dominant social order. In their view, the culture industry generates *false consciousness* among its consumers, encouraging the masses to buy mindlessly into the belief systems or ideologies that allow industrial capitalism to thrive. It is important to note that Adorno and Horkheimer began their theories of media as Jewish intellectuals in Germany during the rise of Nazism in the 1930s, and continued them as refugees in the United States. Their view of media was thus initially formulated in a time and culture where the media was being used effectively to create a particularly destructive and murderous national Fascist ideology.

According to the Frankfurt School view, the "real" conditions of existence—the fact that class oppression and domination are unfair and not a natural aspect of everyday life—are distorted by a mass *ideology* that generates myths about the good life under capitalism. These myths are generated and made to seem natural and inevitable by the mass culture industry. In this view, ideology is a distortion of the realities of the capitalist economy (hence the term "false consciousness"). It is through these media-generated ideologies that the ruling classes of the United States and Europe maintain their dominance at home and abroad. This is a traditional Marxist view of ideology, which we discussed at greater length in Chapter 2. According to Marx, those who own the *means of production* are also in control of the ideas and viewpoints produced and circulated. Members of the dominant class that own, control, or have their interests represented in the newspapers, television networks, and the film industry are able to control the content generated by these media forms. Media, in this view, is a means of domination. It is controlled by the ruling class, which dominates the masses of people who occupy other economic classes by "selling" them ideas through the media.

It can be argued that even public media such as public television in the USA and in France, Britain, and other countries, are not free of this sort of control. Typically public television is funded by both governments and corporations. In the USA, corporations such as Exxon or Philip Morris often have their names prominently displayed as contributors to public television, and hence their logos acquire the cachet of high culture. The role of government in funding television in Britain and other European countries is, of course, never outside of the political domain. In the Frankfurt School view, the pull of ideology is so strong that even those whose interests are not directly served by the ruling classes will help to reproduce it by mindlessly working for its benefit. Frankfurt School theorists, among other critics, emphasized that the mass media made palatable, and even seemingly inevitable, the domination and oppression inherent in a capitalist economy.

The question of what the "masses" or viewers in general might actively do with the mass media was not a central concern of the Frankfurt School or its followers. Though they were concerned with the effects of media on the

Audience wearing
3-D glasses, New
York, 1950

masses, they did not consider just how people interpret and use the media forms they encounter. The ideas of resistant viewing, cultural appropriation, and subjective or psychical factors were introduced by other theorists to modify their model later, in response to the criticism that their view was too universalizing. The Frankfurt School theorists had also set up a divide between art and mass culture, and in so doing established a high and low culture dichotomy. Whereas they regarded consumers of high culture as educated and informed, they saw popular media consumers as mindless dupes of the culture industry and the capitalist system it supported. While the Frankfurt School model of media is flawed in its condescension toward the viewer, and its inability to examine the complex negotiations that take place between viewer and cultural products, their criticism of the effects of the industry of culture—summarized in the phrase, "the whole world is made to pass through the filter of the culture industry"—still resonates today.[2] In part due to the Frankfurt School's contributions, it has become something of a commonplace idea that we experience life in and through our practices of looking at and experiencing media and art.

The Frankfurt School model of mass media concentrates on a top-down way of conceiving how mass media works. However, this is only part of the picture. As we noted in Chapter 2, viewers are not empty receptacles waiting to receive media messages. Since the late 1980s, critics have questioned the high art/mass culture divide, suggesting that our experiences with the media during the late twentieth century are too complex and varied to be adequately characterized in sweeping categories such as mass consciousness or mass culture. We have many cultures, many media industries, and many ways of representing meaning, hence the concepts of a unified mass culture and a singular media industry are not useful for talking about present conditions.

Behind both of these views is the idea that there is no longer one mass audience. Rather, the populace is fragmented among a range of cultures and communities, some of which may respond to art and media in ways that challenge or even transform the dominant meanings generated by the mainstream culture industry. Moreover, the culture industry no longer makes a unified set of products. It increasingly produces a diverse range of art and media designed to appeal to niche audiences. Hence, the media can include *counter-hegemonic* forces that challenge dominant ideologies and the social orders they uphold. This position on mass media states that popular media is not all homogenizing and conformist. How the media function in the realm of the social and the political depends in large part on how we make use of these media within our specific communities and cultures.

The mass media and democratic potential

While the anxious and fearful view of how the mass media can change a society has proliferated throughout the twentieth century, there is also a counter-view that regards the mass media as a promising tool for democratic ideals. This view sees communications technologies as wonderful new tools for use by the mass citizenry that will promote an open flow of information and exchange of ideas, thereby strengthening democracy. It emphasizes the potential for various individual media forms to be used by individuals and groups to advance positions of resistance or countercultural perspectives. For instance, the two-way model of media communication on the Internet has been seen by many of its users as highly democratic in this sense. It offers an alternative to the top-down communications model of broadcasting and challenges the standard culture industry concept of production and consumption. Community-based television, which is produced at low cost by members of the community and is geared toward local audiences, has been subsidized in the USA through Federal Communications Commission regulations and mandates on the cable industry.

Though minimal, this kind of initiative is driven by a democratic idea of a mass media that should also serve diverse or "minority" needs and interests.

The view of media as potentially democratic challenges the very idea of a mass media or a mass society. It stresses instead the potential of individual media forms for the development of community and identity on a much smaller scale. For example, the range and variety of television programming on cable, despite the fact that it contains many channels that emulate network television, presents too varied a terrain to offer a unified idea of what public culture can and should be. Cable network channels are typically geared toward specific audiences, such as Spanish-, Chinese-, or Korean-speaking diasporas. However, cable television can also have a more global appeal, as in the case of Cable News Network (CNN), which aims for national and international audiences.

There are many things to question in this approach to the mass media. The television and advertising industries have shown us that narrowcasting and consumer-driven models are no less firmly driven by the forces of capitalism and may in fact service only those who have the means to gain access to the media, and always at some cost. Nonetheless, this line of thought is an important trend in late-twentieth-century media criticism, one that breaks from the tired paradigm of visual media as a destructive force.

Among those who have seen media as having great democratic and liberatory potential, Canadian communication theorist Marshall McLuhan, who wrote most influentially in the 1950s through the 1970s, has had the most widespread impact. McLuhan was known for coining catchy phrases, of which *"the medium is the message"* and *"global village"* have had the most longevity. McLuhan argued that television and radio were like natural resources, waiting to be used for the benefit of increasing mankind's collective and individual experiences of the world. He also stated that the media were simply extensions of our natural senses, helping us better to hear, see, and know the world and, moreover, helping us to connect ourselves to geographically distant communities and bodies. His analysis in the 1960s and 1970s of how the speed of information's flow through the media has affected local, national, and global cultures was tremendously influential.

McLuhan's well-known phrase "the medium is the message" can be seen as a *technologically determinist* way of viewing media because it implies that content (the "message") is not as important as the medium through which you receive it. Yet, McLuhan was referring to the fact that the medium has an impact on content, and that we understand and evaluate messages in ways that are profoundly influenced by the medium itself. McLuhan felt that media technologies give greater potential for power to our individual bodies by extending our senses and thereby extending our power in the world. Part of the "message" of the medium is the new, bigger scale that is introduced to individual experience through the very act of using a technology that increases the scope of connectivity. One of his examples is a hypothetical man in Africa who does not understand English but listens to BBC radio news every night. According to McLuhan, just hearing the sounds of the broadcaster's voice makes this man feel empowered. The content is not essential. The "message" consists in this man's relationship to the world, enriched and expanded through global media access. Interestingly, McLuhan chose an example in which we can imagine a recent colonial relationship between the man's country (presumably an ex-colony of England, since it receives the BBC) and the media's national source (England). In contrast to McLuhan, we might want to ask, can it be that the man might have a more contradictory relationship than one of "empowerment" through this association with the media broad-cast of a past colonial power?

Both McLuhan's optimistic view of media's potential and the Frankfurt School's critical view were popular in the late 1960s and early 1970s, at a time when there was a keen sense that a communications revolution was possible. (These views resurfaced in the late 1980s and early 1990s.) The Frankfurt School critique of mass media as promoting the interests of industry and cap-italism resonated with the leftist and counterculture movements at the time. McLuhan's liberatory view of connecting through media appealed to political movements that were discovering new media. Portable, consumer-grade video technology became available in the late 1960s, making it possible for artists, activists, and local community and political groups to make their own video-tapes for the first time. Some saw this as a means of countering dominant television and news messages with militant, activist *guerrilla television*. Proponents of guerrilla television argued that to put the means of production in the hands of ordinary citizens would empower these citizens to express themselves more freely and define themselves rather than being molded and "brainwashed" by the mass media. This was regarded as a positive outcome of the new communications revolution that could foster a global media village. For instance, in 1972 a group of video activists calling themselves TVTV (for

TVTV, *Four More Years*, 1972

"Top Value Television") took their Portapak video equipment to the Republican National Convention that re-elected President Richard Nixon to make their tape *Four More Years* (1972) ("four more years" was the slogan of Nixon's re-election campaign). TVTV used their access to the convention to actually interview the press, and get a view of the convention from many perspectives, such as that of anti-Nixon protestors, that were not included in network television coverage.

Today, the proliferation of home video cameras can be seen as both liberating and mundane. Consumer-grade and public access video technology gives local groups and individuals the capacity to represent their own issues instead of having them defined by the media. But this technology also facilitates the production of lots of amateur video that is modeled after television rather than questioning it. While it can be said that the possession of a video camera no longer is the revolutionary act it was in the late 1960s, it does signal an important shift in the relationship of production and consumption in media in general over the last thirty years.

Many of McLuhan's ideas are now being recycled as ways of looking at new media, especially the Internet and the World Wide Web. In 1965, McLuhan stated that "There are no remote places. Under instant circuitry, nothing is remote in time or in space. It's now."[3] His words now seem prescient in defining the world of electronic circuitry, personal computers, data bases, web sites, and Internet chat groups that exploded in the 1990s. We will discuss this global context of new media more extensively in Chapter 9. McLuhan's notion of the global village resonates in profound ways in contemporary cyberculture, where those who have access to the Internet are plugged into a global media network.

Television and the question of sponsorship

The rise of the mass media, which culminated in the twentieth century with television, has also been tied in complex ways to the structure of sponsorship and the funding of programs. While television forms a central example of these structures, they also can be understood in part through an important nonvisual precedent, the aural medium of radio. Radio began as an amateur medium used by enthusiasts who actively produced shows and built their own sets. By the early 1920s, many people were enthralled by the prospect of becoming part of a national audience linked across great distances by real-time voice and musical recordings, without ever having to leave their own living rooms. It was eventually determined that radios would be built and operated by the private sector, within certain regulatory parameters. Following heated debate and struggle among radio enthusiasts, the industry, and the government in the USA, radio came to be supported by corporate not consumer dollars, with bandwidth distributed according to the terms of public interest as set out in the Radio Act of 1927. US television also eventually followed the same model of federally regulated private-sector ownership paid for by advertising, and overseen by the Federal Communication Commission, the agency that in 1934 was officially given oversight of all telecommunications in the public's interest. Until satellite and cable television came on the scene, the individual (or household)

Family gathered
around radio,
Provincetown,
Mass., 1 Jan.,
1942

viewer's costs for access to television were limited to the initial cost of the television set and the relatively minimal cost of electricity used to operate it.
Access to television was more or less free to consumers within broadcast
range, after purchasing the proper equipment. Advertisers paid networks for
air time—and viewers "paid" indirectly, by watching corporate messages and
logos embedded in the programs they viewed.

An important paradox about practices of looking is embedded in this model:
consumers watch television primarily to see programs, but what keeps television afloat is viewers' not-so-incidental exposure to the products advertised
throughout these programs. With few exceptions, in the USA, corporate
network programming has always been laced with advertising content,
whether overtly or subtlely. To recall the title of a 1973 art video by artist
Richard Serra, "television delivers people"—that is, the medium hands consumers over to commercial industries seeking expanded markets. An NBC
executive predicted, in a radio speech aired in 1948, that "advertising on television will be a potent educational force, and consequently will be of almost as
much value to our American way of life as the entertainment itself."[4] As television historian William Boddy has written, despite the opposing view at the time
that advertising had been bad enough on radio, and that television advertising
had the potential to be a horror, broadcast advertising has been the rule,
though its value has remained a vexed question.

In US television's early years, product endorsements were enmeshed with programming itself, making it difficult to separate the product from the program. Corporate sponsorship was explicit, often appearing in the name of the program, as in NBC's *Colgate Comedy Hour*. Sponsors had major control over the content of the programs they sponsored, from scripts to the choice of actors and directors. The "soap opera," a long-time staple of daytime television and radio, got its name from the fact that the sponsors controlling content of that genre were manufacturers of soaps and household cleaning products. These were the products displayed in advertisements geared toward the women who, industry-sponsored audience research indicated, comprised the bulk of the soap opera's viewing audience. The visual and aural aspects of the television text, then, were heavily determined by sponsor interest and were filled with logos, pitches, and product images. Clearly, then, advertisers shaped what viewers saw on early television in major ways, by weaving their products and messages into the very content of the shows.

By the early 1950s, broadcast networks began to tire of the control of image and content by single sponsors. Increasing program length from fifteen to thirty minutes allowed broadcasters to increase program costs for sponsors, making it harder for a single corporation to afford to control an entire show. When NBC introduced the *Today* show in 1952, they gave it a three-hour slot for which they sold thirty- or sixty-second spot ads to an array of sponsors. This effectively put control of the show back in the hands of the network. Another strategy that limited sponsors' control was the introduction of the "spectacular" (the television special), for which networks sold spot ads to advertisers interested in the large audiences these extravaganzas were expected to attract. The real watershed, though, was the quiz show scandal of the late 1950s. Quiz shows were rigged by corporate sponsors who were eager to control the drama of winner and losers, and the flow of prize money. When these practices were discovered, the ensuing scandal culminated in a grand-jury probe and congressional investigation in 1959. The quiz show scandal forced the issue of removing sponsors from the business of programming. It introduced a whole new way of looking, in that programs and advertisements were now separate, signaling viewers to adopt two viewing modes—that is, to recognize the difference between programs (and their codes and conventions) and advertisements (and their codes and conventions). This episode also spawned public distrust of a medium that many had previously believed could provide wholesome entertainment and even education to the American home, even through advertisements. It can be said that viewers acquired more skeptical viewing practices after the scandal exposed the structure of television sponsorship.

The sponsorship of television is also tied to its structure. Broadcasting is dependent on the geographic scope of a given network's potential audience. In the early years of US television, most local station operators, when they did get off the ground, immediately affiliated with one of the two dominant network firms rather than launch independent programming. By affiliating with the major networks, local operators were guaranteed a certain amount of programming that was proven to be successful in other markets. However, in some regions, affiliation was not possible because the coaxial cable that linked the major networks to distant sites was not yet widely enough installed. This limitation resulted in some interesting local programming.[5] With the laying down of coaxial cable in the 1950s, local stations became affiliates of the national networks, foreclosing on the potential for the growth of television as a community-based medium. By the 1960s, each of the three major television networks had around 200 affiliated stations giving over 60 percent of their airtime to national network programming. This system has been criticized for creating a centralized stronghold of three companies over the images and messages circulating nationally (and, eventually, globally). Viewing this from the perspective of visual culture, we might say that television went from a model in which local communities produced and consumed images among themselves, to one in which images are produced at a central source and marketed as broadly as possible to an ever-growing public. This trajectory suggests to many critics that televisual practices of looking were rendered generic and passive.

This argument is made even with the explosion of choice available with the expansion of cable television since the late 1970s. Although available in the form of noncommercial, community-based television as early as 1948, US cable took off as a commercial entity in 1972 with the establishment of Home Box Office. Its success was guaranteed when the FCC lifted restrictions on satellite delivery of cable in the late 1970s and instituted other forms of industry deregulation into the 1980s. Cable is a good example of the paradox of global media. The cable system has multiplied the number of network and program choices viewers have, allowing for highly specific sorts of programming geared toward specific identity groups of all sorts: there is television for women, for blacks, for sports enthusiasts. One would think that with this many choices viewers would have a plurality of practices of looking available.

But cable has also made possible a kind of media globalization, as in the examples of the world-wide casting of news by CNN (Cable News Network) or Telemundo's appeal to a global population of Spanish-speaking people.

In Great Britain, the development of television presents a different paradigm and history of national looking practices. England was the first country to have regular television service available through home sets. The government-established and sponsored BBC (British Broadcasting Corporation) began a television service in the 1930s that remained a monopoly until commercial television made inroads with its own collective monopoly in the 1950s. Commercial television was instituted only when the Conservative Party came to power and set up a commercial channel to rival the BBC. This drove the latter to work toward appealing to a mass audience, which it did, maintaining a strong place in the British television market through the 1990s, and even introducing the innovative Channel Four in 1982 to feature independent producers and alternative viewpoints. The BBC model suggests a mode of looking in which the government plays a strong role in determining what the collective viewing audience sees. Unlike the FCC, which oversees and regulates US television but is not involved in programming, the BBC actually contracts directly with producers. The government thus is a more active player in the overall industry, in programming, and in national looking practices.

Public broadcasting has thus been a central model for television, with Canada, England, France, and Germany opting for state-controlled television over the private industry-driven system. In the USA, public television began in the 1960s as a nonprofit alternative to advertiser subsidy, market rule, and industry interests. The idea behind its formation was to create a venue for dissenting voices, in the spirit of a democratic medium, without commercial intervention. It suggested that the medium could support alternative and minority interests and viewing practices without corporate subsidy of any sort. It is commonly believed that the US Public Broadcasting System (PBS) was introduced to advance liberal viewpoints, but one of the strongest forces behind it was the Department of Defense, which wanted the government to invest in a broadcast network that could aid in propaganda along the lines of Radio Free Europe and Voice of America.[6]

Though public television was introduced in the USA to allow for freedom of expression and minority viewpoints, its potential has been diminished by the argument that television should be freed from government control over how we exercise choice. Television, according to this perspective, should be shaped by free market forces, not government regulation. In addition to federal subsidy and viewer support, US public television now relies on corporate sponsorship with minimal advertising.

In Chapter 9, we will discuss the exportation of American television, and the globalization of television as a medium. Here, we would like to note how the development of television as a central mass medium, with both broadcasting and narrowcasting, has been shaped by the question of its sponsorship. Increasingly, the US model of commercial television is becoming global. These issues are crucial precisely because of the central role that television plays in the experience of public culture and in the construction of concepts of national audience and the nation.

Media and the public sphere

As we stated earlier, the concept of a public culture is an important element in how the mass media is conceived. In what ways are contemporary media forms contributing to a sense of public life or public discussion, and in what ways are they detrimental to it? It is important to note that even those media forms which are one-way, such as radio and television, contribute to a sense of shared audience among viewers. When we watch the national evening news, for instance, we experience ourselves as part of a national audience regardless of our political stance toward the issues it reports. This is particularly the case during times of national crisis, when viewers of the news are *interpellated* as citizen-viewers and often respond by seeing themselves as members of a national audience. This sense of oneself as part of a public dialogue through the media is overtly played out in media broadcasts that incorporate public responses—through the letters to the editor section of newspapers, for instance, or in the reading of listeners' letters on public radio.

This idea of media as dialogue was staged in a very interesting way during the height of the media's attention to the ongoing AIDS crisis in the late 1980s. The US investigative news program *Nightline* invited members of the public to come to a "town meeting" before a panel of AIDS experts, advocates, artists, and activists. Public health officials spoke alongside prostitutes and playwrights while the cameras made frequent forays into the audience, in order to show viewers at home the show's "democratic" inclusion of a representative and diverse population, which apparently included lesbians and gay men selected for prime seating because their appearances conformed to codes of lesbian and gay style. In this instance, primetime network television attempted to function as a public forum for participatory democracy.

The idea of a *public sphere*, in which public discussion and debate takes place, has been influenced by the ideas of German theorist Jürgen Habermas. A public sphere is ideally a space—a physical place, social setting, or media arena—where citizens come together to debate and discuss the pressing issues of their society. Habermas postulated that the public sphere that was participated in by the liberal middle class of the nineteenth century was destroyed in the twentieth century by various forces including the rise of consumer culture, the rise of the mass media, and the intervention of the state in the private sphere of the family and home. Habermas saw the public sphere as a group of "private" persons who could assemble to discuss matters of common "public" interest in ways that mediated the power of the state. In addition, Habermas believed the public sphere was a public space where private interests (such as business interests) were inadmissible, hence a place where true public opinion could be formulated.

A unified, singular public is a utopian ideal that does not adequately account for differences among those who supposedly inhabit this hypothetical sphere. Habermas himself acknowledged that his ideal was never realized. US journalist Walter Lippmann proposed, in the 1920s, that the public sphere was nothing more than a "phantom"—that it was not possible for average citizens to keep abreast of political issues and events and give them due consideration given the chaotic pace of industrial society. Yet, as a phantom, the public sphere has prompted an important discussion about what a public is and how it functions. This model is based on the idea that there are distinctly separate public and private spheres, and that the state is separate from private market interests. Yet, the political terrain of Western capitalist countries has always involved, to varying degrees, elements of private interest. Furthermore, the idea of a separation of public and private spheres is based on traditional notions of gender and race that must be rethought. The concept of a private, domestic sphere in which the public does not intervene depends as well on traditional gender roles, where women are relegated to the domestic sphere of the home and men to the public arena of business, commerce, and politics. The nineteenth-century public sphere described by Habermas was restricted to the participation of white men, and criticisms of his work have seen the exclusion of others such as women, blacks and other ethnicities, and lower-class people as not simply the problem of the restrictions of a previous society but as constitutive aspects of this way of conceiving the public. In other words, this criticism states that the idea of a unified public sphere is not only a fallacy but is also based on exclusion (hence not truly public). Consequently, contemporary attempts to understand how the public converges and functions have proposed the idea of multiple public spheres and counterspheres. For instance, political theorist Nancy Fraser has pointed out that historically women were relegated to the private domestic sphere of the home, and elided from the public spaces and discourses of middle- and upper-class European and white men. She puts forth the useful alternative theory of a women's and a feminist countersphere, among other counterspheres of public discourse and agency. Theorists like Fraser suggest that we can envision many publics that can overlap and work in tension with each other: working-class publics, religious publics, feminist publics, nationalist publics, and so on.

In these multiple and overlapping public spheres, debate and discussion is fostered through many media, including newsletters, journals, bookstores, conventions, conferences, festivals, zines, web sites, chat groups, and other forms of community media. Those media forms that have decentralized over the past twenty years, such as television and the cinema, can be seen as both targeting specific market audiences and functioning as a means for various publics to be formed. The explosion of the Internet and the World Wide Web in the 1990s indicates the ways in which the media can be used as a forum for the cultivation of diverse kinds of publics.

Yet, we can look at the idea of the public sphere, or the notion put forward by Lippmann of a "phantom public," as challenges to consider the status of contemporary public debate and the role of the media within it. Where does our sense of a public exist today? What role does the media play in fostering a sense of a public, or in discouraging it? Where does public discussion take place and who has access to it? Is it in public squares, cafes, bars, and town meetings, in the editorials and letters of newspapers, on radio and television talk shows, or in Internet chat groups and World Wide Web sites? What role do visual media play in building a sense of the public?

One of the forms of traditional mass media that can be seen as a force in public spheres and the formation of public opinion is television. Because of its capacity for instant transmission, in other words, its material condition of electronic transmission, and its situation within the domestic sphere of the home,

Television viewers watching the Kennedy-Nixon debate, 1960

television has played a primary role in fostering a sense of a collective public sphere. John F. Kennedy's use of the medium during his presidency and his representation on television is a case in point. Kennedy was the first US president to televise live press conferences. During the 1961 events known as the Bay of Pigs and the Cuban Missile Crisis of 1962, Kennedy used television broadcasts to speak to the nation and garner support for his administration's actions, in the way that Franklin Roosevelt had used the radio for "fireside chats" before him.

However, it was Kennedy's tragic death that demonstrated the power of television and the photographic image both nationally and globally in the mid-twentieth century, with the impact of the film image of his death and the television coverage of his funeral. The Zapruder film of Kennedy's assassination was seen publicly only as still images for many years after his death, until an illegal copy of it was shown on television in 1975. The footage, taken by Abraham Zapruder on his home movie camera, has become synonymous with the assassination itself and is now considered to be an essential historical document. Indeed, the US government paid the Zapruder family $16 million in 1999 for ownership of the original film. Like many iconic images, the Zapruder film has been endlessly re-enacted, in the popular film *JFK* and the 1975 re-enactment *The Eternal Frame* by video activist groups Ant Farm and T. R. Uthco, who restaged the event in Dallas in order to comment upon the power of the image itself. In the late 1990s, the

Ant Farm/T. R. Uthco,
The Eternal Frame, 1975

Zapruder film was re-enacted again in a parodic music video by singer Marilyn Manson.

Zapruder's documentary footage is not the only means through which Kennedy's death became a media event. The networks covered the events surrounding Kennedy's death and his funeral over many days with uninterrupted television coverage, making of the events a public spectacle and creating an opportunity for mass-mediated participation in the ritual of mourning. Well-known television producer Fred Friendly commented on the coverage in a way that highlights the tremendous importance of the media in constructing a space of public mourning: "It was broadcasting's finest hour. And I think it may have saved this country. . . . Television was for those four days the sinew, the stabilizing force, the gyroscope that held this country together."[7] This footage became a moving-image icon of the era etched indelibly in collective national memory.

Similarly, in the 1997 funeral of Princess Diana, as visual theorist Nicholas Mirzoeff writes, global mourning was facilitated by extensive international coverage.[8] In events such as these, the media serve to create a sense of community at local, national, and global levels. (In the image on the next page, we see the news media setting up for the funeral itself.) It could be said that global events such as Diana's funeral create simultaneously a global audience and a

Television crews set up outside Buckingham Palace, London, 5 Sept. 1997, for the funeral of Princess Diana

specifically national audience, speaking not only to the British citizenry but to all viewers as British citizens. The funeral thus affirmed the nation of Britain while it demonstrated Diana's global appeal. Television thus aids in generating the sense that a national culture exists, even as it fosters the movement of images around the globe.

Television is also a forum for the airing of controversial issues, in particular in the context of television talk shows. In this form, there are multiple audiences: the studio audience, the home audience, and then subsequent audiences such as those of television shows which talk about the talk shows—news shows if a program has been particularly controversial, as well as the "lunch room" discussions at work and school that the shows might generate among viewers. Television talk shows span the range from news shows, comedy shows, and celebrity guest shows to tabloid-like programs often accused of fabricating guests' stories. The genre creates a forum for contemporary issues and thus promotes the formation of public spheres.

The status of talk shows as an arena for public influence and debate is exemplified in the case brought by Texas beef cattle ranchers against Oprah Winfrey. In her popular television show, *Oprah!*, Winfrey hosted an expert on Mad Cow Disease and openly stated her own negative feelings about eating beef following his presentation. The prosecution stated that Winfrey and her show exerted great influence on public opinion and hence damaged the cattle industry in voicing her own views. Though the Texas ranchers lost, this case demonstrates the broad acceptance of the idea of the talk show as public sphere. Likewise, through her monthly book club, Winfrey has been tremendously influential in promoting not only specific books but the idea of reading as an important cultural activity. Her widely popular show can thus be seen as succeeding in fostering public debate and discussion.

Some critics have faulted the media for sensationalizing events involving stars and notorious individuals over important global news, such as wars, famine, and international politics. In the late 1990s there emerged a perception even among members of the media that the public was not being adequately served by its media. Importantly, this demonstrates that the media is not a monolith but is comprised of conflicting views and even self-critical voices. This criticism of the media as a force out of control followed the international outcry against the media following the death of Princess Diana. In the view of many, the media literally drove this international media icon to her death in their frenzy to get a photograph of the woman who was among the most photographed female icons of the twentieth century. This event helped to further the view that the media is a monstrous force that will stop at nothing to get and create news. The accident that killed Diana was both representative and symbolic of the media's unconscionable feeding of a media-hungry society that ate up representations of this princess and socialite's every fashion move, haircut, and social engagement. Ironically, the tragedy spurred a spate of news stories, features, and books, extending the media apparatus that constructed her life for the public. This provides evidence of the way in which the media can appropriate critiques about its practices into its ongoing programming.

New media cultures

The global media landscape of the late twentieth and early twenty-first centuries is highly complex. It is diverse at both the level of the media themselves and at the level of national and cultural boundaries.

Indeed, it is hard to say what constitutes a medium in itself any longer. Traditional forms such as newspapers, for example, are distributed quickly over wider terrains through the electronic transmission of text, and now have on-line components. Hence, newspapers are not just a print medium, they are also sometimes a digital and electronic medium. Films are shown in theaters, rented on videotapes, and shown internationally on television in addition to being distributed in highly developed black markets throughout the world. Moreover, the film industry has for decades relied on electronic means to produce special effects and graphics, and it is widely anticipated that most movie theaters will switch to digital projection in the next decade. In this sense film is also partly an electronic and digital medium.

The Blair Witch Project is a film and advertising phenomenon that demonstrates the crossover among media forms that became commonplace in the 1990s. The fictional film is a faux documentary about a crew of film students who trek out into the backwoods of rural Maryland to make a film about the legendary locations of some gruesome murders reputedly performed under the power of the witch of the film's title.

The film was unique in its use of the Internet to generate the sense that the film is in fact a documentary not fiction production. A year prior to the film's release in 1999, *The Blair Witch Project* had become the subject of an ever-changing web site whose popularity increased dramatically toward the release of the film. By the late 1990s, web sites had become a routine way to advertise upcoming films. But this site was different in that it did not reveal its own status as advertisement explicitly but instead generated an ever-changing update on the background of the Blair Witch myth and the "documentary" film's production process. Visitors to the site, many of whom happened to be teens fascinated with the spooky theme and the daring "documentary" venture of their youth peers, generated e-mail reports of their emotional responses not only to the idea of the project, but to the "real-life" film itself. Even after the release of the film, the e-mail lists devoted to the project were the site of revelations from 14-year-old viewers about the hoax, and defenses from other teens about the truth of not only the legend but the film documentary. The market value of the film was not lost on distributors tracking the web site traffic prior to the film's release. Initially a student production, the film got a major release that finally put an end to the hoax about the film and the legend, though not before the local Maryland township became the site of youth pilgrimages. It is thus not possible to state that this cultural production

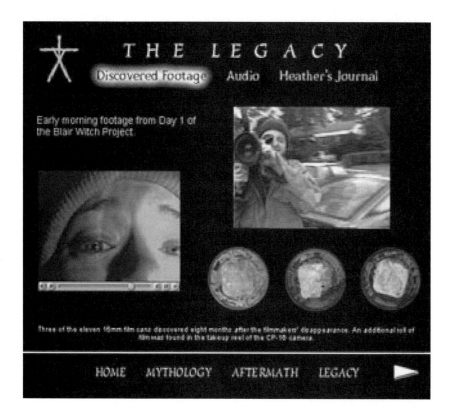

was only a film; it is in fact a complex set of media used to create a media event.

Not only does the contemporary media environment mean that the distinctions among media are less definable, it also means that there are opportunities for media to be less monolithic and centralized. The Frankfurt School view that the media serve the singular purpose of servicing the interests of those who hold economic and political power thus no longer has the same currency. One striking example of the way that even the most centralized media context can be resisted is the Chinese student rebellion in Tiananmen Square in 1989. Though the Chinese government blocked media coverage, fax machines were used to circulate news information internationally. There are many ways in which the media can aid in political resistance, even in the most repressive of situations.

The media and their messages flow through various and diasporic communities, and can be essential elements in productive sorts of cross-cultural exchange and collaboration. As we will discuss further in Chapter 9, while it is possible to see the ways that, for instance, the exportation of American television throughout the world has constituted a kind of *cultural imperialism*, this situation has prompted local and national cultural responses, including protest, media appropriation, and mediated debate. These responses are also part of the media context. It is also important to note the ways programs can acquire new meaning among audiences and are subject to appropriation, reconfiguration, and dramatically resistant and transformative uses. Sub- and countercultural uses of media make a difference, especially in a complex and diversified world where we can no longer speak of a singular mass culture.

It is thus important to see the constant negotiation of power that exists in the media. The media are indeed in the control of powerful entities, and they do influence our thinking. However, audiences in a wide range of cultural and national settings resist, appropriate, and transform media texts not only at the level of consumption, but as producers of new texts. Moreover, media consumers are also tinkerers who transform the technologies they use, adapting them to new settings and new uses. The contradiction between media as the product of global powers and media as technologies for local meaning and use exists not because the theories we rely on to assess the media are faulty, but because the status of media in contemporary cultures is contradictory and mixed in exactly this way. No contemporary circumstance better demonstrates this contradiction than the status of computer communication in the 1990s and the early twenty-first century. It is widely known that the Internet was founded through the research and development efforts of the US military and was intended to be a national information system that would not fail in the event of military attack on US land. But the system was quickly appropriated by workers for limited discussion forums and developed a life of its own as a new sort of public sphere. Yet, like other media and communications systems, the Internet has not been immune to corporate interests. In Chapter 9, we will discuss the Internet as a mass medium in the context of the globalization of media.

Notes

1. Guy Debord, *The Society of the Spectacle* (Detroit, Mich.: Black and Red Books, [1967] 1970), passages 3–5 in section 1, "Separation Perfected."
2. Theodor Adorno and Max Horkheimer, "The Culture Industry: Enlightenment as Mass

Deception," in *The Cultural Studies Reader*, edited by Simon During (New York and London: Routledge, 1993), 33.

3. Paul Benedict and Nancy DeHart, eds., *On McLuhan: Forward through the Rearview Mirror* (Toronto: Prentice Hall Canada, 1996), 39.

4. As quoted in William Boddy, "The Beginnings of Television," in *Television: An International History*, Second Edition, edited by Anthony Smith (New York and Oxford: Oxford University Press, 1998), 33.

5. See James Baughman, *The Republic of Mass Culture: Journalism, Filmmaking, and Broadcasting in America since 1941*, Second Edition (Baltimore and London: Johns Hopkins Press, 1997).

6. See James Ledbetter, *Made Possible By: The Death of Public Broadcasting in the United States* (New York and London: Verso), 1997.

7. Fred Friendly, quoted by Michael Tracey in "Non-Fiction Television," in *Television: An International History*, 73.

8. See Nicholas Mirzoeff, *Introduction to Visual Culture* (New York and London: Routledge, 1999), ch. 7.

Further Reading

Theodor Adorno and Max Horkheimer. "The Culture Industry: Enlightenment as Mass Deception." In *The Dialectics of Enlightenment*. Translated by John Cumming. New York: Seabury Press, 1969. Reprinted in *The Cultural Studies Reader*. Edited by Simon During. New York and London: Routledge, 1993, 29–43.

Robert Allen, ed. *Channels of Discourse, Reassembled: Television and Contemporary Criticism*. Chapel Hill, NC and London: University of North Carolina Press, 1992.

Robert S. Alley and Irby B. Brown. *Murphy Brown: The Anatomy of a Sitcom*. New York: Delta, 1990.

Jean Baudrillard. *Simulacra and Simulation*. Translated by Sheila Glaser. Ann Arbor: University of Michigan Press, [1981] 1995.

James L. Baughman. *The Republic of Mass Culture: Journalism, Filmmaking, and Broadcasting in America since 1941*. Second Edition. Baltimore and London: Johns Hopkins University Press, 1997.

Paul Benedict and Nancy DeHart, eds. *On McLuhan: Forward through the Rearview Mirror*. Toronto: Prentice Hall Canada, 1996.

William Boddy. "The Beginnings of American Television." In *Television: An International History*. Second Edition. Edited by Anthony Smith. New York and Oxford: Oxford University Press, 1998, 23–37.

——*Fifties Television: The Industry and Its Critics*. Urbana: University of Illinois Press, 1992.

A. H. S. Boy. "Biding Spectacular Time." *Postmodern Culture*, 6 (2) (January 1996), ⟨http://www.monash.edu.au/journals/pmc/issue.196/review-2.196.html⟩.

Deirdre Boyle. *Subject to Change*. New York and Oxford: Oxford University Press, 1997.

David Buckingham, ed. *Reading Audiences: Young People and the Media*. Manchester: University of Manchester Press, 1993.

Guy Debord. *The Society of the Spectacle*. Detroit, Mich.: Black and Red Books, [1967] 1970. A more recent edition: translated by Donald Nicholson-Smith. New York: Zone Books, 1994.

——*Comments on the Society of the Spectacle*. Translated by Malcolm Imrie. New York and London: Verso, 1990.

Stuart Ewen and Elizabeth Ewen. *Channels of Desire: Mass Images and the Shaping of American Consciousness*. New York: McGraw Hill, 1982.

John Fiske. *Reading the Popular*. London: Unwin Hyman, 1989.

——*Understanding Popular Culture*. London: Unwin Hyman, 1989.

Nancy Fraser. "Rethinking the Public Sphere." In *The Phantom Public Sphere*. Edited by Bruce Robbins. Minneapolis and London: University of Minnesota Press, 1993, 1–32.

Jürgen Habermas. *The Structural Transformation of the Public Sphere*. Translated by Thomas Burger. Cambridge, Mass. and London: MIT Press, 1989.

Andreas Huyssen. "Mass Culture as a Woman: Modernism's Other." In *After the Great Divide: Modernism, Mass Culture, Postmodernism*. Bloomington: Indiana University Press, 1986, 44–62.

Linda Kintz and Julia Lesage, eds. *Media, Culture, and the Religious Right*. Minneapolis and London: University of Minnesota Press, 1998.

Paul F. Lazersfeld and Robert K. Merton. "Mass Communication, Popular Taste and Organized Social Action." In *Media Studies: A Reader*. Edited by Paul Marris and Sue Thornham. Edinburgh: Edinburgh University Press [1948] 1996, 14–23.

James Ledbetter. *Made Possible By: The Death of Public Broadcasting in the United States*. New York and London: Verso, 1997.

Paul Marris and Sue Thornham, eds. *Media Studies: A Reader*. Edinburgh: Edinburgh University Press, 1996.

Marshall McLuhan. *Understanding Media: The Extensions of Man*. New York: McGraw-Hill, 1964.

Eileen R. Meehan. "Why We Don't Count: The Commodity Audience." In *The Logics of Television*. Edited by Patricia Mellencamp. Bloomington: University of Indiana Press, 1990, 117–37.

Virginia Nightingale. *Studying Audiences: The Shock of the Real*. New York and London: Routledge, 1996.

Marlon Riggs. *Color Adjustment*, 1991. Videotape, distributed by Facets Media.

Bruce Robbins, ed. *The Phantom Public Sphere*. Minneapolis and London: University of Minnesota Press, 1993.

Andrew Ross and Constance Penley, eds. *Technoculture*. Minneapolis and London: University of Minnesota Press, 1992.

Herbert Schiller. *Culture, Inc: The Corporate Takeover of Public Expression*. New York and Oxford: Oxford University Press, 1989.

Anthony Smith, ed. *Television: An International History*. New York and Oxford: Oxford University Press, 1995.

Susan Smulyan. Selling Radio: The commercialization of American Radio, 1920–1934. Washington, D.C.: Smithsonian Institution Press, 1994.

Lynn Spigel. *Make Room for TV: Television and the Family Ideal in Postwar America*. Chicago and London: University of Chicago Press, 1992.

Michael Tracey. "Non-Fiction Television." In *Television: An International History*. Second Edition. Edited by Anthony Smith. New York and Oxford: Oxford University Press, 1998, 69–84.

Raymond Williams. *Television: Technology and Cultural Form*. New York: Schocken Books, 1974.

Consumer Culture and 6
the Manufacturing of Desire

Images are not free. Visual images play a primary role in the commerce of contemporary societies. For instance, works of art are considered to have financial worth and fuel the commerce of the art market, and news images are bought and sold because of their value in depicting current and historical events. Images also have a primary role in the functioning of commerce through advertisements. This means that images are a central aspect of *commodity* culture and of consumer societies dependent upon the constant production and consumption of goods in order to function. Such advertising images are central to the construction of cultural ideas about lifestyle, self-image, self-improvement, and glamour. Advertising often presents an image of things to be desired, people to be envied, and life as it "should be." As such, it necessarily presents social values and ideologies about what the "good life" is. It is also a central strategy of advertising to invite viewers/consumers to imagine themselves within the world of the advertisement. This is a world that works by *abstraction*, a potential place or state of being situated not in the present but in an imagined future with the promise to the consumer of things "you" will have, a lifestyle you can take part in. Indeed, advertising often speaks the language of the future. In the IBM ad on the next page, for instance, a young child reaches out toward the orbiting earth, signifying both innocence and a sense of possibility. The child reaches out to a world that communications technologies (through companies like IBM) will put within his reach. The ad projects its meaning into the future, working to equate this sense of a new world of global communications with the logo of the company itself.

New challenges. New thinking. IBM

We are confronted with advertising images constantly through the course of our daily lives, in newspaper and magazines, on television, in movie theaters, on billboards, on public transportation, on clothing, on the World Wide Web, and in many other contexts in which we may not even notice them. Ads speak to us in a broad range of voices and through an array of *strategies*. In some companies, advertisements are produced by in-house design groups. However, most companies work with advertising agencies whose business it is to design a visual identity for corporations, products, and services. In today's complex media environment, the people who produce advertisements are compelled to constantly reinvent the ways in which they address and hold the attention of increasingly jaded consumers, who are always on the verge of turning the page or hitting the remote control. As we discussed in Chapter 2, as viewers we have a range of *tactics* with which to interpret and respond to the images of advertising, to negotiate meaning through them, or to ignore them. As one strategy to deal with the potentially resistant viewer, contemporary advertising often presents itself as an art that no longer speaks to the viewer directly as a consumer, but takes on many different voices and modes of address. In the world of advertising, images can be presented as art, science, documentary evidence, or personal memories. Our understanding of advertising images is thus influenced by our experience of images in many different social roles and in diverse modes of presentation.

Consumer society

Advertising is a central component of consumer societies and *capitalism*. Capitalism is an economic system in which investment in and ownership of the means of production, distribution, and exchange of goods and wealth are held primarily by individuals and corporations. Advertising is one of the primary means through which this exchange of goods is promoted, whether on product packaging or in print, television, radio, or the Internet. Historically, consumer cultures are a rather recent development. Consumer societies emerged in the context of modernity in the late nineteenth and early twentieth century with the rise of mass production, in the wake of the Industrial Revolution and with the consolidation of populations in major urban centers. A consumer society is one in which the individual is confronted with and surrounded by an enormous assortment of goods, and in which the characteristics of those goods change constantly. There would be no reason for advertisers to constantly create new ads about products if those products always remained the same and were sold through the same strategies. In a consumer society there are great social and physical distances between the manufacture of goods and their purchase and use. This means that workers in an automobile factory may live far from where the cars they help build are bought and sold, and may never be able to afford to buy one. Increased industrialization and bureaucratization in the late nineteenth century meant a decrease in the number of small entrepreneurs and an increase in large manufacturers; this in turn resulted in people traveling longer distances to work. This is in contrast to feudal and rural societies of the past, for instance, where despite trade and traveling salesmen, there was generally proximity between producers and consumers, such as a shoemaker who would make a product that was sold and used in the small village where he made it. As places filled with mobile crowds, mass transit and city streets became forums for advertising. In the middle twentieth century, with the increased distances traveled by people in automobiles in the city and countryside, billboards became a central venue for advertising. The photograph on the next page, taken in 1936 by Walker Evans, shows a rural billboard in Alabama. In this ad, the passing drivers are asked to imagine themselves within the living room depicted on the billboard.

Walker Evans, *Billboard, Birmingham, Alabama,* 1936

In a consumer society, there is a constant demand for new products and the need to constantly repackage and sell old products with new slogans and ad campaigns. In *Marxist theory*, this is understood as the way that capitalism is dependent upon the overproduction of goods and the need for workers to be consumers and spend large sums on mass-produced goods. A capitalist society produces more goods than are necessary for it to function, hence the need to consume goods is an important part of its *ideology*. In a consumer society a large segment of the population must have discretionary income and leisure time, which means that they must be able to afford goods that are not absolutely necessary to daily life but which they may want for an array of reasons, such as style or status. Consumer societies are thus integral to aspects of *modernity*, such as industrialization and urbanism, that we discussed in Chapter 4. The mass production and marketing of goods depended until the late twentieth century on large sectors of the population living in concentrated areas, so that the distribution, purchase, and advertising of goods had an available audience. This has changed with the rise of e-commerce and telemarketing in the 1990s, phenomena that have made telephone and on-line virtual shopping a real possibility, eliminating the necessity for the overhead costs of a physical retail space (a store, a mall) for the sale of goods to consumers. E-commerce is a new phenomenon, but it also recalls the nineteenth and early twentieth-century practice wherein those people living in rural areas relied on mail-order catalogs to purchase many of their goods.

In the emergence of the consumer society of the late nineteenth century, the workplace, the home, and commerce became increasingly separated, which in turn had a significant effect on the structure of the family and gender relations. As people moved increasingly into urban centers and away from agrarian lifestyles in which all members of the family play crucial roles in production, the distance between the public sphere of work and commerce and the private sphere of the home increased. Women were relegated to the domestic sphere while men were delegated to the public sphere. In this context, women and men were increasingly perceived by manufacturers and advertisers as two distinct kinds of consumers, who could be targeted through different kinds of strategies linked to different sets of goods.

Fundamental changes in the experience of community in the rise of the consumer society came through an increased complexity and diversity of the urban population, increased immigration, and a loosening of the hold of small and stable communities and families on social values. The new experience of urban life and modernity of the late nineteenth and early twentieth centuries has often been characterized as the sensation of standing in a crowd, being surrounded on a daily basis by strangers who one will never know, and the both giddy and overwhelming feeling of the city as a kind of organism. In this modern context we can see another important aspect of consumer societies: the source of concepts of the self and identity are constituted in a larger realm than the family. In the modern city, many people were subject for the first time to many influences beyond those of their families. It has been argued that people derived their sense of their place in the world and their self-image at least in part through their purchase and use of commodities which seemed to give meaning to their lives in the absence of the meaning derived from closer-knit community. Indeed, some theorists have gone so far as to say that advertising replaced what had previously been the social fabric of communities, becoming, in effect, a central source of cultural values. This is why, perhaps, people jokingly refer to shopping as a form of "retail therapy."

One aspect of late nineteenth- and early twentieth-century modern consumer society was the rise of the department store as a site of commerce. The department store announced itself as a site of both commerce and leisure, and was constructed in order to display the largest possible number of goods

to a consumer who was imagined as strolling through its aisles. The big windows of department stories were set up as forms of spectacle, that extended the store onto the street. The photograph, of a Parisian shop window in 1925, taken by French photographer Eugène Atget who photographed the streets of Paris in the early twentieth century, shows the conventions of merchandise display during this period. These conventions of using mannequins to display clothing, and creating scenarios for the window shopper, have changed little over time. Stores were designed with an emphasis on the visual display of goods, to make movement through them exciting and to create the idea of shopping as a leisure activity. Window shopping or browsing thus gained a kind of currency (interestingly, an activity that is recalled in the activity of browsing on the World Wide Web). Department stores were important to several new forms of commerce, including buying on credit, the idea that it is patriotic to both consume and acquire debt, and the escalation of consumption to promote rapid turnover of goods. They were also central to the general encouragement by manufacturers of planned obsolescence, the deliberate shoddy manufacture of goods in order to necessitate their replacement with new ones every few years.

Eugène Atget, *Magasin, avenue des Gobelins (Store Window, avenue des Gobelins)*, 1925

Window shopping is, in many ways, a modern activity, one that is integral to the modern city that is meant for pedestrians, strolling, and crowds. As film scholar Anne Friedberg has written, the visual culture of window shopping in the late nineteenth and early twentieth century was related to the more mobile vision of modernity.[2] Evidence of this can be seen in the nineteenth-century interest in panoramas, large 360-degree paintings that the spectator viewed while turning in the center, dioramas, or theatrical compositions of objects and images moved before immobile viewers, and the emergence of photography in the early nineteenth century and motion picture film at its end. French poet Charles Baudelaire wrote about nineteenth-century urban land-scapes as the visual terrain for the *flâneur*, a man who strolled the streets as an observer, never quite engaging with his surroundings but taking an inter-est in them. Walter Benjamin, whose work we discussed in Chapter 4, also wrote about the *flâneur* and the complex shopping arcades of nineteenth-century Paris, elaborate enclosed spaces that were the predecessors of today's shopping malls. Friedberg introduces the concept of the *flâneuse*. In the nineteenth century, *flâneurs* were mostly men, because respectable women were not allowed to stroll alone in the modern streets. As window shopping became an important activity, in particular with the rise of the department store, this allowed for the *flâneuse*, as a window shopper, to emerge in more contemporary contexts. Friedberg notes that theories of film spectatorship, which we discussed in Chapter 3, can also help us to under-stand the broader function of spatial, mobile practices of looking in the con-sumer culture of the city. There are many kinds of gazes at play in the visual culture of modernity, from cinematic predecessors such as the panorama to the cinematic gaze, to the gazes at work in the urban environment of pedes-trians, commerce, and window display. In modern society, new ways of con-suming were linked to new ways of looking. These were not limited to shopping but extended into all areas of urban life.

One of the fundamental changes in turn-of-the-century Euro-American societies that was integral to the rise of consumer culture was the emergence of what historian T. J. Jackson Lears calls the "therapeutic ethos." These societies shifted over a period of time from valorizing a Protestant work ethic, civic responsibility, and self-denial to legitimating ideas of leisure, spending, and individual fulfillment. An older concern for saving gave way to a new emphasis on spending and on imagining that the path to betterment was through the increased acquisition of goods. In this changing culture, the feeling that life was often troubling and overwhelming prevailed. As a result, the idea that everyone was potentially inadequate and in need of improvement took hold. This resulted in a rise of commodities that were intended to aid in self-improvement. This therapeutic discourse is an essential element of consumer culture. Modern advertisements were able increasingly to speak to problems of anxiety and identity crisis, and to offer harmony, vitality, and the prospect of self-realization, all recently shared values in the emerging modern culture. Today, consumption continues to be thought of as both a form of leisure and pleasure and as a form of therapy. It is commonly understood that commodities fulfill emotional needs. The paradox is that those needs are never truly fulfilled as the forces of the market lure us into wanting different and more commodities—the newest, the latest, and the best. This is a fundamental aspect of contemporary consumer culture— that it gives us pleasure and reassurance while tapping into our anxieties and insecurities.

In contemporary consumer cultures, modern industrial capitalism has evolved into what is now referred to as late, or postindustrial, capitalism. Corporations are multinational, goods move globally, and consumers purchase goods that have been manufactured across the world. This means that the physical and social distances between the production and the distribution and consumption of most goods have grown even larger. For instance, much of the clothing that is sold in North America and Europe is manufactured by underpaid workers in Taiwan, Indonesia, and India. Computers are constructed from parts made in Taiwan, Mexico, and Silicon Valley, all very different and distant places. Late capitalism is also based more on the exchange of new forms of commodities such as services and information rather than material goods. In this contemporary context, commerce is increasingly global and advertising is also produced for global markets. However, there are many issues of cultural difference that limit the capacity of ads to be understood in different cultures. As we noted in Chapter 1, US magazines rejected a famous ad from the global Italian-based Benetton company of a black woman nursing a white infant because of the cultural connotations of the ad. In the US context, the ad signified the enslavement of black women as wet nurses in slavery. The specificity of this response suggests that the global marketplace of late capitalism has not necessarily produced a global advertising audience. The targeting of advertisements geared to specific demographics organized according to region, age, culture, gender, and class is very much the case, even for global brands like Coca-Cola. In Chapter 9, we will examine more closely the spread and limitations of global visual culture.

Commodity culture and commodity fetishism

A consumer culture is a commodity culture—that is, a culture in which commodities are central to cultural meaning. Commodities are things that are bought and sold in a social system of exchange. The concept of commodity culture is intricately allied with the idea that we construct our identities, at least in part, through the consumer products that inhabit our lives. This is what media scholar Stuart Ewen has termed the *commodity self*, the idea that our selves, indeed our *subjectivities*, are mediated and constructed in part through our consumption and use of commodities. Clothing, music, cosmetic products, and cars, among other things, are commodities which people use to present their identities to those around them. Advertising encourages consumers to think of commodities as central means through which to convey their personalities. For instance, for many years Dewar's Scotch Whisky had a well-known campaign, the "Dewar's Profile," in which various well-accomplished individuals are profiled according to their profession, interests, hobbies, favorite book, and, of course, their favorite drink. The campaign suggests that if one wants to acquire the qualities of creativity and achievement of these individuals, one should drink Dewar's. It speaks to the concept of a commodity self, making the assertion that this commodity will become a part of one's self-identity and how one projects that self into the world.

This raises the very important question of what precisely it is that ads sell. It is commonly believed that the function of advertisements is to sell products; the consumer sees an ad and is persuaded by it to purchase the product. However, many cultural theorists have argued that advertising is not nearly as successful in this intent as its critics and proponents would like us to believe, and that advertising functions in a much more indirect way to sell lifestyle and identification with brand names and corporate logos. Communication theorist Michael Schudson has argued that the ability of advertising to sell specific products is much overrated.[3] Advertisers are more often than not guessing rather than accurately assessing consumer desires and attitudes. In addition, Schudson states that advertising is only one part of a broader commercial environment, that includes direct marketing, different product placement and display, and complex distribution networks. Advertising is simply the most obvious element of these aspects of marketing.

Advertisers have viewed advertising as an art form since the 1960s, when the field underwent a creative revolution. Ads became more entertaining and intriguing as the rigid hard-sell conventions of the 1950s were relaxed. As cultural theorist Thomas Frank has argued, advertising began in the 1960s to appropriate the language of the counterculture, and to aim to attach to products the signification of being hip. This trend has only increased since that time, and today many products are sold through associations with youth culture and the idea of being cool.

It remains the case, however, that advertising is central to the way in which commodities are given particular qualities and values that they do not have innately. Analyses of commodities and how they function come to us primarily through Marxist theory. Marxist theory is both a general analysis of the role of economics in human history and an analysis of the ways that capitalism functions. A Marxist critique of capitalism understands advertising to be a means to create demand for products, which makes people buy more than they really need. Marxist theory has analyzed in particular the relationship between *exchange value* and *use value* in capitalism. Exchange value refers to what a particular product costs in a given system of exchange. Use value refers to its use within that society. Marxist theory critiques the emphasis in capitalism on exchange over use value, in which things are valued not for what they really do but for what they're worth in abstract, monetary terms.

We will use perfume ads to illustrate exchange value and use value. One might argue that certain food products have a relatively equal exchange and use value. Rice, for instance, is a useful food staple which is relatively affordable, hence its use value is equal to, if not greater than, its exchange value, which is relatively cheap. Expensive perfume, however, is quite another story. A perfume that costs $40 per ounce has a very high exchange value, yet does it have use value? Can a society function well without perfume? Certainly it cannot without food. One could argue, for instance, that a relatively inexpensive Honda car has the same use value as a very expensive Mercedes-Benz, although their exchange value is dramatically different. Yet, that exchange value carries with it a broad array of social meanings that each owner acquires with these cars. The idea of use value is tricky, since the concepts of what is and is not useful are highly ideological—one could argue endlessly about whether or not certain so-called leisure goods are "useful." In an elite culture, ownership of a Mercedes-Benz might buy one a certain social status and respect that another car would not. But it is difficult to assess the use value of qualities like pleasure and status.

One of the most important concepts in the Marxist analysis of advertising is the idea of *commodity fetishism*. This refers to the process by which mass-produced goods are emptied of the meaning of their production (the context in which they were produced and the labor that created them) and then filled with new meanings in ways that both mystify the product and turn it into a fetish object. For instance, a designer shirt does not contain within it the meaning of the context in which it is produced. The consumer is given no information about who sewed it, the factory where the material was produced, or the culture in which it was made. Rather, the product is affixed with logos and linked to advertising images that imbue it with cultural meanings quite apart from those of its specific production conditions and context. Products are most often marketed far from where they were produced. Handmade objects, such as objects made by particular craftspeople, more often retain *signifiers* of their production. Commodity fetishism can be seen as an inevitable outcome of mass production and distribution of goods to many different consumers. It demands, however, that labor and working conditions are made invisible to the consumer. This erasure of the labor process devalues the experience of work, and makes it harder for workers to take pride in what they have produced. Commodity fetishism can thus be seen as a system of mystification that empties objects of the meaning of their production and then fills them with commodity status.

It is often easy to understand commodity fetishism by looking at moments when it fails. For instance, in the early 1990s Nike shoes for women were promoted as signifiers of self-empowerment, athletic women, feminism, and hip social politics. Public outcry later in the decade about the dire working conditions in Nike's factories led to an ironic revelation. These symbols of female empowerment were produced by low-paid women who labored under terrible conditions in Indonesian factories. As these conditions were exposed, the process of commodity fetishism was momentarily ruptured. The shoes could no longer be stripped of the meaning of their conditions of production and "filled" with the signifiers of feminism. The company had to respond to this criticism and change some of its practices.

As the primary means of commodity fetishism, advertising functions to attach certain meanings to products that they would not necessarily have in themselves. In the process, it often awards them complex and emotional attributes; in other words, it can give them an *aura*, to use a term that we discussed in Chapter 4. Commodity fetishism operates through *reification*, a process by which abstract ideas are assumed to be real and concrete. In advertising this means that objects (commodities) acquire human qualities (are perceived as sexy, romantic, or cool, for instance), and human relations can become increasingly objectified and devoid of emotional meaning. This is most obvious in products that are so clearly initially devoid of meaning, such as perfume. We could ask, what is perfume but scented water? Yet, various perfumes are awarded heightened meanings that consumers then supposedly acquire when wearing them. A perfume like Chanel No. 5 carries *connotations* of wealth, class status, and tradition, whereas Calvin Klein's CK signifies not only hipness but androgynous sexual status. Ads for these products attach these specific qualities to them which consumers are then encouraged to feel that they can subsequently acquire through purchasing and using the product.

Condemnations of consumer society and commodity culture have proliferated throughout the twentieth century. The *Frankfurt School* theorists, who were discussed in Chapter 5, saw the role of commodities as a kind of death knell for meaningful social interaction. For these theorists, commodities were "hollowed out" objects which propagated a loss of identity and eroded our sense of history. For them, to think, for instance, that a specific consumer item might make one's life meaningful was to engage in a corruption of the really valuable aspects of existence. In the 1960s, the Frankfurt School ideas re-emerged in a political and social context in which commercialism was condemned as one of the symptoms of a society gone wrong. During this time, the newly emergent counterculture eschewed notions of material success and commodity culture. Yet, at the same time, in the art world, *Pop Art* in the late 1950s and 1960s engaged with mass culture in a way that did not condemn it. As such, Pop was an attack on distinctions between *high* and *low culture*. Pop art took what was considered to be low culture, such as television, the mass media, and popular culture like comic books, and declared it to be as socially significant as high art, in the realm of fine art, classical music, and other artistic products that are elitist and upper-class by association.

By incorporating television images, advertisements, and commercial products into their work, the artists who produced Pop Art were responding in a very different manner from the Frankfurt School to the pervasiveness of

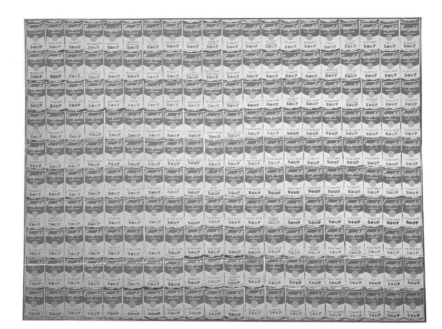

Andy Warhol, *Two Hundred Campbell's Soup Cans*, 1962

Roy Lichtenstein, *Drowning Girl*, 1963

commodity culture. They were doing so not by condemning mass culture but by using it, demonstrating their love of and pleasure in popular culture. Andy Warhol painted and printed images of Campbell's soup cans to question the boundaries between art and product design, and celebrate the aesthetic repetition of mass culture. Warhol's painting has a flattening effect which seems to comment on the banality of popular culture and mass production. The multiplicity of the soup cans refers to the inundation and overproduction of goods in a commodity culture, where repetition prevails. Yet at the same time it is an affectionate homage to package design and consumer culture. Other artists turned to "low culture" forms like comic strips and television. In search of a means to paint an "ugly" picture, Roy Lichtenstein made comic strip paintings, which commented not only on the flat surface of the comic form but also the stories that they told. Lichtenstein's highly formal works were smooth and pristine, in contrast to the painterly brushstroke style of *Abstract Expressionist* painting. In their detail of the dotted surface of the screen-printed comics, these works are a tribute to this commercial form. Lichtenstein's work is a kind of large, oversized comic, blowing up the grain of the comic image so that the viewer can see its dot textures. In this image of a "drowning girl," the artist ambiguously plays off of the conventions and clichés of the self-sacrificing romantic heroine.

Addressing the consumer

Like other images, advertising images *interpellate* their viewers in particular ways, hailing them as ideological subjects. As explained in Chapter 2, interpellation is the process by which we come to recognize ourselves in the *subject position* offered in a particular representation or product. In her discussion of advertising, cultural critic Judith Williamson calls this *appellation*. Ads speak to us through particular modes of address, and ask us to see ourselves within them. Often this is done with written text that specifically speaks to the viewer as "you." In recontextualizing an historical image, a photograph of President Kennedy aboard Air Force One, the ad on the next page works to establish an image of the communication technologies of the past, present, and future. At the same time, its speaks to the viewers as those who believe they should be plugged in constantly, who embrace the world of new technology. Many ads speak in emphatic tones to viewers/consumers, as if the voice of the ad knows what "you" need and want.

It is also the case that many contemporary advertisements speak to consumers in voices that depart from the overbearing narrations of ads in the past that explicitly told consumers what to do. In an attempt to humanize both their address to consumers and their product, some ads speak to consumers in folksy tones, as if the ad and the consumer were having a nice chat. In this Saturn ad, for instance, the story of the correspondence between a school teacher and the Saturn workers who built her car gives the product a very different set of meanings than a car ad that emphasizes speed or convenience. Indeed, the Saturn campaign is notable for its emphasis on the factory workers who produce the cars. In this ad, emotional connection with a commodity, and the folksy relationship between the producer and the consumer, are used to give the car the meaning of an individualized product. It could be said, then, that this ad works against commodity fetishism in that it talks about the workers who produce the car. Yet, at the same time this is an idealized, mythic view of the relationship between the worker and the consumer.

Interestingly, the "you" that advertising addresses, either specifically through text or by constructing viewer positions through interpellation, is

always spoken to or implied to be an individual. The implication is that the product being sold will make the consumer unique, special, and highly individual. In other words, ads perform the very contradictory work of convincing many different consumers that a mass-produced product will make them unique and different from others. Some perfume ads actually make the claim that the scent will smell different on everyone. In Frankfurt School theory, this concept is known as *pseudoindividuality*, a false idea of individuality. Pseudoindividuality is the means by which consumer culture sells a form of homogenization to consumers while proclaiming that it will produce individuality. Indeed, a commodity is only successful when it is purchased by many people.

Hence, it can be said that advertising asks us not to consume commodities but to consume *signs* in the *semiotic* meaning of the term that we discussed in Chapter 1. This means that ads set up particular relationships between *signified* (the product) and *signifier* (its meaning) to create signs in order to sell products as well as the cultural meanings and connotations we attach to those products. When we consume commodities, we thus consume them as

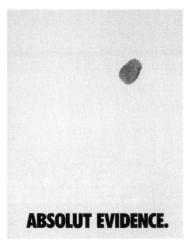

commodity signs—we aim to acquire, through purchasing a product, the meaning with which it is encoded.

Advertising uses particular codes and conventions to convey messages quickly and succinctly to viewers. While some ads intend to shock us or capture our attention through their difference, most advertising provides information through the short-hand language of visual and textual conventions. Hence, most ads speak a mixture of familiarity and newness. One of advertisers' primary strategies is to turn a product into a recognizable brand. A brand is a product name that we know about whether or not we own or ever intend to purchase the product. For instance, Absolut vodka is advertised by a campaign that uses the shape of its bottle as an ongoing motif, often in very playful ways. In these ads, the Absolut bottle refers to nineteenth-century author Mary Shelley, who wrote the novel *Frankenstein*, Las Vegas as a site of conventions (where people have to wear name tags), and to the use of fingerprints as evidence (of whoever stole the vodka bottle). Absolut is established as a brand name because its advertising campaign is well-known, highly visible, and consistent enough over a long period of time as to be instantly recognizable. Even people who have never purchased or tasted Absolut vodka know its brand name. In addition, Absolut has turned its ad campaign into a work of art, not only commissioning famous artists (Andy Warhol, Kenny Scharf, Keith Haring, and Ed Ruscha, among others) to do ads, but also publishing a book specifically about the campaign. In order for a product to be turned into a brand an advertisement must add value to it. The product must acquire particular attributes, indicate a kind of lifestyle, and produce an image of its potential consumer. In the case of Absolut, it gains the added value of being sophisticated and arty through its well-known campaign.

This strategy of repeating a motif in an advertising campaign can be used not only to establish familiarity with a product for viewers, but also to keep viewers' attention by varying the elements within a motif. For instance, the "Got Milk?" campaign, which advertises not a brand but the general product milk, uses images of celebrities, such as the rock band Kiss, all wearing a white "milk mustache" to promote the consumption of milk. The campaign thus aims to give milk the glamour attributes of these famous people, to convince adults that milk is not simply a drink for children, and to attach a kind of hipness to what is thought of as a stodgy product. It affirms this by repeating this form and slogan from ad to ad.

It is a convention in advertising that ads speak in important terms about products that may in the long run have very little importance. Ads operate with a *presumption of relevance* that allows them to make inflated statements about the necessity of their products—the idea, for instance, that the status of one's hair is a key factor in changing one's life or that wearing a new perfume will miraculously produce a handsome man at one's side. In the real world, these statements would be absurd, but in the world of advertising they make perfect sense. In the world of the ad, these claims have relevance. This is in

part because ads create and speak in a world of fantasy. The world presented by an advertisement is fictional. We know, for instance, that the image of a car being driven through a complex set of obstacles in the desert, a common strategy of sports car advertising, is one of artifice.

The presumption of relevance of contemporary advertising also extends to the various elements that are connected in an ad. Ads create a relationship of *equivalence* between elements within the frame and between the product and its signifier. In this perfume perfume ad, an equivalence is created between a woman and an animal. Borrowing on notions of the exotic, the ad attributes the qualities of mystery and sensuality associated with cats to the figure of the woman. The woman gazes directly at the viewer/consumer in a pose that is meant to be both enticing and predatory.

Equivalence can also mean that an advertisement establishes direct connections for the viewer/consumer between the product and a figure of some kind. For instance, a contemporary Gap campaign uses vintage photographs of artistic figures such as Pablo Picasso, Ernest Hemingway, Jack Kerouac, Sammy Davis Jr., Gene Kelly, and Marilyn Monroe wearing khaki pants. Each ad contains the slogan, "Picasso wore khakis" or "Sammy wore khakis," which forms the first part of a sentence that implies ". . . and so should you." The very average khakis thus become signifiers of creativity, uniqueness, and potential fame. The campaign is clearly geared toward middle-aged

ANIMALE
Pure Instinct

Available Exclusively at I.MAGNIN. 1-800-227-1125

consumers in its use of artistic figures of the past. It works to make khaki pants simultaneously signify both tradition and creative talent.

In the same way that ads construct relationships of equivalence between various objects, figures, and qualities, they also indicate relationships of difference and opposition from other products. Companies *differentiate* products from their competition. While this often happens by implication, it has become increasingly common since the 1970s for advertisements to name their competition and to position themselves in opposition to it. Hence, 7-Up produced a successful campaign by calling itself the "Uncola" and Avis car rentals became a well-known brand by selling themselves as the No. 2 competitor behind Hertz, with the now legendary slogan "We Try Harder." Coke and Pepsi have spent decades differentiating their products from each other either directly or indirectly in their campaigns. Why is differentiation an important strategy of ads? Precisely because many products actually are quite similar. Certainly, one could argue that Coca-Cola and Pepsi have spent millions differentiating their products in ads precisely because there is in actuality little difference between their kinds of cola. The difference between them is ultimately taste—not flavor, but the class and cultural aesthetics associated with the respective colas in their ad campaigns.

Images and text

Through these processes of equivalence, differentiation, and signification, ads are doing the work of creating commodity signs. It is important to the meaning of most advertisements that they use photographs to construct their messages. In that photographs always carry with them the connotation of *photographic truth* yet are also a primary source of fantasy, they provide important dual meanings in many advertisements. As we discussed in Chapter 1, photographs derive their power from evoking both evidence of the real and a magical quality that can prompt emotion in the viewer. They are, in Charles Peirce's terms, *indexical*, and thus carry the meaning of offering a trace of the real. It is through complex compositions of photographs, text, and graphics that ads speak to consumers.

Text can often have a powerful effect in establishing the meaning of an advertisement, and changing the meaning of the photograph or image presented. This is particularly effective in ads that intend to shock or in public service advertisements that aim to jar the viewer/consumer. Part of a now famous

Lemon.

This Volkswagen missed the boat.
The chrome strip on the glove compartment is blemished and must be replaced. Chances are you wouldn't have noticed it; Inspector Kurt Kroner did.

There are 3,389 men at our Wolfsburg factory with only one job: to inspect Volkswagens at each stage of production. (3000 Volkswagens are produced daily; there are more inspectors than cars.)

Every shock absorber is tested (spot checking won't do), every windshield is scanned. VWs have been rejected for surface scratches barely visible to the eye.

Final inspection is really something! VW inspectors run each car off the line onto the Funktionsprüfstand (car test stand), tote up 189 check points, gun ahead to the automatic brake stand, and say "no" to one VW out of fifty.

This preoccupation with detail means the VW lasts longer and requires less maintenance, by and large, than other cars. (It also means a used VW depreciates less than any other car.)

We pluck the lemons; you get the plums.

Volkswagen campaign from the 1960s, this ad captures the viewer's attention through its use of text. The ad was shocking in its time precisely because it did what an ad was not supposed to do—it insulted the product being sold. The smaller ad copy explains that this particular car was a lemon and hence would never be sold. The use of text here is thus crucial in creating a contradiction that the viewer is invited to figure out by reading further. The Volkswagen campaign is well known in advertising history because it broke the rules of advertising conventions in its time. It was spare, humorous, and irreverent in a way that spoke to consumers in a new form of address, as informed consumers.

Many public service ads use text to enhance dramatic impact. These ads deploy the conventions of advertising, and are usually placed in the commercial venues of advertising such as magazines and billboards and public transportation, in order to create meaning through juxtaposition with other ads. Thus, an image that could advertise fur becomes, with the text, an anti-fur poster. Or, an image that first signifies cookware, which then evokes violence with the bold type, turns out, when the interested viewer reads further, to be about eating habits. The effect of these anti-ads is to play off the conventions of advertising's mix of text and image, in which advertising copy usually guides

It takes up to 40 dumb animals to make a fur coat.

But only one to wear it.

LYNX

Fighting the fur trade

If you don't want animals gassed, electrocuted, trapped or strangled, don't buy a fur coat. P O Box 509 Dunmow, Essex Tel: 0371 2016

While few people have ever been hit over the head with a frying pan, many have been hit in the heart. The prostate gland. And the colon.

Because fried foods, as part of a high-fat diet may increase the risk of heart disease as well as certain cancers —

including breast cancer. For a free booklet on how to help reduce your risk through low-fat eating, call 1-800-EAT-LEAN.

After all, the purpose of food is to sustain life, not take it away.

1-800-EAT-LEAN

EVERY YEAR THOUSANDS OF PEOPLE ARE KILLED WITH A FRYING PAN.

A public service message from The Henry J. Kaiser Family Foundation.

the viewer on how to read the meaning of the image. In these ads, it is precisely the way that text forces the reader to look again and re-read the image with new meaning that creates the impact of the ad.

These kind of juxtapositions work in part through the power that is awarded to photographs not only in advertising but in our culture in general. In Peirce's terms, which we discussed in Chapter 4, ads combine *iconic signs* in the form of drawings or graphs, *indexical signs*, such as photographs, and *symbolic signs* in the form of text. Contemporary advertising, with its complex combinations of words, photographs, drawing, sound, and television images deploys all three kinds of signs to construct selling messages. The relationship of text and photographs in advertisements is the combination of symbolic and indexical signs. This is also important in ads that emphasize the indexical quality of photographs by contrasting them with iconic images. As an indexical sign, a photograph carries the cultural weight of depicting the real and relaying a sense of authenticity.

Envy, desire, and glamour

All advertisements speak the language of transformation. They tell consumers that their products will change their lives

for the better if they buy a particular product. As we noted earlier, this relates to the therapeutic ideology that ads participate in when they promise to improve our lives. In speaking to viewers/consumers about changing themselves, they are always interpellating consumers as in some way dissatisfied—with their lifestyles, appearances, jobs, relationships, etc. Many ads imply that their product can alleviate this state of dissatisfaction. They often do this by presenting figures of glamour that consumers can envy and wish to emulate, people who are presented as already transformed, and bodies that appear perfect and yet somehow attainable. John Berger has written, "The state of being envied is what constitutes glamour."[1] The idea of glamour is central to advertising, both in the use of well-known celebrities to sell products and in the depiction of models who appear to be happy, without flaws, and satisfied.

The world created by advertisements can also appear to be precious, artistic, and valuable. The attachment of the value of art, in particular fine art, to a product gives it a connotation of prestige, tradition, and authenticity. Many contemporary advertisements make reference to art works of the past in order to give their products the connotation of wealth, upscale leisure, and cultural value attributed to works of art. Some ads reference art by presenting artistic poses and styles, such as the "art becomes you" ad that we discussed in Chapter 4. Other ads speak to consumers who are familiar with the

codes of classical painting, by both referencing art and playing off those conventions to the knowing consumer. In still other ads, direct references to specific paintings and painting styles distinguish a product. In placing the jeans in a painting in the style of *Impressionist* painter Pierre-Auguste Renoir, who worked in the late nineteenth and early twentieth centuries, this ad differentiates these jeans from other jeans and awards them the meaning of tradition. Art is used to present a world that is both enviable and nostalgic and to flatter the consumer for his/her *connoisseurship*.

The enviable world of advertising is thus presented to viewers/consumers as a fantasy of what their lives could be, and it entices consumers to believe that this life is attainable through the act of consumption. Ads thus entreat us to construct commodity selves and to work to acquire the attributes attached to certain products through their use. Sometimes this means that ads speak to consumers as if their bodies exist in separate parts. Since the 1970s, ads have increasingly represented women's bodies in fetishized parts—legs, lips, breasts, etc. Detached from the rest of the bodies and the people of whom they are a part, these body parts represent ideals to consumers. Even when they declare that perfection is unattainable, these ads ask consumers to believe that it can be attained through hard work, maintenance, and consumption. The bodies that are represented in these advertisements have been

rendered to perfection through the sophisticated imaging techniques of airbrushing, color enhancement, and digital manipulation. These images retain the power of the photograph as an indexical sign—the idea that they represent real people—while they are actually highly constructed images which bear little or no relationship to the codes of documentary realism. This is, of course, part of the paradox of what these ads sell—an unattainable highly constructed world which is held out as an attainable ideal.

The world of advertising speaks the language of self-management, self-control, and conformity. These are *docile bodies*, to borrow a term from Michel Foucault—bodies that are socially trained, regulated, and managed by cultural norms. Consumers are incited by ads to seek individuality by conforming to particular standards of beauty, to control their body's odors, movements, food intake, desires, and urges. We are addressed by ads as if we can choose our bodies and reshape them into new forms and sizes.

Advertising thus actively speaks to consumers about their identities, and appears to offer solutions to perceived problems of self-image. As such, it projects anxiety upon consumers. Behind the message of self-improvement is, of course, the message that you should be anxious about what you do not have yet and who you should be. The consumer appellated by advertising is thus not only dissatisfied but also worried. Ads that use anxiety to sell products work by suggesting to consumers the ways in which they may be not only inadequate but potentially endangered or weakened without a particular product. Advertising about technology and financial services often deploy this strategy.

This ad places the consumer in the uncomfortable position of confronting a policeman. The direct address of the ad, through both text and image, thus constructs the viewer as a potential suspect, a startling image that is intended to grab our attention through the anxiety it produces.

It is an essential element of advertising that it promises to us an abstract world which we will never experience. When John Berger wrote that advertising is always situated in the future, he was referring to the way in which the present is depicted in advertising as lacking in some way. Here, it is helpful for us to return to the *psychoanalytic theory* of Jacques Lacan. He suggests that desire and lack are central motivating forces in our lives. Our lives are structured by a sense of *lack* from the moment that we recognize that we are separate entities from our mothers. This separation, experienced as a splitting, marks the point from which we recognize ourselves as subjects apart from others. We are always searching to return to some state of wholeness that we believe we once had prior to this moment of recognition. We constantly strive, through relationships and activities like consuming products, to fill that lack. It is our drive to fill our sense of lack that allows advertising to speak to our desires so compellingly. Advertisements often recreate for us fantasies of perfect ego-ideals, facilitating a regression to this childhood phase.

Yet, it is an essential aspect of lack that it is necessarily always unfulfilled. There is never a moment, in psychoanalytic terms, when lack is replaced by satisfaction, precisely because of its origins in various stages of infantile and childhood development that we keep replaying and the fact that lack is primarily nostalgic. Nostalgia is a longing for a prior state, often perceived to be innocent, which will always remain unfulfilled because this state is irretrievable—indeed, it never existed. Advertising is adept at speaking to consumers in nostalgic terms. This can take the form of evoking earlier times, when life seemed less complicated, or it can be a reference to a time period when, for instance, the potential consumer was younger. In today's advertising, this often takes the form of marketing products to consumers of the post–World War II baby boomer generation by reviving the symbols of their youth, such as the signifiers of the 1960s. In the late 1990s, Volkswagen's campaign for the new Beetle, shown on the next page, evoked the nostalgia for the original Beetle and what it represented about lifestyles and attitudes in the 1960s. The spare and "clean" style of the image, with the car situated in a white space, also evokes the earlier Volkswagen ad campaign.

If you were really good in a past life, you come back as something better.

Many ads reach back into the past to attach concepts of memory and history to their products. In creating equivalence between products and symbols of the past, these ads are packaging memory into easily understood signs. Often, these ads aim to evoke not only nostalgia in viewers/consumers, but also a sense of lineage and tradition. Tradition is sold in these ads as something that will authenticate the product and give it the value of reliability, the test of time, and the approval of our forefathers. In this Motorola ad, the cell phone is not being sold through the predictable signifieds of speed, convenience, and competitive pricing. It is being sold as the child of the wireless radio of World War II, a device described as a war "hero" which saved lives. Encoded in the cell phone is thus a sense of tradition as well as heroism, dependability, and life-saving importance.

Belonging and difference

Advertisements sell both concepts of belonging (to a community, nation, family, or special group or class of people) and difference (from others). Sometimes when advertisements ask us to consume commodity signs, they attach to their products concepts of the nation, family, community, and democracy. Hence, the ideological function of many adver-

tisements takes the form of speaking a language of patriotism and nationalism, in order to equate the act of purchasing a product with a practice of citizenship. In other words, ads that use an image of America or Britain or other nations to market products are selling the concept that in order to be a good citizen and to properly participate in the nation, one must be an active consumer. These products are presented as the means by which we can participate in national ideology.

Because the idea of the nuclear family is central to most national ideologies, it often emerges as a focus of advertisements. The concept of "family values" is a central aspect of political debates, and many advertisements depict the family as nuclear, concerned, and, above all, consumerist. In many ads, the family is a site of harmony, warmth, and security, an idealized unit with no problems that cannot be solved by commodities. Indeed, commodities are presented as the means by which the family is held together, affirmed, and strengthened. In these ads, people relate to each on the most intimate levels through commodities, which are shown as facilitating familial emotion and communication. For instance, the well-known AT&T slogan "reach out and touch someone" promotes the telephone (and AT&T service) as a means to create emotional attachment.

Advertising about the nuclear family exemplifies the Marxist critique of reification, the process by which products are awarded human qualities and human relations are mediated through commodities. McDonald's can be successful in selling a fast-food meal as the proper replacement for a home-cooked family meal. In many McDonald's ads, the restaurant is presented as the place where family togetherness is reaffirmed because going to McDonald's is something the family members agree on and which they can share. In therapeutic terms, McDonald's makes up for what the family cannot do (find time to have both a meal and a meaningful experience together at home). McDonald's achieves this message, and the presumption of relevance within it (in order for viewers to not ask the question, why is an evening out at a fast-food restaurant the perfect family meal?), in part because it has established itself as a patriotic symbol through years of advertising.

Ads that sell concepts of the nation and the family as norms speak to viewers as if they are members of these social realms. Membership in an exclusive club is often a selling point that allows consumers to feel that they can aspire to such exclusivity while feeling anxious about whether or not they really do belong there. In this ad, American Express establishes its product as not simply a credit card but a club in which one is a member (and to which famous people—in this ad, basketball player Lisa Leslie—who are unidentified

in the ad, belong). The ad poses its question in a way that can promote anxiety. The concept of membership is underscored by the fact that images of the celebrities are actually embedded within the design of the card itself. In addition, many advertisements establish particular codes for class difference and represent class relations. Ads for high-end, expensive products establish the class to which they belong through understood conventions such as classical music, references to fine art, and other codes of wealth and prestige. These ads interpellate all consumers as potential members of a class regardless of their actual class status.

In the same way that advertising sells the idea of belonging, it also establishes codes of difference in order to distinguish products. Ads often establish norms by demonstrating things that are different from the norm through marking. As we discussed in Chapter 3, the *unmarked* category is the unquestioned norm and the *marked* category is the one seen as different or *other*. For instance, a white model is unmarked, the normative category, precisely because consumers are not meant to register the fact of his/her whiteness, whereas a nonwhite model is marked by race. Traditionally, race has been used in advertising to give a product a kind of "exoticism" and foreignness.

For example, there has been a long tradition of advertisements that use images of the "islands" and unidentified exotic locales to sell things such as cosmetic products and lingerie. These unidentified locales are coded as closer to nature and offering access to the "primitive." These ads situate the tropics as the source of beauty aids precisely because they are represented as more natural, less tainted by modernity, and as the source of innocence and beauty. They work both to erase colonial politics and the reality of life in the Third World (where, in fact, most of the low-paid labor that produces First World products takes place) and to re-code these places as sites of leisure and playlands for tourists. Here again, we can see how commodity fetishism operates as a process of mystification, obscuring the complex reality of colonized places and former colonies in order to attach the meanings of difference to products. Ironically, while these products promise to white consumers the qualities of *otherness*, commodity culture is about the denial of difference, in that it encourages conformist behavior through the act of consumption.

Increasingly, markers of ethnicity and race are used in advertisements to demonstrate social or racial awareness and to give a product an element of cultural sophistication. There are an increasing number of ads that use models of many different ethnicities in an attempt to both unmark race and to attach to their products the meaning of social awareness. The most obvious example of this is the advertising of United Colors of Benetton. Benetton ads are intended to signify racial harmony and ethnic diversity. While they have produced a famous advertising campaign using documentary images, which we will discuss in Chapter 7, in their advertisements that display clothing the company always uses models of many different races posed together. In these advertisements, cultural difference sells.

Hence, Benetton's ads both unmark race and mark it quite consciously. Viewers are meant to register the many races represented by the models and to read this diversity as progressive and hip. This campaign can be said to reduce the concept of racial identity to one simply of skin color as something fashionable, an association that simplifies the complexity of cultural and ethnic identity. In other words, racial difference is an integral part of one's identity and culture, it is not simply a color that one takes on and off. Through its association with the product of Benetton clothing, the idea of racial harmony is reduced to the idea of putting on and taking off different colored clothing.

Benetton is selling a celebration and erasure of difference and a kind of universal humanism. At the same time, the company is promoting multiculturalism as something that one can buy. The concept of multiculturalism in some cases has been tied to commodity culture, as if one might buy one's way into another culture. Many people see themselves as participating in multiculturalism simply by purchasing products from other cultures and eating in "ethnic" restaurants. Consuming otherness is central to commodity culture in the global era.

Bricolage and counter-bricolage

The idea of a commodity self, and consumer feelings of belonging and difference in response to advertisements, demonstrate the ways that consumers negotiate meaning through ad images and commodity culture. As we discussed in Chapter 2, there are a range of strategies that viewers/consumers use when reading images, and in the case of advertisements they can run from responding positively to an ad's message to resisting its claims. As a form of dominant culture, advertising is also subject to *counter-hegemonic* forces. In Chapter 7, we will discuss some of the ways that advertising has responded with *postmodern* strategies to the increased sophistication of viewers/consumers. Here, we would like to note the ways that counter-ads have been constructed and how the commodities sold by advertisements are often used by consumers in unintended ways.

Although the products advertisements sell to us often give us pleasure and satisfaction, they can never entirely achieve the promises of fulfillment that advertisements offer. Yet, all consumers have the potential to reconfigure the meanings of the commodities that they purchase and own. As we noted in Chapter 2, many youth *subcultures* use commodities as central elements of their style—low-slung pants over boxer shorts, jackets worn backwards, Tommy Hilfiger sweat shirts, or big work boots. The redeployment of commodities for new purposes and meaning—the wearing of a safety pin as body decoration, for instance—is a practice called bricolage. *Bricolage* is a mode of adaptation where things are put to uses for which they were not intended and in ways that dislocate them from their normal or expected context. What happens to a cultural object or commodity when it has been dislocated—how do we read it as a *sign*? These subcultural signs reappropriate objects to make new signs, producing new meanings that can then in turn change the meaning of a commodity.

Yet, the dynamic process of cultural practices and power relations is such that the activities of marginal subcultures are often quickly coded as "cool" and identified by mainstream marketers and advertisers as potential new fashions and trends. As we noted earlier, since the 1960s, advertising has borrowed many of the cultural signifiers of hipness in order to attach these meanings to products. This means that many ads do the work of creating commodity signs of youthfulness. The selling of youth is not simply about selling the idea that a product will make one feel or look more youthful, it is about selling the posture of youth to older consumers. Many slogans for ads, such as Pepsi's "Be Young. Drink Pepsi," thus do the work of filling a product with the meaning of youth.

At the same time, contemporary marketers are constantly in search of products, styles, and commodities that are understood to be cool on the street, which will then appeal to a broad range of middle-class consumers who want to acquire products with the signification of cool. Fashion designers and advertisers use a form of *counter-bricolage* to appropriate styles which have reconfigured commodities. They repackage the youth styles that use bricolage to change the meaning of commodities, and resell those ideas to mainstream consumers. For instance, the youth style of wearing boxer shorts visibly above one's pants has produced a fashion trend for designer boxer shorts. Contemporary advertising thus often uses codes of the street, urban hipness, and subculture fashion to repackage products and sell them to consumers as authentic.

Many contemporary advertising campaigns aim to attach abstract concepts not specifically to products, but to corporate logos. In attempting to speak in new ways to consumers, advertisers thus increasingly produce ads that neither look like traditional ads nor address the consumer as traditional ads do. We will discuss strategies of postmodern advertising at more length in Chapter 7. Here, we would like to note the ways that corporations attempt to acquire new voices as strategies of counter-bricolage. For example, Apple Computer's "Think Different" campaign used important figures of the twentieth century such as Mahatma Gandhi, Amelia Earhart, Mohammed Ali, and others, as a means of establishing its corporate logo as original and unique, as globally significant and forward thinking. The fact that a historical figure such as Gandhi led a lifestyle that was antithetical to technology is

unimportant to the commodity sign of the ad. In other cases, even the logo may be difficult to decipher in an anti-ad. First viewers/consumers must search for what the ad is selling. The ad gets the viewer's attention by initially withholding information rather than providing it.

Just as advertisers have taken on the codes of youth culture, many have also used the language of feminism to produce images of control and body management. Feminist concepts of empowerment and strength are translated into the mandate that working out and producing a tight, lean, muscled female body is equivalent to having control over one's life. As a kind of "commodity feminism," according to Robert Goldman, these ads sell concepts of feminism by attaching them to products such as running shoes.

These ads draw on the language of self-control, empowerment, and self-realization that underlies mainstream feminism in order to speak to female consumers who identify with those values. In some ads, this takes the form of celebrating women's liberation through their capacity to be active consumers, in others it means joking about the past of women's oppression, as a means of establishing the present as liberated. In still other ads, this means establishing the values of fashion comfort and practicality as specifically feminist. Many contemporary ads speak to female consumers as though particular

**YOU WERE BORN
A DAUGHTER.
YOU LOOKED UP TO
YOUR MOTHER.
YOU LOOKED UP TO
YOUR FATHER.**

**YOU LOOKED UP AT
EVERYONE.
YOU WANTED TO BE
A PRINCESS.
YOU THOUGHT YOU
WERE A PRINCESS.**

YOU WANTED TO OWN A HORSE.
YOU WANTED TO BE A HORSE.
YOU WANTED YOUR BROTHER TO BE A HORSE.
YOU WANTED TO WEAR PINK.
YOU NEVER WANTED TO WEAR PINK.

Air Pegasus

YOU WANTED TO BE A VETERINARIAN.
YOU WANTED TO BE PRESIDENT.
YOU WANTED TO BE THE PRESIDENT'S VETERINARIAN.
YOU WERE PICKED LAST FOR THE TEAM.
YOU WERE THE BEST ONE ON THE TEAM.
YOU REFUSED TO BE ON THE TEAM.

YOU WANTED TO BE GOOD IN ALGEBRA.
YOU HID DURING ALGEBRA.
YOU WANTED THE BOYS TO NOTICE YOU.
YOU WERE AFRAID THE BOYS WOULD NOTICE YOU.
YOU STARTED TO GET ACNE.
YOU STARTED TO GET BREASTS.
YOU STARTED TO GET ACNE THAT WAS BIGGER
THAN YOUR BREASTS.
YOU WOULDN'T WEAR A BRA.
YOU COULDN'T WAIT TO WEAR A BRA.
YOU COULDN'T FIT INTO A BRA.

Air Elite' Lite

YOU DIDN'T LIKE THE WAY YOU LOOKED.
YOU DIDN'T LIKE THE WAY YOUR PARENTS LOOKED.
YOU DIDN'T WANT TO GROW UP.

Air Healthwalker Plus

YOU HAD YOUR FIRST BEST FRIEND.
YOU HAD YOUR FIRST DATE.
YOU HAD YOUR SECOND BEST FRIEND.
YOU HAD YOUR SECOND FIRST DATE.
YOU SPENT HOURS ON THE TELEPHONE.
YOU GOT KISSED.
YOU GOT TO KISS BACK.
YOU WENT TO THE PROM.

YOU DIDN'T GO TO THE PROM.
YOU WENT TO THE PROM WITH THE WRONG PERSON.
YOU SPENT HOURS ON THE TELEPHONE.
YOU FELL IN LOVE.
YOU FELL IN LOVE.
YOU FELL IN LOVE.
YOU LOST YOUR BEST FRIEND.
YOU LOST YOUR OTHER BEST FRIEND.
YOU REALLY FELL IN LOVE.
YOU BECAME A STEADY GIRLFRIEND.
YOU BECAME A SIGNIFICANT OTHER.

Air Cross Trainer' Low

YOU BECAME SIGNIFICANT TO YOURSELF.

*Sooner or later, you start taking yourself seriously.
You know when you need a break. You know
when you need a rest. You know what to get worked
up about, and what to get rid of.*

*And you know when it's time to take care
of yourself, for yourself. To do something that makes
you stronger, faster, more complete.
Because you know it's never too late to have a life.
And never too late to change one.*

Just do it.

products—in particular athletic wear—are coded as feminist, self-empowering, and individualistic. In this Nike ad, a woman's life journey is enacted like a script, one that creates a kind of ad book as it spans many magazine pages, thus asking the viewer to invest time in reading it. Under the guise of feminism, these ads sell an equally normalizing image of the perfect body—one which is taut, tight, and muscled, a body in control and on which one has to work hard. On the one hand, women viewers/consumers might feel good about an ad that speaks to them in the language of feminism and empowerment; on the other hand, it raises the question: what does it mean when complicated ideas such as feminism or social awareness become something that can be attached to a product and sold? When a brand name can thus connote feminism, advertisers have succeeded in reducing important political principles to the simple act of selling.

The brand

The role of the brand is central to commodity culture. The 1934 film *Imitation of Life*, directed by John Stahl, includes a shot of a factory conveyor belt upon which box after box of pancake mix rolls by imprinted with the image of a black domestic worker. The white businesswoman who is the main protagonist of the film will strike it rich with this recipe, which originated with her maid—the very woman whose face becomes synonymous with the product. Like the infamous Aunt Jemima® pancake syrup so popular in the USA, this national brand indicates the link between stereotypes of identity and the marketing of products. Ironically, the woman who became synonymous with the product and its quality reaped few benefits from her image's function as commodity sign. The "Aunt Jemima" image has been reproduced in many places, including the quilt pictured on the next page, made from Aunt Jemima sacks in the 1940s. This is a cultural artifact that, incidently, preceded Andy Warhol's reproduced commodity images like the soup cans by two decades. This raises the question of who owns images, and what is the relationship between brand names, identity, and ownership?

As we explain in the next chapter, philosopher Jean Baudrillard has suggested that the late nineteenth century saw the emergence of a commodity culture in which the distinction between objects and images eroded. Instead of a "real" world of objects to which advertisements refer, we see the emergence of a culture in which the image itself is what we live through and

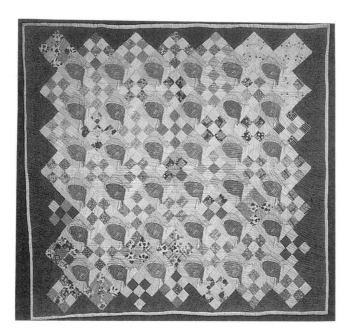

Aunt Jemima sack quilt, Texas, 1940s

consume. Identity is no longer the signifier of a product. Rather, identity is the pure product that we consume, either as information or as image. Advertisements are not the only means through which we experience the images and signs of commodity culture. They are lived through the insignias and logos affixed to the clothes we wear, the products we use, and the food we eat. One manifestation of this function gone awry (from the standpoint of corporations) is the generic use of trademarks. If you were to say that you might "Xerox" pages from this book, you would be using language that takes the global brand name for the generic activity of photocopying. Rosemary Coombe, a professor of law and anthropology, explains that lawyers refer to the way that trademarks become part of public culture as "genericide."[4] The owner of the mark loses rights to the product name as it takes on a meaning for the generic type in the market, rather than for the particular brand of the product. Manufacturers of Coke® and Kleenex® are eager to get us to identify their products with quality, but are not eager to have us kill off their product's difference by using its name for the generic type. To remain profitable, even those brands that go global need to retain their distinguishing features, their identity, in the marketplace. When the mark of a product gains true universality, it is no longer owned by the company and loses its ability to function as a profit-generating commodity.

Coombe discusses the circulation of brand names, trademarks, and logos as means through which identities are constructed in late capitalism not only for goods and corporations, but for people who appropriate those signifiers of products for a style or aspect of themselves or their culture. In the 1990s, the Nike® slash was ubiquitous not only in the USA but in Europe and some Third World cities as well. As a global brand name signifying not just sports but a certain kind of trendy, quality sports style, Nike developed a cachet such that its products—all with the simple curved slash logo—became near-universal signifiers of hip urban youth culture, so much so that there was discussion of its logo being "overexposed." As we discussed in Chapter 2, Doc Martens® was the trademark shoe of various subcultures of the 1980s and mainstream youth culture of the 1990s. First manufactured by a doctor named Maertens as orthopedic shoes in Germany in 1947, they were licensed in Britain as work shoes in 1960. As a global brand, Doc Martens have become synonymous with youth subcultures of many different stripes. The product has clear visual identifying features that "read" in a fairly universal and clear way—thick soles, trademark top-stitching where the upper meets the sole, a discreet fabric tag with the company name imprinted at the back of the ankle. The shoe came to be understood as a signifier of cultural resistance, a message that took on less of an edge with the popularization of the brand as a mainstream signifier of the casually hip. Hipness, in this case, is linked to identification with the working class. Fashion, in embracing industrial chic, turned up its nose at high culture and championed instead the everyday styles of those working-class people who wear such shoes at their blue-collar jobs.

The combining and framing of product and brand-name signifiers to form a personal image is a crucial aspect of postmodern identity, which we will discuss in Chapter 7. But the process of crafting a commodity-based identity is not always performed consciously or intentionally. Rather, signifiers collect on and around us as we acquire, use, and consume the multitude of products that surround us. Coombe describes a teenager she encounters on Queen Street, a hip street in urban Toronto. Her observation and analysis of the teenager emphasizes the youth's engagement in the appropriation of logos as a means of constructing identity. But more importantly, Coombe shows us that this accrual of identity is sometimes offhand and occurs by chance through our encounters with the signifiers of everyday life. In the process of relating this story, Coombe also models the way we as viewers engage in acts of public looking and interpreting that require knowledge about brands and the cultural meanings and discourses that stick to them:

A teenager on a streetcar I board shrugs off a leather jacket adorned with a stitch-on emblem, a cameo of the Colonel (you know the one); this genteel Southern gentleman's face is overlaid with skull and crossbones. Food tampering, I wonder? No, too literal — maybe the treatment of the chickens the company purchases. I ask her if she knows why there is a skull and crossbones over the Kentucky Fried Chicken® logo. Glancing quickly and curiously at the jacket, she says, "it's my boyfriend's, but I think you can buy them." "Do you know who makes them?" I ask. She looks at me as if I had requested the name of her narcotics source and murmurs something noncommittal.[5]

We quote from Coombe's account at length because it illustrates so well how trademarks and logos circulate as images appropriated as signifiers of identity. It also shows us how wearers employ humor, irony, and critique in their bodily display of product names and images usually associated with storefronts and billboards. The KFC logo's alteration indicates a level of critique or commentary the meaning of which, interestingly, the wearer herself is unsure about. Intentionality is not the name of the game. Coombe, as the one who looks at the walking display of commentary, engages in a dialogue with the teenager that results in new and subtle meanings emerging from this lesson in looking practices. We learn that the defamation of the logo is covert, underground—the bearer of the logo cannot or will not reveal her source. The jacket in itself—and its apparent meanings—are in fact appropriated from someone, and a person of another gender (the boyfriend). The teenager is in effect a billboard for the signifiers her boyfriend constructed to wear on his own body. This anecdote is rich in its demonstration of the many levels at which logos and product signifiers works in their life on the streets, on our bodies, and in our chance visual and verbal exchanges in the public spaces of modernity. There is no clear author of the signifiers borne by this teenager, no definitive meaning to be derived from the jacket's function as it circulates from back to back and from context to context. Logos are thus the quintessential free-floating signifiers of late modernity. Freed from ties to specific media and subject to cross-industry flows facilitated by deregulation and corporate vertical integration, logos turn up everywhere we look. Not only are they on billboards and magazine pages, they are in the most intimate and the most mundane places. We find them on the edges of our bedsheets and sewn into the seams of our underwear. They are emblazoned on our mousepads and inscribed along the ridges of pencils. The tie-in is a phenomenon of the twentieth century in which movies and television shows became the source for marketing other consumer goods. Featured merchandise became something more than a product for a secondary set of markets as the commodity sign itself preceded and almost always overtook the "original" source of the movie in revenues and popularity. Children of the 1990s woke between Little Mermaid® sheets wearing Batman® pajamas and rose to eat cereal out of Tarzan® plates while drinking Sesame Street® juice boxes while watching Teletubbies® in Pooh® chairs. Corporate conglomerate "authors," such as Disney/Capital Cities/ABC, have launched a rich intertextual world populated by myriad logos and trademarked characters. Advertising has become not just a way of selling goods but an inescapable mode of everyday communication in the new commodity culture of the twenty-first century.

Anti-ad practices

So far, we have discussed what consumers do with ads and products, but advertisements can be themselves directly the subject of resistant cultural practices. The public service ads that we discussed earlier are exemplary in their use of advertising's dramatic text and image juxtapositions to emphatically present political and public service messages. The form of advertisements themselves has also been the focus of work by artists who are interested in critiquing commodity culture. Artist Hans Haacke has created a whole series of works that use the codes of advertising as forums for political critique. In 1978, he reworked a series of advertisements for Leyland Vehicles, which make Jaguars and Land Rovers, in which he incorporated information about the company's practices in South Africa during Apartheid, and created new slogans for the company, such as "a breed apart" and "nothing can stop us now," in order to comment on its elitism. Haacke has consistently produced works that address the workers who are rendered invisible by the process of commodity fetishism, and the costs to these workers of their labor. In a 1979 image pictured on the next page, Haacke used the famous Breck shampoo campaign of the 1970s that featured the motif of a well-coiffed "Breck girl" to make a political critique of Breck's labor practices. The text refers specifically to the fact that American Cyanamid, Breck's parent company, gave women workers of child-bearing age whose jobs posed reproductive health risks the

Hans Haacke, *The Right to Life,*
1979

"choice" of losing their jobs, transferring, or being sterilized. Haacke's "ad" is thus not only a parody of Breck's campaign, it is a political statement about the treatment of workers and the kinds of oppressive practices that corporations are allowed to use against workers. The image is thus explicitly about the absence of the female Breck worker in the original Breck ad, and her differences from the idealized Breck girl. As such, it offers a biting commentary on the way in which advertising sells a superficial concept of choice.

Advertisements are not only the subject of artistic parody, they can also be the site of on-site political messages. For instance, in Australia in the mid-1970s, a movement took place in which a series of billboards were "re-written" or vandalized by activists wielding spraypaint who were offended by the advertising messages and wanted to change them. Members of the group, and many others, signed their work "BUGA UP," an acronym for Billboard Utilizing Graffitists Against Unhealthy Promotions, which is pronounced "bugger up," meaning to screw up. They achieved, for a period of time, popularity for their work in changing the messages of ads. BUGA UP would change slogans such as this one, from Southern Comfort to Sump Oil, "Marlboro" to "its a bore" and "Eyewitness News. Always First" to "We are witless nits: always are." Others were explicit critiques of advertising's underlying

BUGA UP billboard

Two billboards by the
Billboard Liberation
Front (BLF)

messages, such as a billboard of two hands grasping a beer can that was labeled "masturbation fantasy #133." For the time period in which they were on display, these billboards were anti-ads and political statements about commodity culture, as well as other issues.

Since the late 1970s, a group in San Francisco, called the Billboard Liberation Front, has also been reworking billboards against their intended messages. The group redesigns billboards so that it is not readily obvious that they have been tampered with. For instance, the early cigarette ad, on the previous page, was changed to state "I'm real sick. I only smoke FACTS." The BLF states that the group is not anti-billboard (in fact, several of its members work in the advertising industry); it believes that billboards should be available to all. They state, "to Advertise is to Exist. To Exist is to Advertise. Our ultimate goal is nothing short of a personal and singular Billboard for each citizen."[6] The BLF continues their work at a time when advertisers are increasingly attempting to coopt styles of anti-corporate messages. For example, the group reworked the Apple Computer "Think Different" slogan which is itself intended to get viewers to stop and attempt to identify the person in the image, by rewriting it as "Think Doomed" and "Think Disillusioned." BLF also reworked a Levi's Jeans billboard to include mass murderer Charles Manson as its spokesperson, and rewrote a Kent cigarette ad to read "Kant—The Choice is Heteronomy." The work by groups such as BUGA UP and BLF has been defined by cultural critics as "culture jamming," a term that refers to the CB radio terms for jamming someone's broadcast and which was coined by the band Negativland.[7] Writer C. Carr notes that these guerrilla artists are working out of the tradition of the Situationists of the 1960s, which we mentioned in Chapter 5, and its analysis of the role of spectacle in producing a banal experience of "pseudo-life." The interventions of billboard artists, whether shock or humor is their strategy, thus changes the messages of the marketplace, startling viewers into thinking about those messages differently. It is the case, though, that advertisers are also using these self-mocking techniques to get attention, and thus the distinction between ads and anti-ads is increasingly difficult to make.

These processes testify to the complex ways in which processes of hegemony and counter-hegemony function in a continuous dynamic. Cultures are always in flux and are being constantly reinvented; they are always the site of struggles for meaning. In the culture of late capitalism, when the meanings of coolness and hipness are understood to be central to the exchange of commodities, there is a continuous appropriation of the styles of marginal cultures, which are in turn in a constant state of reinvention. And, in the cultural realms of art, politics, and everyday consumer life, mainstream values are constantly questioned and political struggles are waged. As subversions and resistances at the cultural margins are appropriated into the mainstream, new forms of cultural innovation and refusal are found. Thus, in late capitalism, the boundary between the mainstream and the margins is always in the process of being renegotiated.

Notes

1. John Berger, *Ways of Seeing* (New York and London: Penguin, 1972), 131.
2. Anne Friedberg, *Window Shopping: Cinema and the Postmodern* (Berkeley and London: University of California Press, 1993).
3. Michael Schudson, *Advertising, the Uneasy Persuasion: Its Dubious Impact on American Society* (New York: Basic Books, 1984).
4. Rosemary Coombe, *The Cultural Life of Intellectual Property* (Durham, NC: Duke University Press, 1998).
5. Coombe, *The Cultural Life of Intellectual Property*, 3.
6. Jack Napier and John Thomas, <http://www.billboardliberation.com/home.html>.
7. C. Carr, "Guerrilla Artists Celebrate 20 Years of Culture Jamming: Wheat Pasting against the Machine," *Village Voice* (28 April–4 May 1999) <http://www.villagevoice.com/columns/9917/carr.shtml>.

Further Reading

Theodor Adorno and Max Horkheimer. "The Culture Industry: Enlightenment as Mass Deception." In *The Dialectics of Enlightenment*. Translated by John Cumming. New York: Seabury Press, 1969. Reprinted in *The Cultural Studies Reader*. Edited by Simon During. New York and London: Routledge, 1993, 29–43.

Jean Baudrillard. *Simulations*. Translated by Paul Foss, Paul Patton, and Philip Beitchman. New York: Semiotext(e), 1983.

John Berger. *Ways of Seeing*. New York and London: Penguin Books, 1972.

Susan Bordo. *Unbearable Weight: Feminism, Western Culture, and the Body*. Berkeley and London: University of California Press, 1993.

Rosemary Coombe. *The Cultural Life of Intellectual Property: Authorship, Appropriation, and the Law*. Durham, NC and London: Duke University Press, 1998.

Stuart Ewen. *All Consuming Images: The Politics of Style in Contemporary Culture*. New York: Basic Books, 1988.

Thomas Frank. *The Conquest of Cool: Business Culture, Counterculture, and the Rise of Hip Consumerism*. Chicago and London: University of Chicago Press, 1997.

Anne Friedberg. *Window Shopping: Cinema and the Postmodern*. Berkeley and London: University of California Press, 1993.

Henry Giroux. "Consuming Social Change: The United Colors of Benetton." In *Disturbing Pleasures: Learning Popular Culture*. New York and London: Routledge, 1994, 3–24.

Robert Goldman. *Reading Ads Socially*. New York and London: Routledge, 1992.

——and Stephen Papson. *Sign Wars: The Cluttered Landscape of Advertising*. New York and London: Guilford, 1996.

Hans Haacke. "Where the Consciousness Industry is Concentrated: An Interview with the Artist by Catherine Lord." In *Cultures in Contention*. Edited by Douglas Kahn and Diane Neumaier. Seattle: Real Comet Press, 1985, 204–35.

Dick Hebdige. *Subculture: The Meaning of Style*. New York and London: Routledge, 1979.

Sut Jhally. *The Codes of Advertising: Fetishism and the Political Economy of Meaning in the Consumer Society*. Second Edition. New York and London: Routledge, 1990.

Peter King. "The Art of Billboard Utilizing." In *Cultures in Contention*. Edited by Douglas Kahn and Diane Neumaier. Seattle: Real Comet Press, 1985, 198–203.

T. J. Jackson Lears. "From Salvation to Self-Realization." In *The Culture of Consumption: Critical Essays of American History 1880–1980*. Edited by Richard Wrightman Fox and T. J. Jackson Lears. New York: Pantheon, 1983, 3–38.

William Leiss, Stephen Kline, and Sut Jhally. *Social Communication in Advertising: Persons, Products and Images of Well-Being*. Second Edition. New York and London: Routledge, 1990.

Celia Lury. "Marking Time with Nike: The Illusion of the Durable." *Public Culture*, 11 (3) (Winter 1999), 499–526.

Michael Schudson. *Advertising, the Uneasy Persuasion: Its Dubious Impact on American Society*. New York: Basic Books, 1984.

Ellen Seiter. "Semiotics and Television." In *Channels of Discourse: Television and Contemporary Criticism*. Edited by Robert C. Allen. Chapel Hill, NC and London: University of North Carolina Press, 1987: 17–41.

Kaja Silverman. *The Subject of Semiotics*. New York and Oxford: Oxford University Press, 1983.

Judith Williamson. *Decoding Advertisements: Ideology and Meaning in Advertising*. London: Marion Boyars, 1978.

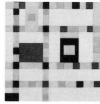

Postmodernism and Popular Culture 7

French philosopher Jean Baudrillard has described the late twentieth century as a period during which images became more real than the real. We have passed from an era in which *reproduction* and *representation* were the most crucial aspects of how images work. Regarding contemporary images, he writes, "if they fascinate us so much it is not because they are sites of the production of meaning and representation—this would not be new—it is on the contrary because they are sites of disappearance of meaning and representation, sites in which we are caught quite apart from any judgement of reality."[1] For Baudrillard, one of the main theorists of the role of the image in the late twentieth century, *simulation* is the new image paradigm that replaces representation. We live in a culture dominated by the dull flickering screens of our computers and television sets, a culture in which America has become the paradigm for global looking practices ruled by the simulacra of virtual media images. Unlike representations, which make reference to a real, simulacra stand on their own without requiring recourse to real objects or worlds elsewhere. Within Baudrillard's terms, the *hyperreal* overtakes the real, and simulacra rise, partly through new media forms, as the new forms of *postmodern* existence. Baudrillard is only one theorist of the looking and imaging practices of the late twentieth century that have come to be regarded as postmodern. But his ideas give us an immediate and dramatic sense of the role of the image as it is transformed through the new media forms of the period after the 1960s.

A wide array of styles can be found in the different images that have circulated since the last decades of the twentieth century. These images span from conventional ones that use traditional codes and genres to highly complex ones designed to speak to media-savvy, visually literate viewers who are bored with the usual formulas. Contemporary image styles and products of popular culture thus represent many different approaches and ways of thinking about viewing. The terms "postmodern" and "postmodernism" have been used to describe some of the styles and approaches to making images that have circulated more prominently since the late 1970s. They have also been used to describe the set of *ideologies*, or the ethos of the late twentieth-century world in its particular phase of late *capitalism*, and with its high-powered technologies and media systems. This chapter considers the meaning of these terms, postmodern and postmodernism, with respect to art, popular media, and advertising of the last decades of the twentieth century and on to the twenty-first.

Is postmodernism a period, a style or set of styles, an ethos, a set of sensibilities, or a politics of cultural experience and production in which style and image predominate? Postmodernism, unlike *modernism*, has been such a mass cultural phenomenon that we probably all know something about it. In 1988 MTV launched *Postmodern TV*, a program whose title and context clues us in to the fact that postmodernism is at home with the very popular culture so criticized and disdained by many modernist cultural critics and producers. Postmodernism may not be about style alone, but style is one of the chief characteristics of a postmodern ethos. The term "postmodern" has been used to describe fashions, and was even used to describe those politicians in the 1990s who used the media quite heavily in their campaigns. It can be argued, along the lines suggested by Baudrillard's concept of simulacra, that they used the media to produce something other than simply representations of themselves. They actually produced themselves through myriad media images and texts, generating identities as simulacra—hyperreal identities with no recourse back to a real person, their composite media image being more real than real. Whereas modernist art and theory were distinguished by their elitism toward media and the popular, postmodernism has been at one with the popular from its origins. Although postmodernism is not only style and image, it relies heavily on style and image to produce its worlds. In the period associated with late (post–World War II) modernist thinking and movements, critics spoke from positions they imagined to be outside—specifically, politically or aesthetically above—popular culture in order to criticize that culture, or to reveal the ideological investments hidden beneath the glitzy *surface* of representations and images. Postmodernism dispels the idea that surface does not contain meaning in itself, or that structures lie beneath the mask of surface appearances. The modernist way of thinking about structure did not stop with the emergence of postmodernism; this approach to art, criticism, and theory continues throughout the 1980s and 1990s, overlapping with tendencies associated with the postmodern. One signpost of the difference between a modern and a postmodern critical sensibility is the acknowledgement within the latter that we cannot occupy a position outside of the milieu we analyze; we cannot get beneath the surface to find something more real or more true. As postmodern theorist Santiago Colás puts it, "We may attempt to forget or ignore mass culture, but it will neither forget nor ignore us."[2] Postmodernism complicates the divisions between *high* and *low culture*, elite and mass consciousness, and in doing so makes it impossible to occupy a critical viewpoint on culture from outside or above it.

This attitude is not limited to criticism. It can be found even within advertising. We can identify a postmodern sensibility, for example, in those advertisements that give us a fragmented, cryptic set of images or story line followed by a brief and discrete logo on the screen, or tucked into the corner of the print ad image. No product, no mention of company name is needed for the viewer who is so thoroughly steeped in the world of media and consumption. Indeed, it would be an insult for manufacturers to think they needed the prompting of goods or direct *signifiers* of the company in an address to the consumer who lives its products as a part of his or her identity. Moreover, these advertisements need not sell their viewers on function or quality. They promote their goods as embodiments of style—style we can live by wearing or using these products. One of the aspects of postmodernism we are getting at here, then, is that it entails a reflexive recognition of our lived relation within the world of the simulacra. This is a world lived at the level of consumption, images, media, and the popular.

It is hard to identify a precise origin for postmodernism, though most critics associate it with the period after 1968. Opinions differ as to whether postmodernism is a period, a set of styles, or a broader set of politics and ideologies. Some theorists have used the term "postmodern" to describe the postwar "cultural logic of late capitalism," a phrase famously used by cultural critic Fredric Jameson as the subtitle of his 1991 book on postmodernism.[3] This definition of postmodernism emphasizes the formative role of economic and political conditions including postwar *globalization*, the emergence of new information technologies, and the breakdown of the traditional nation-state in the emergence of postmodern modes of cultural production. Others begin with the cultural objects themselves, identifying postmodernism as a set of styles—indeed, as a creative explosion of style and surface image in reaction to the rigid attention to form and underlying structure in modernism. The latter approach has been criticized for implying that postmodernism is simply a style an artist or producer might choose to embrace or reject, rather than a cultural trend that is integral to changes in culture, the economy, and politics. Postmodernism has often been characterized as a response to the conditions of late modernity linked to late capitalism. But it is widely agreed that there is no precise moment of rupture between the modern and the postmodern. Rather, postmodernism intersects with and permeates late modernity, a period during which modernist approaches continue to be generated. The proliferation of images and image-producing apparatuses like the cinema, video, and digital imaging devices that can be characterized as postmodern have been met by criticism steeped in modernist ways of thinking. At the same time, other writers have actively embraced a "postmodern" approach to cultural criticism. It is important to remember, then, that aspects of postmodernism and modernism have coexisted throughout and since the last decades of the twentieth century. One of the criticisms of some postmodern theory is that it does not take the historical into account. It is our perspective that to understand the terms of "postmodern" and "postmodernism," we first need to consider what we mean by the terms "modern," "modernism," and "modernity," and how postmodernism emerged from and exists alongside these concepts and this context.

Modernism

The term "modern" in its most familiar sense means of present or recent times, contemporary, or in fashion. In relation to art and culture, however, the term takes on a different set of meanings. German scholar Jürgen Habermas explains that the concept of the modern has been used over and over again by societies since as long ago as the late fifth century. In these uses, the term expresses the self-consciousness of an epoch that relates itself to a past in antiquity, in order to view itself as the result of a transition from old to new or to model itself on a classical past. *Renaissance* artists, for example, revived and built upon Greek standards of form and beauty. The idea of being modern on the model of the classical changed, Habermas explains, with the

Enlightenment. As we explained in Chapter 4, the Enlightenment was an eigh-teenth-century cultural movement associated with a rejection of tradition and an embrace of the concept of reason. Enlightenment thinkers and practition-ers emphasized rationality and the idea of moral and social betterment through scientific progress. Science took on a new role in the arts and culture during the period of the Enlightenment, emerging as the model for such con-cepts as rational thought, knowledge, truth, and progress in areas of culture. The Enlightenment, then, was future-oriented rather than basing itself on a relation to the past. In the nineteenth century, there emerged a radicalized version of modernity that freed itself even more from the tendency to look back to specific historical precedents and tradition for models of the new.

Modernity, as we explained in Chapter 4, reached its height in the nine-teenth century and into the early twentieth century, with the increased move-ment of populations from rural communities into cities and the escalation of industrial capitalism. It is characterized by the experience of upheaval and change, yet also of optimism and a belief in a better, more advanced future. The experience of modernity is thus that of increased urbanization, industri-alization, and technological change that results from industrial capitalism with its ideological faith in progress. The modern belief in a linear sense of progress saw technological and social change as imperative and beneficial. Indeed, it can be said that modernity was in many respects quite uncynical about progress and the benefits of technology and commerce. Yet, modernism also involved a concern about increased social *alienation* and a sense of living at the edge of the abyss in the experience of the modern city. A metaphor for modernity often used in literature is the urban experience of being in a crowd of strangers whom one will never know, as opposed to living in a small village. The feeling that life was undergoing a revolutionary change also produced a general cultural anxiety. The breaking down of traditions allowed for people to have a sense of infinite possibilities, yet also generated fears about the loss of the security of those traditions.

Modernism was based on the traditional idea of the human *subject*. The subject is understood in this context as self-knowing, unified, and whole. This idea of a subject fully endowed with consciousness and authenticity, as an independent source of action and meaning, is derived in part from the Western philosophical tradition that began with René Descartes in the seventeenth century. Descartes famously stated, "I think, therefore I am," thus creating the idea that consciousness establishes individual presence and completeness.

The modern city street, New York's Times Square, 1937

This concept of the subject was revised by a broad array of contemporary thinkers during the period of modernity. Freud, for example, wrote in the early twentieth century about the subject as an entity governed by the forces of the *unconscious*, forces held in check by and in tension with consciousness. This is a far cry from the model of the self-knowing, self-willed individual. Marx, through his ideas about class and the effects of economics on individuals in the late nineteenth century, criticized the idea that human beings were self-determining individuals. Instead, he emphasized that they were collectively the products of and in the control of the forces of labor and capital. He saw individuals as part of a collective organized in relation to the forces of the capitalist system of labor. Foucault, who can be described as a modernist thinker whose work influenced postmodern ideas about the subject, saw the subject as an entity produced within and through the *discourses* and institutional practices of the Enlightenment. As we explained in Chapter 2, Foucault's subject is never autonomous, but is always constituted in a relationship of power.

Although much of his work focused on earlier periods in history, Foucault's theories about sexuality in particular reworked Freud's theses about the unconscious and Marx's ideas about collectivity and the forces of labor. Challenges, such as Foucault's, to the idea of the unitary subject ruled by conscious action can be thought of as part of modernism's contribution to the destabilization of the concept of the subject. This destabilization is one of the chief characteristics of postmodern thought. One aspect of Foucault's thinking that gives some insight into the ways modernism challenged ideas about the individual is his reworking of Freud's theory of *repression*. Foucault took Freud's idea that we repress emotions, desires, and anxieties unconsciously in order to keep them in check, and proposed instead that repression does not result in leaving things unsaid or in inaction. Instead, according to Foucault, repression is productive of activities, meanings, and sexualities. Foucault argues that repression produced a particular discourse of sexuality as it was lived in the late nineteenth century and the twentieth century that was about regulating sex rather than repressing it.

We can also talk about the modernist subject in terms of its role in relationship to embodied looking. If the modern subject was the free-floating observer of the new consumer spaces and spectacles of the city, as Anne Friedberg has argued, the postmodern subject of late modernity is epitomized in the shopper at the suburban mall.[4] The modern *flanêur*, which we discussed in Chapter 6, is thus replaced by the postmodern mall shopper. The mall space is covered in mirror surfaces, and constructed in a *pastiche* of architectural facades and styles borrowed from different periods and contexts. An array of consumer worlds is constructed with goods, advertisements, media displays, and this architectural pastiche of references to place and time. The consumer is fragmented and dispersed into myriad *virtual* worlds of consumption, experiencing (some would argue) a level of alienation and fragmentation more extreme than that produced in capitalism's shop-lined city streets.[5]

In art, modernism was characterized by radical styles that questioned traditions of representational painting. The role of art was reconceived in modernism to consider form as a primary focus. The *avant-garde* artists of the early twentieth century took apart the conventions of representational art by creating abstract paintings whose content was the form itself. For Dutch artist Piet Mondrian, for instance, the simple compositions of line and the primary color in a work like *Broadway Boogie Woogie* (1942–43), seen on the next page, demonstrated the essential form of painting and the medium's potential to reflect objectivity and formal order. Mondrian's paintings and drawings consisted of the simplest elements of form—straight lines and primary colors. He used line and abstract shape to create different formal

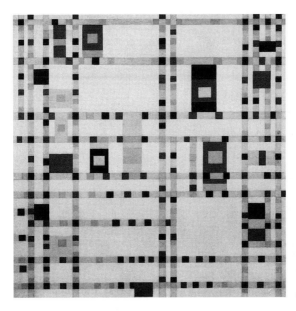

Piet Mondrian, *Broadway Boogie Woogie*, 1942–43

arrangements. His intent was to create a kind of pure form as the content of his work, and to use painting not to represent reality but as a means of depicting basic elements like visual rhythm. The title *Broadway Boogie Woogie* is meant to suggest that painting without literal objects, like music without lyrics, can convey the abstract rhythms of modern spaces like New York City's Broadway, a vital city street that is typical of the modern cityscape of the *flanêur*. Mondrian's paintings were carefully plotted systems of rhythmic color, shape, and line devoid of realistic content.

One of the interests of some modern artists was the very materiality of paint on canvas and the act of making marks "documented" in the painting. The "drip and splash" style that was *Abstract Expressionist* Jackson Pollock's trademark emerged in his paintings of the late 1940s, and is evident in his painting titled *Number 1, 1948*. To create paintings like this one, Pollock placed his canvas on the floor or the wall and poured and dripped his paint from a can right onto the surface. Instead of using brushes, he manipulated the paint with sticks, trowels or knives, sometimes adding to it sand, broken glass, or other materials. Action painting had in common with *Surrealist* theories of automatism the idea that this process resulted in a direct expression or revelation of the unconscious of the artist at the moment of its production. Elements such as line, color, shape, scale, and form are seen as direct translations or expressions of the mental state of the painter. The emphasis was on the action and

Jackson Pollock,
Number 1, 1948, 1948

expressive movement used to produce the work, rather than the system used to create the piece, or the resulting composition's appearance.

Concept, process, and performance were essential aspects of many modern artists' practices, and were the source of categories designating sub-types of modern art (*conceptual art*, process art, and performance art). Conceptual art involved the production of works in which the idea or concept was more important than the visual product. Artist Yves Klein, in a technique he used during the 1950s that combined the conceptual with process, performance, and action, directed nude models to roll in paint and then roll their bodies over canvas before audiences, producing paintings that were imprints of their action. This kind of body art, which resulted not only in paintings but photographic documentation of these performances, subverted the tradition of "painting from life" in which studio artists observed posed nude models and painted representations of them. Klein's body art took the body of the model and used it as a direct source of imprinting, and as a means of documenting their physical bodies in motion. Recordings of these events added another level of meaning. One work from Klein's series of body images has a title, *Anthropometrie*, that directly evokes the nineteenth-century practices of measuring bodies to derive information about health and intellect (we discuss these practices further in Chapter 8). Klein's paintings were so notorious that the particular color of paint he used for these pieces became something like his trademark. The phrase "Yves Klein blue" brings to mind a definite cobalt-blue hue among modern art aficionados.

Many of the trends of modern art illustrate the tendency toward a radical break with the past. We will look at one particular example, Soviet *Constructivism* in the period following the Russian Revolution in 1917. During and following the revolution, some pro-Soviet artists adopted an avant-garde aesthetic politics that broke with older paradigms, deploying a new iconography that rejected not only the content but the form and composition of previous works. Form, it was suggested by a few artists, embodies the politics and ideology of a culture as much as if not more than content. New formal principles were devised by architects, artists, and filmmakers based on the theories of Karl Marx and Soviet leader Vladimir Lenin, and an embrace of technological and engineering advancements as key forces in the movement to change the material conditions of Soviet life to reflect the new and modern political ethos.

As a style of modernism, Constructivism, a label associated with works produced in the spirit of the Soviet revolution, was a movement that broke with the idea that art is spiritual and mysterious or *sublime*. The sublime, as a kind of veneration of the image, was associated with a society based on the values of religion and monarchy that had characterized the previous political system in Russia. While some artists were intent on producing realist representations of the conditions of Soviet life after the revolution, others including those associated with Constructivism made work that embodied the principles of the changing Soviet world. Science and technology were regarded as models in the transformation from the old Russia to the new, modern Soviet state. Constructivist painters used dynamic lines of force and principles of geometric construction of form in their abstract pieces. They wanted to capture the vitality and dynamism of the latest engineering and architectural forms and technologies the Soviet Union was eager to embrace in this time of transition. Soviet sculptor and painter Vladimir Tatlin and other artists were exposed to the *Cubist* constructions of French artists including Pablo Picasso in the early 1910s. They saw in Cubism the potential for representing structure and technology as the embodiment of the new Soviet process of restructuring society according to the theories of Marx and Lenin. Tatlin's *Monument to the Third International*, which was never built but was constructed in model form in 1919–20, was intended to be a 1,312-foot-high structure consisting of a metal spiral frame tilted at an angle, enclosing three glass structures (in the shape of a cylinder, a cone, and a cube) housing conference spaces. All three units were to revolve slowly at intervals, emphasizing dynamism and *dialectical* change, with rotating chambers that displayed political meaning in their form. The executive block on top, for instance, would turn once a day while the lower chamber of the legislative council would rotate one degree every day, or a complete rotation every year. In its embrace of technology as an expression of the Soviet ethos, and in its focus on form as an expression of cultural meaning, this work is emblematic of modernism. The monument, available to us only in the form of Tatlin's model, was never built because government policy changed in favor of more realist approaches to representation.

It is important to note that while Constructivism and other abstract art movements are often used to illustrate a paradigm of modernist art, there were many and varied political and aesthetic approaches to art within the framework of modernism, and even realist art works continued to be produced and supported alongside abstract art movements. One of the under-considered aspects of modernism is the place of realism within it. In the Soviet Union, abstraction came to be thought of as a reactionary tendency by many, a view supported by the fact that those artists who continued to work in

Vladimir Tatlin, model for the *Monument to the Third International*, 1919

abstract modes under Stalin got little or no support and were even persecuted for the political transgression of making abstract art. In a climate where art was meant to service the advancement of the state, to produce an art form that challenged the party line was a serious offense.

An emphasis on form in modernism was also expressed as a kind of *reflexivity* in which the artwork comments on itself and its own process of production. Reflexivity is the practice of making viewers aware of the material and technical means of production by featuring them in the image or as the "content" of a cultural production. Soviet filmmaker Dziga Vertov took on a *nom de plume* that in Russian means "spinning top" to reflect his own physical existence as an observer caught up in the giddy motion and excitement of the new Soviet city and the post-revolutionary move to industrialize the nation. His newsreels of the 1920s, titled *Kino Pravda* (or, film truth), captured life on the streets of Russia as viewed through the eyes of this "spinning top" cinematographer. Like the *flâneur*, the cameraman of Vertov's films seems to float through the dizzying spectacle of the new urban vistas under construction, his camera-eye moving from sight to sight in modernity's display of architectural and engineering. Although Soviet culture of the 1920s was not imbued with the consumer culture that shaped the modern spectacles observed by the *flâneur* in the capitalist metropolis, it was nonetheless engaged in stunning technological transformations of space and architecture. *Man with a Movie Camera* (1929) is a film in the vein of the "city symphony" (a phrase used to describe lyrical film celebrations of the spectacular sight of urbanization) in which Vertov reflexively exposes the presence of the cameraman as a roving eye capturing the city for the pleasure of its Soviet viewing subjects. Reflexive footage of the cameraman's encounters with his subject matter emphasizes the conventions of filmmaking and viewing. The filmmaker documents the city, turning the camera out to "look back" at the camera filming him (and thus at "us" seated collectively in the audience). The seats of an empty film theater shot from a position at the rear of the audience fold open mechanically as if to invite us to be aware of our own status as viewers, and to invite us to participate in this mass spectacle of urban transformation. Unlike Tatlin's unbuilt Monument, the film embodies a kind of realism in its attention to the day-to-day life of the Soviet people, albeit captured and edited together in a somewhat abstract and fragmented, non-narrative fashion. But what is abstracted is not so much the city itself (and Soviet life) as the mode through which the

Dziga Vertov, *Man with a Movie Camera*, 1929

film leads us to observe it. Vertov's film-truth approach worked very much in an observational mode in which what "we" observe through the eye of the cameraman is seen in the distracted and fragmented fashion of a subject caught up in the distractions of urban, industrial modernization. He offers his viewers a practice of looking that glances and abstracts in the movement of the camera-eye's framing and in the editing, allowing the viewer to see things from new perspectives. But he does not necessarily offer an abstract image. In this sense, his work retains ties to representational realism. Not only did this make his work less problematic from the standpoint of Soviet policies about abstraction, it allowed it to become a basis for *cinéma verité* and *direct cinema* in the 1950s and 1960s. Directors active in these documentary film movements in France, England, and the United States placed the camera to capture spontaneous action, minimizing the interference of direction, camerawork, and editing with events as they unfolded.

It would be misleading to suggest that modernism was solely linked to left politics and revolutionary movements. Cubism, for example, did not tie political change to modernist aesthetics as Constructivism did. *Futurism*, another art movement of the period of the 1910s and 1920s, bears ties to the mentality that gave rise to a very different politics—Fascism in Italy. Most modernist movements from this period through the 1970s, however, did share the general principles of breaking with past conventions, foregrounding form over content, and attending explicitly to the language and/or materiality of the medium. Reflexivity is apparent throughout many of the movements linked to modernism in art, film, and literature from the 1910s on. This approach reaches its fullest expression in the minimalist and structural art and film movements of the 1970s.

There is a paradox embedded in the concept of the modern. Habermas explains that to be modern is not simply to be contemporary, let alone stylish or trendy. That which is truly modern, even if it breaks with its own historical past, "preserves a secret tie to the classical," even as it breaks with the classical past.[7] Modern works of art, for example, gain meaning within their own self-enclosed canon and set of modernist principles. Modernist movements frequently operate on the basis of a kind of self-referential approach that we do not encounter in works labeled postmodern. We can thus speak of a classical modern work of art—a work that embodies the concepts and style of modern art as an historical style that is as rule-based as any classical form. To be modern is not to be contemporary, but to fit within the framework of modern art movements that began to dissipate in the 1970s. Hence, museums that emerged in the early to mid-twentieth century that called themselves museums of modern art in order to connote ideas of being up to date and cutting edge are now faced with the reality that they are devoted to historical rather than contemporary works. These works are increasingly seen as examples of a past modernist set of principles and standards for art—principles and standards that are no longer the primary criteria for judging contemporary works of art.

Postmodernism

As we stated earlier, modernism and postmodernism both contrast and overlap with one another. There is no precise moment of transition between the modern and the postmodern, rather postmodernism intersects with and permeates late modernity. It is correct, then, to say that postmodernism describes a set of conditions and practices occurring in late modernity. Modernism and postmodernism are not concepts that are strictly period-specific. Aspects of postmodernism can be seen in the early twentieth century, and in the late twentieth and early twenty-first centuries, aspects of modernity and postmodernism, as well as modern and postmodern styles, coexist.

The term "postmodernity" refers to the experience of living in a postmodern culture, and the upheaval of modernist principles and frameworks that involves. There are important social aspects of postmodernity that can be distinguished from those of modernity. Modernism was characterized by a sense of knowing that was forward-looking and positive, and believing one could know what was true and real as well as what was for the best in a given society. The postmodern is characterized by questioning these sorts of knowledges and the belief in progress: Do we really know that progress is always a good thing? Can we really know the human subject? How can any experience be pure or unmediated? How do we know what truth is? Whereas modernity was based on the idea that the truth can be discovered by accessing the right channels of knowledge, the postmodern is distinguished by the idea that there is not one but many truths and that the notion of pure truth is an illusion. As such, the postmodern entails a crisis of cultural authority, that is, a profound questioning of the very foundations of social structure and the means of theorizing social relations and culture.

For these reasons, postmodernism is often described as a questioning of the *master narratives* (or metanarratives) of society. A master narrative is a framework which purports to explain society, if not the world, in comprehensive terms, such as religion, science, Marxism, psychoanalysis, Enlightenment myths of progress, and other theories that intend to explain all facets of life.

Metanarratives involve a sense of an inevitable linear progress toward a particular goal—enlightenment, emancipation, self-knowledge, etc. French theorist Jean-François Lyotard characterized postmodern theory as profoundly skeptical of these metanarratives, their universalism, and the premise that they could define the human condition. Hence, postmodern theory has undertaken to examine philosophical concepts which were previously perceived to be beyond reproach or question, such as the idea of value, order, control, identity, or meaning itself. It has involved a scrutinizing of social institutions, such as the media, the university, the museum, medicine, and the law, in order to examine the assumptions under which they operate and the ways that power works within them. One could say that postmodernism's central goal is to put all assumptions under scrutiny in order to reveal the values that underlie all systems of thought, and thus to question the ideologies within them that are seen as natural. This means that the idea of *authenticity* is always in question in postmodernism.

One of the primary aspects of postmodernism is the critique of the idea of *presence*, a concept that is fundamental to the modern concept of the subject. Presence refers to an idea of immediate experience, the direct understanding of the world through one's senses and perceptions as both reliable and real. Postmodernism says that this idea of presence, or immediate experience, is a myth, and that everything we experience is mediated through language, images, social forces, etc. In other words, postmodernism asserts that there is no such thing as a pure, unmediated experience. The work of postmodern theory has been to examine these aspects of the postmodern condition and to make sense of the complexity of contemporary social interaction, meaning, and cultural production. This does not mean that all aspects of contemporary societies are postmodern, rather that they work in tension with modern aspects and other influences.

Postmodernism emphasizes ideas of pluralism and multiplicity. The idea of difference is central to postmodern thought. There is an emphasis in postmodernism on the concept of multiple subjectivities, that is, the concept that our identities consist of a variety of identity categories—race, gender, class, age—and are the product of our social relations to social institutions. This way of thinking about identity is quite different from the idea of the unified subject of modernity. Postmodernism thus has been contemporaneous with the focus on cultural pluralism and diversity. Postmodern thought has emerged simultaneously in dialogue with social movements of the late twentieth century that have brought to the table questions of gender, race, sexuality, and class: the civil rights, feminist, and gay rights movements. The concept of identity politics arose out of critical theories of the 1980s and 1990s that emphasized the cultural identity of authors and subjects as crucial aspects of the politics being articulated in texts. Following earlier forms of class, race, and gender-based theory including feminism, those authors working within the loose framework of identity politics brought to the fore the fundamental question of cultural difference and the question of who it is that speaks through a given text. It matters whether the subject being discussed, and the subject speaking, is male or female, black or white, Asian or Latino, gay, straight, or transgendered. In other words, these social and theoretical movements intervene in the idea that one can speak of the human subject in universal terms. With its emphasis on the differences between subjects, and by extension viewers/readers, postmodern criticism in a more general way emphasizes that images will be interpreted differently by different viewers. Some postmodern theory places an emphasis on the question of *polysemy*, the idea that texts can have many meanings.

It is not only criticism and theory that can be described as postmodern in its approach to its objects. Many postmodern image texts, be they television shows, films, or advertisements, have more than one preferred reading and may be interpreted by viewers in different ways. The idea of multiple meanings existing in one text is well illustrated in the example of *hypertext*. A concept used to describe computer texts with multiple links to various threads of a narrative or various points within a larger set of data, hypertext is emblematic of the postmodern condition in using a network model with multiple pathways rather than linear narrative to organize knowledge and information. Baudrillard introduced the concept of simulation to describe the collapse between counterfeit and real, original and copy that exists in the digitized culture of the late twentieth and early twenty-first centuries. It could also be argued that Disneyland's depiction of Main Street USA simulates a middle American street so convincingly that visitors may take their image of main-street America from Disneyland rather than from an actual small town.

Postmodernism has a very different analysis from modernism of popular culture, mass culture, and the surface world of images. While opposition to mass culture and its saturation of the world with images is one of the hallmarks of modernism, postmodernism emphasizes *irony* and a sense of one's own involvement in low or popular culture. The forms of low, mass, or commercial culture so disdained by modernists are understood, in the context of post-modernism, as the inescapable conditions in and through which we generate our critical texts. *Appropriation, parody*, nostalgic play, and reconfiguration of historical forms and images are just some of the approaches used by some artists and critics of the 1980s and 1990s whose works are associated with the term "postmodernism."

Reflexivity

Earlier, we discussed the conscious ways in which reflexivity emerged as a style in modernism. The practice of making viewers aware of the means of production by incorporating them into the content of the cultural product was often a feature of modernism. Much of postmodern art and culture takes this modern concept of reflexivity further. Self-awareness of one's inevitable immersion in everyday and popular culture has led some post-modern artists to produce works which reflexively examine their own position in relation to the artwork or the artwork's institutional context.

The early work of photographer Cindy Sherman is a good example of this approach. Sherman produced a series of photographs in which she struck poses evoking actresses in film stills. These images do not reproduce partic-ular film stills. Rather, they evoke the style of a particular moment or genre, such as the Hollywood studio film of the 1930s and 1940s. A similar strategy was used by the Los Angeles Chicano art collective, Asco. This group made "No-Movies" comprised of film stills for movies they never actually made, never intended to make—because the group lacked the budget to produce one. This fact functioned as the instigation for an ironic joke about the func-tion of the film still, an entity that requires no *referent* or "real" film to exist. It is well known in the industry that these stills are not frame enlargements from the actual film, but publicity stills—photographs made to advertise the film in production to the press before the film is complete. Posed to look like the film itself, these images have no referent, as the film is most often not even com-plete at the time the still is shot.

Sherman's photographs can be seen as self-portraits that are not actually about herself, since she is always disguised and playing a role. Hence, viewers are not meant to understand these pictures as images of Sherman or of actual

Cindy Sherman, *Untitled Film Still #21*, 1978

film stills, but as ironic readings, deliberate imitations, and self-conscious interpretations of style, gesture, and stereotypes. Sherman's work is a response
to an era of feminist modernist criticism that challenged representations
of women, an era whose defining essay was that watershed in feminist film
theory, "Visual Pleasure and Narrative Cinema". In this 1975 essay, which we
discussed in Chapter 3, Laura Mulvey argued that in classical Hollywood
cinema the male position is the active viewing position, while the female position is that of the passive object of male visual pleasure. This argument
launched a whole field of feminist theory about structures of identification.
Feminist film critics asked some of the following questions throughout the
1980s: How do Hollywood films, as one expression of patriarchal culture,
organize our looking practices in ways that render the male viewing position
one of authority and pleasure, and the female position that of specular object?
How do women, as objects within this gaze, identify within a position of active

looking? If woman is image and man the bearer of the look, can women assume a male looking position? If we use Freud's theories of subject formation in relation to language and meaning to assert the masculine nature of image production, where do women stand in relation to the subjective experience of looking and making meaning of images of women?

Sherman's photography indirectly but powerfully engages these theories of looking and sexual difference by giving us visual texts that comment reflexively on women's place on both sides of the camera, as bearer of the look and as image. Indeed, many of Sherman's earliest photographs show her dressed in the garb of the height of the Hollywood studio era (the 1930s and 1940s). Her compositions reflexively pose questions about spectatorship, identification, the female body image, and the appropriation of the gaze by the woman photographer as self-portrait subject. But Sherman, unlike critical writers, actively inserts herself into the media she reflexively critiques. Rather than taking a critical stance from outside the image and its mode of production, Sherman inserts herself not only into the image but into the process of its production. She enmeshes herself in the very world being critically interrogated in her work. This is one of the key things that distinguishes her commentary as postmodernist against the modernist critical-readings-from-above offered by feminist film criticism of roughly the same period.

Nostalgic references to other historical periods is another hallmark of postmodern art captured in Sherman's photographs. Like much postmodern advertising and media culture of the 1980s and 1990s, Sherman's photographs feed our nostalgia for bygone eras. Her double position as both producer of the scene and object of the gaze, however, introduces an edge of irony and reflexivity that sets her work apart from its more popular counterparts (Madonna, for example, as we will explain further). Irony refers to a deliberate contradiction between the literal meaning of something and its intended meaning (which can be the opposite of the literal meaning). Irony can border on sarcasm—that is, when someone says "nice picture" when they really mean "terrible picture." In a broader sense, irony can be seen as a context where appearance and reality are in conflict. Sherman's photographs comment not only on the conditions of that past, but ironically on the artist-producer's awareness of her enmeshment in the visual culture of nostalgic fantasy she evokes. By situating herself as both artist and subject, Sherman invites us to think reflexively about subjectivity and gendered processes of identification, cultural memory, and fantasy in postmodern visual culture. This makes her photographs ironic images that also instruct us in seeing practices of looking as historical and situated.

Reflexive attention to self-image and the cultural producer's own engagement in media culture is also apparent, with varying degrees of irony, in the construction of public image by various pop performers. Punk and New Wave artists of the late 1970s and early 1980s raided thrift stores to acquire clothes reflecting the various musical and artistic styles referenced in their works. Clothing and music were venues for parodic send-ups of the values of the Hollywood studio era and its culmination in youth rebellion in the 1950s and 1960s. In the 1980s, cultural producers became obsessed with the transformation of self-image as a means of critical expression.

This strategy of appropriation and parody of fashion was popularized by Madonna, who adopted a Marilyn Monroe look, followed by numerous transformations of style and image over the course of her career. Madonna can be described as the quintessential postmodern pop figure of the 1980s and early 1990s in that she made the transformation of style a stylistic signature in itself. Sherman, too, appropriated the Marilyn look, but to a more insightful and critical end than Madonna's use of the image to capitalize on its mass appeal. Also in the 1980s, pop singer Michael Jackson exhibited a similar penchant for bodily transformation as a means of nostalgic reference to past icons, undergoing a series of surgeries and treatments to make his face over in the likeness of Elizabeth Taylor. These two vocal artists' construction of themselves as images, transforming their looks according to a familiar cultural referent, is emblematic of postmodern culture.

This focus on image was followed in the 1990s by artists adopting a more direct approach to the transformation of image and/as identity. Ru Paul, for example, made overt transgendered performance his trademark. French performance artist Orlan underwent a series of cosmetic surgeries performed by plastic surgeons in art galleries with the public present, resculpting her face after well-known female figures in various masterpiece paintings including the *Mona Lisa* and Botticelli's *Venus*. In the case of Orlan's surgical performances, the concept of nostalgia is important, but a more crucial factor (one might say fantasy) is that body and identity become infinitely malleable in a culture where the image is the ultimate register of experience. Orlan's work suggests that there is no "real," original body to which we might return in our quest to model ourselves after some fantasy of what we hope to become: the image of an image. In the modernist period the image's function as a register of truth and meaning came under scathing scrutiny. Postmodernism follows not by going beyond the image to some newer, more accurate register of truth, but by embracing the surface—the way that images supercede the real and the true. Postmodern theory sees the surface as the primary element of social life, as opposed to the idea that the true meaning is hidden underneath. According to Baudrillard, the surface is all we see and all we can have access to. The image transcends the idea of the real, taking on a new importance in millennial culture. We can no longer look below the surface for depth and true meaning, because we will find nothing there.

Reflexivity also takes the form in postmodern style of referencing context or framing in order to rethink the viewer's relationship to an image or narrative. One postmodern narrative style is to refuse viewers the opportunity to become absorbed in the narrative and lose themselves, to forget their role as viewers. This is sometimes done by breaking the conventions of cinematic storytelling, by pulling back the camera to reveal the framing devices or set, or by talking directly to the consumer about how the ad was made within the ad itself. Whereas within the modernist period critical writers asked us to pay attention to the framing and process of production of a work, in the postmodern period there is no implied criticism in this reflexive process.

Modernist reflexive narrative tactics involved asking viewers to notice the structure of the show and distance viewers from the surface pleasures of the text. This idea of distancing is an important one, because it means that viewers are engaged at a critically conscious level. Bertolt Brecht, a well-known German Marxist playwright and critic of the 1920s and 1930s, proposed the concept of distanciation as a technique for getting viewers to extract themselves from the narrative in order to see the means through which it gets us to buy into ideology. Reflexivity is, in this modernist light, a way that the critical viewer can undermine the illusions of a media complicit in the values of capitalism. Yet, in postmodern reflexive texts, it is the advertisers and media producers themselves who offer us these techniques of "disillusionment." However, they offer them as a pleasurable process, not necessarily as a tool for critical and distanced reflection on the real economic and cultural conditions behind the text.

Postmodern styles tend to break many of the conventions of image-making.

Films that incorporate postmodern style, for instance, defy the conventions of cinematic language by shuffling narrative elements and using jump cuts to call attention to the editing. Conventional cinematic language is based on a seamless text in which the illusion of a continuous story is created through specific editing techniques, lighting effects, and camera movements. Some postmodern films break these codes through the strategy of discontinuity. With discontinuity, the form is not invisible but, rather, is made obvious to the viewer. This can involve using jump cuts, mixing of black-and-white and color images, oblique or unexplained camera angles, or unmatched consecutive action. Since they were introduced in the early 1980s, music videos have often incorporated these strategies to tell stories in unconventional styles. Indeed, music videos are considered to be primary examples of postmodern style, with their mix of varied, often disconnected, story elements, their combinations of different kinds of images, and their status as both ads and television texts. It is an irony of media history that the techniques and conventions of discontinuity, reflexivity, narrative fragmentation, and multiplicity of meanings in a previous era were tied to the political project that aimed to get viewers to disengage from and oppose the capitalist media's illusionary images and looking practices. These techniques were meant to generate radical looking practices. Instead, they have become the codes of jaded viewers who are aware of the conditions of illusion and find nothing significant beneath them to ponder.

A film like *Pulp Fiction* (Quentin Tarentino, 1994), which tells its story in a nonchronological fashion with events taking place in a shuffled order, is an example of a postmodern text in the sense that it plays with the order of the narrative, making time a malleable entity. Each time that the story doubles back, the viewer is forced to think about the film's structure and to work to figure it out. Like discontinuous editing, this technique does not allow viewers to sink into any illusion of the cinematic narrative. But in this film, learning about the way continuous narratives give us an illusion of reality is simply a pleasurable exercise, not a political statement about the seductions of capitalist media.

The copy, pastiche, and institutional critique

Can there ever be new ideas and images, things that have not been thought of or done before? Does it matter? The world of images today consists of a huge variety of remakes, copies, parodies, *replicas*, and reproductions. In the arenas of art and architecture, as well as popular culture, the idea of an original image or form seems to have been thoroughly subverted.

This can be seen readily in postmodern styles of architecture. One of the foundational texts of postmodernism is Robert Venturi, Denise Scott Brown, and Steven Izenour's *Learning from Las Vegas*, a 1977 book that takes readers through a tour of the architectural appropriations that line the glitzy, sordid consumer-oriented streets of Las Vegas at the low end of popular architectural culture. Food stands and strip joints—sites that appropriate iconography and symbolism from all classes of architecture and iconography—can tell us more about the history of architecture and the history of our culture, this book suggests, than the most sophisticated work of architecture. This book opened the door for a new reverence in "high" architecture for architectural "low" culture and its unaffected ironic humor and imagination.

A postmodern architectural edifice in the vein of the postmodern might borrow on many different styles of architecture—modern, classical, gothic, etc.—and mix them together with no apparent sense of correctness concerning their historical meanings. Postmodern architecture can be seen as a kind of plagiarizing, quoting, and borrowing of previous and current styles. The very notions of architectural lineage and authenticity are radically called into question. For example, Philip Johnson's well-known design for the AT&T building in New York is a modern tower topped with a sculpted motif derived from Chippendale furniture. This mixing with no reference to history or sense of rules about what is "right" for design is known as pastiche, which refers to a quoting, borrowing, pilfering, and combining of different styles, genres, and forms. Pastiche works in defiance of the concept of progress—the idea, for instance, that styles get better as they evolve. The notion of progress so fundamental to modernism dies a resounding death in postmodernism's studied disregard for the new. In modernism, style follows a linear course, each new style building on and progressing forward from the last by introducing more functionality, or a better design. In postmodernism, styles can be mixed with no sense that we are moving toward something better.

In addition, many elements in postmodern buildings defy the notion of architecture as functional. An arch may have no structural function, and its use may reside in the humor of existing without a function, as mere decoration. A passage may lead nowhere, a facade may conceal nothing, and a Greek column might stand next to a Gothic arch. This is all done toward a playful undermining of some basic architectural principles and a celebration of surface that works simultaneously as a joke about architecture's functional role. Pastiche allows elements of architectural form to act as free-floating signifiers, detached from their original historical or functional context, which can constantly change meaning from different angles and in different contexts. In keeping with the respect for low and consumer culture epitomized in *Learning from Las Vegas*, many of the most famous architectural designs of the postmodern period have been spaces of public consumption, such as shopping malls.

The notion that perhaps nothing new can be made, which implies to a certain degree that the idea of something completely new is a fallacy, is a fundamental aspect of postmodern art. Here, then, not only does the copy have the same value as the original, it often functions to completely undermine the idea of original value and authenticity. Artist Sherrie Levine makes this point in a series of works in which she simply rephotographed famous images—in blatant violation of their copyright, the signifier of authorship and authenticity—and displayed them as her own. In *After Weston*, Levine photographed Edward Weston's famous image of his son, Neil, entitled *Torso of Neil* (1925). Weston's image is situated in a long history of male nudes, which Levine's

Philip Johnson, AT&T
Building, New York

"theft" disrupts precisely because it is self-consciously presented as stolen, rather than concealing its status as a copy. However, her choice of this male nude is provocative, given that Weston was known for his depictions of the female nude. Levine's work is a defiant critique of the idea of an original and a feminist critique of the idea of the male artist as master. It presents the viewer with a questioning of the differing value of images and the entire question of reproduction. In addition, like new technologies that allow images to be easily "re-authored," Levine's aesthetic style questions the very foundations of authorship.

One of the principles put in question in Levine's work is the idea of the original. Levine's photographic appropriations, like the photographs of Cindy Sherman, raise questions about the role of the artist. Who is the "real" artist here, Levine or Weston, and which is the "real" work of art, the copy or the original? Is Sherman's image her own? Is the "real" or the "true" a concern in the late twentieth-century world of endless reproduction? Both of these artists are questioning the traditional idea of the artist as someone who acts autonomously, as the sole creator of the unique work. Like that of other postmodern artists, their work questions the idea of originality in art and the auratic value that is placed upon it in museums, galleries, and the art market. In works

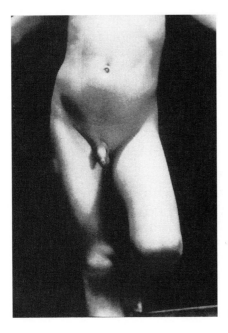

Sherrie Levine, *After Weston #2*, 1980

like these, the question of *semiotics* becomes quite complicated. What do these images signify and what are the referents they represent? In the case of a photograph, does it make sense to speak of "original prints"? Levine's images are exact replicas that are distinguished from the originals specifically in terms of their conceptual elements—the irony of remaking an image, the titling of each to make clear its difference from the original. These images are reworkings of representations, which are part of a potentially endless reworking of images for which the original referent is no longer identifiable.

Much postmodern art is not concerned with representing reality but with rethinking the function of art and emphasizing the role of institutional context in producing meaning. Many such works focus on the institutions of art and the power relations created by them. For instance, the question of context generated a whole set of works of the 1990s devoted to the museum as an institution that is commonly regarded as a repository of truth and value. Fred Wilson is one artist who has produced a number of art installations for museums and galleries that reflexively interrogate the structuring function of the museum and its ways of ordering knowledge and managing art, people, and information. In *Mining the Museum*, an installation of 1992 done in collaboration with the Maryland Historical Society, Wilson put on display objects and data from the collection to demonstrate how knowledge is produced in the techniques of collecting and archiving. The work suggests that the representation and omission of people of color is an issue we need to consider with respect to the museum's collecting and archiving practices. In his work *Guarded View* (1991), seen on the next page, Wilson displays life-size headless statues of museum guards, forcing viewers to ponder directly those very institutional subjects who are rendered invisible by the dynamics of the gaze at work in the museum. Whereas many of the guards in US art museums are black and Latino, most of the patrons are white. This installation foregrounded the issue of race in relation to labor and marketing practices of museums. It was included in the "Black Male" exhibition at the Whitney Museum of American Art. Curated by Thelma Golden in 1994, this exhibition raised awareness of the racial dynamics of the art institution in unprecedented ways. Andrea Fraser, another artist who engaged in reflexive institutional critique in the 1980s and 1990s, performed as a museum docent, interrogating the role of the docent or guide in shaping public knowledge about the art displayed in museums and galleries in the course of her tours. In 1992, she began a series of works based on interviews with museum board members and other

Fred Wilson, *Guarded View*, 1991

personnel to uncover the hidden social and economic side of art institutions. The recordings and transcripts were edited into audio-tours, audio-installations and publications which accompanied exhibitions of works by other artists. In work like Wilson's and Fraser's, reflexivity takes place from within the institution, not from outside it. Moreover, the work of art takes on the whole institutional structure that surrounds it rather than focusing on the textual meanings inherent in a given work. Wilson and Fraser also allow us to think about the "invisible" people who make art's display and consumption possible, not the curators but the guards and docents. The low-paid labor and invisibility of these people stand in stark contrast to the value and visibility of the work of art and the artist him- or herself as commodity and public image.

Popular culture: parody and reflexivity

Reflexivity is not only a feature of postmodern art, it has become a central aspect of postmodern style in popular culture and advertising. It often can take the form of noting the "frame" of the text—the set of a TV show or the border of an advertisement. In the ad on the next page, the torn page calls attention to the frame of the

Andrea Fraser
performing *Museum
Highlights: A Gallery Talk*,
1989 at the Philadelphia
Museum of Art

ad and acknowledges to the viewer the ad's placement within a magazine, while at the same time using this device to illustrate doing "half the job."

Reflexivity also takes the form of referencing other texts, be they other images, ads, films, or TV shows, through *intertextuality*. This literally means the insertion of another text, with its meaning, within a new text. One of the fundamental aspects of intertextuality is its presumption that the viewer knows the text that is being referenced. Intertextuality is not a new aspect of popular culture or specific to postmodernism. After all, the use of celebrities to sell products can be seen as an intertextual tactic—the stars bring to the ad the meaning of their fame and the roles they have played. However, contemporary intertextuality operates on a level that is much more ironic and complex. It often presumes a significant amount of media literacy and familiarity with many cultural products on the part of viewers. It *interpellates* a media and visually literate viewer who is familiar with image conventions and genres. For instance, in *Pulp Fiction*, John Travolta and Uma Thurman visit a restaurant where all the waiters are dressed as Hollywood icons: Marilyn Monroe, Buddy Holly, Jayne Mansfield. The drinks are named after famous comedy teams, such as a "Martin and Lewis" for Dean Martin and Jerry Lewis, and an Ed Sullivan imitator runs a dance contest. Finally, the character played by Travolta references his own previous film role in *Saturday Night Fever* in a dancing segment of the film. These intertextual references form a reworking of nostalgia that is both affectionate homage and a reconfiguration of history.

In advertising, intertextuality is a means to tap into consumers' memories of other ads, and to speak to consumers as savvy viewers. When Pepsi produced a series of ads with musician Ray Charles, the advertising agency inserted several jokes which made reference to previous Pepsi campaigns. In one scene, Charles, who is blind, takes a sip from a can that someone has switched from Pepsi to Coke. He then laughs and declares that he gets the joke. The joke of this ad refers back to previous advertising of the cola wars, when Pepsi and Coke would do "blind taste tests" with "consumers" in order to have them identify their brand.

Sometimes, intertextuality is deployed for the purpose of evoking nostalgia—the use of songs from the 1960s, for instance, to sell products in the 1990s. This kind of intertextuality can occasionally backfire when viewers feel strongly about the texts being referenced. In the 1980s, when Nike used the Beatles' song "Revolution" as the basis for a rapidly edited series of black-and-white images to sell its sneakers, there was an outcry among baby-boomer

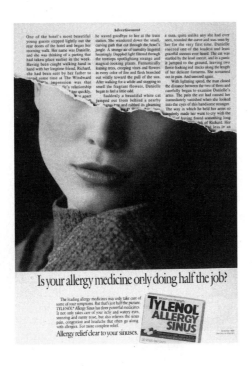

Quentin Tarantino, *Pulp Fiction*, 1994
© Miramax Films

consumers for whom the song had nostalgic value. Some listeners felt that the political message of the original song was being disrespected in this blatantly commercial appropriation of a song that had been something of a political anthem. Because this was the first time that a Beatles song had been used in an advertisement, the concern was that the political meaning of the word "revolution" had been reduced to the idea that there was a "revolution" in sneakers. This was, of course, nothing new, since advertisers have been using the word "revolution" for ages. However, the Beatles' song was explicitly about social upheaval. Hence, its use in an advertisement reminded consumers of how commercialized the 1960s image had become, and how stripped of authentic political meaning. This definitely worked against the preferred meaning of the ad—that Nike is hip to the ideals of the 1960s.

Increasingly advertising campaigns refer to other ad campaigns, either of competing products, generic campaign strategies, or as a co-campaign with another product. Not only do these ad campaigns disguise their status as ads, they actually work to emphasize this role. The Energizer bunny moves in and out of other ads, as a signifier of its slogan that it keeps "going and going," propelled by the Energizer battery. It is simultaneously an advertisement for the battery and a commentary on the nature of advertising itself. The bunny is usually used to poke fun at the pretensions of other ads at the same time that it is intended to capture viewers' attention by violating the conventions of ads, interrupting the message so to speak. While the bunny acquires inter-textual meaning which it carries into these other texts, the ad campaign also playfully remakes and parodies well-known texts. The irony of these references is increased by the longevity of the campaign, so that viewers now expect each new Energizer ad to up the ante of the last one. Like many postmodern texts, this ad manages to identify (one could even say "critique") the very nature of advertising while still selling its product. This is typical of the double position occupied by many postmodern texts—it attempts to sell its product while simultaneously critiquing the process of doing so.

Ironic humor is a strategy used in many contemporary advertising campaigns. This ad for ABC is designed to capture viewer's attention specifically through its ironic humor. It makes fun of the critical view of television through its message that "TV is good." In doing so, it speaks to viewers, who are used to thinking of television watching as guilty pleasure, in an unexpected way. The yellow background of the image, with the computer text print simply dis-played, has the effect of a yield sign, and echoes aspects of computer commu-nication. The simplicity of the ad acts as a kind of deadpan statement, underscoring its message.

A parody assumes a viewer who is familiar with many different texts, and who will enjoy the activity of guessing references and getting the joke. It could be said that many of these parodies and intertextual references work on several levels, one for the all-knowing viewer and one for the viewer who may not know the references at hand. A television show like *The Simpsons*, which often remakes old films in its storylines, can work this way. When the show remade *Dracula*, it did so by incorporating particular plot elements of the film into its existing locale and characters. Not only that, it remade the Francis Ford Coppola version of the film, *Bram Stoker's Dracula* (1992), which was in turn a remake of the 1931 original. With many humorous and absurd plot lines, the episode of *The Simpsons*, pictured on the next page, did not ask viewers to take its reworking of the Dracula story seriously, merely to share in its homage and parody.

This returns us to the initial question, is it possible to make something new in a context of constant remakes, parodies, and references? Clearly, *The Simpsons'* parody of *Dracula* and other films is not a substitute for the original or an attempt to redo it. It depends on the original for its meaning. Its retelling of the story is always coded with irony precisely because viewers are never meant to be absorbed in the story without remembering that it is a remake. This form thus demands a self-consciousness on the part of viewers, in which they are constantly noting the form, style, genre, and conventions (and parodic departures from them) rather than the story itself. As we stated earlier, this does not constitute the kind of reflexive style deployed by modernists who wanted viewers to acquire a political distance from the message

The Simpsons, 1992

of a media work, but rather suggests a deliberately playful engagement with the idea of the forms of popular culture.

Addressing the postmodern consumer

All of these stylistic strategies rework the relationship to the viewer/reader/consumer. Rather than thinking of viewers/consumers as dupes or as easily manipulated, these cultural products assume that viewers are media literate and a bit jaded by contemporary popular culture. They posit viewers who are informed about the conventions of popular culture, who know enough to understand intertextual references to other popular texts, and, in the case of advertisements, who are always potentially bored and ready to hit the remote control. Advertisements in particular tend increasingly to speak to consumers with a tone of knowing collusion. Advertisers address the consumer in a sly insider voice, a voice that says, "we know that you know how ads work and that you are not easily fooled. We are not going to condescend to you but rather are going to bring you into the process." This is a form of *metacommunication*, in which the ad speaks to the viewer as a postmodern strategy about the process of viewing the ad. It speaks not directly, but at a "meta" or reflexive level, in other words, the subject of the exchange (between viewer and the voice of the ad or text) is the relationship between the two. Hence, the ad is talking to the consumer not about buying the product, but about the process of looking at the ad. This technique allows advertisers to address jaded consumers in a new way and hence to get their attention. This metacommunication has the same goal as earlier forms of address in advertising—it is still about selling the product, brand, logo, or company image.

Metacommunication can be thought of as a postmodern strategy of addressing viewers/consumers, in that it appears to address viewers as more sophisticated and knowing. In always making reference to strategies of advertising, these ads appear to invite the viewer into the conference room of the advertising agency and to let them in on the secrets of the selling campaign. Yet, their actual goal is to get viewers' attention long enough to create a *commodity sign* for their product.

In the 1992 ad on the next page, Kenneth Cole displays not a product but a handwritten memo which mocks typical fashion ads. This ad establishes metacommunication with the viewer by discussing the decisions that supposedly went into the ad. It is designed to allow the viewer/consumer to feel that designer Kenneth Cole is speaking directly to them. This technique interpellates consumers who understand the conventions of fashion ads and are presumably bored with them. The metacommunication of the ad captures the viewer's attention but, most importantly, establishes Kenneth Cole shoes as hip, smart, and feminist. This is a company, the ad implies, that will not condescend to women consumers by showing them yet another image of airbrushed models wearing their goods. The handwritten note, which conveys a spontaneity and familiarity, thus aims to make the viewer/consumer feel they have a particular personal connection with the company.

Styles of metacommunication in advertisements often take the form of anti-ads. As we discussed in Chapter 6, these are ads in which the product is not shown, and the primary intent is to convey a sense of knowing or hipness. Often these ads use codes of *hyperrealism* to create this effect. The handwriting and askew angle of the Kenneth Cole memo makes it seem like a real memo lifted from the famous designer's desk. A hyperreal text is one that seems to be saying "this is real, take note of that!" Realism is perceived in our culture to be authentic, of the highest value, and better than something constructed. In

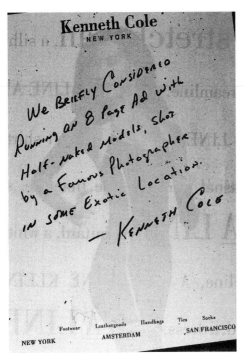

advertising, this strategy is in part a reaction against the increased slickness of ads and an attempt to make them look more spontaneous, intimate, and less artificial. This can be done through the use of grainy images, or in the case of TV ads, jerky hand-held camera movement, unexpected camera angles, "natural" sound, and the use of nonactors or out-takes.

In general, postmodern anti-ads discuss their products little if at all. Instead, they do the work of establishing a tone which will then be associated with their brand name. More often than not, this style is about establishing a product or brand name as hip or cool, or socially aware and concerned. This is meant to engage viewers by piquing their curiosity—to generate curiosity, as in, what is this ad about, and how can I get "in" on its exclusive world of meaning? This Moschino ad makes no reference to its product, but rather presents a series of political slogans. It works both to attach concepts of social concern to the name Moschino, and to get viewers to stop and examine the ad because it is unclear what it is selling. In this Diesel ad, the model selling the jeans is surrounded by strange men, all painted in gold, with no explanation. This campaign includes many images of bizarre scenes designed to make Diesel stand out as cool and enigmatic. The campaign is intended to shock the viewer through images of the grotesque and the bizarre. This is a tactic used by advertisers to stop the "page traffic" of someone casually leafing through a magazine.

This strategy is taken further in many Benetton ads that do not show Benetton clothing or products. They consist instead of dramatic documentary images, or highly charged staged images that refer to social injustice, racial diversity, and global disaster. The only reference to Benetton is the logo set across each image. These images pictured on the next page are enigmatic. While the first two are clearly meant to signify racial harmony and the ways in which the races are tied (chained, handcuffed) together in life, the third is harder to decipher. This man seems to be a soldier in an unidentified war, perhaps in Africa. What kind of bone is he holding? Is this a war of both rudimentary and sophisticated weapons? A guerrilla war? Close-up framing is used in all of these images to withhold information, to create a sense of mystery, and to depict the sometimes claustrophobic spaces in which people of

different races are forced to engage with each other. The unexplained aspects of this image allow it to become a free-floating signifier, detached from the specifics of a particular situation. It refers to social strife and conflict only in an abstract sense. What, then, is the meaning that Benetton wants viewers/consumers to attach to their product? As we explained in Chapter 6, their advertising is marketing social concern in the context of global fashion.

Benetton is capitalizing in these ads on the importance of the photograph, in particular the documentary photograph, as an *indexical sign* that carries the cultural assumptions of photographic truth. These images are recoded when they are accompanied by a logo, yet Benetton deploys them without any contextual information, as a means of stopping page traffic, rather than as a means of informing consumers about particular conflicts or political contexts around the world.

Through this campaign and subsequent campaigns, including the use of disabled children to model clothing and a series on death-row inmates that included interviews, Benetton has achieved considerable notoriety. Indeed, precisely because of the difference of its ad campaigns, and its breaking of the codes of advertising, the company has been the subject of countless media articles. Its name is now approaching the brand recognition of Coca-Cola. Oliviero Toscani, the man who designs Benetton campaigns, has said, "My dream is that some day Benetton won't have to spend another penny on advertising in newspapers or magazines." Both Toscani and Luciano Benetton have said that they felt that the codes of advertising had become too boring. Benetton states, "We felt obliged to get out of the traditional advertising formula. Of course, our advertising has to have a traditional function too—to make Benetton known around the world and to introduce the product to consumers. But for us just showing the product at this point is banal."[7] It is important to note the kind of blurring of boundaries indicated by such campaigns between the documentary and the advertising image. Not only does this rework the role played by the advertising image, but it also has an impact on the cultural status of the documentary image, given that it is so easily employed to sell mundane products. One could argue that in postmodern style, images are reduced to this kind of decontextualization and play, and stripped of their potential capacity to move and affect us in meaningful ways as viewers.

All of these ads engage in postmodern strategies that are about reinventing style and selling to media-saturated consumers. All of them acknowledge that showing the product to the consumer has become banal. For some advertisers, this fact means that ads must speak to consumers in reflexive tones, acknowledging the ad process. For others, such as Benetton, this means that ads should do another kind of work, such as addressing social issues. However, when such issues are raised in the context of an ad, whose primary goal is to sell a product or brand name, social concern is packaged and sold in a way that reduces its meaning. What then is the status of social concerns and political movements, when such statements are so easily coopted in the name of commerce? Does a political statement have any force when it is an integral part of an ad selling a product?

Postmodern style often raises such kinds of questions. Postmodernism addresses viewers as both complex readers and media and image conscious individuals. It is an ironic mode of viewing the complexities of contemporary culture. And, it is deeply cynical (in opposition to the uncynical aspects of modernism) about the level at which all facets of life appear to be commercial. Postmodernism is not necessarily liberating; just because it breaks with the tenets of modernism does not necessarily mean that it breaks with or is resistant to dominant ideology. Indeed, it can be seen as deeply implicated within the ideologies of consumer culture. In its rejection of nostalgia, universal humanism, and a single concept of truth, postmodernism is also about acknowledging the overlap between the categories of art, commerce, news, and advertising. This means that there is both increased blurring of these boundaries as well as an acknowledgement that they were never as separate as imagined in modernism. Postmodernism signals the rise of a generalized self-consciousness, which can be seen in both the reflexivity and the metacommunication of postmodern style and in the constant questioning of traditional metanarratives in all facets of everyday life.

Notes

1. Jean Baudrillard, *The Evil Demon of Images*, translated by Paul Patton and Paul Foss. (Sydney: University of Sydney, 1988), 29.
2. Santiago Colás, *Postmodernity in Latin America: The Argentine Paradigm* (Durham, NC and London: Duke University Press, 1994), ix.
3. Fredric Jameson, *Postmodernism, or, the Logic of Late Capitalism* (Durham, NC and London: Duke University Press, 1991).
4. Anne Friedberg, *Window Shopping: Cinema and the Postmodern* (Berkeley and London: University of California Press, 1993).
5. Fredric Jameson, *Postmodernism, or, the Logic of Late Capitalism*, 39–45.
6. Jürgen Habermas, "Modernity—An Unfinished Project," in *The Anti-Aesthetic*, edited by Hal Foster (Port Townsend, Wash.: Bay Press, 1983), 4.
7. Ingrid Sischy, "Advertising Taboos: Talking to Luciano Benetton and Oliviero Toscani," *Interview* (April 1992), 69.

Further Reading

Perry Anderson. *The Origins of Postmodernity*. London: Verso, 1998.

Jean Baudrillard. *The Evil Demon of Images*. Translated by Paul Patton and Paul Foss. Sydney: University of Sydney, 1988.

——*Simulacra and Simulations*. Translated by Sheila Faria Glaser. Ann Arbor: University of Michigan Press, 1994.

Lawrence Cahoone. *From Modernism to Postmodernism: An Anthology*. Cambridge, Mass. and Oxford: Blackwell Publishers, 1996.

Santiago Colás. *Postmodernity in Latin America: The Argentine Paradigm*. Durham, NC and London: Duke University Press, 1994.

Anne Friedberg. *Window Shopping: Cinema and the Postmodern*. Berkeley and London: University of California Press, 1993.

Thelma Golden, ed. *Black Male: Representations of Masculinity in Contemporary American Art*. New York: Whitney Museum of American Art, 1994.

Robert Goldman. *Reading Ads Socially*. New York and London: Routledge, 1992.

—— and Stephen Papson. *Sign Wars: The Cluttered Landscape of Advertising*. New York and London: Guilford, 1996.

Jürgen Habermas. "Modernity—An Unfinished Project." In *The Anti-Aesthetic*. Edited by Hal Foster. Port Townsend, Wash.: Bay Press, 1983, 3–15.

Andreas Huyssen. *After the Great Divide: Modernism, Mass Culture, Postmodernism*. Bloomington: Indiana University Press, 1986.

Fredric Jameson. *Postmodernism, or, The Cultural Logic of Late Capitalism*. Durham, NC and London: Duke University Press, 1991.

Jean-François Lyotard. *Postmodernism: A Report on Knowledge*. Translated by Geoff Bennington and Brian Massumi. Minneapolis and London: University of Minnesota Press, 1984.

Angela McRobbie. *Postmodernism and Popular Culture*. New York and London: Routledge, 1994.

Kynaston McShine. *The Museum as Muse: Artists Reflect*. New York: Museum of Modern Art, 1999.

Robert Venturi, Denise Scott Brown, and Steven Izenour. *Learning from Las Vegas: The Forgotten Symbolism of Architectural Form*. Cambridge, Mass. and London: MIT Press, 1972; Revised Edition 1977.

Brian Wallis, ed. *Art After Modernism: Rethinking Representation*. New York: New Museum, 1984.

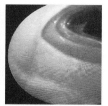
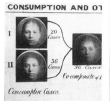
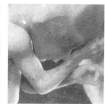

Scientific Looking, Looking at Science 8

Images play many different roles in visual cultures. They provide information in the media, sell goods through advertisements, evoke personal memories, and provide scientific data. Throughout this book, we have emphasized the ways that images in certain contexts affect the way that we view images in other social arenas. We have stressed that our experiences and interpretations of images are never singular, discrete events but are informed by a broader set of conditions and factors. The term "visual culture" encompasses a wide range of forms ranging from fine art to popular film and television to advertising to visual data in fields that we tend not to think about in terms of the cultural—the sciences, law, and medicine, for example. Because scientific imagery often comes to us with confident authority behind it, whether we view it through the press or through professional work and study, we often assume it represents *objective* knowledge. But as we will see in this chapter, scientific looking is as culturally dependent as the other practices of looking we have examined. Our view of scientific images will take into account the culture and experience of looking at art and popular media and the way in which we look at advertising images, because scientific looking does not occur in isolation from these other contexts.

Since the origins of photography in the early nineteenth century, scientific images have been an important area of photography's history and development. The role that photographs have played as scientific and legal evidence has been significant. With the rise of computer and digital imaging in the late twentieth century, images and visual inscriptions of data are a major part of the way that different fields of science conduct experiments, render information, and communicate ideas. There has been a worldwide shift toward visual means of representing knowledge and evidence, one that has escalated with the increased importance of digital media as a preferred mode of information. This increased use of visual images and combinations of visuals and text changes not only *how* we know what we know, but *what* we know. In other words, knowledge itself changes with this shift in the mediation of knowledge, with the ways it comes to us in images. It is important to keep in mind that science and culture are not discrete entities. Science intersects with other areas of knowledge and culture and draws on those systems in its day-to-day practices. In this chapter, we consider the various ways that images come into play both in scientific practice and in media appropriations of scientific methods and approaches. We put forward the view that scientific looking is always caught up in culturally influenced forms of looking.

Images as evidence

The mechanical nature of image-producing systems, such as photography and film, and the electronic nature of image-making systems such as television, computer graphics, and digital images, bear the legacy of *positivist* concepts of science in the nineteenth century and before. As we noted in Chapter 1, the notion of *photographic truth* hinges on the idea that the camera is an objective device for the capturing of reality, and that it renders this objectivity despite the subjective vision of the person using the camera. Hence, the photographic image has often been seen as an entity stripped of intentionality, through which the truth can be told without media-tion or subjective distortion. Yet, as we have seen, photographic images are highly subjective cultural and social artifacts that are influenced by the range of human belief, bias, and expression. Much of the meaning of camera-generated images is derived from the combination of the camera's role in capturing the real and its capacity to evoke emotion and present a sense of the unattainable—in other words, to appear to be both magical and truthful at once.

Images have been important in scientific *discourse* and the practice of science since well before the origins of photography, but we will begin our dis-cussion with photography because our primary interest is to consider the role of images in science since the nineteenth century. In addition to the initial explosion of portrait photography in the mid-nineteenth century, photography was taken up by scientists and in medical institutions to provide a visual record of experiments, to document diseases, and to register scientific data. In *modernity*, the idea of seeing farther, better, and beyond the human eye had tremendous currency; photography as the quintessential modern medium aided in this quest. The camera was imagined by some as an all-seeing instrument. Photographers took cameras up in hot-air balloons to photograph aerial views that few had seen before, and scientists attached photographic cameras to microscopes in order to magnify views of structures too small for the human eye to see. Later, when X rays were invented in the 1890s, they were perceived to offer a new vision of the human body. These were just some of the scientific frontiers that photography helped to traverse. This embrace of the image or the imaging instrument as that which helps us see further than the human eye continues to be a theme in scientific discourse. In this ad, the implication is that new imaging technology in medicine allows the doctor to see the patient with a new vision, one that is beyond human sight. It speaks the language of a modernist belief in the capacity of science and technology. Scientific images are thus understood as providing the capacity to see "truths" that are not available to the human eye.

This belief in the capacity of the photograph to see beyond the human eye and to create a sense of new frontiers of vision was coupled with its increased use for institutional regulation and categorization or archiving of people according to types. Hospitals, mental institutions, and government agencies all employed (and many still employ) photography to catalog subjects, diseases, and citizens in the late nineteenth century. This practice of cataloging bodies drew in part on the pseudo-sciences of phrenology, popular between 1820 and 1850, and craniology, a slightly later phenomenon of the nineteenth

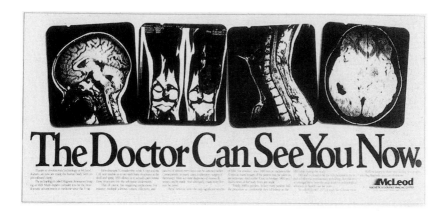

century. These "sciences" believed that the outward physical human body could be read for signs of inward moral, intellectual, and social development. Physiognomy—interpreting the outward appearance and configuration of the body, and the face in particular—was popular prior to the 1900s, as represented in the work of Barthélemy Coclès in his *Physiognomonia* of 1533, which went so far as to "read" the eyelashes of men as *signifiers* of, for example, pride and audacity.[1]

With the rise of photography in the 1830s, physiognomy had a potential new tool to refine this sort of physical representation and measurement. Readers of Sherlock Holmes may have puzzled over the line uttered by Moriarity who, upon meeting Sherlock Holmes, observes: "You have less frontal development than I should have expected." This comment reflects the popular sentiment that the face and the formation of the skull could be read for signs of intelligence, breeding, and moral standing. These qualities were linked to race, as is evident in *The Races of Man*, written in 1862 by John Beddoe, who would become a president of the Anthropological Institute. Beddoe argued that there is a difference, both physical and intellectual, between those in Britain with protruding jaws and those with less prominent jaws. The Irish, Welsh, and the lower classes were among those with protruding jaws, he argued, whereas all men of genius had less prominent jaws. Beddoe also developed an Index of Nigressence, from which he stated that the Irish were close to Cro-Magnon man and thus had links with what he called the "Africinoid" races. Here, we clearly can see how a visual "science" of the body had ties to racist *ideology*.

The science of eugenics, which was devoted to the practice of both studying and controlling human reproduction as a means of improving the human race, was founded by Sir Francis Galton, author of a book titled *Hereditary Genius* (1869). Of course, in eugenics, not all races were deemed worthy of reproducing. Galton, who was British, used measurement and the new method of statistics to "read" medical and social pathology off the surface of the body. The frontispiece that appears in his 1883 *Inquiries into Human Faculties* shows us many of his photographs of criminals, prostitutes, and people with tuberculosis. He was interested in producing a visual archive of deviant types within the realm of medical and social pathologies. He even went so far as to make composite portraits of various people thought to represent a given condition (as in the superimposition of portraits of people with consumption in the frontispiece reproduced here), with the idea that these composites would better represent the general type.

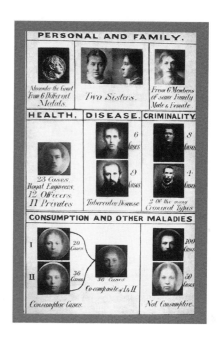

Francis Galton, Frontispiece from *Inquiries into Human Faculties* (1883)

Race was far from the only category so analyzed. As we discussed in Chapter 3, criminality, prostitution, mental illness, and a host of other behaviors and differences were thought to be visible on the bodily exterior. During the nineteenth century, medical researchers, hospitals, prisons and the police, psychiatrists, and lay photographers cataloged people's bodies on photographic film, effectively creating archives of types of pathologies for institutional records. In the mid-nineteenth century, Duchenne de Boulogne, a French physician, used photographs to document his experiments of applying electronic shock to subjects' faces in order to create a system for understanding facial expression. Duchenne's aim was to establish the universality of human expression, and photography was an essential tool in his project. In the image pictured on the next page, the subject is placed before the camera in a pose not unlike that of the criminal in a mug shot. There were many other such uses of photography. In the late nineteenth century the French neurologist Jean Martin Charcot devoted himself to the analysis of what he diagnosed as hysteria, mostly in women. He had his staff launch a battery of visual studies of subjects in various stages of hysterical episodes. These studies included live performances, drawings from life and photographs, photography sessions, measuring changes in position over time in sequential photographs, and even

Guillame Duchenne de Boulogne/Adren Tournachon, Figure 58 of Illustrations for *"Mécanisme de la physionomie humaine,"* 1854

making visual motion studies. Charcot believed in observation as a key to knowledge, and saw the photograph as an ideal means for extending one's ability to observe.

The creation of images of the *other* was thus enabled by the use of the camera in the name of scientific inquiry. This took place not only in the medical and biological sciences but also in the social sciences such as anthropology. In this image, taken in the late nineteenth century, the photograph is defined within the discourses of medicine and race, as well as the discourse of *colonialism* (in which certain nations assumed they had the right to take over—by military force, economically, and culturally—other territories and nations). The image on the opposite page is an example of anthropometry, a science of the time that used measurement to make distinctions between races. That these kinds of racist studies are now discredited should help us to consider the ways in which contemporary ideas about "truth" in scientific practices are the product of particular discourses at this moment in history, and can change in time as well, even if their recording technologies make it seem as if they have captured "universal truths." The nakedness of the figure of the Chinese man serves a very different purpose than the nude figures of art images or the partially clad figures of fashion models. His nakedness is coded within a discourse of science that establishes him as an object under study, and hence succeeds in effacing his *subjectivity*. The grid of the image defines him within scientific codes of body type and normalcy. The photograph does not allow the viewer to treat him as an individual, but rather as a racialized subject, defined as other from the viewer.

Scientific images span a broad set of roles, from categorization and the establishment of likeness and difference, to the presentation of evidence, to the evocation of new scientific frontiers. As we noted in Chapter 1, photography originated when a context of *positivist* science—in which the idea that we can know things positively and factually without the mediation of language or representation systems—was firmly in place. Today, however, there is a sense, even within the realms of science, of the power of language and representation systems, such as visual images, to affect not only how we see something but also our basic understanding of what we identify as objects of study and evidence itself. Thus, the role of images in science and as evidence is caught up in the debates about what *empirical* evidence is and how, if it all, it can be established.

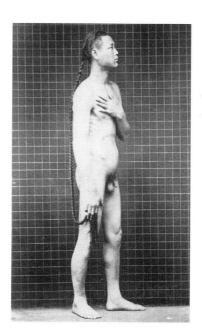

Anthropometric study taken according to the John Lamprey system of photographic measurement, 1868

Scientific looking

In the setting of a courtroom, science is sometimes evoked to convince viewers of the accuracy of the imaging system and hence the *authenticity* of the documents presented. In many of these contexts, the discourse of science is tacitly or explicitly evoked through images to lend authority to particular arguments. Images are seen as "scientific" when they are held to present accurate, self-evident proof of certain facts. Increasingly, though, the ideological limits of such claims to truth through positivist representation have become evident and are subject to debate.

One example in which the role of images as science and evidence was enacted in controversial ways in the courtroom is the 1992 trial of Los Angeles police officers for the beating of motorist Rodney King. A videotape of the beating, which took place after King was pulled over by officers, was made by George Holliday, a citizen who happened to witness the incident from his apartment window and, having his new home video equipment in its box nearby, taped the event. Holliday first brought the tape to the police. However, their lack of interest influenced him to turn it over to a local news station. The videotape was subsequently excerpted and broadcast widely on television news, and eventually became crucial evidence in the 1992 trial. King's lawyers introduced the tape in court because they thought it held incontrovertible evidence that the officers used excessive force on King. However, there was a surprise turn of events when the defense turned the tables, using the exact same

George Holliday, video
of Rodney King beating,
1991

footage to argue that the police acted appropriately and that King had been out of line.

For many viewers, as for the prosecution, this video carried a high degree of authenticity. Certain formal conventions contributed to the truth-value of the video. Since the emergence of video practices in the late 1960s, the use of low-tech, consumer-grade video and film has been associated with high authenticity in various genres and forms. For instance, in *direct cinema*, a documentary film style that emerged in the 1960s and 1970s, directors used grainy black-and-white film, hand-held cameras, and long takes to capture unscripted action as it unfolded spontaneously in "real" situations. In "reality television" shows of the 1990s, producers follow police on chase and rescue missions, using small hand-held cameras to document crises as they unfold, to create a sense of realism. Some contemporary advertisements use the realist codes of black-and-white video and hand-held shakiness to make their ads seem like amateur documentaries and hence their products more authentic. Similarly, in the Holliday video, the camera's unsteady focus indicated that it was shot by an amateur untrained in the manipulation of visual evidence. The video, in its original state, was unedited, suggesting it offered an unselective reflection of events as they unfolded. The position and angle of the camera made the image somewhat difficult to interpret at points, but they nonetheless conveyed a sense that the footage was shot spontaneously and not through selective framing and planning. The prosecution relied on this association of real-time, hand-held, spontaneous footage with reality to make their case that the video showed the facts as they happened.

There was great interest and concern among media scholars when the defense countered by using the same video footage to demonstrate a very different interpretation of it—that King made threatening moves toward officers and provoked the beating through his own behavior. The defense supported its argument with the same video footage displayed and altered through various techniques including slowed projection, freeze framing, blowups of portions of the full frame, digitized markings on the frame directing viewers where to look, and computerized stills (frame grabs) excerpted from the tape.

The method of time and motion study used by the defense is a familiar one in scientific settings. The idea behind it is that by slowing down or stopping a moving image, we can see things we might have missed when events fly by in

LAPD defense with still
of King video

real time. But this sort of abstraction can also have the effect of eliminating time-dependent aspects of the event, and hence can construct some meanings while blocking others. The original footage shows King's body reacting to the blows of the officers' batons and the jolts of a stun gun. In the slow motion and stop-action technique so familiar in televised sports replays, King's movements are separated by greater time from the blows, making his reaction seem like unprovoked action and his defensive movements appear aggressive. Ultimately, the defense won over the jury with these tactics of framing and interpreting the "raw" footage, so that the image appeared to document Rodney King "in complete control" of the situation, in the words of one juror.

The argument about representation cannily suggested by the defense's manipulation of the footage is that "raw" documentation does not tell us the whole story. We must break down and analyze what is there in the footage in order to see what the eye, or the camera, does not make obvious. The defense argued that appearances are deceiving, hence we need to analyze appearances to see what lies beneath. The defense's technological analysis of Holliday's footage recalls two different traditions of interpreting visual data. The most immediate one is the history of film analysis. Since the 1970s, film theorists have conducted analyses of motion pictures in which individual frames of the continuous flow of 16- or 35-millimeter images are slowed and selectively frozen. These frames are reproduced as stills and subjected to comparative analysis to discern aspects of meaning lost to the viewer during the images' rapid and fleeting projection. The idea behind this sort of analysis is that we can scientifically break down, abstract, and decode the discrete elements of a visual text in order to arrive at meanings embedded in a film's textual structure.

This precedent recalls a second, even earlier use of frame analysis in scientific experiments. At the turn of the century and later, scientists in physiology and other fields used photographs and motion picture film to conduct frame analyses in order to reveal aspects of a living or moving entity (such as a body or a machine). The idea was that by breaking down and freezing moments in the flow of a body's or a machine's continuous process, we might learn something new about its function—something imperceptible to the eye, imperceptible in the unaltered footage. Charcot's staff produced photographic series for this purpose. In the late nineteenth century, Eadweard Muybridge used photography in a now-famous study of animal locomotion. Muybridge set up elaborate systems of cameras and trip wires to take a series of images of animals and humans in motion in order to study locomotion. He began this work to settle a famous bet on whether or not there is a moment when a horse ever has all four hooves off the ground when galloping (the answer is yes). His project was one of many scientific and popular uses of the photographic motion study in North America and Europe during this period. Muybridge's images were understood at the time to be reliant on the codes of science, but it is easy to see the inevitable influence of culture and ideology on those codes.

Eadweard Muybridge, *Woman, Kicking*, 1887

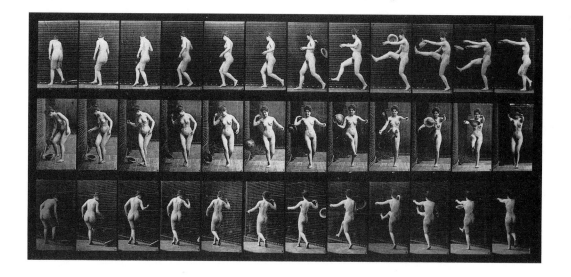

In the gender-coded roles of the time, many of these images documented naked men doing athletic activities, such as wrestling, boxing, and throwing a ball, and naked women performing seemingly mundane domestic tasks, such as pouring a jug of water, carrying a bucket, and sweeping. While the nudity of these figures is coded as dispassionate science, it has since been argued that these photographs can be understood both as gendered portrayals and as relying on codes of sexual representation and pleasure.[2]

The century-old process of time and motion study has been refined with the techniques of computer enhancement and image manipulation. Those who prepared the Holliday footage for the defense were able to change the image in ways that were perceived as clarifying, not altering, the facts. For example, computer rendering was used to sharpen Holliday's sometimes out-of-focus image and to emphasize areas of interest while diminishing others. Graphic markers such as circles and pointers were used to draw attention to aspects of the image. These techniques are common in the management of scientific data. Whereas scholars trained in visual analysis would see these techniques as ways of changing meanings, those trained in scientific imaging techniques often regard image manipulation as essential to the process of allowing evidence to emerge. Even more crucial to the defense's argument was the use of interpretive language that evoked the physiognomist's attribution of deviant behavior to racial types. King's body was described using terms that made it seem implicitly dangerous. For example, his leg was described by one witness as "cocked," likening it to a gun. The tacit assumption behind this approach to scientific imaging practices is that meaning is not self-evident in visual documents. To derive meaning from sources, we must first subject them to a process of abstraction or refinement that uncovers masked meanings. As we have previously noted, the relationship of all images to the truth is problematic. However, in the case of the King trial, the reduction of moving images to stills by the defense took it to another level of distortion, precisely because of the way each still could be made to tell an individual narrative. There are multiple ways to present a given set of images, and no one manner of presentation allows us to reach the unbiased truth. Indeed, even the prosecution engaged in their own interpretation of the moving image as closer to the truth. Rather, it is important to focus on the means of analysis themselves to reveal the ways that they embed meanings in the text. Images do not embody truth, but always rely on context and interpretation for their meanings.

Images in biomedicine:
sonograms and fetal personhood

Different imaging techniques have been central to how the interior of the body has been imaged and imagined throughout history. The process through which images change meaning according to variations in context, presentation, textual narrative, and visual re-framing is well illustrated in the history of the X ray image. When X rays were introduced as a means of medical diagnosis in the late 1890s, the public responded with tremendous curiosity and fear. The X ray image, essentially a picture of bone density, suggested to some that the X ray gave its practitioners superhuman visual powers, allowing them to invade the private space of the body. This fantasy took on an erotic cast, as seen in the work of some illustrators who made humorous cartoons, such as this one from 1934, and altered photographs dramatizing this fantasy in scenarios of a male cameraman using the rays to peer through women's clothing and flesh.

Ultrasound images provide another example of a kind of medical looking that has been invested with public meaning and cultural desires. Ultrasonography, the process of imaging the internal structures of an object by

Ballyhoo's Candid X-Ray Cameraman
"See's All—Knows All"

Mr. and Mrs. T. Sufferin Catts out for a stroll on the Avenue.

The Sea, the Beautiful Sea! Our Candid X-Ray Cameraman see through the Bathing Beauties at Malibou Beach.

Right: Our cameraman catches a

measuring and recording the reflection of high-frequency sound waves that are passed through it, became a cornerstone of diagnostic medical imaging in the 1980s. Whereas X rays create images of dense structures (such as bones) and involve the use of potentially harmful ionizing radiation, ultrasound allows doctors to discern softer structures and (debatably) does not damage tissue. The technique was particularly well received in obstetrics, where practitioners had long sought a means of imaging the fetal body and tracking its development and the identification of abnormalities without exposing the fetus or the pregnant woman to X rays. However, less than a decade into the sonogram's use in obstetrics, studies began to show that pregnancy outcomes were only minimally affected by the technique—in other words, it was not a crucial diagnostic procedure to monitor the normal pregnancy through these images. Why, then, was this imaging technique so popular among obstetricians, and why does its use continue in the routine monitoring of normal pregnancies?

One answer is that the fetal sonogram serves a purpose beyond medicine; in other words, it is not simply a scientific image but a cultural image. As we have noted before, images can change social roles and be used in new contexts, with art in advertisements and police photos on news magazine covers. It is a well-known fact that the sonogram became a cultural rite of passage in the industrialized West through which women and their families got their first "portrait" of the child-to-be. Future parents relate to the sonographic image, pinning it up on the refrigerator and showing it to coworkers at the office as one would display a first baby picture. Sonograms routinely turn up as the first image in a baby book. Similarly, science images are used in personal contexts. Beginning in the 1990s, patients undergoing ultrasound and endoscopic procedures (where a tiny camera is passed into narrow orifices and channels to record a moving image of the interior) frequently get to view their procedure in real time, and are then given copies of the tape to take home. Medical images like ultrasounds and MRIs (magnetic resonance images) have also been integrated into nonmedical advertisements to signify special care of the body or to evoke the authority of scientific knowledge. The role of the fetal sonogram as an icon of one's imagined future family is evident in this 1996 advertisement that plays on Volvo's reputation as the safe family car. This advertisement features a fetal sonogram with the message "something inside you is telling you to buy a Volvo."[3] It appeals to an imagined maternal desire to protect the fetus, while also playing on cultural anxieties about women's

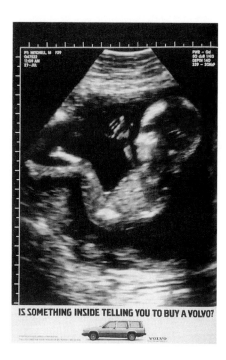

IS SOMETHING INSIDE TELLING YOU TO BUY A VOLVO?

bodies not being a safe enough vehicle for the fetus's well-being. It is the image of this partly formed "child," through its persuasive address as icon of family, that "tells" the viewer she must conform to cultural messages about the woman's obligation to minimize fetal risks. Here, the fetus not only resembles a child, it is also positioned as if in the driver's seat, thus drawing a parallel between intrauterine "safety" and car safety.

The idea that women visually bond with their future children through the image of the sonogram has circulated in the medical profession since the early 1980s, and prompted the claim, reported in one study, that the sonogram image may encourage women who are ambivalent about their pregnancies to choose not to terminate them. In other words, the image is understood to have the power to encourage emotional bonding much more than textual descriptions of the fetus ever could.

This has sparked a debate among cultural analysts and medical practition-ers, and it remains a vexed issue in part because the boundaries between the medical and the personal are blurred.[4] However, one point of agreement is that in the case of the fetal sonogram the biomedical image takes on the *aura* of a portrait, a document of the fetus's status as a social being (as a person) and not just a biological entity. We do not often hear accounts of people bonding with, say, an X ray or a bone scan, but the fetal image has evoked a kind of response more typically associated with a family photograph or home video.

This view of the sonogram as a social document helps to award to the fetus the status of personhood (and a place in family and community) more typically attributed to the infant after birth. Expectant parents and families thus project onto the sometimes barely legible sonogram character traits and aspects of personhood that are incongruent with the fetus's actual developmental stage. In this sense, sonograms serve a nonmedical cultural function that justifies the technique's use, despite the fact that there have been questions about its clinical or diagnostic usefulness in treating normal pregnancies. By saying that this function is nonmedical, we do not mean to imply it is merely cultural. The concept of a fetus as a person has been a central factor in legal cases that have allowed the fetus to be represented in legal terms by adults who feel they may speak on its behalf, and are pitted against the wishes or rights of the pregnant woman.[5] In these cases, the cultural aspect of fetal personhood shows itself to have an active life in law and the many other areas of life where moral values and social policy coincide.

Scientific images as advocacy and politics

The image of the fetus, whether as a photograph or an ultrasound, thus acquires meanings beyond its most literal medical meaning in diagnosis. Science is never separate from social meaning or cultural issues. Throughout the history of Western science, the idea that science is a separate social realm, one unaffected by ideologies or politics, has been a central doctrine of the hard sciences. Scholarship in science studies of the last few decades has forcefully pointed out, on the contrary, that what science signifies depends on social, political, and cultural meanings, and what kind of science is practised and rewarded is a highly political issue. We need only refer back to the now mostly discredited racist scientific practices of the nineteenth and twentieth centuries—such as the practices of physiognomy and craniology (skull measurement) to establish racial superiority of whites or the callous use of black men with syphilis as experimental subjects in the now famous Tuskegee Institute studies—to see the ways in which the ideologies that dictate scientific practice have changed over time. Hence, in Michel Foucault's terms, we can analyze how the *discourses* of science, like all discourses, change over time, allowing for new *subject positions* to emerge and new ways of speaking about science to come into being.

To continue with our example of fetal imaging, images of the fetus have become central icons in the debate over abortion in the United States. The compelling fantasy of fetal personhood that is projected onto the sonogram has provided powerful fodder for the anti-abortion movement. This was made clear early in the history of obstetrical ultrasound in 1984 with the release of the videotape *The Silent Scream*. In this production, ex-abortion doctor Bernard Nathanson mounts a case against the practice of abortion through various tactics including showing the viewer what he describes as real-time ultrasound images of a twelve-week-old "unborn child," an abortion, and images supposedly of aborted fetuses. Nathanson explicitly states that the moving image convinced him to change his political stance because it led him to believe he was seeing a "living unborn child" and not a mere fetus.

The Silent Scream provides many examples of the visual and extra-visual manipulation of images to demonstrate certain "truths." A rebuttal tape made by Planned Parenthood reveals that *The Silent Scream* consistently uses older fetuses to give the impression of a bodily form, and manipulates time and motion to make the ultrasound image of an abortion appear to produce the image of it "screaming." In attempting to portray the view that the fetus "sensed danger" with the insertion of instruments used in abortion, Nathanson sped up the supposedly real-time ultrasound image to make the fetus appear agitated and seem to throw back its head in a "silent scream," something the rebuttal tape assures us it does not have the developmental capacity to do. In their rebuttal tape, Planned Parenthood experts show viewers the "real-time" footage only to demonstrate truths not evident on its surface. Techniques like those used by Nathanson, the Planned Parenthood experts suggest, are deceptive and manipulative.

Whereas *The Silent Scream* banks on the power of images to reveal the truth, *Response to the Silent Scream* makes the argument that images are easily manipulated and can seduce people into believing things that are not true. Yet, the history of images demonstrates that the simple process of debunking a manipulated image is not enough to eliminate its power. In exposing Nathanson's manipulation of images, Planned Parenthood failed to address a crucial fact: images generate strong emotional responses in their viewers, whether or not they are "truthful" in what and how they represent, and whether or not we are aware of their manipulations. The prevalence of ultrasound suggests that people are moved by its images whether or not they are medically useful, and they construct narratives about fetal personhood despite what is known to be true about fetal life and development. Many of the people who participate in the culture of obstetrical ultrasound construct narratives about fetal personality, identity, and familial roles whether or not they know and believe the facts about fetal development—and about the potential of images to "lie" or "tell the truth" depending on how they are used.

It could thus be said that viewers/consumers of images often choose to read particular meanings into them for emotional and psychological reasons, and to ignore those aspects of an image that may work against this response. In his book *Enjoy Your Symptom!*, cultural critic Slavoj Žižek explains that consumers of popular media are not dupes of the media industry; they know they are participating in systems of ideology that work against their interests, but they participate all the same—and they enjoy this participation, as they should. Hence, women who pin their fetal sonogram up on the refrigerator and place it in the family scrapbook as the first portrait of their "child" are not naive victims of the culture industry that makes medical images into fodder for fantasies about family and fetal personhood. Rather, they are appropriating medical culture's artifacts to construct cultural narratives inflected by other aspects of their worlds. Likewise, viewers of *The Silent Scream* can be moved by Nathanson's drama despite what they know about his tactics of staging and narration.

It is this profound emotional response to images that has fueled the political nature of fetal images since the first photograph of a fetus was produced in the 1960s by well-known medical photographer Lennart Nilsson. Nilsson's images, which have been popularized by the book *A Child is Born*, depict fetuses at various stages of gestational development until birth. The book presents medical photography and other forms of interior biomedical imaging as nothing short of a miracle of modern culture. The "miracle" refers both to the process of human reproduction and development, but also, by implication, to the miracle of scientific imaging—the fact that the photographic camera can actually produce these images. The book is filled with glowing color images celebrating the reproductive process, lending credence to the belief that the visual is at the core of modern science and culture.

Some feminist critics of science have noted that Nilsson's images do more than provide compelling images of fetuses, they also have the effect of erasing

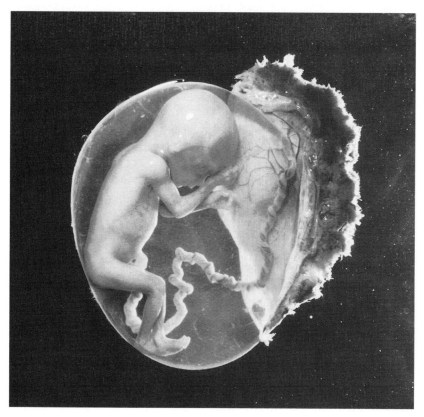

Lennart Nilsson, Fetus at 16 weeks

the mother. Taken when many of these fetuses were actually outside the womb, these images depict fetuses as floating in space, as if they are not actually within the body of a woman.[6] Hence, it has been argued that these images, along with ultrasound images, provided the emotional and political means for the interests of the fetus to be seen in opposition, in medical and legal terms, to its mother. The capacity to think of the separation of the fetus from its mother in social and legal terms was an unanticipated effect of these scientific images. It has encouraged a pro-life emphasis on the fetus's rights over the rights of the pregnant woman.

Images of fetuses obviously outside the womb and no longer living have been central to the anti-abortion debate. The intensity of this debate has hinged in part on the powerful effect these images can produce. While the reproductive rights movement has sometimes attempted to counter these images with equally horrific images of women who have died of illegal abortions, the image "war" in this context has clearly been "won" by those who have within their political discourse the image of a dead potential child. These images, which their advocates legitimate as science, are usually presented without any contextual information. They rely on shock value rather than reason to make their case. In the contest of advocating a particular political position, it can be said that an image that appears to award life, such as the Nilsson photographs, and an image of gore (such as those of dead fetuses) "speaks" louder than words.

Vision and truth

Underlying both of these stories is a tension between the idea that truth is self-evident in the surface appearance of things, and the contrasting idea that truth lies hidden elsewhere, in internal structures or systems of the body, and that scientific representational techniques may uncover evidence of these hidden truths. The idea that the truth lies beneath the surface, and needs to be seen to be fully understood, has predominated in Western culture since the time of the Greeks. It is a common sign in contemporary culture to use the image of looking inside someone as seeing their "true" identity. In this ad, understanding is equated with the capacity to see into someone's interior with an MRI image.

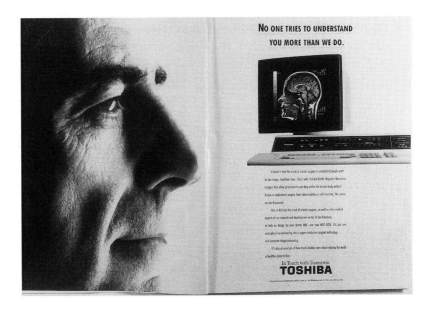

The idea that truth can be made visible was a topic of particular interest to French philosopher Michel Foucault. His book *Birth of the Clinic*, an account of the creation of hospital-based teaching and research in 1790s France, is pertinent to discussions of science and visuality, though its particular focus is the clinic and not obstetrics or law. Foucault describes the replacement of traditional methods of diagnosis by reading the surface symptoms of an illness with the practice of anatomical dissection and looking for empirical evidence beyond the physical surfaces of the body. In Chapter 3, we discussed the institutional gaze identified by Foucault in terms of surveillance and inspection. He was also interested in the identification of signs and symptoms, specifically how the "medical gaze" elicited truths hidden within bodies, rather than through direct self-evidence of pathology. Dissection rejected older ideas about where to look for the "truth," but it still adhered to an ideology of visual truth in which it was assumed that all a doctor had to do was gaze into the depths of the body for its truth to be unveiled positively and positivistically.

In the rise of the natural sciences in the nineteenth century and in biomedicine today, vision is understood as a primary avenue to knowledge and sight takes precedence over the other senses as a primary tool in the analysis and ordering of living things. Hence, an ultrasound image taken by a doctor will be perceived as more reliable than a woman's description of her bodily sensations of pregnancy—or what has been termed "felt evidence." Foucault identifies the introduction of a new (clinical) regime of knowledge in which vision plays a distinctive role in our regard of bodies and subjects. At the same time, vision can play different roles in contemporaneous regimes of truth; there is not one but multiple medical and scientific ways of looking.

The looking Foucault describes is crucially linked to other activities that give meaning to what vision uncovers: experimenting, measuring, analyzing, and ordering, for example. These are the activities that separate the idea of appearances as self-evident from the analytical clinical gaze Foucault describes. The clinical gaze leaves its mark in the particular "scientific" approach to images taken in the LAPD analysis of the Holliday footage, and in the Planned Parenthood analysis of Nathanson's use of ultrasound images, though to different ends. While these are not the only approaches to the visual we can find in contemporary science, they represent one major tradition. The paradox of the clinical gaze and its legacy, then, is that vision may predominate, but is nonetheless dependent upon other sensory and cognitive processes. This paradox becomes all the more pronounced as we move into the twenty-first century and the age of the digital image.

Once again, ultrasound provides an instructive example of how what we think of as visual material and visual knowledge in the digital era is in fact highly dependent on factors other than sight. We tend to think of the ultrasound image as a kind of window into the body. Through it, we see structures previously unseen and in some cases unknown. But in fact ultrasound involves the visual only in the last instance, almost as an afterthought to a process that is markedly lacking in any aspect of visuality.

Ultrasound had its foundation in military sonar devices designed to penetrate the ocean with sound waves and measure the waves reflected back as indicators of distance and location of objects. In this technique, sound is utilized not for hearing or communication *per se*, but as an abstract means of deriving measurements. The data measurements of sound waves acquired through sonar are computed to assemble a record of object location and density in space, but this record need not be visual. It could take the form of a chart, a graph, a picture, or a series of numbers. Adapted to the analysis of human bodies, the data derived from sonography is analyzed with computers and sometimes translated into graphic images on computer or video monitors or the construction of objects in three dimensions. Ultrasound is visual only in the translation of its data. In other words, we can derive roughly the same information from sonography without rendering it in images.

The paradoxical nature of this "visual system" that involves imaging in the last instance is compounded by the fact that sonography is a "sound" system that involves neither hearing nor the production of noise *per se*. It is because there exists a cultural preference for the visual that ultrasound's display capabilities have been adapted to conform to the visual conventions of the photograph and not to the standard of, say, the graph or the numerical record. In the practice of ultrasound, then, looking and the visual are, paradoxically, all-important afterthoughts. The visual may "steal the show," but it is not the whole picture of biomedical knowledge.

Genetics and the digital body

The desire to visualize the interior of the body has been a central aspect of Western medicine for its entire duration. Science has consistently embraced visual technologies throughout its history and those technologies have in turn redefined the ways that scientists, medical professionals, and the general public think about the human body. As we saw in our discussion of images of fetuses, the capacity to look within the body fundamentally alters how it is understood in cultural and political terms. During the last decades of the twentieth century, biomedicine introduced a broad range of imaging technologies such as MRIs, CAT scans, ultrasound, and fiber optics, in addition to the historical technology of X rays, to produce images of the body's interior. Increasingly, *digital* rather than *analog* technology is being used to map the body, such as the MRI image, and this means in turn that cultural concepts of the body have begun to reflect concepts of the digital. This is particularly the case with the emergence of the Human Genome Project, which aims to create a genetic "map" of the human genome.

Genetics captured the scientific and popular imagination at the end of the twentieth century. During the 1990s, genetics was the field that scientists and the public turned to for clues about the origins of everything from smoking to schizophrenia, from cancer to criminal behavior. This decade saw the rise of specialties like gene therapy, genetic counseling, and genetic testing as the world of science was harnessed to the task of mapping the human genetic code. Genetic science is not simply about identifying the genes that constitute the human chromosome, it is also about identifying genes linked to disease, behavior, physical appearance, and a host of other conditions and factors. Genetic therapy understands genes as they relate to medical aberrations and pathologies. Just as nineteenth-century scientific practices of measurement were used to shore up ideologies of racial difference, gene therapy is used to map differences among human subjects and has the potential to be used to designate those who are outside the "norm" in profoundly troubling ways. Echoing Foucault, Dorothy Nelkin and Susan Lindee explain that with the shift to a genetic model, "Images of pathology have moved from gross to hidden body systems. Once blacks were portrayed with large genitalia and women with small brains. Now the differences are in their genes."[7] Genetics has thus emerged as a new and deeply problematic marker of biological and cultural difference, taking the place of nineteenth-century physiognomy. Why has it been so quickly embraced as a measure of humankind? The answer lies in part in its rendering of the body as a kind of accessible digital map, something easily decipherable, understandable, and containable—a body that is seemingly less mysterious than the body that is popularly conceived and individually experienced.

The new genetics relies on a regime of knowledge involving different practices of looking to construct its truths. *Secrets of Life*, a public television series produced by WGBH Boston in 1993 and devoted to the history and status of genetics, captures in its title the status of scientific visuality in the 1990s. The secrets of life, this series suggests, are held within the chromosomes, which contain "instructions" or a "blueprint" for every living thing. One of the primary aims of the Human Genome Project, a multinational consortium of scientists, is to "map" the "codes" of the human genome, leaving no chromosomal structure untraced. Metaphors of maps, blueprints, instructions, and codes (as in the codes of life) abound in descriptions of the new genetics. It is important to note that metaphors about science are not simply ways of talking about these processes, they affect how they are undertaken and understood. These metaphors are not the constructions of a misguided media that fails to "see" science accurately. Rather, they are the chosen metaphors of geneticists themselves, who adopt these models to describe their own work.

In *Secrets of Life* viewers see row upon row of file drawers each containing sheaves of paper on which are printed genetic code. Genetic researcher David Suzuki periodically gestures to and rifles through these papers. He stresses the importance of completing the task of filling in the blank sheets with newly discovered code. When the project is completed, he indicates, we will have the fullest representation of the human body we have ever had access to. The image he offers viewers is that of a human body transcribed into thousands of pages of code—line upon line of letters in various orderings. This, he acknowledges, will be far too much data for scientists, much less the public, to view or comprehend. The task following the assembly of the data, then, is to make sense of this code.

Suzuki perfectly lays out for us another configuration of the paradox we have been describing. Genetics constructs the "truth" of the body as a secret that science cannot readily see. It claims that this truth can be uncovered if scientists around the globe work hard enough to track and make sense of the minute, invisible, and abstract code or blueprint in human chromosomes. Yet, even now that the goal of "unlocking" the code and transcribing it has been completed (in 2000), we are still unable to "see" the body. Another level of interpretation is necessary. To simply see the body and its surface attributes (hair color, pigmentation) becomes less meaningful as we become convinced that the real meaning lies hidden within, and cannot be reached by visual techniques alone despite tremendous advances in imaging technologies. The enigma of that which is beyond the visible increasingly takes precedence over the goal of making things visible as we move into the realm of genetic "language" or "code"—the body's new secrets.

The idea of the body as a communication center has been central to many biomedical scientific practices in the twentieth century. Medical researchers talk of the brain as a "communication center" for the body, and their use of language such as "code" and "messages" transfers onto bodily processes the human activity of communication. As José Van Dijck explains, during the same period that Marshall McLuhan espoused the view that the medium is the message, geneticists (and other scientists) mined his communications theory for metaphors to describe the body (its DNA) as a medium of communication. The body is represented as an entity that enacts its own sign system independent of the social subject.

In earlier epochs of science, we have shown, practices of looking were central to discriminatory systems. The identification of visible and measurable differences in skin tone and color and body shape and size were (and still are) means through which stereotypes are constructed and discriminatory practices are carried out. Today, these appearance-related markers of natural difference are supplemented or replaced by the supposedly more accurate sign of the invisible gene as a marker of difference. But when the marker of difference is invisible, are the marker and difference itself taken out of the realm of influence and debate? As an invisible marker, genetic code seems more fixed and more factual, far from the field of discourse, outside of historical context and the social field of power and knowledge. If differences are genetically determined and therefore immutable (except perhaps through gene therapies), as the outpouring of press reports during the 1990s would lead us to believe, it becomes easy to imagine that socialization may not be responsible for or effective in changing differences of mental capacity, physical skill, and other attributes of human beings. Nelkin and others have asked, is the establishment of genetic difference just a new way of justifying discriminatory social practices and eliminating social programs geared toward changing society? For instance, a hypothetical genetic argument could say that criminals commit crime because they are genetically predisposed to do so, hence we need not waste money on programs designed to improve their social environment and behavior. The uses of genetic knowledge thus far, from nineteenth-century eugenics to Nazi science of the 1940s to the far less sinister practice of genetic disease testing of the 1990s, suggest that the metaphors and representations of genetics have in fact been a compelling force behind the interpretation of cultural differences as natural and unchangeable at the level of the social. In other words, science does not necessarily become freer of ideology but finds new ways to make that ideology less evident and therefore more embedded and insidious.

The imagining of the body as digital takes place not only in genetic mapping, which produces an image of the body as a set of *bits*, but also through the increased use of digital imaging that makes bodies appear mutable and plastic, easily combined and reassembled. These concepts of the body can be seen as aligned with concepts of the *postmodern* that we discussed in Chapter 7. The visual technique of *morphing*, for instance, makes it difficult to distinguish between one person and another, thus collapsing the boundaries between bodies that were once considered inviolable. Morphing techniques are sometimes used to make statements about universal humanity and the blending together of races. Ironically, these morphed images recall the nineteenth-century composite photographs of Sir Francis Galton, which we described earlier. For example, in 1993, a special issue of *Time* magazine was devoted to "The New Face of America: How Immigrants are Shaping the

World's First Multicultural Society", a feature essay that revived Galton's composite technique from a century earlier. *Time* presented a computer-generated composite of racial types, represented in a portrait of a young woman with dark hair and eyes and a medium skin tone. "Take a good look at this woman," the cover sidebar reads. "She was created by a computer from a mix of several races." The image was produced with Morph 2.0, the same software package used in the production of *Terminator 2: Judgement Day* (1991) and the legendary Michael Jackson video, *Black or White*. It is a computer composite that is 15 percent Anglo-Saxon, 17.5 percent Middle Eastern, 17.5 percent African, 7.5 percent Asian, 35 percent Southern European and 7.5 percent Hispanic. Whereas Galton's composites gave us types in hopes of breeding out those racial types deemed inherently pathological, *Time*'s suggests an amalgamation of races that appears to embrace a more multicultural future society.

The visual culture of computer graphics fuels the popular imagination of genetics, creating fantasies for the forging of new peoples and new worlds in imagined and emergent genetic specialties such as cloning and selective breeding. But, as Evelynn M. Hammonds argues, this cover story enacts both a fear of racial mixing and a fantastic construction of a generic woman of color.[8] This fear and generalization about racial others are quite close to the conditions that gave rise to Galton's eugenics. Stereotypic racial typologies remain in place as this attractive, idealized woman of color becomes an icon reflecting the unattainable desires of those who brought her to life on the screen. As the *Time* article reveals, "Little did we know what we wrought. As onlookers watched the image of our new Eve begin to appear on the computer screen, several staff members promptly fell in love. This is a love that must forever remain unrequited."[9] While people wanted to think of this woman as a person, she is a *virtual* person, with no *referent* in the real world. Composite photography had long been in use in forensics and criminal identification, and the digital software of morphing and composites was partly an outcome of this sort of practice. Visual constructions like the "Face of America," then, are not simply benign imaginings. They can serve as material "blueprints" for the scientific and social practices that they invoke, including selective breeding. They make these practices seem natural, easy, and inevitable.

Artist Nancy Burson has been a major force in the development of morphing not only in the art world, but in the crossover between art, science, and the broader culture. In the late 1980s, Burson was instrumental in developing computer software that contributed to the ability to take a photograph of an individual and make it "age"—that is, to create a virtual rendering of the person as they could be predicted to look many years after the photograph was taken. This technique was an important breakthrough in the branches of government and social service devoted to locating missing persons and criminals, and images with "age progression" are now commonly circulated on flyers of those who have been missing for long periods of time. Burson's composite photographs and virtual renderings suggest some of the ways that the visual cultures of art and science are not as distinct as one might think. In the late 1990s, Burson created a series that commented in important ways on the legacy of physiognomy. Her series *About Face* is composed of portraits of children with facial anomalies. Rather than taking these portraits in clinical, context-stripped settings and poses so common in the institutional imaging of aberrant facial structures, Burson shows us these faces in intimate, highly personalized framings that evoke everyday life and the routine normalcy of those deemed physically anomalous.

In the 1990s, a number of artists turned to scientific renderings of the body as inspiration for art in the form of personal portraiture, commentary on questions of racial and sexual identity in science's visual culture, and as a critique of science's approach to HIV/AIDS. Mona Hatoum, a Lebanese artist living in exile in Britain, uses the body as a metaphor for social struggle. Hatoum turns the feminist phrase "the personal is political" to an investigation of the body

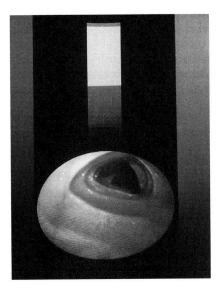

Mona Hatoum, *Corps étranger*, 1994

as a site of contested meanings and political struggle. In her installation *Corps étranger*, Hatoum includes a video projection of an endoscopic survey of the interior of the body (stomach, intestines, vagina). She explains that this introduction of a "foreign body"—the camera—into the human body represents a threat of invasion and violation that is experienced at other levels of identity and existence as well.

Contemporary imaging techniques such as morphing and *virtual reality* are indicators not only of the changing concepts of the postmodern, digital body, but also of the relationship between the body and technology. In many ways, Hatoum's work, as well as the work of many other artists, can be seen as engaging with the idea of the *cyborg*. The concept of the cyborg, or cybernetic organism, defines an entity that is part technology and part organism. The cyborg has its roots in early computer science. It was prominently theorized by cultural and science studies theorist Donna Haraway in her essay "The Cyborg Manifesto" as a means to think about the transformation of subjectivity in a late capitalist world of science, technology, and biomedicine.[10] Rather than suggesting that subjects experience technology solely as an external and oppressive force, Haraway wrote of the body-technology relationship as one filled with potential for imagining and building new worlds. Much contemporary work in cyborg theory postulates that we are all cyborgs, given our complex and bodily relationships with technology, for example, that the Walkmans on our heads become inseparable from our bodies.

While these artistic and theoretical engagements with biomedicine and digital technology have worked to re-imagine contemporary bodies and subjectivities, there have also been artistic interventions in the question of how science is institutionalized and funded. Artist-activists, specifically in the context of AIDS activism, have produced a large body of visual images that address the structure of science and the role of the media in reporting on scientific issues. In Chapter 2, we discussed the innovative use of posters to raise public awareness of facts about HIV/AIDS during a period when public officials in areas most hard-hit by the epidemic gave the issue little funding and attention. The work of ACT-UP (AIDS Coalition to Unleash Power) in the 1980s and 1990s introduced a whole new era of political visual culture. ACT-UP explicitly challenged not only cultural perceptions about AIDS, but also political policies around science and medical funding and research. ACT-UP's visual campaigns, which included performances, sit-ins, videos, and posters, were an important venue for the distribution of accurate information about AIDS

Gran Fury, *The Government Has Blood on its Hands*, 1988

transmission at a time in history when science and medicine were not working to get out the message. ACT-UP used images as an integral aspect of their provocative public interventions that aimed to get mainstream media to pay attention to the AIDS crisis. ACT-UP used images such as these, distributed as posters and stickers, to shock the public in the urban cityscape into thinking about the presence of people with AIDS and the inaction of the government in addressing the growing health crisis. The visual culture of AIDS activism constitutes one of the most transformative and effective interventions by nonscientists in the culture of science to date.

Popular science

As we have suggested earlier, science is not created in a vacuum or in a world that is separate from social and cultural meaning. Scientific ways of looking have influenced thinking in other social realms, and as the example of science adopting the communications metaphor suggests, the popular media are not without their influence over the thinking of scientists. Hence, there is a cross-fertilization of ideas and representations that exist with science and culture, which can be seen as well in popular culture. The representation of science in the popular media can have a reciprocal influence on how scientists do science. It is certainly a central aspect of how science is understood by the general public.

The genre of science fiction in literature, film, and television has had an important influence on the popular imagination of science and scientific practices. While much of science fiction can be seen as a distortion of what scientists actually do, it can also be examined as an important cultural domain in which both the fears about and promise of science are represented. For instance, the 1931 film *Frankenstein*, which was based on the 1818 novel by Mary Shelley, visualized the scientist Henry Frankenstein in a world of elaborate beakers filled with unidentified liquids and wrestling complex contraptions of electric voltage and switches. Science in this depiction is a mysterious and unexplained world that has the potential, through arrogance, to produce monsters and threaten humanity. Throughout the mid-twentieth century, in particular in the 1950s, science fiction film produced a broad set of images of science as the means by which the modern world would move confidently into the future, and, in the case of some films, the means by which the United States would win the Cold War. At the same time, many films depicted science as a potential source of destruction when placed in the wrong hands. Many popular films play into public fears about scientific practices that are not

James Whale,
Frankenstein, 1931

generally understood. *Jurassic Park* (1993) portrays science as an activity that is distorted by corporate interests. In this case, genetic science is seen as highly dangerous, with the capacity to create monsters, in the form of real live dinosaurs, that cannot be contained. Science fiction is a cultural realm in which both the desire for scientific knowledge and the fear of science out of control are played out. Some theorists have noted that science fiction has not only provided an arena in which public anxieties and desires about science are enacted, but has also had the effect of producing new, futuristic ideas about science that may affect the ways that scientists think about research as well.

Moreover, when the media and popular culture express fears about science often this is not because the media (or the public) do not have the capacity to grasp scientific knowledge, but because scientific findings may have implications and meanings for us that scientists themselves may not intend or comprehend. For instance, when X rays first came into medical use experimentally at the end of the nineteenth century, the popular and news media responded with fear and objections that these mysterious imaging rays might harm people. Amateur and professional scientists using the technique scoffed at these objections, chalking them up to ignorance and superstition. Yet for some time they were no more knowledgeable than the public about what constituted these "mysterious rays" and, moreover, their perception of X rays as harmless proved dead wrong. Indeed, the public's "intuitive" concerns were remarkably accurate and even prescient. Science and the popular and news media, then, work in complexly interwoven ways to forge new ways of looking, and new ways of receiving these new ways of looking.

Similarly, the realm of consumer culture and advertising is central to the popular understanding of science. Advertisers often use the discourse of science to attach to their products not only the meaning of scientific authority but also the allure of scientific mystery. It has long been an advertising strategy, for instance, to show the body in pseudo-scientific charts and animated graphics to represent what a product will do. A common example of this is the depiction of the human digestive systems as a set of organs, apparently separate from the body itself, through which medications pass. Advertisers often use actors dressed in lab coats like doctors as figures of authority when advertising over-the-counter medications, a tactic that produced the

Why do I use Curél?
Because for dry skin, it's the best
lotion on the shelf.

Amy Maskin, Pharmacist

I can use any moisturizer on the shelf. Why do I choose Curél® lotion?
Because as a pharmacist, I know clinical studies prove Curél
moisturizes better than Lubriderm®, Keri® and other leading lotions. As
a woman with dry skin, I know Curél works. It just heals dry skin better.

You can see the Cure in **Curél**™

well-known Anacin campaign in which actor Robert Young, who played the role of doctor Marcus Welby in the 1970s TV drama *Marcus Welby M.D.* states, "I'm not a doctor, but I play one on TV." In addition, actual medical professionals are used frequently in advertisements to lend a quality of medical professionalism to the product. In this ad, the endorsement of the pharmacist is intended to confer upon the product the prestige of science, precisely because she notes that clinical studies, as scientific evidence, convince her to use the product.

The use of scientific discourse to sell products is also evident in the marketing of cosmetics in conjunction with other discourses of gender and aesthetics. Science, these ads promise, will provide the technology to make you beautiful. Often, the distinction between scientific language and the language of beauty and appearance is made clear through juxtaposition. The evocation of science in an ad thus allows cosmetic ads, for instance, to evoke the authority of science, and to conjure the impression that a product has been researched in a laboratory and endowed with transformative properties. The Jergens ad on the next page also works to humanize science, by calling Jergens cleansers, "science you can touch."

Unlike the popular media and fine arts, science does not rely on a public audience in the same way for its approval and support. Until recently, it has operated with a degree of remove and autonomy, making it difficult to transpose methods for reading the "consumer" side of science. Entertainment, leisure, and culture are terms relatively remote from the way we think of science. Yet science has increasingly come to figure more centrally in the techniques and topics of our entertainment and leisure. We may dissect medically accurate and detailed simulations of bodies in CD-ROM games. Likewise, doctors in training will soon operate on simulated bodies so real that they bleed, in settings so well simulated that they are virtually real. We may participate in virtual reality environments fabricated by high science, and we use sophisticated workplace technologies on a daily basis with little thought to their intricate design and cost. Practices like computer morphing and genetic cloning or home video and institutional surveillance show us just how permeable are the boundaries between science and culture. Indeed, the term "science" in the twenty-first century may become as all-encompassing as the term "culture" was in the twentieth.

Notes

1. See the entry on physiognomy at the web site of *The Skeptic's Dictionary*, by Robert Todd Carroll, <http://skepdic.com/physiogn.html>, 1998, update 19 March 1999.
2. See Linda Williams, "Film Body: An Implantation of Perversion," in *Narrative, Apparatus, Ideology: A Film Theory Reader*, edited by Philip Rosen (New York: Columbia University Press, 1986), 507–33.
3. See Janelle Sue Taylor, "The Public Fetus and the Family Car: From Abortion Politics to a Volvo Advertisement," *Public Culture*, 4 (2) (1992), 67–80; and Carol Stabile, "Shooting the Mother: Fetal Photography and the Politics of Disappearance," *Camera Obscura*, no. 28 (January 1992), 179–205.
4. See, for instance, Rosalind Petchesky, "Fetal Images: The Power of Visual Culture in the Politics of Reproduction," in *Reproductive Technologies*, edited by Michelle Stanforth (Minneapolis and London: University of Minnesota Press, 1987), 57–80.
5. See Valerie Hartouni, "Containing Women: Reproductive Discourse(s) in the 1980s," in *Cultural Conceptions: On Reproductive Technologies and the Remaking of Life* (Minneapolis and London: University of Minneapolis Press, 1997), 26–50.
6. See Petchesky, "Fetal Images," and Stabile, "Shooting the Mother: Fetal Photography and the Politics of Disappearance."
7. Dorothy Nelkin and M. Susan Lindee, *The DNA Mystique: The Gene as a Cultural Icon* (New York: W. H. Freeman, 1995), 102–03.
8. Evelynn M. Hammonds, "New Technologies of Race," in *Processed Lives: Gender and Technology in Everyday Life*, edited by Jennifer Terry and Melodie Calvert (New York and London: Routledge, 1997), 113–20. See also Lauren Berlant, *The Queen of America Goes to Washington City* (Durham, NC and London: Duke University Press, 1997), ch. 5.
9. *Time*, "The Face of America" (Fall 1993), 2.
10. Donna Haraway, "The Cyborg Manifesto," in *Simians, Cyborgs, and Women: The Reinvention of Nature* (New York and London: Routledge, 1991), 149–81.

Further Reading

Anne Balsamo. *Technologies of the Gendered Body*. Durham, NC and London: Duke University Press, 1996.

Lauren Berlant. *The Queen of America Goes to Washington City: Essays on Sex and Citizenship*. Durham, NC and London: Duke University Press, 1997.

Robert Todd Carroll. 1998 *The Skeptic's Dictionary*. Physiognomy entry. <http://skepdic.com/physiogn.html>, 1998, update 19 March 1999.

Lisa Cartwright. *Screening the Body: Tracing Medicine's Visual Culture*. Minneapolis and London: University of Minnesota Press, 1995.

Kimberle Crenshaw and Gary Peller. "Reel Time/Real Justice." In *Reading Rodney King/Reading Urban Uprising*. Edited by Robert Gooding-Williams. New York and London: Routledge, 1993, 56–70.

Robbie Davis-Floyd and Joseph Dumit, eds. *Cyborg Babies: From Techno-Sex to Techno-Tots*. New York and London: Routledge, 1998.

Barbara Duden. *Disembodying Women: Perspectives on Pregnancy and the Unborn*. Translated by Lee Hoinacki. Cambridge, Mass. and London: Harvard University Press, 1993.

John Fiske. *Media Matters: Race and Gender in US Politics*. Minneapolis and London: University of Minnesota Press, 1996.

Michel Foucault. *The Birth of the Clinic: An Archaeology of Medical Perception*. Translated by A. M. Sheridan Smith. New York: Vintage, [1963] 1994.

Chris Hables Gray, ed. *The Cyborg Handbook*. New York and London: Routledge, 1995.

Evelynn M. Hammonds. "New Technologies of Race." In *Processed Lives: Gender and Technology in Everyday Life*. Edited by Jennifer Terry and Melodie Calvert. New York and London: Routledge, 1997, 108–21.

Donna Haraway. *Simians, Cyborgs, and Women: The Reinvention of Nature*. New York and London: Routledge, 1991.

Valerie Hartouni. *Cultural Conceptions: On Reproductive Technologies and the Remaking of Life*. Minneapolis and London: University of Minneapolis Press, 1997.

Mona Hatoum. Art catalogue. New York: Phaidon Press, 1996.

N. Katherine Hayles. *Chaos and Order: Complex Dynamics in Literature and Science*. Chicago and London: University of Chicago Press, 1991.

Ruth Hubbard and Elijah Wald. *Exploding the Gene Myth*. Boston: Beacon, 1993.

Roberta McGrath. "Medical Police." *Ten. 8*, 14 (1984), 13–18.

Dorothy Nelkin and M. Susan Lindee. *The DNA Mystique: The Gene as a Cultural Icon*. New York: W. H. Freeman, 1995.

Lennart Nilsson, with Mirjam Furuhjelm, Axel Ingelman-Sundberg, and Claes Wirsen. *A Child is Born*. New York: Dell, 1966.

Constance Penley and Andrew Ross, eds. *Technoculture*. Minneapolis and London: University of Minnesota Press, 1991.

Rosalind Petchesky. "Fetal Images: The Power of Visual Culture in the Politics of Reproduction." In *Reproductive Technologies*. Edited by Michelle Stanforth. Minneapolis and London: University of Minnesota Press, 1987, 57–80.

Carol Stabile. "Shooting the Mother: Fetal Photography and the Politics of Disappearance." *Camera Obscura*, no. 28 (January 1992), 179–205.

Marita Sturken. *Tangled Memories: The Vietnam War, the AIDS Epidemic, and the Politics of Remembering*. Berkeley and London: University of California Press, 1997, ch. 7.

Janelle Sue Taylor. "The Public Fetus and the Family Car: From Abortion Politics to a Volvo Advertisement." *Public Culture*, 4 (2) (1992), 67–80.

Time. Special Issue. "The Face of America." Fall 1993.

Paula Treichler, Lisa Cartwright, and Constance Penley, eds. *The Visible Woman: Imaging Technologies, Gender, and Science*. New York: New York University Press, 1998.

José Van Dijck. *Imagenation: Popular Images of Genetics*. New York: New York University Press, 1998.

Linda Williams. "Film Body: An Implantation of Perversion." In *Narrative, Apparatus, Ideology: A Film Theory Reader*. Edited by Philip Rosen. New York: Columbia University Press, 1986, 507–33.

Slavoj Žižek. *Enjoy Your Symptom!: Jacques Lacan In Hollywood and Out*. New York and London: Routledge, 1992.

The Global Flow of Visual Culture 9

Images are not only produced and consumed, they also circulate within cultures and across cultural boundaries. The media landscape of the late twentieth century and early twenty-first century has changed with the rise of a worldwide communications infrastructure and multinational corporations, the decline of the central power of the sovereign nation-state, and the resulting emergence of new forms of local and global cultures. Three central terms of these changes are *globalization*, *convergence*, and *synergy*. With the wiring of the world, the rapid development of wireless communications, and the rise of multinational corporations, many critics feel there has been a collapse of geographic distance and national boundaries—hence a globalization of economics, technology, and culture. The convergence of previously discrete media industries and technologies allows media to be integrated into the lives of people across geographic boundaries more smoothly and effortlessly. For example, the computer has moved in three decades from being a text-only instrument to integrating sound, image, and text, and will soon incorporate television and an increased mobility of images. The ability to transmit text, image, and sound in one medium and through a network facilitates global interconnectivity. The growth of media conglomerates in the 1990s, with ownership across the realms of print media, television, radio, the music industry, and consumer products, amplifies the power of the corporation to influence cultural practices on a global scale. This creates a synergy in which programming, production, and distribution are all held together by single corporate entities that market globally. This set of conditions has prompted seemingly contradictory tendencies toward globally shared visual cultures, on the one hand, and the rise of an abundance of local discourses and *hybrid* media cultures that defy categorization according to geography and nationality, on the other.

In previous chapters, we discussed the ways that images can move from one social realm, such as art, advertising, or law, to another, and acquire new meaning in that move. We emphasized how images are composed, and how viewers see them. In this chapter, we will look at the ways that media images, texts, and programs circulate in and across cultures. Our emphasis will thus shift from the individual's experience of looking and the qualities of images themselves, to the issue of how images circulate in an era of globalization—away from the materiality of the image and toward the more abstract terms of information and transmission. This chapter addresses how looking practices develop and are shared across places and among disparate peoples. It considers the politics of the global movement of images, in particular in the development of television and the *Internet*, with a focus on the place of looking and visual media in this world picture.

There is a limit to what we can say about specific viewers in the global context. In Western societies, there has been a large quantity of research conducted about looking practices and the meanings produced on the basis of particular sorts of images. Less research of this sort has been conducted on subjective experience and audience reception in regions outside the industrialized West. Discussions of the global often address how images are transmitted, but not how they are received and used. This dynamic will change as more research is done on the specific concerns and responses of non-Western audiences. For the moment, most research about global media and imaging practices tends to focus on populations and countries, not communities and localities.

The media have been important forces in the changing status of the nation-state and the move toward a global economy. Transnational and *diasporic* cultures, in which peoples are dispersed across national boundaries, are linked in part by consumption patterns and media cultures. Religious communities are increasingly forged across broad geographic areas through programming that includes radio shows, television shows, web sites, videos, books, magazines, and Internet listservers.[1] Popular television programs are imported and exported around the world, and in many countries television includes channels in multiple languages directed at specific ethnic groups. Television news has been globalized with Cable News Network (CNN), which distributes stories throughout the world. The Internet allows for global communications and international access not only to millions of *World Wide Web* sites, but to radio broadcasts and print media articles. Previously discrete media industries are converging on the ground of shared and overlapping reliance on *digital* technologies, as in the example of Internet radio and television access. The wiring of and increased use of wireless communication in the *Third World* is predicted to result in a further collapse of distance and boundaries of nation and culture, resulting in new markets for information and goods. Media and information travel more quickly throughout the world, crossing boundaries of nation, culture, and language.

Visual culture, which generally does not observe differences in language and levels of literacy, is key in this climate of globalization. Understanding how images circulated and what role they played to support the growth of a global information economy in the late twentieth century is crucial to understanding practices of looking in the twenty-first century. Among those media through which images circulate, television and the Internet are primary examples. Television, the Internet, and the World Wide Web have been extolled for erasing national boundaries and creating cross-cultural exchange. One popular take on the Internet, represented in the writing of Net guru Howard Rheingold, is that this medium realizes McLuhan's vision of a media-based *global village*, which we discussed in Chapter 5. In this view, the Internet democratizes society and collapses distances and cultural differences, forming communities based on shared interests across geographic, national, and cultural boundaries. This increased global traffic of cultural information also creates new markets. For corporations, for instance, the capacity to traverse great distances and the wiring of the Third World will create new markets for information, products, and services.[2]

The globalization of media and industry has also been criticized for facilitating unchecked capitalist interests at the expense of communities. Media scholars Herbert Schiller and James Ledbetter, for example, hold that the new digital media are in fact the tools of big business. Multinational corporations increasingly acquire businesses across the media and entertainment industries, expand their markets nationally and overseas, and exploit cheap labor and new markets in Third World regions, deepening the global economic divide between the haves and the have-nots. Their argument is that the corporate expansion of the late twentieth century is not dissimilar to the political practice of *colonialism* that existed in the nineteenth and early twentieth centuries. Corporate mergers such as the creation of Disney/Capital Cities/ABC in 1996 are particularly troubling, according to Ledbetter. This merger brought together five film production companies, four magazines, a book publishing company, a hockey team, a utility company, multiple TV channels, eight newspapers, and a radio network with 3,400 affiliates, to list just some of the company's holdings. A single corporation thus has an enormous hold on global visual culture. Resources behind this image-machine are vast: the Disney-Capital Cities liaison alone created a company with combined assets of more than $30 billion and a market capitalization of $50 billion. This global enterprise is capable of creating, packaging, and distributing entertainment, news and sports programming in the USA and overseas.[3] Entertainment analysts agree that the linking of companies in this manner has sparked dramatically heightened opportunities for market expansion—what the industry calls "synergy"—by vertically integrating production, programming, and distribution and also horizontally integrating across a geographic scope that no one entity could have reached alone.

Synergy, Ledbetter points out, is not limited to media and entertainment entities alone. Two of the big three-and-a-half US networks are owned by military contractors and the makers of nuclear power plants at home and abroad, ensuring that news and hence public debate about nuclear power will be controlled from within the industry itself. Schiller makes the case that the global expansion of corporations hardly translates into access to media production and information for Third World countries. What corporations are seeking is cheap labor, natural resources, and new audiences or consumers for their services and goods. However, the term "globalization" is applicable not only to this increased conglomeration of corporate interests on an international scale, but also to the movement of cultural products across national boundaries. We will turn now to the history of how television has functioned as a local, national, and global medium.

Television flow: from the local to the global

In Chapter 5, we discussed how television was developed in the USA, Britain, and throughout the world through different models of sponsorship—as both public and commercial television. Television has been a central tool in constructing concepts of the local and the national. In some of its manifestations, television has been the site of narrowcasting to local and community audiences, particularly in cable. In

Watching televison in
Abidjan, Ivory Coast

many of its uses, television has been a fundamental tool in the creation of national audiences. However, television is also central to the increased globalization of media, and has emerged by the early twenty-first century as a global medium. By marketing commercial programs overseas, networks sell practices of looking and ways of using media images to a global public along with programs themselves. With the globalization of markets, the US model of commercial television has made its way around the world, where indigenous programming produced through national services contends with US imports. The US system is often maligned abroad because it is so completely driven by corporate interests. However, at the same time, the high production values of US television programs appeal to audiences in other countries. This is in part because many countries do not have the capital invested in television equipment and facilities to make shows that are as slick as those produced in the USA and because US producers aggressively market their programming, just as industries market their products, in other countries. The US networks can offer their programs quite cheaply to the overseas market and still make a significant profit. *I Love Lucy*, *Kojak*, *Dynasty*, and *Santa Barbara* are just a few of the series that have had global audiences through syndicated runs overseas. For example, the global circulation of the children's television series *Rugrats* can be followed on the web site <http://saginaw.simplenet.com/ontv.htm>, where viewers can click on any of the more than thirty countries where the show was broadcast to get information about when and which episodes aired.

Third World countries were, and still are, an important market for US television programs. The term "Third World" was coined in the post–World War II period, during the years of decolonization. Western political theorists, after World War II, divided the world into two camps: East and West, with two major superpowers, the USA and the USSR. The countries of Africa, Asia, and Latin America, it was presumed, would have to join sides with one or the other of these "worlds." However, these countries decided to band together and establish themselves as a "Third World" rather than taking sides with Eastern or Western superpowers. With the decline of the Cold War, the shifting status of the autonomous nation-state, and the wiring of many Third World countries for global media and information systems in the 1990s, the concept of a Third World is losing currency, but continues to hold important historical meaning.

Television emerged in Third World countries not because of local popular or market demands, but because of smart global marketing plans on the part of mostly American and European industrial interests.[4] Some of the earliest Third World television markets were established by US corporations and, later, by US-European multinationals. In the 1940s soap operas were brought to Latin American audiences by US soap manufacturers such as Colgate-Palmolive and Lever Brothers. Called telenovelas, this form has become even more important to Latin American audiences. Telenovelas, 100-hour movies shown in one-hour segments, form a booming multi-million dollar industry with worldwide distribution. A typical telenovela is shown five or six days a week in the evening, and has about 75 to 150 episodes broadcast over the course of three to six months. Unlike American soap operas which go on forever (or until they are canceled), Latin American telenovelas roll to definite climatic endings.

The attempt to secure markets in Latin America was never completely successful for these founding corporations. The local junior partners who set up local stations in these countries were quick to capitalize on US expertise and squeeze out the foreign competition, and some countries set up quotas to limit the amount of import television air time. A similar pattern followed in some areas of Africa. In the Middle East and North Africa, the introduction of television was the subject of debate about the compatibility (or lack thereof) between television and religious values. American practices of looking were not compatible with those of less secular nations, where religious bans on the worship of idols and the representation of sexuality posed problems for the dissemination of imported television programs.

However, as these countries began to set up their own national programming and people acquired TV sets, it was discovered that program transmission did not obey the laws of national boundaries. Television historian Dietrich Berwanger points out that, for example, American programs aimed at US citizens working in oil companies in the Middle East would spill over into living rooms throughout the Gulf states. This spillover replicated itself in just about every region where the USA had troops stationed (such as the Philippines and South Korea). This situation inspired US companies to actively develop viewer markets in these areas. Similarly, India began broadcasting in Bangladesh, to the consternation of Bangladesh authorities, who then implemented their own national industry to respond to the penetration of the national imaginary by Indian propaganda. By the mid-1970s, every country of the Third World with a population over 10 million had introduced TV (with the exception of South Africa, which straggled behind because it was trying to develop separate programming for whites and blacks—ultimately a doomed idea).[5]

The prospect of imported programming raised the question of national sovereignty. What would become of national practices of looking, national image cultures, and national identity in the face of these trends toward imported programming and transnational image circulation? Who would be empowered to regulate the global circulation of images? Technical and non-technical international groups like the International Telecommunications Union (ITU) and UNESCO became increasingly involved in oversight. Television thus participated in the seemingly contradictory trends of localism and globalism. It has spread amidst a climate where claims to national sovereignty, expressed in the rise of national programming and regulations, came up against the fluidity with which global media including television, marketing, and the Web ignore the laws of borders. National identities and "local" ways of looking were readily tied to corporate marketing strategies that pushed global brands and global ways of looking through narrowcast marketing to specific populations. As Robert Foster explains, the global brand Coca-Cola is marketed through local strategies that make identification with the brand an aspect of an emergent national identity in Papua New Guinea.[6] It can be said that the national and the global are in constant, fluid tension. While the increased globalization of media venues may erode the centrality of national programming, it is also the case that media like television still function to affirm national ideologies and to give people a sense of participating in a national audience. Concepts of the nation, what it means to be an American or British or French citizen, for instance, are often an integral part of programming that traverses national boundaries.

The critique of cultural imperialism

There are several frameworks that we can use to understand the circulation of images around the world. One framework is the concept of *cultural imperialism*. Cultural imperialism refers to how an *ideology*, a politics, or a way of life is exported into other territories through the export of cultural products. Communications theorists including Armand Mattelart and Herbert Schiller argue that television is a means through which world powers like the USA and the USSR invade the cultural and ideological space of a country with images and messages, in place of an all-out military invasion. Television images and messages permeate the minds of the country's people with ideas about the value of US products, ideologies, and politics. In this view, television is able to cross boundaries and literally invade cultures in ways that bodies cannot. Television would get people around the globe to make global markets for US products, and promote global acceptance of US political values.

An extreme example that illustrates this point is the US government's Cold War era practice of transmitting a radio broadcast, called the Voice of America, into the frequency range of communist Cuba. In 1985, the Reagan administration instituted Radio Marti, a similar venture, and in 1990 Congress put $7.5 million toward TV Marti. These media venues were intended to provide the message of democracy to Cuba. After coming to power in 1959, Fidel Castro made Cuban television a national (as opposed to private) industry and used the medium as a tool for the establishment of a new social order. Castro spoke for hours on television every evening, announcing new policies and even staging trials of captured infiltrators from the USA and opponents of the new regime.[7] Some saw the radio and television *propaganda* broadcasts of Radio and TV Marti as necessary interventions in Castro's own media propaganda. Others saw this form of media intervention as an act of cultural imperialism rather than an attempt to make democratic choices available to a population held captive by Castro's media rule. We might see this as a war carried out at the level of looking practices. TV Marti, according to some critics, violated the spirit, if not the word, of the 1982 International Telecommunications Convention that determined that a country's air space, like its land, was a part of its domestic property and hence these boundaries must not be violated. TV Marti raised important questions about the right of a nation to protect the "space" of media transmissions, and to control the circulation of images in their seemingly immaterial state as they are transmitted over the airwaves. The debates over TV Marti have much to tell us about the limits of media globalization in a world in which information is quickly becoming the most fluid and transmissible of global commodities, and many speak of unchecked information flow as a democratic ideal.

The case of TV Marti vividly demonstrates that cultural products (images, sound, information) move across national boundaries with increased ease, primarily from cultural powers like the USA outward. Other analyses have shown that so-called innocent products of popular culture can have much more complex meanings when they travel across cultural boundaries. Communication scholar Armand Mattelart and cultural critic Ariel Dorfman wrote a scathing analysis of the role played by the seemingly innocuous figure of Donald Duck in promulgating US imperialism in Latin America, titled *How to Read Donald Duck*. They argue that Donald Duck and various other "innocent" Disney characters and stories presumably aimed at child audiences in fact were targeted also at adult viewers; that the narratives of these cartoons modeled for their adult Third World viewers a relationship of dutiful respect for and submission to US paternal authority. Donald Duck and Mickey Mouse covertly "sell" to South Americans the belief that the United States is a place whose values and cultural practices should be emulated, and whose economic presence should be welcomed. Mattelart and Dorfman point out that Disney along with the US government worked to promote "good neighborliness" in South America in the 1940s, just as US corporations were beginning to seek new markets for products and exploit the natural products and cheap labor available in South America. These authors share much with the thinkers of the *Frankfurt School* and their concepts of the domination of the culture industry which we discussed in Chapter 5. They believe that in a *postcolonial* world where overt measures of domination were no longer feasible, the innocuous visual images of Donald Duck and his cartoon cohorts were ideal venues for charming unwitting Latin American audiences into submission and conformity, making their adoption of US ideology palatable and even pleasurable. Donald Duck, for Mattelart and Dorfman, is an insidious icon of US imperialist paternalism.

Likewise, it has been suggested that logos of products with global markets—the Coca-Cola trademark logo, for example, and the image of the red Coke can itself—symbolize the global dominance of the multinational corporations that produce these goods. As texts, these images (as graphic logos and advertisements) carry widely shared meanings easily read across cultures, classes, and vastly distant geographic spaces. But they also contribute to the forging of local and emerging national identities through advertisements geared toward specific cultures. The growth of multinationals and the related emergence of a global information system to carry advertisements and other information results in homogenization—a collapse of borders and distances, and of differences of taste, language, and meaning. But they also result in the emergence of specific cultural and national identities under the sign of the brand, rather than under the sign of an empire. In some contexts, such as mainland China prior to the 1980s, the symbol of Coke carried the meaning of cultural imperialism, symbolizing the spread of US capitalism around the world. In late twentieth and early twenty-first century China, however, cultural imports such as McDonald's have become status symbols rather than symbols of cultural imperialism. Rather than signifying cheap fast food, McDonald's in major Chinese cities is now a place where young people who want to associate themselves with the symbols of emerging capitalism like to congregate and spend time.[8] In a globalizing world, images and logos can take on transcultural meanings. Andy Warhol's pop-art take on Campbell's soup cans, which we discussed in Chapter 6, conveys this sense of the product as symbolizing mass production and bland American universality—Campbell's soup, like McDonald's and Coke, his works suggests, is everywhere.

Markets of the Third World

While the idea of the global has taken on a particular value at this turn of the century, when corporations want to market themselves as having a global reach and transnational power, the local has also emerged as a marketable concept. Many advertisements attach the meaning of local regions to their products to give them a folksy connotation and counter their image as distant corporate conglomerates. This marketing of the local in relation to the global can be seen in the rise of the Body Shop, a successful multinational chain retailer of body-care goods and beauty products. The Body Shop refers to itself as a "multi-local" corporation, and promotes itself in the language of the *global village*. The global village is a concept, discussed in Chapter 5, that emerged in the 1960s through the work

THE BODY SHOP

skin & hair care preparations

vol. 8

BY MAIL · THE BODY SHOP · BY MAIL

free shipping
on orders over $40 through feb. 28, 1994

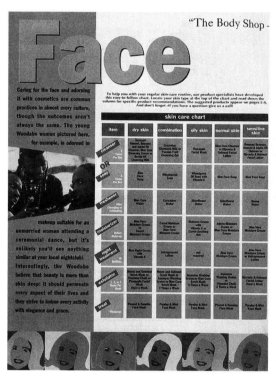

"The Body Shop -

Face

Caring for the face and adorning it with cosmetics are common practices in almost every culture, though the outcomes aren't always the same. The young Woodabe woman pictured here, for example, is adorned in makeup suitable for an unmarried woman attending a ceremonial dance, but it's unlikely you'll see anything similar at your local nightclub! Interestingly, the Woodabe believe that beauty is more than skin deep: it should permeate every aspect of their lives and they strive to imbue every activity with elegance and grace.

To help you with your regular skin-care routine, our product specialists have developed this easy-to-follow chart. Locate your skin type at the top of the chart and read down the column for specific product recommendations. The suggested products appear on pages 5-9. And don't forget -If you have a question give us a call!

skin care chart

item	dry skin	combination	oily skin	normal skin	sensitive skin

the issues

What color is The Body Shop?
Green, of course!

Since the day Anita opened the first store, way back in 1976, the phrase "Reuse Refill Recycle" has been at the heart of The Body Shop's corporate philosophy. Many of our original environmental policies — like using simple plastic bottles, minimizing packaging, and offering our customers a refill service — were adopted as good housekeeping.

But we also realized that taking these measures would also help reduce The Body Shop's impact on the environment. Last spring, in our shops across the United States, we ran a major education campaign, encouraging our customers to "Give Us Back Our Bottles!" And they do: by November 1, 1993 we had refilled 24,000 bottles and recycled another 300,000 that customers had returned to us.

ALUMINIUM

Where do all those bottles — as well as other waste plastic from our day-to-day operations — go? To a Long Island plastics recycling plant that manufactures plastic lumber, which is then used for playground equipment, park benches, and other outdoor furnishings.

The Body Shop works to protect the environment in other ways too. Many of our shops participate in park, beach, river front and highway clean-up projects, and some have even adopted their own "green space" that they visit and clean up on a regular basis. Through our mail order

business, we've run a tree planting program, helping customers to plant well over 2000 new trees across the country.

In Europe, we've also done public education campaigns with organizations like Friends of the Earth and Greenpeace. In the US, we're planning to initiate standardized environmental audits in both our corporate offices and our shops. This is part of our overall commitment to full accountability and transparency.

We will publish details of our environmental audits.

of Marshall McLuhan and in the context of global media expansion. It refers to the concept that the media extend our reach across political and geographic boundaries, bringing the world together—shrinking it, as it were. The Body Shop specializes in selling products produced in specific Third World locales to consumers throughout the world. It emphasizes education and awareness of other cultures through the consumption of products that were made by "others." The company does not directly advertise but produces brochures and educational materials that let the consumer know that it supports women and underprivileged workers in the Third World in the manufacture of their products. In this case, educational brochures about the environment and animal rights, a "community trade" policy, and even an international human rights award given by the company stand in for product advertisements in promoting the company. As Caren Kaplan explains, the Body Shop paradoxically was able to emerge as a successful multinational corporation by trading on its image of sensitivity to local politics and environmental concerns.[9]

Just as the Third World emerged as a viable market image in the 1980s, so it remained a strong market for the selling of US media images. Programs, production facilities, and ideologies were not the only things exported to the Third World. In almost all cases, television sets had to be imported. These imports constituted a major market for Japanese, American, and European corporations that had saturated their markets at home. In a given Third World household, the TV set is likely to be the most expensive family purchase, and in many places it exists in the absence of a refrigerator or even a bicycle. In the Amazon region of Brazil, battery-powered TV sets are found in river homes without refrigeration or electricity, and neighbors gather to watch the latest American series import outdoors.

Why is television so important to these developing countries that limited funds would be invested in the medium rather than in health or other areas of the economy? What are the meanings that are produced by this circulation of programs? Most of the approaches to analyzing global television stress the negative impact of cultural imperialism through media and information technologies. Whereas critics like Mattelart identify programming content as the conveyor of imperialist messages, communications specialists like Harold Innis stress the imperialistic potential of media export in itself, regardless of the messages transmitted. Frankfurt School criticism by and large gave short shrift to Third World media, focusing instead on US and European contexts and American industry dominance. But their theories laid the ground for theorists, like Schiller, who stress the negative impact of media images, messages, and flows.

Alternative circulations:
hybrid and diasporic images

In this global media environment, the different relationships of production and consumption are caught up in power relations in complex ways. Yet, this global circulation of cultural products such as television, and other forms of popular culture and news, clearly does not remain only within the model of cultural imperialism. Many contemporary theorists have analyzed the global movement of people and commodities as indicative of the ways that the model of Third and First World divisions no longer make sense, if they ever did. The movement of people and images around the world in the early twenty-first century is increasingly complex, with significant numbers of immigrants and refugees, a growth of *diasporic* communities (in which people are living in numbers away from their homelands), and *postcolonial* cultural contexts. *Hybridity* is a term used in the sciences to refer to plants or animals originating from different species or a person of mixed origins. It has been appropriated by cultural theorists to describe the mixing of peoples and of cultures in the era of globalization. With the geographic dispersal of peoples, the breakdown of nation-states, and the hybridization of cultures, media images are infused with a mix of conventions and meanings that derive from these various origins. Given these conditions, the idea of a First World that is neatly distinct from a Third World no longer makes sense. Moreover, First World conditions and peoples can be found within the Third World, just as Third World conditions and peoples can be found within the First World.

One model for rethinking the distinctions between cultures undergoing globalization has been suggested by anthropologist Arjun Appadurai.[10] He uses the suffix "-scapes," derived from the geographical metaphor of landscapes, as a framework for thinking about particular sorts of global flows. Ethnoscapes are groups of people of similar ethnicities who move across borders in roles such as refugees, tourists, exiles, and guest workers. The term "mediascapes" captures the movement of media texts and cultural products throughout the world. Technoscapes frames the complex technological industries that circulate information and services. Financescapes describes the flow of global capital. Ideoscapes represent the ideologies that circulate with these cultural products, capital, and movement of populations. Analyzing global flow according to "scapes" allows for a critique of the different power relations within these cultural and economic movements and exchanges of products, people, and capital. It also provides an alternative to the traditional model of one-way cultural flow, allowing us to see the complex directions and scope of an image's or text's global circulation beyond the implied one-way reach of, say, broadcasting, or imperial rule.

It is important to keep in mind that critics who use the term "cultural imperialism" do not always take into account the complex movements of an image or media text's flow, or the specific practices used by viewers to mediate and appropriate imported cultural products and images. As we have discussed in previous chapters, viewers do not receive media texts as producers intend them to be seen, or at face value. Viewers make meanings based in part on the context in which they experience images. Meanings are also shaped by experiences and knowledges brought to the circumstances of viewing. Viewers may appropriate what they see to make new meanings, meanings that may be not just different from but even oppositional to the ideologies intended or received in these texts' original contexts. While the dominance of cultural producers in creating and disseminating messages to varying markets of consumers is evident, it is also the case that cultural difference may allow for a broad range of responses to images.

Visual and cultural anthropologists have done the most toward providing accounts of how specific Third World cultures produce and use technologies and images imported from the industrialized West. Visual anthropologists long have been among the most innovative critics and scholars in the move to both study and facilitate the agency of Third World subjects in the production and circulation of images and media texts, rather than to market media to them or study them as consumers. Since the 1950s, some visual anthropologists have emphasized the need for active collaboration and sharing of power between media producers and the subjects of their productions. French anthropologist Jean Rouch produced a series of films in the 1950s in which he tried to get Western audiences to see the world through the eyes of the African people he filmed, inviting these subjects to participate with him in the scripting process and training them in film production. In the USA, anthropologists Sol Worth and John Adair taught members of a Navajo community in Pine Springs, Arizona to use film equipment in what became known as the Navajo Film Project in 1966. They allowed members of the community to develop their own techniques and conventions of filming, composition, and editing, rather than training them in standard cinematic techniques, and then showed these films as a way of seeing through Navajo eyes, rather than seeing the Navajo through Western eyes.[11] One film, *Intrepid Shadows*, by Al Clah, garnered attention for its unique approach to imaging, in which Clah explores images as a means of reconciling the tensions between Navajo beliefs and Western religion.

More recent efforts include the work of anthropologists such as Vincent Carelli and Terence Turner in Brazil and Eric Michaels and Faye Ginsburg with the aboriginal population of Australia. They launched various studies that supported the use of video by indigenous peoples as a means of empowering local communities and facilitating their unique practices of image-making and looking. Indigenous groups in Australia and Brazil have thus used television to document their culture and preserve memories and local knowledge. *Video in the Villages (Espirito da TV, Festa da Moca, Pemp)* is one example of work with and by indigenous groups for outside audiences. The project is part of the Centro de Trabalho Indigenista, a non-governmental organization. It began in the 1980s and receives funding from a variety of sources including US foundations and Brazilian non-governmental organizations. Making videos is only a small part of the project's function; the organization provides technical assistance to indigenous organizations who want to use video, and it archives

The Navajo Film Themselves, 1966

Al Clah, *Intrepid Shadows*, 1966

tapes. The project, which was directed by Vincent Carelli, a Brazilian video producer, consists of several documentaries. The first, *Espirito da TV*, is an essay about the way the Waiapi, a small and recently contacted Tupi-speaking group in far northern Brazil, have used television to document their own cultural practices. They have used video to discover the existence of other Tupi-speaking groups they had not known about, and to learn about the experience of other indigenous groups that have confronted common problems such as land rights. The third, titled *Pemp*, documents the recent history of the Gaviao tribe in the eastern Amazon. In the 1960s, the Gaviao were widely considered so decimated by contact with the West that their continued survival as a group was impossible. The video demonstrates through interviews, oral histories, and scenes of people at work, that the group has not only survived but has developed some approaches to living on the interface with Brazilian culture, both through its resistance to development projects (mining, a hydroelectric dam) and through participation in commerce.

Accounts from fieldworkers such as Carelli, Turner, Michaels, and Ginsburg all provide strong evidence of alternative uses and meanings of media among specific local populations, against the forces of cultural imperialism. These projects collectively suggest a much less universal and fatalistic picture of media globalization than a focus on advertising and corporate practices would suggest. In other words, there is room for autonomy and resistance to the forces of media globalization.

There are many non-anthropological examples of programming in the contemporary global media environment that demonstrate the power of cultural products to reaffirm ethnic and local values over the homogenizing forces of global media networks. In 1982, the Inuit people of the Northern Canadian

Arctic founded a television broadcasting network based on their satellite experiments, which had been in existence since the 1970s. The Inuit Broadcasting Corporation (IBC) was established to link Inuit communities dispersed across the continent, and to offer indigenous programming produced and broadcast in the Inuit language, Inuktitut, and representing their own cultural values. The IBC, with its Inuit superhero, Super Shamou, seen on the next page, and its own popular and educational programming and images, presents a powerful alternative to mainstream Canadian television and popular media images already consumed by Inuit people. The example of the IBC suggests that indigenous and autonomous practices of looking can not only survive in an era of globalization; they can thrive by using global technologies wisely. As the IBC web site explains, their use of media technology not only links peoples who are geographically dispersed, it also helps to both preserve and reinstate cultural traditions and language practices that had been lost. The IBC is, indeed, a model for using global media technologies to support cultural and political autonomy in the face of globalization.

IBC Programming Chart

Television series	Language	Subject
Kippinguijautiit	Inuktitut	Arts/Entertainment
Qanuq Isumavit?	Inuktitut	Live phone-in
Qimaivvik	Inuktitut	Cultural
Qaggiq	Inuktitut	Current Affairs/News
Takuginai	Inuktitut	Children
Takuginai	English	Children
Qaujisaut	Inuktitut	Youth

IBC produces programming that is internationally recognized as one of the most successful communication models for developing nations. Inuit communities are separated by huge distances in Nunavut, a region that makes up one-third of Canada's land mass. The only way in or out of most Inuit communities is by plane or ski mobile. IBC programming travels by satellite via Television Northern Canada. The vast distances between communities makes electronic communication of vital importance to the development of Inuit management

IBC's Super Shamou

of the North. Nunavut now has its own government, and Inuktitut is the offi-cial language of the Territory.

The IBC model is an important exception to the rule of global media impe-rialism in the age of cable. But even cable holds the possibility for supporting alternative and local cultural interests. Whereas in the earlier narrowcast model distance and geography defined the limits of programming, in the cable television era (in particular since the 1980s), "community" television can mean programming for a "local" population that is dispersed around the globe. This means that diasporic communities throughout the world, that is, ethnic com-munities living apart from their homeland, often constitute the audiences of narrowcast programming. For diasporic and exiled peoples, television pro-gramming aired across national boundaries and narrowcast to their own com-munities can be a vital lifeline. "Local" programming across the geographic expanses of a diaspora provides what for some viewers may be a virtual "home." Ethnic programming may link viewers to a community whose geo-graphic origin is no longer accessible—say, because viewers live in exile, because they cannot afford to go home, or because the homeland no longer exists (has been destroyed or overtaken through political upheaval). For example, Iranian exiles living in Southern California and other parts of the USA form the audience for Persian-language television produced by fellow exiled Iranians. This cable programming focuses on Iranian media genres, culture, history, and values. Media scholar Hamid Naficy has written that US-based Iranian television is a new sort of "local" or community-based television production. In its specificity and self-limiting range, it challenges the broadcast model. This kind of cross-cultural programming works in opposition to the model of cultural imperialism to a degree, in that global connectivity supports the maintenance of virtual local cultures in the absence of an actual (geographic) base. Telemundo and Univision similarly offer programming in Spanish with cultural issues and formats meant to appeal to geographically and even culturally broad groups of people (in Spain, the USA, and Latin America, for example). Language, and sometimes religious and cultural values, yet not regional origins or proximity, are what unify this group. But the programming is nonetheless "localized" or narrowcast in its maintenance of a virtual community. Networks like Telemundo demonstrate the viable market that "the local" has become for global media and information corporations.

The Internet: global village or multinational corporate marketplace?

While television provides perhaps the first example of global media, new technologies are now redefining the concept of globalization. Throughout history, the development of new technologies from the era of print onward has been greeted with both optimism and fear. In general, these responses represent technology as either a panacea for social problems or as a threat to the social fabric. The development of the telegraph in the nineteenth century was believed to be a means of achieving world harmony through global communication, as if the technology's capacity to transmit messages quickly would unify the world. The development of television spawned a different set of debates about the ill effects of the mass medium, its negative effect on children, its addictive qualities, and its potential to foster juvenile delinquency. New technologies often are seen as a threat to traditional class and gender relations, as detrimental to the family, and as highly destructive to existing communities.

Many of the utopian and dystopian narratives about new technologies are echoed in contemporary debates about the Internet. Concerns about the Internet circulated in the late 1990s in media stories about loneliness and even depression among users. At the same time, the Internet has been extolled as a forum for self-help and self-health, a means of establishing virtual social community, and a means for improving business productivity, curing social inequities and technology-access limitations, providing more leisure time, and even promoting world peace. The Internet is a worldwide network linking smaller networks of computers. It was begun with US military research in the 1960s and 1970s and by the 1990s it linked users across millions of computers around the world who log on from schools (designated by the .edu address suffix), research centers (.edu or .mil), government agencies (.gov), nonprofit organizations (.org), and commercial entities (.com). While many critics see the Internet as a new, more democratic mode of communication, others see it as a form through which corporations are taking control of public dialog and global markets. One utopian view of the Internet, promoted by the US government, is that it is a global information superhighway that provides access to knowledge and power to all individuals with access to this global network. This view is inherent in proclamations that schools should provide every child with a computer, with the implication that technology access is essential for the most basic achievements in life. Whereas television provides a one-way broadcast flow of information to the passively receptive masses, the Internet, belief has it, allows information about the world to be produced and to circulate more freely among users who interactively post and circulate information, write their own messages, and communicate with each other. Lines of communication are multidirectional and the medium is interactive, hence the experience is more fundamentally democratic than the experience we have with television. Everyone is a potential producer on the World Wide Web, the argument goes, hence the power relations between the culture industry and its audiences will be transformed. This is a very similar argument to that of guerrilla television in the 1970s. As we discussed in Chapter 5, many video activists felt that the very act of putting a camera in someone's hands would change the power structure of media. Some critics of Internet rhetoric caution that this new information infrastructure is really only going to allow freedom of expression within the limits set by those corporations who are rapidly taking over control of Internet "space." How the Internet will develop—whether it will be a global public forum or a global marketplace—is a crucial topic of debate, and parallels in many ways the debates about radio in the 1920s and television in the late 1940s.

The Internet has a strong reputation for its facilitation of interpersonal communication through text-based e-mail. This issue interests us with regard to practices of looking insofar as it suggests deep personal relationships can form on the basis of written exchanges, without experiences of sight and touch. The text-based virtual community model deserves some discussion because it has been such an important aspect of late twentieth-century social life in the industrialized West. We have probably all heard testimony about the Internet as a "world" or a "community" where people make new friends around the world, or where couples have fallen in love thousands of miles apart without ever having laid eyes—or hands—on one another. Many frequent users of the Internet present it as a life-changing integral aspect of their well-being. One of the most well-known proponents of this view is Howard Rheingold, who has written about his experience as one of the original participants in the WELL, an early Internet community. Rheingold's account, echoed anecdotally in hundreds of press accounts of lay Internet experience, emphasizes the strength of interpersonal and community bonds forged in the virtual communities that occupy the more social corners of the Internet.

For people who are unable to communicate in real life (or, in Net parlance, IRL), the Net can provide a vital connection to the outside world. For example, a person with a disability that makes him or her home-bound may find the Net a useful means of linking into public debate and a social life. The Net can be a vital source of emotional contact and even a place for education and work activities for home-bound people. It also gives home-bound people access to discussions with other people who share similar disabilities. For example, people with cystic fibrosis, who are sometimes home-bound, can log onto the CF discussion list and share their innermost feelings with people with CF from around the world. This kind of meeting "IRL" would be financially and perhaps even physically prohibitive for most of the people involved in these sorts of on-line communities. These forums also allow participants to diminish the potential for the experience of discrimination or stigma on the basis of their disability, if it involves visually obvious indicators. For example, a person with a facial anomaly can go on-line with the confidence that he or she will not be subject to discrimination on the basis of appearance. A different logic applies with respect to communication between Deaf and non-Deaf interlocutors online. The mainstreaming of the telephone effectively marginalized the Deaf insofar as the technology relied on precisely the senses and communication medium they did not have access to, eliminating the visibility of the body and the looking practices so essential to sign language. The Internet allows for exchanges that downplay the importance of speech and hearing by relying on text. However, according to French philosopher Paul Virilio, there is a serious social problem afoot when able-bodied people assume a home-bound existence to conduct their social life on-line and through media. He is skeptical about the potential for full social and political action in the realm of the virtually (as opposed to actually) disabled citizen who chooses to communicate electronically over real-life engagement.

These accounts illustrate the importance of the presence and absence of visuality and the visibility of the body especially in the Internet's textual worlds. The Internet has been characterized as a potentially dangerous medium through which people can pretend to be what or who they are not because they are not "seen," acting out on-line in ways that are deceptive and harmful. This ability depends on the potential for erasing one's physical, visible body and creating a textual or iconic body in its place. One famous story that circulates about the Internet concerns a male psychiatrist who, once mistaken for a woman in an on-line communication, actively assumed the on-line personae of a seriously disabled woman.[12] Through this identity, he garnered the trust and personal confidences of women in an on-line discussion group—participants who, upon learning his true identity, reported feeling "raped." Stories about men seducing impressionable female youth by presenting themselves in deceptively appealing descriptions and then setting up secret meetings IRL abound in cautionary news stories and tales of arrests. These stories served as the dramatic imagery for some of the advertisements of the late 1990s supporting commercially available Net censorship programs. Public debates about the unregulated Internet's threat to children have proliferated in public media in the USA at the end of the twentieth century and the beginning of the twenty-first.

For some analysts of the Internet, it is precisely the way in which the Internet facilitates role-playing and the possibility of playing with multiple identities in the absence of a visible and material body that makes it a unique and promising forum for human interaction and social change. For example, cultural theorist and psychologist Sherry Turkle has argued that the shifting of roles and identity on the Internet is indicative of the ways in which many people experience identity as a set of roles that can be mixed, matched, and imaginatively transformed. Internet role-playing thus allows people to create parallel or alternative personae that can facilitate their negotiation and transformation of identity in real life. According to Turkle, much Internet role-playing is testimony to the ways in which our selves are multiple, fragmentary, and complex, in contrast to the traditional *Enlightenment* notion of the self as a unified entity.

How did the Net become such a rich world of social interaction and personal enhancement? The history of the Internet shows us that these were definitely not the uses it was intended for in its early years. The Internet was originally designed as a communications system that would not break down in the event of a nuclear war. It started out as a military defense system, built under the name of ARPANET in the 1970s. The Net was built as a decentralized system to ensure that communications would keep going if parts of the system were destroyed. This model of decentralized communications provided a structure for new kinds of human interaction. The mythology of the Internet's rise includes stories about the government researchers conducting military network research using the system to engage in on-line dialog about science fiction and wine, and finally setting up networks to support such unauthorized and personal discussions. By the mid-1980s, nonmilitary networks had already sprung up to provide venues for people to converse in open forums about matters of culture and pleasure far from the original concern of national defense.

One early on-line model that demonstrates the Internet's potential for democratic exchange is Usenet. Started in 1979 by two graduate students at Duke University, its founders thought the system would be used to raise discussions about computer operating systems and networks. Instead, Usenet evolved into an anarchic body of newsgroups far from academic interests including topics such as alt.sex and alt.drugs. A world-wide public conferencing network, Usenet made it possible for computer users around the world to have public discussions, raise questions or problems so they could get help, and send e-mail to one another. Usenet was the prototype for the use of the Internet as a public space of communications open to everyone, not just to academics and military personnel. In this sense, we can see the Internet as fulfilling many of the concepts of the *public sphere* that we discussed in Chapter 5. But critics of this liberal utopianism are quick to point out that many countries—most notoriously China—have instituted strict Internet censorship and control, making the idea of the global village seem nothing more than a liberal fantasy.

The World Wide Web as
private and public sphere

It is precisely because of its decentralized technology, which has allowed it to be a truly international medium with a global reach, that the Internet is extremely difficult to regulate. The rise of the Internet has thus been accompanied by a rhetoric of freedom of information, and the desire to see the Internet as a new information "frontier" without restrictions of use and flow (in the writings of the Electronic Freedom Foundation, for example). Arguments about the Internet as a free-speech global frontier traversed by pioneering console cowboys hinge on the fact that it is a vast, rapidly growing and changing entity and is thus extremely difficult to regulate. US attempts to regulate the content of the Internet and the World Wide Web have been thwarted not only by the First Amendment right to free speech but also by the fact that some of the material in question is on foreign web sites and hence subject to other national laws. For proponents of Internet free speech and the idea of the Internet as an "electronic frontier," these obstacles to regulation are precisely what makes this medium a unique new form of communication and expression.

A point we want to emphasize here is that the Internet's apparent "freedom" during the 1990s was strikingly dependent on the simple format of text. This nonvisual means of communication took off during the same years that images and visual media were becoming more and more prevalent in other areas of life in which technology was key. Medicine, science, and the entertainment industry all saw tremendous growth in imaging technologies and experienced the introduction of new ways of looking during the same period that the Internet took off so dramatically. It was the introduction of *hypertext* and the area of the Internet known as the World Wide Web in the late 1980s that would bring together the Internet and the various technologies in play in these other areas of life.

The Internet was introduced when computer communications technology was principally text-based; the Internet was not visual because the technology to make it so was not available. The development of computer imaging, multimedia, and hypertext made possible the emergence of the Web as a commercial entity in the early 1990s. The Web is a region of the Internet linking vast quantities of information stored in files of computers around the world. Until recently, all files used one common language (HTML, or hypertext mark-up language). This graphics-rich, hypermedia interface allows access to files containing sound, images, text, and graphics. With the explosion of activity on the World Wide Web in the late 1990s, the Internet became a truly visual and aural medium.

The ethos of universality and the idea of a web-like structure that would make all information universally available are widely regarded as having originated with computer pioneer Vannevar Bush, who wrote of a "memex," a conceptual machine that could store vast amounts of information in "trails" or links of related text and illustrations. This trail could then be stored and used for future reference. This concept inspired computer pioneer Ted Nelson to develop the modern version of hypertext in 1960. Hypertext is a system that links pictures, text, audio, and other data, often in a decentralized structure. Hyperlinks, or simply links, are the "hot" words or icons that generate the connection when the user clicks on them. Nelson believed that the future of humanity was to be found at the interactive computer screen, a concept that was only a vision of the future in 1960. He presciently believed that the new writing and movies would be interactive and interlinked. Indeed, by 2000 one could download movies to one's computer hard-drive. Nelson's projections were bold ideas for his era. In 1989, having followed Nelson's ideas, Tim Berners-Lee developed the World Wide Web as it currently exists through CERN (subsequently called the European Laboratory for Particle Physics). The Web system was motivated in part by the rise of media-based information as a fundamental part of scientific knowledge, and by the fact that scientists working on CERN projects were dispersed all over the globe. CERN needed a communications system that could support text and high-quality images, and could transmit multi-directionally and globally. The system that Berners-Lee designed quickly gained great popularity among Internet users.

It should come as no great surprise that the biggest Web enthusiasts were those companies with goods and services that could be advertised widely and practically for free on the new audiovisual arena of the Internet. As we noted in Chapter 4, the World Wide Web became popular specifically because of its emphasis on visual images and its emergence at the same time that consumer-grade computers began to support *graphical user interface* software, making it possible to both generate and display images and icons. Not only was the visual appeal important in making computers less intimidating to a wide range of users, it also dramatically changed the role of the Internet. It was now possible to have one's own personal Web page, replete with images to which e-mail correspondents could refer. It is possible to e-mail images as file attachments. The nonvisual culture of the Internet was thus relatively short-lived. In the corporate world e-commerce became a booming growth area and a central force behind the growth of the Web. It is now imperative for companies to have web sites, and the moniker of ".com" circulates as a signifier of being plugged in to the future. In this ad, an equivalence is created between the infant and small companies that are "newborn" as a way of humanizing technology. The "dot com" sign is thus used to signify new technology. The e-commerce of dot com companies is dependent upon the image-based and hyperlink context of the Web, and could not have emerged in the same way or as quickly in the text-based realms of the Internet. Commercial web sites thus use images to capture consumer attention, display goods, and function as stand-ins for store aisles and "shopping carts."

The fact that the World Wide Web has quickly become a primary venue for business should not overshadow the fact that it has also opened up new possibilities for personal expression and political activity. Increasingly, people use web sites to create personal home pages in which they talk about their interests, pursue practices of fan cultures and other *subcultures*, disseminate health information, and conduct a whole host of activities that constitute personal forms of publication. Hence, more than the text-based arenas of the Internet, the Web has facilitated a broad range of expressive activities including new kinds of publications, ones that are cheap to make with access to the

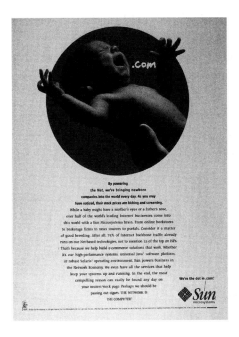

software, and which have potential global audiences. It can thus be said that the Internet and the World Wide Web have dramatically changed the power relations between producers and consumers in the mass media. Previously, in a system like television, only a select few had the capacity to create images that could be transmitted world-wide. Now, a web site potentially can have an audience across the world.

This aspect of the Web has had an important impact on the dissemination of information by political groups, and on the connections maintained among communities spread throughout the world. Many political groups have used the Web effectively to build support for their causes—to give information about their struggles, to raise funds, and to create broader communities. One of the most well known is the Zapatistas, a political movement in Mexico that is centered in the region of Chiapas, Mexico. Supporters of the Zapatistas have effectively disseminated information from the rebels to a world-wide group of supporters. This has involved both high-tech and low-tech networks in which, for instance, messages are hand-carried to those with access to computers. The dissemination of a broad set of texts on the Zapatistas through a variety of networks on the Web, e-mail, and on-line discussion has helped to build broad Mexican and international support for the Chiapas resistance. The Web is an important medium through which members of this political movement can present information on closer footing with the media messages of the Mexican government that they are opposing. The Web, because it is decentralized and requires relatively minimal production and broadcast technologies, provides access to visual production and display in ways that television never has. The Zapatistas have little recourse, for example, to the means to mount a television news campaign on equal footing with that mounted against them by state-controlled Mexican television.

The Web, like cable television, can also facilitate political connections among people who are separated from their homelands, by providing an illusion of a "place" where that group resides. The term "web site" encourages users to think of a physical place, although such a place exists only within virtual space. For people who have been exiled from their homelands for political reasons, this idea of a web site as a place is very meaningful. Pradeep Jeganathan has written about the sites that have emerged in the struggles of the Tamil movement in Sri Lanka.[13] The Tamil nation, called Tamileelam, which is held by its proponents to exist in certain provinces of Sri Lanka, is not recognized by the government of Sri Lanka. Under political duress, many Tamils migrated out from Sri Lanka in the 1980s to places throughout India, Europe, Canada, and Australia. The web sites that sprang up to unite these Tamil populations form a virtual place in which this "nation" can exist. The location of the Tamil nation at eelam.com is somewhere in cyberspace, not in the desired location in Sri Lanka. This cyberspace address is a symbolic site where this diasporic community maintains and generates unity in the absence of a real geographic home. In its existence on the Web, according to Jeganathan, where it is equidistant from all places in the world, eelam.com allows for the possibility that that geographic place will be reclaimed. The difference between this virtual world and that offered in narrowcast cable programming is that information can be communicated much more quickly and fluidly. The site allows for active participation of site participants, who author messages as well as view and read materials that can be posted and changed regularly.

The challenge of the Internet to
privacy, censorship, and free speech

The sites of the World Wide Web are thus "places" where people participate in a diverse set of activities and practices in a global network. The explosion of commerce in the audio-visual medium of the Web has created a context in which the regulation of the circulation of images on a global basis has been challenged dramatically. By comparison, most countries remain able to regulate in some fashion the television programming that is imported to their television systems. The World Wide Web is a highly global entity, making it hard if not impossible to regulate the images that are exchanged on it. One area of the Web in which issues of regulation, access, and rights is played out with great force is on-line pornography. Like every other industry, the pornography industry discovered the benefits of web marketing early on in the Web's existence. Although the Web increased marketing prospects by exploding the geographic market base for pornography companies, it also raised problems having to do with surveillance. No sooner did these sites appear on the Web than watchdog groups and concerned citizens began to petition governments to shut them down, or provide means of regulating access to them. The stated fear was that innocent children might stumble across (or look for) pornographic sites during unsupervised web surfing. In the mid-1990s, the media carried stories about children "caught looking" and children in dangerous encounters with pornographers soliciting photographs and real-life meetings. Web surveillance and regulation became overwhelmingly the demand and the expectation of watchdog groups.

Because in the United States the First Amendment protects freedom of speech, and does not allow restrictions deemed to protect children to keep information from adults at the same time, there have thus far been no attempts to restrict the Internet that have survived legally. This has shifted the focus of concern about the Internet to the level of the users and their capacity to restrict their own access to web sites. In response, a series of US companies began to release software aimed at blocking access to sites. Internet filter programs with such names as SurfWatch, NetNanny, Cyberpatrol, and Cybersitter allow users to limit access to different kinds of web sites, and usually maintain databases of sites that are regarded as not for children and known explicit or obscene web sites. Some of these programs allow parents to keep track of all the sites their children visit and to alert them when their children have accessed new sites. Finally, the US government stepped up its surveillance and control measures and began to close down sites deemed a threat to the public. One of the most publicized attempts to remove a web site in the late 1990s did not involve pornography but rather an anti-abortion group that kept a hit-list of medical personnel that included the name of a Buffalo, New York, physician who was assassinated in his home. All of these attempts to restrict the Web are counter to the ideology of freedom of information that has been central to its proponents.

It is also the case that the demand for image (and text) surveillance and control has had the sometimes unintended effect of restricting other kinds of content on the Web. For instance, a significant amount of material available on the Web serves medical and educational purposes, and may incorporate graphic anatomical imagery that is not restricted to intended viewers. These images of bodies are not intended as pornography, yet can easily be misconstrued by relatively crude censorship programs as pornographic. Some programs have been deliberately designed to prevent access to any site that deals with issues of gay life. These kinds of conflicts indicate the way in which context is particularly important to the specific meaning of images and words. As we have discussed in other chapters, *semiotics* demonstrates that context contributes in a major way to the meaning of images. The Web compounds this issue by rendering context more complex. Anyone can access much of what is "out there" on the Web, and Web-based material can be imported into any context with the right hardware and software. What happens, then, when image context becomes as uncontrolled and arbitrary as it does on the Web? This raises, in addition, the question of image copyright and authorship.

The images on the Web are digital images, which means they are encoded so that they can be easily moved and downloaded. As we discussed in Chapter 4, this dramatically changes the relationship of producers and users. Anyone with access to the Web through a computer can thus have at their disposal a wide range of images that they can manipulate, rework, place in new contexts, and make their "own." As we stated before, the idea of the Internet as a domain in which everyone is a "publisher" has dramatically changed notions of authorship and copyright, in particular in a global framework. Computer graphics reproduction and simulation capabilities make possible the exact replication of digital images in a context such as the Web. This poses a very powerful threat to the traditional tenets of copyright law, which hold that an author or artist has the sole right to commercial gain from the use of their work and the right to restrict its use. Digital reproduction in the context of the Web is even more of a threat to the idea of the valued artistic original, since it can be done without even physically touching the original, given the availability of works on-line. This could prompt a crisis for those who work in various areas of visual culture. Increasingly, individuals and companies that own the copyright to images have secured broad rights to their digital versions. New companies, such as the Bill Gates-owned Corbis, have acquired vast digital image banks in order to profit from the demand for reproductions—a demand that grows in an increasingly media-based society. In this new media context, those without access will become increasingly marginalized in a world where media is currency and being on-line is equated with being publicly active.

The place of the visual in the new millennium

It is impossible to talk about computer media as a purely visual set of forms—forms primarily about looking. We live in an era of media convergence. To speak of images apart from sound, dimensional form, and other modes of representation is to overlook the crucial fact that media convergence is key to the Web's appeal as a global communications system. The idea of convergence has always been implied in the notion of a global village, with its image of connecting people across geographic distances. It is the hope of many communication and technology theorists that this convergence will collapse distances and democratize knowledge. Key to this is the idea that image, text, sound, and objects also converge in the social production of meaning, and can no longer be studied in isolation. Yet at the same time, the global exchange of media in the early twenty-first century demonstrates to us the complex power relations that are always a part of the production and circulation of images. The desire to situate oneself within the local and the national is always in tension with an embrace of the global; the movement of cultural products and visual images throughout the world is always about the production of different kinds of cultural meanings.

In this book, we have examined many of the changes that have taken place in the world of visual images throughout history, and focused in particular on the ways that image technologies of the nineteenth and twentieth centuries have impacted the kinds of images that are produced, how they are consumed and understood, and how they circulate in and across cultures. This complex history shows us how difficult it is to predict the future of images in the twenty-first century. While convergence is the focus of the industry, it is also the case that people have important ritualistic relationships and distinct *phenomenological* experiences with different media that may make them resistant to media convergence. Clearly, the shift toward digital images will continue to impact social notions of photographic truth and the visual aspects of legal and scientific evidence. Yet, at the same time, that may also prompt a renewed interest in the traditional photograph as a cultural artifact. While their technological status may change, the cultural and social roles of images will remain fundamental. If one thing is certain, it is that visual images will inevitably play a central role in the culture of the twenty-first century.

Notes

1. See Linda Kintz and Julia Lesage, eds., *Media, Culture, and the Religious Right* (Minneapolis and London: University of Minnesota Press, 1998).
2. See Frances Cairncross, *The Death of Distance: How the Communication Revolution Will Change Our Lives* (Boston: Harvard Business School Press, 1997).
3. See the Disney web site account of the 1996 merger with Capital Cities/ABC, <http://disney.go.com/investors/annual/capcitie.html>.
4. Dietrich Berwanger, "The Third World," in *Television: An International History*, edited by Anthony Smith (New York and Oxford: Oxford University Press, 1998), 188–200.
5. Berwanger, "The Third World."
6. Robert Foster, "The Commercial Construction of 'New Nations,'" *Journal of Material Culture*, 4 (3) (1998), 262–82.

7. On this issue, see Michael Tracey, "Non-Fiction Television," in *Television: An International History*, 78.

8. Yunxiang Yan, "McDonald's in Beijing: The Localization of Americana," in *Golden Arches East: McDonald's in East Asia*, edited by James L. Watson (Stanford, Calif.: Stanford University Press, 1997), 39–76.

9. This analysis of the Body Shop is based on Caren Kaplan, "A World Without Boundaries: The Body Shop's Trans/National Geographics," *Social Text*, 13 (2) (Summer 1995), 45–66.

10. Arjun Appadurai, "Disjuncture and Difference in the Global Cultural Economy," in *Modernity at Large: Cultural Dimensions of Globalization* (Minneapolis and London: University of Minnesota Press, 1996), 27–47.

11. Sol Worth and John Adair, *Through Navajo Eyes* (Bloomington: Indiana University Press, 1972).

12. See Allucquere Rosanne Stone, *The War of Desire and Technology at the Close of the Mechanical Age* (Cambridge, Mass. and London: MIT Press, 1995), 65–81.

13. Pradeep Jeganathan, "Eelam.com: Place, Nation, and Imagi-Nation in Cyberspace," *Public Culture*, 10 (3) (1998), 515–28.

Further Reading

Robert C. Allen, ed. *To be continued . . . : Soap Operas around the World*. New York and London: Routledge, 1995.

Arjun Appadurai. "Disjuncture and Difference in the Global Cultural Economy." In *Modernity at Large: Cultural Dimensions of Globalization*. Minneapolis and London: University of Minnesota Press, 1996, 27–47.

Pat Aufderheide. "Grassroots Video in Latin America" and "Making Video with Brazilian Indians." In *The Daily Planet: A Critic on the Capitalist Culture Beat*. Minneapolis and London: University of Minnesota Press, 2000, 257–88.

John Perry Barlow. "Crime and Puzzlement." In *High Noon of the Electronic Frontier: Conceptual Issues in Cyberspace*. Edited by Peter Ludlow. Cambridge, Mass. and London: MIT Press, 1996, 459–86.

Dietrich Berwanger. "The Third World." In *Television: An International History*. Second Edition. Edited by Anthony Smith. New York and Oxford: Oxford University Press, 1998, 188–200.

William Boddy. "The Beginnings of American Television." In *Television: An International History*. Second Edition. Edited by Anthony Smith. New York and Oxford: Oxford University Press, 1998, 23–37.

——*Fifties Television: The Industry and Its Critics*. Urbana: University of Illinois Press, 1992.

Frances Cairncross. *The Death of Distance: How the Communication Revolution Will Change Our Lives*. Boston: Harvard Business School Press, 1997.

Vincent Carelli. *O Espirito da TV (The Spirit of TV)*. *Video in the Villages*. Central de Trabalho Indigenista. (1990) 18 min.

Leslie Devereaux and Roger Hillman, eds. *Fields of Vision: Essays in Film Studies, Visual Anthropology, and Photography*. Berkeley and London: University of California Press, 1995.

Ariel Dorfman and Armand Mattelart. *How to Read Donald Duck: Imperialist Ideology in the Disney Comic*. New York: International General, 1984.

Timothy Druckrey, ed. *Electronic Culture: Technology and Visual Representation*. New York: Aperture, 1996.

Elizabeth Edwards, ed. *Anthropology & Photography 1860–1920*. New Haven and London: Yale University Press, 1992.

Robert Foster. "The Commercial Construction of 'New Nations.'" *Journal of Material Culture*, 4 (3) (1998), 262–82.

Elizabeth Fox. *Latin American Broadcasting: From Tango to Telenovela*. Luton, UK: University of Luton, 1997.

Faye Ginsburg. "Indigenous Media: Faustian Contract or Global Village?" *Cultural Anthropology*, 6 (1) (1991), 94–114.

Harold A. Innis. *Empire and Communications*. New York and Oxford: Oxford University Press, 1950.

Inuit Broadcasting Corporation, Suite 703, 251 Laurier Ave. W. Ottawa, Ontario K1P 5J6. e-mail: ibcicsl@sonetis.com, <http://siksik.learnnet.nt.ca/tvnc/Members/ibc.html>.

Pradeep Jeganathan. "Eelam.com: Place, Nation, and Imagi-Nation in Cyberspace." *Public Culture*, 10 (3) (1998), 515–28.

Caren Kaplan. "A World Without Boundaries: The Body Shop's Trans/National Geographics." *Social Text*, 13 (2) (Summer 1995), 45–66.

Linda Kintz and Julia Lesage, eds. *Media, Culture, and the Religious Right*. Minneapolis and London: University of Minnesota Press, 1998.

James Ledbetter. "Merge Overkill: When Big Media Gets Too Big, What Happens to Debate?" *Village Voice* (26 January 1996), 30–35.

Perry Ludlow, ed. *High Noon on the Electronic Frontier: Conceptual Issues in Cyberspace*. Cambridge, Mass. and London: MIT Press, 1996.

Michèle Mattelart and Armand Mattelart. *The Carnival of Images: Brazilian Television Fiction*. Translated by David Buxton. New York: Bergin & Garvey, 1990. Republished by Westport, Conn.: Greenwood.

Eric Michaels. *Bad Aboriginal Art: Traditional, Media, and Technological Horizons*. Minneapolis and London: University of Minnesota Press, 1994.

David Morley and Kevin Robbins. *Spaces of Identity: Global Media, Electronic Landscapes, and Cultural Boundaries*. New York and London: Routledge, 1995.

Hamid Naficy. *The Making of Exile Cultures: Iranian Television in Los Angeles*. Minneapolis and London: University of Minnesota Press, 1993.

Howard Rheingold. *The Virtual Community: Homesteading on the Electronic Frontier*. New York: Harper Perennial, 1993.

Herbert I. Schiller. "The Global Information Highway: Project for an Ungovernable World." In *Resisting the Virtual Life: The Culture and Politics of Information*. Edited by James Brook and Iain A. Boal. San Francisco: City Lights, 1995, 17–33.

Donald A. Schon, Bish Sanyal, and William J. Mitchell, eds. *High Technology and Low-Income Communities: Prospects for the Positive Use of Advanced Information Technology*. Cambridge, Mass. and London: MIT Press, 1999.

Ella Shohat and Robert Stam. *Unthinking Eurocentrism: Multiculturalism and the Media*. New York and London: Routledge, 1994.

John Sinclair. *Latin American Television: A Global View*. New York and Oxford: Oxford University Press, 1999.

Anthony Smith, ed. *Television: An International History*. Second Edition. New York and Oxford: Oxford University Press, 1998.

G. Smith. "Space Age Shamans: The Videotapes." *Americas*, 41 (2) (1989), 28–31.

Roland Soong. "Telenovelas in Latin America," 1999, <http://www.zonalatina.com/Zldata70.htm>.

Allucquere Rosanne Stone. *The War of Desire and Technology at the Close of the Mechanical Age*. Cambridge, Mass. and London: MIT Press, 1995.

Sherry Turkle. *Life on the Screen: Identity in the Age of the Internet*. New York: Touchstone, 1995.

Terence Turner. "Defiant Images: The Kayapo Appropriation of Video." *Anthropology Today*, 8 (6) (1992), 5–16.

Nico Vink. *The Telenovela and Emancipation: A Study of Television and Social Change in Brazil*. Amsterdam: Royal Tropical Institute, 1988.

Paul Virilio. *The Art of the Motor*. Translated by Julie Rose. Minneapolis and London: University of Minnesota Press, 1995.

Sol Worth. *Studying Visual Communication*. Edited by Larry Gross. Philadelphia: University of Pennsylvania Press, 1981.

——and John Adair. *Through Navajo Eyes*. Bloomington: Indiana University Press, 1972.

Yunxiang Yan. "McDonald's in Beijing: The Localization of Americana." In *Golden Arches East: McDonald's in East Asia*. Edited by James L. Watson. Stanford, Calif.: Stanford University Press, 1997, 39–76.

Lenny Zeltzer. "The World-Wide Web: Origins and Beyond," <http://www.zeltser.com/www/#History_Hypertext> copyright 1995, accessed 21 March 2000.

Glossary

Abstract/abstraction The quality of being conceived apart from concrete realities. In art, a nonrepresentational style that focuses on form, shape, color, and texture rather than the representation of reality. In advertising, the term "abstraction" is used to describe the fantasy world that is created by advertisements, in which they abstract us as viewers away from our everyday world, suspend its normal laws, and offer us instead a space of desire defined by imagination.

Abstract expressionism A style of abstract art, which prevailed in the post–World War II era until the mid-1950s in the United States and Europe, that was characterized by an emphasis on abstraction as expressive of contemporary anxiety. Its primary proponents included Jackson Pollock and Willem De Kooning.

Aesthetics A branch of philosophy that is concerned with beliefs and theories about the value, meaning, and interpretations of art. The aesthetic traditionally referred to concepts of the beautiful, but today refers to what is valid and valuable in the arts.

Agency The quality of having the power to act or to make meaning. In some contexts, individuals or groups are disempowered, hence without agency in some way.

Alienation A term that has several different meanings historically. In general, alienation refers to the sense of distance from nature, separation from others, and helplessness that is an effect of modern existence. In Marxist theory, alienation is a specific condition of capitalism in which humans experience a sense of separation from the product of their labor, and hence all aspects of life including human relations. In psychoanalytic theory, alienation refers to split subjectivity and the discovery of the fact that one is not in control of one's thoughts, actions, and desires because of the existence of the unconscious. See *Marxist theory*, *Psychoanalytic theory*, and *Modernism/modernity*.

Analog The representation of data by means of physical properties that express value along a continuous scale. Analog technologies include a photograph, a tape, a vinyl record, a clock with hands, or a mercury thermometer, in which highs and lows, darks and lights, etc. are measured along a scale that shows incremental change, such as that of electrical voltage. Indeed, it could be said that we experience the world as analog, that is, as based on a certain continuity. An analog image such as a photograph is distinguished from its digital counterpart in its basis on continuity in gradation of tone and color, whereas a digital image is divided into bits that are mathematically encoded. See *Digital*.

Apparatus, cinematic The various devices that produce the traditional viewing experience of cinema, including the film projector, movie screen, and seating arrangement. In film theory, the term is extended to include the psychological disposition of the spectator in the movie-viewing context.

Appellation The process in advertising by which an ad speaks directly to the viewer/consumer. This may occur in the use of the term "you" in text or spoken words, or may be implied in the address of the ad. Consumer ads name viewers/consumers through these modes of address by asking them to insert themselves into the ad. In other words, appellation refers to the process by which ads construct their viewers/consumers. Appellation was coined by critic Judith Williamson to signify the ways that advertisements interpellate consumers. See *Interpellation*.

Appropriation The act of borrowing, stealing, or taking over others' meanings to one's own ends. Cultural appropriation is the process of "borrowing" and changing the meaning of commodities, cultural products, slogans, images, or elements of fashion. In addition, appropriation is one of the primary forms of oppositional production and reading, when, for instance, viewers take cultural products and re-edit, rewrite, or change them in some way. See *Bricolage, Trans-coding, Oppositional reading*.

Aura A term used by German theorist Walter Benjamin to describe the quality of unique works of art that exist in only one place. According to Benjamin, the aura of such works is precisely what gives them the quality of authenticity, which cannot be reproduced. See *Reproduction*.

Authenticity The quality of being genuine or unique. Traditionally, authenticity referred to things which were one of a kind and original, rather than copied. In Walter Benjamin's theories of the reproduction of images, authenticity is precisely that quality that cannot be reproduced or copied.

Avant-garde A term imported from military strategy (in which it indicated an expeditionary or scouting force) into art history to describe movements at the forefront of artistic experimentation. Avant-garde is often associated with modernism and is frequently contrasted with mainstream or traditional art that is conventional rather than challenging.

Base/superstructure Terms used by Marx to describe the relations of labor and economics (base) to the social system and consciousness (superstructure) in capitalism. In classic Marxist theory, the economic base dictates the legal, political, religious, and ideological aspects of the superstructure. See *Marxist theory*.

Binary oppositions The oppositions such as nature/culture, male/female, etc., through which reality has been traditionally represented. Although binary oppositions can seem immutable and mutually exclusive, contemporary theories of difference have demonstrated the ways in which these oppositional categories are interrelated and are ideologically and historically constructed. The historical reliance on binary oppositions points to the way that difference is essential to meaning and how we understand things. See *Marked/unmarked, Structuralism*.

Biopower A term used by French philosopher Michel Foucault to describe the processes through which institutional practices define, measure, categorize, and construct the body. Biopower thus refers to the ways that power is enacted upon the body through regulating its activity (in social hygiene, public health, education,

demography, census-taking, and reproductive practices, among others). These processes and practices produce particular kinds of knowledge about bodies, and produce bodies with particular kinds of meaning and capacities. In Foucault's terms, all bodies are constructed through biopower. See *Docile bodies, Power/knowledge*.

Bit The smallest unit of memory and information in a computer. A bit can hold only one of two values: 0 or 1. See *Digital*.

Black-boxed The term "black-boxed" refers to the inability of the user to see inside (metaphorically and sometimes literally) a machine and how it functions. What gets "boxed" are the qualities and capabilities of a particular technology that are not visible to its user.

Bricolage The practice of working with whatever materials are at hand, "making do" with what one has. As a cultural practice, bricolage refers to the activity of taking consumer products and commodities and making them one's own by giving them new meaning. This has the potential to create resistant meanings out of commodities. For instance, the youth practices of wearing sneakers unlaced or baseball caps on backwards can be seen as practices that change the intended meaning of those products. The punk practice of wearing safety pins as body ornamentation is one of the most well-known examples of bricolage. One origin of the term in cultural studies is derived from anthropologist Claude Lévi-Strauss in reference to how so-called primitive cultures differ in their processes of meaning-making from dominant colonial cultures. See *Appropriation, Counter-bricolage*.

Broadcast media Media that are transmitted from one central point to many different receiving points. Television and radio, for instance, are transmitted across broad spectrums, from a central transmission point to a vast number of receivers (TV sets and radios). Low-power and local transmission are not broadcast but narrowcast media. See *Narrowcast media*.

Capitalism An economic system in which investment in and ownership of the means of production, distribution, and exchange of wealth are held primarily by individuals and corporations, as opposed to cooperative or state-owned means of wealth. Capitalism is based on an ideology of free trade, open markets, and individuality. In capitalism, the use value of goods (how they are used) matters less than their exchange value (what they are worth on the market). Industrial capitalism refers to capitalist systems that are primarily industrial, such as those of many Euro-American nation-states in the nineteenth and twentieth centuries. Late capitalism (which is also called postindustrialism) refers to late twentieth-century forms of capitalism that are more global in terms of economic ownership and structure, in which the primary commodities that are traded tend to be services and information rather than manufactured, physically tangible goods. Marxist theory is a critique of the ways that the system of capitalism is based on inequality and exploitation of workers, allowing a few to prosper while many have only limited means. See *Exchange value*, *Marxist theory*, *Use value*.

Cartesian space A term that refers to concepts of space that were originally influenced by the mathematical concepts of seventeenth-century philosopher René Descartes. Descartes's theories concerned a rationalistic, mechanistic interpretation to understanding nature, including the idea that space can be mathematically mapped and measured. A Cartesian grid refers to the definition of space through three axes, each intersecting each other at 90 degrees to define three-dimensional space. Cartesian space is based on Descartes's famous theory of human nature summarized in the phrase "I think, therefore I am," which supposes that humans exist and can know the world in a positive, unmediated way. Cartesian space is thus contingent on the idea of an all-knowing, rational, all-seeing human subject. Concepts of virtual space are considered to be in opposition to this tradition of Cartesian space. See *Virtual*.

Cinéma vérité A movement of documentary cinema in the 1960s, in some contexts referred to as direct cinema, that promoted a naturalistic, supposedly unmediated recording of reality through the use of long takes with minimal editing, hand-held cameras, and the rejection of voice-over narration and scripts. While advocates of cinéma vérité felt that these techniques provided a more authentic way of representing reality, it can still be said that the choices they made through framing and their presence as filmmakers in these situations all had an effect on the "authenticity" of what they shot. Vérité directors include Jean Rouch and Frederick Wiseman, who is also associated with the Direct Cinema style. See *Direct Cinema*.

Classical art Art that adheres to the styles and aesthetics of tradition. Typically the term is associated with ancient Greek and Roman art where it refers to norms of balance, symmetry, and proportion.

Code The implicit rules by which meanings get put into social practice and can therefore be read by their users. Codes involve a systematic organization of signs. For example, there are codes of social conduct, such as forms of greeting or styles of social interaction, that are understood within a given society. One situation in which codes become evident is when they are broken.

Semiotics shows that language and representational media, such as cinema and television, are structured according to specific codes. Cinematic codes include lighting, camera movement, and editing. Codes may cross media, and various sets of codes may inform a single medium. For example, the painterly codes of chiaroscuro lighting or Renaissance perspective may be used in photographs and films.

The term "code" has also been used by Stuart Hall to describe how cultural texts, such as television, can be encoded with meaning by producers, and are then decoded by viewers. See *Decoding*, *Encoding*, *Semiotics*, *Sign*.

Colonialism The policy of a nation by which it extends its power over another people or territory. The term is used primarily to describe the colonization by European countries of Africa, India, Latin and North America, and the Pacific region from the sixteenth through the twentieth century (when struggles for independence produced the conditions of postcolonialism). Colonization was motivated by the potential exploitation of Third World people and resources by these First World nations, and involved both the conquest of countries politically and economically but also the fundamental restructuring of their cultures, with enforced changes in language among other things. See *Imperialism*, *Postcolonialism*.

Commodification/commodity Originally a term in Marxism, commodification is the process by which material objects are turned into marketable goods with monetary (exchange) value. Commodities are goods marketed to consumers in a commodity culture.

Commodity fetishism The process through which commodities are emptied of the meaning of their production (the labor that produced them and the context in which they were produced) and filled instead with abstract meaning (usually through advertising). In Marxism, commodity fetishism is the process of mystification that exists in capitalism between what things are and how they appear. Commodity fetishism also describes the process by which special life powers are attributed to commodities rather than to other elements in social life. For example, to suppose that a car provides self-worth is to engage in commodity fetishism.

In commodity fetishism, exchange value has so superceded use value that things are valued not for what they do but what they cost, how they look, and what connotations can be attached to them. For instance, a commodity (such as bottled purified water) is emptied of the meaning of its production (where it was bottled, who worked to bottle it, how it was shipped) and filled with new meaning (mountain springs, purity) through an advertising campaign. See *Exchange value*, *Fetish*, *Marxist theory*, *Use value*.

Commodity self A term, coined by Stuart Ewen, that refers to how we construct our identities, at least in part, through the consumer products that inhabit our lives. The concept of a commodity self implies that our selves, if not our subjectivities, are mediated and constructed in part through our identification with commodity signs—the meanings that are attached to consumer products which we intentionally acquire through their purchase and use.

Commodity sign A term that refers to the semiotic meaning of a commodity that is constructed in an advertisement. The representation of a commodity, or the product itself, and its meaning together form the commodity sign. Contemporary cultural theorists state that we do not consume commodities, but commodity signs. That is, what we are really purchasing is the meaning of the commodity. See *Commodity*, *Sign*.

Conceptual art A style of art that emerged in the 1960s that focused on the idea of concept over material object. An attempt to counter the increased commercialism of the art world, conceptual art presented ideas rather than art works that could be bought and sold, and thus worked to shift the focus to the creative process and away from the art market. Artist who worked in conceptual art include Joseph Kosuth and Yoko Ono.

Connoisseur A person who is particularly skilled at discerning quality in a particular art. The term "connoisseur" is a class-based concept that has been traditionally used to refer to those with "discriminating" taste, i.e. those of an upper-class status. The concept of connoisseurship has been criticized for representing upper-class taste as something that is natural and more authentic than popular taste.

Connotative meaning In semiotics, all the social, cultural, and historical meanings that are added to a sign's literal meaning. Connotative meanings rely on the cultural and historical context of the image and its viewers' lived, felt knowledge of those circumstances. Connotation thus brings to an object or image the wider realm of ideology, cultural meaning, and value systems of a society. According to Roland Barthes, myth occurs when we read connotative meanings as denotative (i.e. literal) meanings, and thus naturalize what are in fact meanings derived from complex social ideologies. See *Denotative meaning*, *Myth*, *Semiotics*, *Sign*.

Constructivism An art movement in the Soviet Union following the 1917 Russian Revolution that deployed a modernist avant-garde aesthetic. Constructivism emphasized dynamic form as the embodiment of the politics and ideology of a machine-driven culture. The pro-Soviet artists of Constructivism embraced the theories of Karl Marx, ideas of technological progress, and a machine aesthetic. Its primary proponents were Vladimir Tatlin, El Lissitsky, and filmmaker Dziga Vertov.

Convergence A term that refers to the increased combination of media together into one point of access. The potential combination of communication technologies such as computers, television, film, fax, and telephone into one interconnected multimedia system is the vision of media convergence of many proponents of new technology.

Counter-bricolage The practice used by advertisers and marketers of manufacturing and selling as commodities aspects of bricolage style. For instance, counter-bricolage occurs when certain youth styles are created to change the meaning of commodities (such as the practice of wearing oversized, low-slung pants that reveal boxer shorts underneath), and those styles are then appropriated by manufacturers and packaged and sold to consumers. See *Appropriation*, *Bricolage*.

Counter-hegemony The forces in a given society that work against dominant meaning and power systems, and keep in constant tension and flux those dominant meanings. See *Hegemony*.

Cubism An early twentieth-century art movement that was part of the modern French avant-garde. Cubism began with a collaboration between Pablo Picasso and Georges Braque, who were both developing new ways of depicting space and objects. Cubism was a deliberate critique of the dominance of perspective in styles of art, and an attempt to represent the dynamism and complexity of human vision by imaging objects simultaneously from multiple perspectives. See *Dada*, *Futurism*, *Modernism/modernity*.

Cultural imperialism See *Imperialism*.

Culture industry A term used by the members of the Frankfurt School, in particular Theodor Adorno and Max Horkheimer, to indicate how capitalism organizes and homogenizes culture, giving cultural consumers less freedom to construct their own meanings. Horkheimer and Adorno saw the culture industry as generating mass culture as a form of commodity fetishism that functions as propaganda for industrial capitalism. They saw all mass culture as dictated by formula and repetition, encouraging conformity, promoting passivity, cheating its consumers of what it promises, and promoting pseudoindividuality. See *Commodity fetishism*, *Frankfurt School*, *Pseudoindividuality*.

Cyberspace A term that refers to the space defined by the computer, the Internet, and virtual technologies. Cyberspace is the imagining of the sites of electronic exchange, such as surfing the World Wide Web, sending and receiving e-mail, exploring virtual reality systems, etc. as a kind of geography. See *Cartesian space, Internet, Virtual, World Wide Web.*

Cyborg A term originally proposed by Manfred Clynes and Nathan Kline in 1960 to describe "self-regulating man-machine systems" or cybernetic organisms. Since that time, the cyborg has been theorized, most famously by Donna Haraway, as a means to consider the relationship of human subjects to technology, and the subjectivity of late capitalism, biomedicine, and computer technology. It is argued that those who have prosthetics or pacemakers, for instance, are actual cyborgs, and cyborgs have populated contemporary science fiction literature and film. However much of the contemporary thinking about cyborgs is as a means of thinking about how all subjects of contemporary postmodern and technological societies can be understood as cyborgs because of their dependence upon and integral relationship with technologies.

Dada An intellectual movement that began in Zurich in 1916, and later flourished in France with such figures as Marcel Duchamp and Francis Picabia. Dada was defined by the poet Tristan Tzara as a "state of mind" and was primarily anti-art in its sensibilities, with, for instance, Duchamp making "ready-mades" by putting ordinary objects, like a bicycle wheel and a urinal, on display in a museum. It was irreverent, and influenced by Futurism, though did not fully share Futurism's association with fascism and love of the machine. Other important figures were the German writer Richard Hulsenbeck, German artist Kurt Schwitters, and French artist Jean Arp. See *Futurism.*

Decoding In cultural consumption, the process of interpreting and giving meaning to cultural products in conformity with shared cultural codes. Used by Stuart Hall to describe the work done by cultural consumers when they view and interpret cultural products (such as television shows, films, ads, etc.) that have been encoded by producers. According to Hall, factors such as "frameworks of knowledge" (class status, cultural knowledge), "relations of production" (viewing context), and "technical infrastructure" (the technological medium in which one is viewing) influence the process of decoding. See *Code, Encoding.*

Denotative meaning In semiotics, the literal, face-value meaning of a sign. The denotative meaning of a rose is a flower. However, in any given context, a rose is likely to have connotative meanings (such as romanticism, love, or loyalty) that add social, historical, and cultural (connotative) meaning to its denotative meaning. See *Connotative meaning, Semiotics, Sign.*

Dialectic A term from philosophy whose use is varied and often ambiguous. In Greek philosophy, it referred to the process of question and answer promoted by Plato as the means to higher knowledge. The term has generally been used to refer to a conflict or tension between two positions, for example the dialectics of good and evil. However, its use in philosophy refers to a mediation or resolution of this conflict. In Marxist theory, history moves forward not in a continuous progression but through a chain of conflicts that are resolved only to bring new conflicts. Marxism speaks in this respect of theses and antitheses, for example an owner (thesis) and a worker (antithesis), whose antagonism leads to a synthesis through dialectical process. See *Marxist theory.*

Diaspora The existence of various communities, usually of a particular ethnicity, culture, or nation, scattered across places outside of their land of origin or homeland. There are, for instance, large diasporic communities of Jews throughout the world, and of East Indians in England. Work in diasporia studies has stressed the complexity of such communities, who not only negotiate memory and nostalgia for original homelands, but have the shared histories of migration, displacement, and hybrid identity of other local diaspora communities. See *Hybridity.*

Differentiation In advertising, the strategies to differentiate or distinguish qualities of one product or one brand from another. For example, Pepsi and Coca-Cola market similar products, but their advertising campaigns attribute very different qualities, such as youthfulness or world harmony, to their soft drinks.

Digital Representing data by means of discrete digits, and encoding that data mathematically. Digital technologies, which are technologically in contrast to analog technologies, involve a process of encoding information in bits and assigning each a mathematical value. A clock with hands that move around a dial to show the time is analog, and a clock with a numbered readout is digital. A photographic image is analog and continuous in tone, while a digital image is mathematically encoded so that each bit has a particular value. This allows it to be more easily manipulated and copied. See *Analog, Bit.*

Direct Cinema Closely related to cinéma vérité, direct cinema involved recording synchronized sound and footage of real-life action spontaneously, as it unfolded before the camera and crew. This technique broke with the use of voice-over narrative that had continued in some of the work of vérité directors like Jean Rouch, and involved minimal or no scripting, staging of action, editing, and general manipulation of materials filmed and recorded. Ricky Leacock, Robert Drew, Donn Pennebaker, Frederick Wiseman, and Albert and David Maysles are some of the US directors associated with this style. Their focus was primarily people in everyday institutions and their inhabitants, from famous political figures to students and teachers, prison inmates and guards. See *Cinéma vérité*.

Discontinuity In postmodern style, the strategy of breaking a continuous narrative and audience identification with it in order to defy viewer expectations. Discontinuity might include jump cuts, a shuffling of chronological events, or reflexivity. See *Reflexivity*.

Discourse In general, the socially organized process of talking about a particular subject matter. According to Michel Foucault, discourse is a body of knowledge that both defines and limits what can be said about something. While there is no set list of discourses, the term tends to be used for broad bodies of social knowledge, such as the discourses of economics, the law, medicine, politics, sexuality, technology, etc. Discourses are specific to particular social and historical contexts, and they change over time. It is fundamental to Foucault's theory that discourses produce certain kinds of subjects and knowledge, and that we occupy to varying degrees the subject positions defined within a broad array of discourses. See *Subject position*.

Docile bodies A term used by Michel Foucault to describe the process by which social subjects submit bodily to social norms. See *Biopower*.

Dominant-hegemonic reading In Stuart Hall's formulation of three potential positions for the viewer/consumer of mass culture, the dominant-hegemonic reading is one in which consumers unquestioningly accept the message that the producers are transmitting to them. According to Hall, few viewers actually occupy this position at any time because mass culture cannot satisfy all viewers' culturally specific experiences, memories, and desires, and because viewers are not passive recipients of the messages of mass media and popular culture. See *Negotiated reading*, *Oppositional reading*.

Empiricism The science-inspired philosophy that assumes that things exist independent of language and other forms of representation, and can be known unambiguously as positive truths independent of any specific context. An empirical methodology relies on experimentation and data collection to establish particular truths, and is in opposition to theories that see facts and truths as dependent on the context and language system in which they take on meaning.

Encoding In cultural consumption, the production of meaning in cultural products. Used by Stuart Hall to describe the work done by cultural producers in encoding cultural products (such as television shows, films, ads, etc.) with preferred meaning that will then be decoded by viewers. According to Hall, factors such as "frameworks of knowledge" (class status, cultural knowledge, and taste of the producers), "relations of production" (labor contexts of the production), and "technical infrastructure" (the technological context of the production) influence this process of encoding. See *Decoding*.

Enlightenment An eighteenth-century cultural movement associated with a rejection of religious and pre-scientific tradition through an embrace of the concept of reason. The Enlightenment emphasized rationality and the idea of moral and social betterment through scientific progress. Kant defined the Enlightenment as "man's emergence from his self-imposed immaturity," and awarded it the motto of *sapere aude*—Dare to Know. The Enlightenment is associated with broader social changes, such as the decline of feudalism and the power of the Church, the increased impact of printing in European culture, and the rise of the middle class in Europe. It is considered to be an important aspect of the rise of modernity. See *Modernism/modernity*.

Epistemology The branch of philosophy concerned with knowledge and what can be known. To ask an epistemological question about something is to investigate what we can know about it.

Equivalence A term used in applications of semiotics to refer to the establishment in an image of a relationship between elements within the frame or between a product and its signifier. Equivalence means, for instance, that an advertisement establishes direct connections for the viewer/consumer between the product and a figure of some kind. Celebrity endorsement advertisements thus establish an equivalence between the product (Nike Air Jordan shoes) and their spokesperson (Michael Jordan) that allow for the qualities of each to be seen as equivalent (hence awarding the quality of superb basketball skills to the wearers of Nike shoes).

Exchange value The monetary value that gets assigned to a commodity in a consumer culture. When an object is seen in terms of its exchange value, its economic worth (or monetary equivalent) is more important than what it can be used for (its use value). Marxist theory critiques the emphasis in capitalism on exchange over use value.

For example, gold has significant exchange value though very little use value, since there are few practical functions for it; it thus serves to buy status. See *Capitalism, Commodity fetishism, Marxist theory, Use value*.

Exhibitionism In psychoanalytic terms, the pleasure derived from being looked at. Classical Hollywood movies are considered to be exhibitionist in their display of the female form to the spectator. See *Psychoanalytic theory, Scopophilia, Voyeurism*.

False consciousness In Marxist theory, the process by which the real economic imbalances of the dominant social system get hidden and ordinary citizens come to believe in the perfection of the system that oppresses them. The biblical phrase "the meek shall inherit the earth" would be considered by Marxism to be an example of false consciousness, since it tells the downtrodden not to rebel against the system but await later reward. Twentieth-century developments in Marxism see the concept of false consciousness as itself potentially oppressive, since it defines the masses as unaware dupes of the system. In contrast, concepts such as hegemony emphasize the active struggle of people over meanings rather than their passive acceptance of ideological systems. See *Marxist theory, Hegemony, Ideology*.

Fetish In anthropology, an object that is endowed with magical powers and ritualistic meaning, for example, a totem pole. In Marxist theory, an object that is awarded "magical" economic power that is not in the object itself. For example, a dollar bill is a piece of paper that physically has no worth, yet is given economic power by the State. In psychoanalytic theory, a fetish is an object that is endowed with magical powers to enable a person to compensate for psychological lack. For example, a poster of a movie star can give someone a fantasy of possession that would otherwise be unavailable to them. See *Commodity fetishism*.

First World A term used in the post–World War II period to refer to the countries of the West, as opposed to the Second World (the East), or the Third World. In this theory, the world is divided into West (First World) and East (Second World) with two major superpowers, the USA and the USSR. As the Cold War has faded, and the global dynamics of these countries have changed, the term has been considered to be less useful. See *Third World*.

Flâneur A French term first popularized by nineteenth-century poet Charles Baudelaire, and subsequently theorized explicitly by cultural critics such as Walter Benjamin, that refers to a person who wanders city streets, taking in the sights, especially those of consumer society.

In other words, the *flâneur* is a kind of window shopper, with the implication that the act of looking at the gleaming offerings of commodity culture is itself a source of pleasure whether or not one actually ever purchases anything. The *flâneur is* simultaneously in the world of consumerism and detached from the cityscape around him. Originally, the *flâneur* was understood to be male, since women did not have the same freedom to wander the city streets alone, but recent cultural criticism, such as the work of Anne Friedberg, has sought to theorize the concept of the *flâneuse*, as a female wanderer through the seductive sights of the city. See *Modernism/modernity*.

Frankfurt School A group of scholars and social theorists, working first in Germany in the 1930s and then primarily in the United States, who were interested in applying Marxist theory to the new forms of cultural production and social life in twentieth-century capitalist societies. The Frankfurt School scholars rejected Enlightenment philosophy, stating that reason did not free people but rather became a force in the rise of technical expertise, the expression of instrumental reason divorced from wider goals of human emancipation, and the exploitation of people, making systems of social domination more efficient and effective. The key figures associated with the Frankfurt School are Theodor Adorno, Walter Benjamin, Max Horkheimer, Herbert Marcuse, and later Jürgen Habermas. The early members fled Germany with the rise to power of the Nazis. See *Culture industry*.

Futurism An Italian avant-garde movement that was inspired by Filippo Tommaso Marinetti's *Futurist Manifesto*, which was published in 1909. The Futurists were interesting in breaking free of tradition, and embraced the idea of speed and the future. They wrote many manifestos and maintained a provocative and challenging style sometimes associated with fascism. Some of the Futurists painters, such as Giacomo Balla, focused on painting objects and people in motion, and others worked in Cubist styles. See *Cubism, Dada*.

Gaze In theories of the visual arts, such as film theory and art history, the gaze is a term used to describe acts of looking caught up in dynamics of desire—for example, the gaze can be motivated by a desire for control over its object. Theories of the gaze have explored the complex power relations that are a part of the acts of looking and being looked at.

In traditional psychoanalytic theory, the gaze is intimately linked to fantasy. This theory was updated by French psychoanalyst Jacques Lacan who put the gaze at the center of his approach to how individuals deal with their desire. For example, Lacan saw the mirror phase—the moment when a child recognizes and idealizes itself in reflection—as a meaningful visual act that is key to an individual's psychological development. Applying Freud's and Lacan's theories to film, 1970s psychoanalytic film theory posited that in cinema, the gaze of the spectator upon the image was an implicitly male one that objectified the women on screen. Contemporary theories of the gaze have complicated this original model, and now discuss a variety of different kinds of gazes, for example, gazes distinguished by sex, gender, race, and class, that can be deployed by different kinds of spectators.

Michel Foucault uses the term "gaze" to describe the relationship of subjects within a network of power—and the mechanism of vision as a means of negotiating and conveying power within that network—in a given institutional context. For Foucault, social institutions enact an inspecting or normalizing gaze upon their subjects, to keep track of their activities and thereby to discipline them. In this formulation, the gaze is not something one has or uses, rather, it is a spatial and institutionally bound relationship into which one enters. See *Panopticism*, *Psychoanalytic theory*.

Gender-bending Practices that call into question the traditional gender categories of male and female and the sexual norms associated with them. For example, a gender-bending reading of a particular cultural product might point out previously unacknowledged homosexual undertones and codes.

Genre The classification of cultural products into particular types with different intents and formulas. In cinema, genres include the western, the romantic comedy, science fiction, and the action adventure. In television, for example, genres include situation comedies, soap operas, news magazines, and talk shows, among others.

Globalization A term used increasingly toward the end of the twentieth century to describe a set of conditions escalating since the postwar period. These conditions include increased rates of migration, the rise of multinational corporations, the development of global communications and transportation systems, and the decline of the sovereign nation-state, and the "shrinking" of the world through commerce and communication. While some theorists take the conditions of globalization as a given, others see them as ideological, in the sense that their direction and force are not inevitable but are shaped by vying economic, cultural, and political interests. The term "globalization" also works to extend the concept of the local, in that globalization's advancement depends on the formation of new sorts of local communities not geographically bound (such as Internet communities). See *Global village*.

Global village A term coined by Marshall McLuhan to refer to the ways that media can connect people from all over the world into communities, hence to give the collective sense of a village to groups that are separated geographically. McLuhan stated that the global village was created by instant electronic communication. He wrote, "The global village is at once as wide as the planet and as small as the little town where everybody is maliciously engaged in poking his nose into everybody else's business. The global village is a world in which you don't necessarily have harmony; you have extreme concern with everybody's else's business and much involvement with everybody else's life." It is a term that describes both the contemporary frenzy of media events and the connections created by people over distances through communication technologies. The concept of a global village puts a cheery spin on globalization. See *Globalization*.

Graphical user interface The design in computer software and in the World Wide Web that allows users to make choices, enact commands, and move around through the use of graphics and images rather than text. See *Internet*, *World Wide Web*.

Guerrilla television A term used by video artists and activists to describe alternative video practices begun in the late 1960s that used the medium of television to produce videotapes that were oppositional to the styles of mainstream television. Guerrilla television defined work that was shot by participants, rather than distanced broadcasters, and which could be used for political action.

Habitus A term popularized by French sociologist Pierre Bourdieu to describe the unconscious dispositions, strategies of classification, and tendencies that are part of an individual's sense of taste and preferences for cultural consumption. According to Bourdieu, these value systems are not idiosyncratic to each individual but are derived instead from one's social position, educational background, and class status. Hence, different social classes have different habituses with distinct tastes and lifestyles.

Hegemony A concept most associated with Italian Marxist theorist Antonio Gramsci that rethought traditional Marxist theories of ideology away from ideas about false consciousness and passive social subjects. There are two central aspects of Gramsci's definition of hegemony: that dominant ideologies are often offered as "common sense," and that dominant ideologies are in tension with other forces and hence constantly in flux. The term "hegemony" thus indicates how ideological meaning is an object of struggle rather than an oppressive force that fully dominates subjects from above. See *Counter-Hegemony*, *Ideology*, *Marxist theory*.

High/low culture Terms that have traditionally been used to make distinctions about different kinds of culture. High culture distinguishes culture that only an elite can appreciate, such as classical art, music, and literature, as opposed to commercially produced mass culture presumed to be accessible to lower classes. The distinction of high and low culture has been heavily criticized by cultural theorists for its snobbery and elitism and its condescending view of the popular consumer as a passive viewer with no taste.

Hybridity A term referring to anything of mixed origins that has been used in contemporary theory to describe those people whose identities are derived simultaneously from many cultural origins and ethnicities. Hybridity has been used to describe diasporic cultures that are neither in one place or the other but of many places. See *Diaspora*.

Hyperreal A term coined by French theorist Jean Baudrillard that refers to a world in which codes of reality are used to simulate reality in cases where there is no referent in the real world. Hyperreality is thus a simulation of reality in which various elements function to emphasize their "realness." In postmodern style, hyperrealism refers to the use of naturalistic effects to give an advertisement, for instance, the look of a realist documentary—"natural" sound, jerky "amateur" camerawork, or unrehearsed nonactors, yet which is understood to be a construction of the real. See *Postmodernism/postmodernity*, *Simulation/simulaacrum*.

Hypertext A format for presenting text and images, which forms the basis of the World Wide Web, that allows viewers to move from one text, page, or web site to another through hyperlinks. This means that any web site, for instance, can have a number of links to other sites, to audio, video, and other graphics. The importance of this format is that it allows for web users to move laterally through a significant amount of material that is linked. See *World Wide Web*.

Hypodermic effect A theory of mass media that sees viewers as passive recipients of media messages who are not only "drugged" by the media but injected with its ideology. The idea of a hypodermic or narcotic effect of the media specifically refers to the way in which viewers of mass media are allowed the impression that they are participating in a public culture while watching mass media forms such as television, when in fact this viewing has replaced social and political action on their part.

Icon Originally, the term icon referred to a religious image that had sacred value of some kind. In its contemporary meaning, an icon is an image (or person) that refers to something beyond its individual components, something (or someone) that acquires symbolic significance. Icons are often perceived to represent universal concepts, emotions, and meanings.

Iconic sign A term in semiotics used by Charles Peirce to indicate those signs in which there is a resemblance between the signifier (word/image) and the thing signified. For example, a drawing of a person is an iconic sign because it resembles him or her. Peirce distinguished Iconic, Indexical, and Symbolic signs. See *Indexical sign*, *Semiotics*, *Symbolic sign*.

Identification The psychological process whereby one forms a bond with or emulates an aspect or attribute of another person and is transformed through that process. The term "identification" is used extensively to describe the experiences of viewers in looking at film. According to cinema theorist Christian Metz, cinematic identification can involve identification with characters or with the cinematic apparatus itself (and its ways of seeing). One example would be viewer identification with the all-seeing camera that appears to go everywhere. Traditionally in film theory it was thought that viewers only identified with characters who shared their gender, race, or social position, but increasingly it is thought that viewers identify in complex and partial ways across such attributes.

Ideology The shared set of values and beliefs that exist within a given society and through which individuals live out their relations to social institutions and structures. Ideology refers to the way that certain concepts and values are made to seem like natural, inevitable aspects of everyday life. In Marxist theory, the term "ideology" has undergone several definitions, including the following: first, by Marx, to imply a social system in which the masses are instilled with the dominant ideology of the ruling class and that constitutes a kind of false consciousness; second, by French Marxist Louis Althusser, who combined psychoanalysis and Marxist theory to postulate that we are unconsciously constituted as subjects by ideology, which gives us a sense of our place in the world; third, by Antonio Gramsci, who used the term "hegemony" to describe how dominant ideologies are always in flux and under contestation from other ideas and values. See *False Consciousness*, *Hegemony*, *Interpellation*, *Marxist theory*, *Psychoanalytic theory*.

Imperialism Derived from the word "Empire," imperialism refers to the policy of nations that aim to extend their boundaries into new territories, for example through colonization. In Marxist theory, imperialism is one of the means by which capitalism extends its power by creating both new markets that it can sell its commodities to and new labor forces that it can use to make those commodities for low cost. Cultural imperialism refers to how ways of life are exported into other territories through cultural products and popular culture. Because it is the center of the production of global popular culture and has economic power, the United States is often accused of cultural imperialism. See *Colonialism*.

Impressionism An artistic style that emerged in the late nineteenth century, primarily in France, that was characterized by an emphasis on light and color. Impressionist work emphasized a view of nature as unstable and changeable. Painters foregrounded the brushstroke and often painted the same scene many times to evoke how it changed with the light. Prominent Impressionist artists included Claude Monet, Pierre-Auguste Renoir, Alfred Sisley, Camille Pissarro, and Berthe Morisot. Paul Gauguin, Vincent van Gogh, and Paul Cezanne are often referred to as post-Impressionists.

Indexical sign A term in semiotics used by Charles Peirce to indicate those signs in which there is a physical causal connection between the signifier (word/image) and the thing signified, because both existed at some point within the same physical space. For example, smoke coming from a building is an index of a fire. Similarly, a photograph is an index of its subject because it was taken in its presence. Peirce distinguished Iconic, Indexical, and Symbolic signs. See *Iconic sign*, *Semiotics*, *Symbolic sign*.

Internet A network that connects supercomputers, mainframe computers, and personal computers throughout the world through e-mail, the World Wide Web, and file transfer. The Internet functions through a system of protocols that allows computers with different software and hardware to communicate, and a system of packet switching, which allows many computers to communicate and be on-line simultaneously. See *Virtual*, *World Wide Web*.

Interpellation A term coined by Marxist theorist Louis Althusser to describe the process by which ideological systems call out to or "hail" social subjects and tell them their place in the system. In popular culture, interpellation refers to the ways that cultural products address their consumers and recruit them into a particular ideological position. Images can be said to designate the kind of viewer they intend us to be, and in speaking to us as that kind of viewer help to shape us as particular ideological subjects. See *Ideology*, *Marxist theory*.

Interpretant A term used by semiotician Charles Sanders Peirce in his three-part system of signification. The interpretant is the thought or mental effect produced by the relationship between the object and its representation (Peirce's definition of a sign). The interpretant is the equivalent of the signified in Saussure. Peirce stated that the interpretant could be endlessly commuted, that is, that each interpretant can create a new sign which in turn creates a new interpretant, and so on. See *Referent*, *Signified*.

Intertextuality The referencing of one text within another. In popular culture, intertextuality refers to the incorporation of meanings of one text within another in a reflexive fashion. For example, the television show *The Simpsons* includes references to films, other television shows, and celebrities. These intertextual references assume that the viewer knows the people and cultural products being referenced.

Irony The deliberate contradiction between the literal meaning of something and its intended meaning (which can be the opposite of the literal meaning). Irony can be seen as a context where appearance and reality are in conflict, for instance when someone says "beautiful weather!" when in fact they intend to state that the weather is terrible. Irony is more subtle and less direct than sarcasm and satire.

Kitsch Art or literature judged to have little or no aesthetic value, yet which has value precisely because of its status in evoking the class standards of bad taste. Afficionados of kitsch thus re-code these objects, such as lava lamps and tacky 1950s suburban furniture, as good rather than bad taste.

Lack A term used in psychoanalysis by Jacques Lacan to describe an essential aspect of the human psyche. According to Lacan, the human subject is defined by lack from the moment of birth and his or her separation from the mother. The subject is lacking because it is believed to be a fragment of something larger and more primordial. The second stage of lack is the acquisition of language. In Lacan's theory, the human sense of always wanting something that is out of reach or unattainable is the result of lack—there is no person or thing that can fulfill that feeling of lack. In Freudian psychoanalysis, the term lack refers to the woman's lack of a penis/phallus, her lack being precisely what awards power to the phallus. See *Phallus/phallic*, *Psychoanalytic theory*.

Low culture see *High/low culture*

Marked/unmarked In binary oppositions, the first category is understood to be unmarked (hence the "norm") and the second category as marked, hence other. In the opposition male/female, for instance, the category male is unmarked, thus dominant and the category of female is unmarked, or not the norm. These categories of marked and unmarked are most noticeable when the norm is departed from. For instance, until quite recently, in the majority of advertising images, which have traditionally been directed at a white middle-class audience, white models were unmarked (the norm, hence their race was unremarkable) whereas models of other races and ethnicities were marked (that is marked by race). See *Binary oppositions, Other*.

Marxist theory Originating with the nineteenth-century theories of Karl Marx and Friedrich Engels, Marxist theory combines political economy and social critique. Marxism is, on the one hand, a general theory of human history, in which the role of the economic and modes of production are the primary determining factors of history, and, on the other hand, a particular theory of the development, reproduction, and transformation of capitalism that identifies workers as the potential agents of history. Emphasizing the profound inequities that are necessary for capitalism to function, Marxist theory is used to understand the mechanisms of capitalism and the class relations within it. Concepts of marxism have evolved throughout the nineteenth and twentieth centuries with such theorists as Louis Althusser, Antonio Gramsci, Chantal Mouffe, and Ernesto Laclau. See *Alienation, Base/superstructure, Commodity fetishism, Exchange value, False consciousness, Fetish, Hegemony, Ideology, Interpellation, Means of production, Pseudoindividuality, Use value*.

Mass culture/mass society Terms used historically to refer to the culture and society of the general population, often with negative connotation. Mass society was used to characterize the changes that took place in Europe and the United States throughout the industrialization of the nineteenth century and culminated after World War II, when large numbers of people were concentrated in urban centers. The term "mass society" implies that these populations were subject to centralized forms of national and international media, and that they receive the majority of their opinions and information not locally or within their family but from a larger society in which mass media proliferate. The culture of this society has been characterized as a mass culture, and this term is often synonymous with popular culture. It implies that this culture is for ordinary people who are subjected to the same messages, hence one that fosters conformity and homogeneity. Both these terms have been criticized for reducing specific cultures to an undifferentiated mass.

Mass media Those media which are designed to reach mass audiences, and that work in unison to generate specific dominant or popular representations of events, peoples, and places. The primary mass media are radio, television, the cinema, and the press including newspapers and magazines. Computer-mediated communication, such as the Internet, the World Wide Web, and multimedia, is a new form of mass media that expands its definition in many ways. See *Medium/media*.

Master narrative A framework (also referred to as a metanarrative) that aims to comprehensively explain all aspects of a society or world. Examples of master narratives include religion, science, Marxism, psychoanalysis, and other theories that intend to explain all facets of life. French theorist Jean-François Lyotard famously characterized postmodern theory as profoundly skeptical of these metanarratives, their universalism, and the premise that they could define the human condition.

Means of production In Marxist theory, the means of production are the ways in which a society makes use of the natural resources of the world around it to make useful things. For example, in a small-scale agricultural society, the agricultural means of production include individual farmers growing their own produce and constructing their own tools. In industrial capitalism, the means of production include large-scale mass production of goods in factories. In late capitalism, the means of production include the production of information and media industries. In Marxist theory, those who own the means of production are also in control of the ideas that circulate in a society's media industries. See *Capitalism, Marxist theory*.

Medium/media A form in which artistic or cultural products are made. In art, a medium refers to the art materials used to create a work, such as paint or stone. In communication, medium refers to a means of mediation or communication—an intermediary form through which messages pass. The term "medium" also refers to the specific technologies through which messages are transmitted: radio, television, film, etc. The term "media" is the plural of medium, but is often used in the singular, as in "the media," to describe the constellation of media industries that together influence public opinion.

Medium is the message, The A phase popularized by Marshall McLuhan to refer to the ways that media affect viewers regardless of their messages. McLuhan stated that a medium affects content, since it is an extension of our individual bodies, and that one cannot understand and evaluate a message unless one first takes account of the medium through which one receives it. Hence, McLuhan felt that a medium such as television has the power to impose "its structural character and assumptions upon all levels of our private and social lives."

Metacommunication A discussion or exchange in which the topic is the exchange taking place itself. A "meta" level is a reflexive level of communicating. In popular culture, this refers to ads or television shows etc. in which the topic is the viewer's act of viewing the cultural product. An ad that addresses a viewer about the ways that the viewer is looking at the ad is engaging in metacommunication.

Mimesis A concept that originates with the Greeks that defines representation as a process of mirroring or imitating the real. Contemporary theories such as social construction criticize mimesis for not taking into account the way in which systems of representation, such as language and images, shape how we interpret and understand what we see, rather than merely reflecting it back to us.

Mirror phase A stage of development, according to psychoanalytic theorist Jacques Lacan, in which the infant first experiences a sense of alienation in its realization of its separateness from other human beings. According to Lacan, infants begin to establish their egos at about 18 months through the process of looking at a mirror body-image, which may be their own mirror image, their mother or another figure, and not necessarily a literal mirror image of their own body. They recognize the mirror image to be both their self and different, yet as more whole and powerful. This split recognition forms the basis of their alienation at the same time that it pushes them to grow. The mirror phase is a useful framework to understand the emotion and power invested by viewers in images as a kind of ideal, and has been used to theorize about film images in particular. See *Alienation, Psychoanalytic theory.*

Modernism/modernity A term with meanings in culture, art, literature, and music, modernism/modernity refers both to a particular time period and a set of styles associated with that time. Modernity refers to the time period and world view beginning approximately in the eighteenth century with the Enlightenment, reaching its height in the late nineteenth and early twentieth centuries, when broad populations in Europe and North America were increasingly concentrated in urban centers and in industrial societies of increased mechanization and automation. Modernity is a time of dramatic technological change that embraces a linear view of progress as crucial to humankind's prosperity and an optimistic view of the future at the same time that it embodies an anxiety about change and social upheaval.

In art and film, modernism refers to a set of styles that emerged in the late nineteenth and early twentieth centuries that questions traditions of representational painting and emphasizes the importance of form. Modern art values linearity, form, and the mechanical, and embraces abstraction over realism. Most modernist art movements share the general principles of breaking with past conventions, foregrounding form over content, and reflexively drawing attention to the materiality of the medium. See *Postmodernism/postmodernity.*

Morphing A computer imaging process by which one image is seamlessly merged into another, creating images that are combinations in between. A morphing of one image of a face into another would thus go through many combinations of both faces before finally taking the form of a third image.

Multidirectional communication Media that operate in several directions, in contrast to broadcast media that transmit in one direction only. The Internet, which allows information to be exchanged among a broad range of participants, is an example of multidirectional communication. See *Internet.*

Myth A term used by French theorist Roland Barthes to refer to the ideological meaning of a sign that is expressed through connotation. According to Barthes, myth is the hidden set of rules, codes and conventions through which meanings, which are in reality specific to certain groups, are rendered universal and given for a whole society. Myth thus allows the connotative meaning of a particular thing or image to appear to be denotative, hence literal or natural. In Barthes's famous example, an image in a popular magazine of a black soldier saluting the French flag produces the message that France is a great empire in which all young men regardless of their color faithfully serve under its flag. For Barthes, this image affirms French colonialism at the level of myth. Myth is roughly equivalent to the term "ideology." See *Ideology, Semiotics, Sign.*

Narrowcast media Media that have a limited range through which to reach audiences, and hence are capable of carrying programming tailored to audiences that are more specific than broadcast audiences. Cable television is a primary example of narrowcast programming, with many channels narrowcasting to specific communities (on local city or municipal channels) or to audiences with specific interests (such as independent film). See *Broadcast media*.

Negotiated reading In Stuart Hall's formulation of three potential positions for the viewer/consumer of mass culture, the negotiated reading is one in which consumers accept some aspects of the dominant reading and reject others. According to Hall, most readings are negotiated ones, in which viewers actively struggle with dominant meanings and modify them in numerous ways because of their own social status, beliefs, and values. See *Dominant-hegemonic reading, Oppositional reading*.

Objective/objectivity The state of being unbiased and based on facts, usually referring to scientific fact or ways of seeing and understanding the world that involve a mechanical process rather than human opinion. Debates about the inherent objectivity of photographs, for instance, have centered on whether a photographic image is objective because it was taken mechanically by a camera or is subjective because it was framed and shot by a human subject. See *Subjective*.

Oppositional reading In Stuart Hall's formulation of three potential positions for the viewer/consumer of mass culture, the oppositional reading is one in which consumers fully reject the dominant meaning of a cultural product. This can take the form not only of disagreeing with a message but also of deliberately ignoring it. See *Dominant-hegemonic reading, Negotiated reading*.

Orientalism A term defined most recently by cultural theorist Edward Said that refers to the ways that Western cultures conceive of Eastern and Middle-Eastern cultures as other and attribute to them qualities of exoticism and barbarism. Orientalism is thus used to set up a binary opposition between the West (the Occident) and the East (the Orient) in which negative qualities are attributed to the latter. For Said, Orientalism is a practice that can be found in cultural representations, education, social science, and political policy. For instance, the stereotype of Arab people as fanatic terrorists is an example of Orientalism. See *Binary oppositions, Other*.

Other, The A term used to refer to the category of subjectivity that is set up in binary opposition to dominant subjectivity. The Other refers to that which is understood as the symbolic opposite to the normative category, such as the slave to the master, the woman to the man, the black person to the white person, etc. In contemporary theories that question the functions of binary oppositions in understanding society and social relations, the Other is that which defines the opposite of the dominant pole of the binary opposition (black being defined as not-white) and which can be understood as disempowered through this opposition. The concept of the Other has been taken up by various theorists including Edward Said to describe the psychological dynamic of power that allows those who identify within a position of Western dominance to imagine a racial or ethnic Other, against which he or she may more clearly elaborate his or her own (dominant) self. In Freudian psychoanalytic theory, the mother is the original mirror-like other through whom the child comes to understand his or her self as an autonomous individual. See *Binary oppositions, Marked/unmarked, Orientalism*.

Overdetermination A term that in its usage in Marxist theory (most associated with French theorist Louis Althusser) indicates a case in which several different factors work together to make up the meaning of a social situation. For example, the popularity of the *Mona Lisa* is overdetermined both by artistic qualities within the painting and by mythologies surrounding the woman in the painting as well as the fact that it is known as one of the most famous paintings. See *Marxist theory*.

Panopticism A theory used by French philosopher Michel Foucault to characterize the ways that modern social subjects regulate their own behavior. Borrowing from nineteenth-century philosopher Jeremy Bentham's idea of a panoptic prison, in which the prisoner could always be observed by the guard tower yet not know when that gaze was directed upon him, Foucault suggested that in contemporary society we behave as if we are under a scrutinizing gaze and therefore internalize the rules and norms of the society. See *Gaze*.

Parody Cultural productions that make fun of more serious works through humor and satire while maintaining some of their elements such as plot or character. For example, the film *Airplane!* is a parody of aviation disaster films. Cultural theorists see parody (as opposed to the creation of new and original works) as one of the key strategies of postmodern style, though it is not exclusive to postmodernism. See *Postmodernism/postmodernity*

Pastiche A style of plagiarizing, quoting, and borrowing from previous styles with no reference to history or a sense of rules. In architecture, a pastiche would be a mixing of classical motifs with modern elements in an aesthetic that does not reference the historical meanings of those styles. Pastiche is an aspect of postmodern style. See *Postmodernism/postmodernity*.

Perspective A technique of visualization that was invented in Renaissance Italy in the mid-fifteenth century that indicates the Renaissance interest in the fusion of art and science. To use perspective to create a painting, a painter would deploy a geometric procedure to project space onto a two-dimensional plane. The central aspect of linear perspective is the designation of a vanishing point within the image, with all objects within the image receding in size toward that point, that directs the eye of the viewer to a dominant focal point. The introduction of perspective technique was enormously influential in painting styles of realism, in part because it was understood as scientific and rational. Debates about the dominance of perspective in Western art have proliferated, and many modern styles of art, such as Impressionism and Cubism, are resistant to its concept of human vision. Central to the critique of perspective is its designation of the viewer as a single, unmoving spectator. See *Renaissance*.

Phallus/phallic In psychoanalytic terms, the symbol of the power that men have in patriarchal society. Psychoanalytic theorists, including Jacques Lacan, have debated the extent to which the phallus is equated with the penis as the specific object that awards power. Nonetheless, to call something phallic is to attribute to it both aspects of male power and the symbol of the penis. The representation of a gun, for instance, is considered to be phallic because it is a powerful object that also physically evokes the shape of the penis. See *Lack, Psychoanalytic theory*.

Phenomenology A philosophical position that centers on the dimensions of subjective human experience in how we react bodily and emotionally as well as intellectually to the world around us. Phenomenology emphasizes the importance of the lived body in how we experience and make meaning of the world. Phenomenologists thus talk of being-in-the-world, meaning that we are rooted in the here and now of bodily experience. The mainstream of phenomenology does not see this experience as socially (or sexually or racially) determined. Instead phenomenology talks about "bracketing out" the social context to imagine a direct encounter of people with the world around them. Applications of phenomenology to visual media have focused primarily on the specific capacities of each medium that effect the experience of viewers. Its main theorists are Edmund Husserl and Maurice Merleau-Ponty.

Photographic truth As images produced by the mechanical device of a photographic camera, photographs have the power to project images of the truth and to be seen as unmediated copies of reality. The myth of photographic truth means that photographs are understood to be evidence of actual people, events and objects of the past, even though they are relatively easy to manipulate. The truth-value of photography and camera imaging is the subject of ongoing debate, one that has been heightened by the introduction of digital imaging techniques.

Polysemy The quality of having many potential meanings. A work of art whose meaning is ambiguous is polysemic because it can have many different meanings to different viewers.

Pop art An art movement in the late 1950s and 1960s that used the images and materials of popular or "low" culture for art. Pop artists took aspects of mass culture, such as television, cartoons, advertisements, and commodities, and reworked them as art objects and in paintings, and in so doing formulated a critique of the so-called high/low culture divide. Its primary proponents were Andy Warhol, Roy Lichtenstein, James Rosenquist, and Claes Oldenburg.

Positivism A philosophic position that is strongly scientific in inspiration and that assumes that meanings exist out in the world, independent of our feelings, attitudes, or beliefs about them. Positivism assumes that the factual nature of things can be established by experimentation and that facts are free of the influence of language and representational systems. It believes that only scientific knowledge is genuine knowledge and that other ways of viewing the world are suspect. For example, the assumption that photography directly gives us the truth of the world is a positivist assumption.

Postcolonialism A term that refers to the cultural and social context of countries that were formerly defined in relationships of colonialism (both colonized and colonizer), in the contemporary mix of former colonies, neocolonialism, and continuing colonialism. The term "postcolonial" refers to the broad set of changes that have affected these countries, and in particular to the mix of identities, languages, and influences that have resulted from complex systems of dependence and independence. Postcolonial contexts, for instance, can be identified both in the former colonies of England and within England itself. Most theorists of postcolonialism insist that the breakup of older colonial models is never complete, and does not put an end to forms of domination between more and less powerful countries. See *Colonialism*.

Postmodernism/postmodernity Used to describe particular styles in art, literature, architecture, and popular culture, to define particular aspects of contemporary theory, and to designate a particular way of viewing the world (often seen as a time period) in the late twentieth century, postmodernism is often seen as both imprecise and multiple in its meanings. Broadly, the term has been used to describe a set of social, cultural, and economic formations that have occurred "post" or after the height of modernity, and that have produced both a different world view and different ways of being in the world than that of modernity.

Postmodernity has thus been used to describe a radical transformation of the social, economic, and political context of modernity, while at the same time it is often understood as an extension of modernity. It has been referred to as a postmodern questioning of "metanarratives" by French philosopher Jean-François Lyotard, and of the premise within them that they could define the human condition. It has also been described by Fredric Jameson as a historical period that is the cultural outcome of the "logic of late capitalism." Postmodernism has been characterized as a critique of concepts of universalism, the idea of presence, the traditional notion of the subject as unified and self-aware, and of the modern faith in progress.

In terms of its application to art and visual style, postmodernism has been used to describe a set of trends in the art world in the late twentieth century that question, among other things, concepts of authenticity, authorship, and the idea of style progression. Postmodern works are thus highly reflexive with a mix of styles. In popular culture and advertising, the term "postmodern" has been used to describe techniques that involve reflexivity, discontinuity, and pastiche, and that speak to viewers as both jaded consumers and through self-knowing metacommunication. See *Discontinuity, Hyperreal, Metacommunication, Modernism/modernity, Parody, Pastiche, Reflexivity, Simulation/simulacrum, Surface.*

Poststructuralism A loosely used term that refers to a range of theories that followed and criticized structuralism. Poststructuralist theories examine those practices that are left out of a structuralist view of society. For example, desire, play and playfulness, and ambiguities of meaning especially in the arts. Its primary theorists are Roland Barthes (in his later work), Gilles Deleuze, Paul de Man, and Jacques Derrida. See *Structuralism.*

Power/knowledge A term used by Michel Foucault to describe the ways that power impacts what gets to count as knowledge in a given social context, and how in turn knowledge systems within that society are caught up in power relations. Foucault thus posited that power and knowledge are inseparable, and the concepts of truth are relative to the networks of power and knowledge systems (such as educational systems that award degrees and the designation of expertise) of a given society.

Practice An important concept in cultural studies that refers to the activities of cultural consumers through which they interact with cultural products and make meaning from them. Thus, one can speak of practices of looking as the activities undertaken by viewers of art, the media, and popular culture to interpret and make use of these images.

Presence The quality of immediate experience that has been traditionally contrasted with representation and with those aspects of world that are the product of human mediation. The quality of being "present" has thus been understood historically to mean that one can be in the world in a way that is direct and experienced through the senses, and unmediated by human belief, ideologies, language systems, or forms of representation. Postmodernism criticizes this concept of presence as the illusion that we can actually experience the world in a direct and complete way without the social baggage of language, ideology, etc.

Presumption of relevance In advertising, the manner of speaking that makes the presumption that the issues presented are of utmost importance. In the abstract world of advertisements, for instance, the statement that having shiny hair is the most important aspect of one's life does not register with viewers as absurd because of the presumption of this as relevant within the ad's message.

Propaganda A term with negative connotations that indicates the imparting of political messages through mass media or art with the intent of moving people in calculated ways to precise political beliefs. For example, in Nazi Germany the film *Triumph of the Will* was intended to propagandize for the Nazi cause in its depiction of Hitler as a charismatic leader.

Pseudoindividuality A term used in Marxist theory to describe the way that mass culture creates a false sense of individuality in cultural consumers. Pseudoindividuality refers to the effect of popular culture and advertising that addresses the viewer/consumer specifically as an individual, as in the case of advertising actually claiming that a product will enhance one's individuality, while it is speaking to many people at once. It is "pseudo" individuality if one attains it through mass culture, "pseudo" because the message is predicated on many people receiving a message of individuality at the same time, hence not on individuality but on homogeneity. See *Marxist theory*.

Psychoanalytic theory A theory of how the mind works derived originally from Austrian psychoanalyst Sigmund Freud (1856–1939) that emphasizes the role of the unconscious and desire in shaping a subject's actions, feelings, and motives. Freud's work emphasized bringing the repressed materials of the unconscious to the surface through what was called the talking cure. It focused on the construction of the self through various mechanisms and processes of the unconscious as laid out in Freud's writings and accounts of his analyses. In its beginnings, psychoanalysis was much maligned in the United States, where ego psychology held sway during Freud's heyday in Europe.

Psychoanalytic theory is the application of many of these ideas not as a therapy practice but to analyze systems of representation. French theorist Jacques Lacan updated many of Freud's ideas in relationship to language systems, and inspired the use of psychoanalytic theory to interpret and analyze literature and film. See *Alienation, Exhibitionism, Fetish, Gaze, Lack, Mirror phase, Phallus/phallic, Repression, Scopophilia, Unconscious, Voyeurism*.

Public sphere A term which originated with German theorist Jürgen Habermas that defines a space where citizens come together to debate and discuss the pressing issues of their society. Habermas defined this as an ideal space in which well-informed citizens would discuss matters of common public interest outside of the context of private interests. It is generally understood that Habermas's ideal public sphere has never been realized because of the integration of private interests into public life, and because it did not take into account relations of class, race, and gender and how these define unequal access to public space. The term has been used more recently in the plural to refer to the multiple public spheres in which people debate contemporary issues.

Queer Originally a derogatory term for homosexuals that has been re-appropriated as a positive term for sexual identities that do not fit within dominant heterosexual norms. The term "queer" is thus a good example of appropriation in action, in changing a negative term to a positive, even progressive, one. A queer reading of a cultural product reads against the grain of dominant sexual ideology to look for unacknowledged representations of gay, lesbian, or bisexual desire. See *Appropriation Trans-coding*.

Referent In semiotics, a term that refers to the object itself, as opposed to its representation. Semiotician Ferdinand de Saussure famously referred to the referent, in the example of a horse, as "what kicks you," meaning that while you would not be kicked in real life by the representation of a horse, you could be by a real horse. In semiotics, some theorists such as Roland Barthes use a two-part model to explain signification (signifier-signified), whereas others such as Charles Peirce, use a three-part system (sign, interpretant, object), thus making a distinction between the representation (word/image) of an object and the object itself. The term "referent" is helpful to explain the difference between representation (the re-presentation of real-world objects) and simulation (the copy that has no real equivalent or referent). See *Interpretant, Representation, Semiotics, Signified, Signifier, Simulation/simulacrum*.

Reflexivity The practice of making viewers aware of the material and technical means of production by featuring those aspects as the "content" of a cultural production. Reflexivity is both a part of the tradition of modernism, with its emphasis on form, and of postmodernism with its array of intertextual references and ironic marking of the frame of the image and its status as a cultural product. For instance, in the film *Pulp Fiction*, Uma Thurman says to John Travolta, "don't be a square," and draws a square with her fingers, while a square line appears on the image, reminding the viewer that they are watching a film screen. Reflexivity functions to prevent viewers from being completely absorbed in the illusion of an experience of a film or image, hence it is thought of as a means to distance viewers from that experience. See *Modernism/modernity, Postmodernism/postmodernity*.

Reification A term from Marxist theory that describes the process by which abstract ideas are rendered concrete. This means, in part, that material objects, such as commodities, are awarded the characteristics of human subjects, while the relations between human beings become more objectified. For instance, in an advertisement, a perfume may be given the human attributes of sexiness or femininity, and described as "alive" or "vibrant." Marxist theorists use the term reification to refer to the alienation that is experienced by workers in their identification with the means and products of production, thus causing them to lose their sense of humanity while at the same time, commodities are perceived to be human.

Renaissance A term first coined in France in the nineteenth century to look back on a particular period of history that began in Italy in the early fourteenth century and reached its height throughout Europe in the early sixteenth century. As a time period, it was characterized by a resurgence of cultural, artistic, and scientific activity and a renewed interest in classical literature and art. The Renaissance is understood as marking a broad transition between medieval time—which was mistakenly characterized as a time period with little intellectual or artistic activity—and the modern era. The art of the Renaissance, which flourished in particular in Italy, emphasized both the technique of perspective and a fusion of science and art through such figures as Leonardo da Vinci, Sandro Botticelli, Michelangelo, and Raphael. See *Perspective*.

Replica A copy of an art work that was produced by the original artist or under his/her supervision. A replica of a painting therefore would be another painting that had been made to be as close to it as possible. Replicas differ from reproductions in that they are composed in the same medium and are not easily reproducible. A replica is thus not an exact copy or a reproduction. This tradition became less popular with the rise of techniques of mechanical reproduction. See *Reproduction*.

Representation The act of portraying, depicting, symbolizing, or presenting the likeness of something. Language, the visual arts, such as painting and sculpture, and media such as photography, television, and film, are systems of representation that function to depict and symbolize aspects of the real world. Representation is often seen as distinct from simulation, in that a representation declares itself to be re-presenting some aspect of the real, whereas a simulation has no referent in the real. See *Mimesis, Simulation/simulacrum, Social construction*.

Repression A term in psychoanalytic theory that refers to the process by which the individual relegates to and keeps within the unconscious those particular thoughts, feelings, memories, or desires that are too difficult to deal with. Freud postulated that we repress that which produces fear, anxiety, shame, or other negative emotions within us, and that this repression is active and ongoing. He felt that it was only through this repression that we can become functioning and normative members of a society. Michel Foucault offered another approach, in which he argued against the idea that these desires are hidden and unexpressed. Foucault wrote that systems of control are productive rather than repressive. By this, he meant that social structures encourage such desires to be expressed, spoken, and rendered visible, thereby allowing them to be named, known, and regulated. For example, in a Foucaultian approach, talk shows in which people confess their bad behavior and secret wishes would be seen as a context

in which desires can be cataloged and therefore controlled. See *Power/knowledge, Psychoanalytic theory, Unconscious*.

Reproduction The act of making a copy or duplicating something. Reproduction of images refers to the means through which original works are rendered into multiple copies in the form of prints, posters, postcards, and other merchandise. German theorist Walter Benjamin wrote a famous essay in 1936 on the impact of "mechanical reproduction" of art images. Benjamin emphasized the importance of the role of the copy in changing the meaning of the original image (in his case, a painting). See *Replica*.

Resistance In the context of popular culture, the term "resistance" refers to the techniques used by viewers/consumers to not participate in or to stand in opposition to the messages of dominant culture. Bricolage, or the strategies by which consumers transform the meanings of commodities from their intended meaning, is an example of a resistant consumer practice. See *Appropriation, Bricolage, Oppositional reading, Tactic, Textual poaching*.

Scientific Revolution The time period covering the fifteenth to seventeenth centuries that was characterized by scientific development and a struggle for power between the Church and science. This time period includes the Renaissance, the great navigations of European countries to the new world, the Protestant Reformation, and the emergence of Spain as the first great world power. It was a time period of scientific discovery in astronomy (with Copernicus and Galileo), the development of perspective in art, the development of experimental method by Frances Bacon in the seventeenth century, the philosophy and mathematics of René Descartes, and the discovery of gravity by Isaac Newton. By the beginning of the eighteenth century, science had emerged as an unquestioned pursuit of human endeavor, with a separation of the moral world of the Church and the goals of science. See *Renaissance*.

Scopophilia In psychoanalytic terms, the drive to look and the general pleasure in looking. Freud saw voyeurism (the pleasure in looking without being seen) and exhibitionism (the pleasure in being looked at) as the active and passive forms of scopophilia. The concept of scopophilia has been important to psychoanalytic film theory in its emphasis on the relationship of pleasure and desire to the practice of looking. See *Exhibitionism, Psychoanalytic theory, Voyeurism*.

Semiotics A theory of signs, sometimes called semiology, concerned with the ways in which things (words, images, and objects) are vehicles for meaning. Semiotics is a tool for analyzing the signs of a particular culture and how meaning is produced within a particular cultural context. Just as languages communicate through words organized into sentences, other practices in a culture are treated by semiotic theory as languages made up of basic elements and the rules for combining them. For instance, wearing tennis shoes with a tuxedo (as film director Woody Allen frequently does) communicates a different meaning because of the codes of fashion (which can be thought of as a language with its own forms of correct and incorrect grammar).

The two originators of semiotics are the Swiss linguist Ferdinand de Saussure at the beginning of the twentieth century, and the American philosopher Charles Peirce in the nineteenth century. Contemporary applications of semiotics follow from the work of French theorists Roland Barthes and Christian Metz and Italian theorist Umberto Eco in the 1960s. Their work provides important tools for understanding cultural products (images, film, television, clothing, etc.) as signs that can be decoded. Roland Barthes used a system of signifier (word/image/object) and signified (meaning) as the two elements of a sign. Charles Peirce used the term "interpretant" to designate the meaning that a sign produces in the mind of the person. Peirce also divided signs into several categories, including indexical, iconic, and symbolic signs.

Semiotics is central to understanding culture as a signifying practice, that is the work of creating and interpreting meaning on a daily basis in a given culture. See *Iconic sign, Indexical sign, Interpretant, Referent, Sign, Signifier, Signified, Symbolic sign.*

Sign A semiotic term that defines the relationship between a vehicle of meaning such as a word, image, or object and its specific meaning in a particular context. In technical terms, this means the bringing together of a signified (word/image/object) and signifier (meaning) to make meaning. It is important in semiotics to note that word and images have different meanings in different contexts. For example, in a classic Hollywood film, a cigarette might signify friendship or romance, but in an anti-smoking ad would signify disease and death. See *Semiotics, Signified, Signifier.*

Signified In semiotic terms, the element of meaning within a sign, so called because it was what is signified by a signifier. For example, in an advertising image, a sports car can signify speed, wealth, and youthfulness. These are the signifieds communicated by the signifier

sports car, and each forms a sign with that signifier. See *Semiotics, Sign, Signifier.*

Signifier In semiotic terms, the word, image, or object within a sign that conveys meaning. For example, in an advertisement for sports shoes, an inner-city basketball court is a signifier of authenticity, skill, and coolness. The relationship of a signifier and a signified (its meaning) together forms a sign. Semiotic theory often refers to a free-floating signifier, by which it means a signifier whose sense is particularly not fixed and which can vary a great deal from context to context. See *Semiotics, Sign, Signified.*

Simulation/simulacrum Terms most famously used by French theorist Jean Baudrillard that refer to a sign that does not clearly have a real-life counterpart. A simulacrum is not a representation of something, but is more difficult to distinguish from the real. Hence, it can be considered to be a kind of fake real that could potentially supercede the real. Baudrillard stated that to simulate a disease was to acquire its symptoms, thus making it difficult to distinguish between the simulation and the actual disease. For example, a casino or amusement park simulacrum of the city of Paris can be seen as creating a substitution for the actual city, and can perhaps for some viewers seem to be more real than the city itself. The term "simulation" is often used to describe aspects of postmodern culture in which copies and realities get blurred. See *Postmodernism/postmodernity, Representation.*

Social construction A theory that gained primacy in the 1980s in a number of fields that, at its most general level, asserts that much of what has been taken as fact is socially constructed through ideological forces, language, economic relationships, and so forth. This approach understands the meaning of things to be derived from how they are constructed through systems of representation, such as images and language, rather than to have a meaning separate from human interpretation. Thus, we can only make meaning of the world around us through these systems of representation, and they, in effect, construct that material world for us. For example, in science studies, social constructionists examine the social factors (class, gender, ideology, etc.) that influence laboratory experimentation.

Spectacle A term that generally refers to something that is striking or impressive in its visual display. The term "spectacle" was used by French theorist Guy Debord, in his book *Society of the Spectacle*, to describe how representations dominate contemporary culture, and all social relations are mediated by and through images.

Spectator A term derived from psychoanalytic theory that refers to the viewer of visual arts such as cinema. In early versions of this theory, the term "spectator" did not refer to a specific individual or an actual member of the viewing audience, but rather was imagined to be an ideal viewer, separate from all defining social, sexual, and racial influences. This abstract category allowed film scholars to generalize about certain types of viewing relationships and the role of the unconscious and desire in shaping film meanings.

In contrast, film theory in the late 1980s and 1990s emphasized specific identity groups of spectators, such as female spectators, working-class spectators, queer spectators, or black spectators. This work shifted away from the abstraction of the category to include more culturally specific aspects of identity. In addition, film theory has increasingly emphasized how one need not occupy an identity group to identify within that group's spectator position. For example, in action films, one does not have to be male to take up the position of the male spectator. See *Identification, Psychoanalytic theory*.

Strategy A term used by French theorist Michel de Certeau to describe the practices by which dominant institutions seek to structure time, place, and actions of their social subjects. This is in contrast to the tactics by which those subjects seek to reclaim a space and time for themselves. For example, the television programming schedule is a strategy to make viewers watch programming in a particular order, whereas an individual's use of a remote control is a tactic to decide viewing in their own way. See *Tactic*.

Structuralism A set of theories that came into prominence in the 1960s that emphasized the laws, codes, rules, formulas, and conventions that structure human behavior and systems of meaning. It is based on the premise that cultural activity could be analyzed objectively as a science, and structuralists emphasize elements within a culture that created a unitary organization. This often takes the form of defining the binary oppositions that structure ways of viewing the world and cultural products as well. Structuralism is considered to have originated with the structural linguistics of Swiss theorist Ferdinand de Saussure in the early twentieth century, and in the mid-1950s through the work of Russian linguist Roman Jakobson. It was explored in influential ways by French anthropologist Claude Lévi-Strauss, who applied it to studying various cultures.

In popular culture, structuralism has been used to identify the recurrent patterns and formulas in genres of film or literature. For example, Italian theorist Umberto Eco wrote a well-known structuralist analysis of the James Bond spy thriller novels of Ian Fleming, in which he argues that no matter how much the details change from story to story, the structure remains the same. Eco saw this structure organized around a limited set of binary oppositions, such as Bond/villain, good/evil, etc., that lead to a defined and limited set of plot elements that recur in each story. Analyzing these elements and pinpointing their regularity is a practice of structuralism. Much of the theory that followed structuralism, which is often called poststructuralism, criticized structuralism for emphasizing structure at the expense of other elements that do not fit into these formulas or conventions. See *Binary oppositions, Genre, Poststructuralism*.

Subculture Distinct social groups within wider cultural formations that define themselves in opposition to mainstream culture. The term "subculture" has been used extensively in cultural studies to designate those social groups, usually youth groups, who use style to signify resistance to dominant culture. Subcultures, which might include punk rockers, followers of rave, or subgroups of hip-hop, use style in fashion, music, and lifestyle as signifying practices to convey resistance to norms. Bricolage, or the use of commodities in ways that change their meaning (such as wearing jackets backwards or extra-large pants slung low) is a central practice of subcultures. See *Bricolage*.

Subject A term, used in both psychoanalytic and cultural theory, that defines those aspects of human individuals that individuals are not in control of and that are actually shared among humans. To speak of individuals as subjects is to indicate that they are split between the conscious and unconscious, that they are produced by the structures of society, and that they are both active forces (subjects of) history but also acted upon (subjected to) all the social forces of their moment in time.

Subjective Something that is particular to the view of an individual, hence the opposite of objective. A subjective view is understood to be personal, specific, and imbued with the values and beliefs of a particular person. See *Objective*.

Subject position A term used to define those ways that images, whether as films or paintings, etc., designate an ideal position for their intended spectators. For instance, it can be said that particular films offer to their viewers an ideal subject position. There is an ideal spectator of the action film, regardless of how any particular viewer might make personal meaning of the film, and the subject position of a traditional landscape painting is that of a spectator who luxuriates in the fantasy of ownership of sublime and bountiful nature. As theorized by Michel Foucault, subject position is the place that a particular discourse asks a human subject to adopt within it. For example, the discourse of education defines a limited set of subject positions that individuals can occupy in which some are authoritative figures of knowledge such as teachers and others are relegated the position of students, or recipients of that knowledge. See *Discourse*.

Sublime A term in aesthetic theory, specifically in the work of eighteenth-century theorist Edmund Burke, that sets out to evoke experiences so momentous that they inspire intense veneration in the viewer or listener. The history of traditional landscape painting, for instance, was about imaging the sublime in that it intended to create in viewers a deep awe of the limitless splendors of nature.

Surface The idea in postmodernism that objects have no depth or profound meaning, but instead exist only at the level of surface. This is in contrast to the idea in modernism that the real meaning of something is below the surface and can be found through acts of interpretation. See *Postmodernism/postmodernity*.

Surrealism An art movement of the early twentieth century in both literature and the visual arts that focused on the role of the unconscious in representation and in dismantling the opposition between the real and the imaginary. The Surrealists were interested in unlocking the unconscious, in Freudian terms, and working against the rational. Surrealist practices included automatic writing and painting and the use of dreams to inspire writing and art. The movement's primary proponents were André Breton, Salvador Dali, Giorgio de Chirico, Max Ernst, and René Magritte.

Surveillance The act of keeping watch over a person or place. Camera technologies such as photography, video, and film have been used for surveillance purposes. For French philosopher Michel Foucault, surveillance is one of the primary means through which a society enacts control over its subjects. See *Panopticism*.

Symbolic sign A term in semiotics used by Charles Peirce to indicate those signs in which there is no connection between the signifier (word/image) and the thing signified except that imposed by convention. Language systems are primarily symbolic systems. Peirce distinguished Iconic, Indexical, and Symbolic signs. For example, the word "university" does not physically resemble any actual university (in other words, it is not

iconic) nor does it have a physical connection to the university (so it is not indexical), hence it is a symbolic sign. See *Iconic sign, Indexical sign, Semiotics*.

Synergy A term used in industry to describe the ways that corporate conglomerates own aspects of cultural production, programming, and distribution across many media and into many geographic locales. Synergy thus refers to the capacity of corporations that own across many media such as broadcast networks, cable television, movie studios, film distribution companies, magazines and other publishing entities, to both vertically integrate across programming and distribution and horizontally market products globally.

Tactic A term used by French theorist Michel de Certeau to indicate those practices deployed by people who are not in positions of power to gain some control over the spaces of their daily lives. De Certeau defined tactics as the acts of the weak which do not have lasting effect. He contrasted this with the strategies of institutions. For example, sending a personal e-mail while at work might be a tactic to give oneself a small feeling of empowerment in the alienation of one's workplace, while a company's monitoring of employee e-mail usage is a strategy. See *Strategy*.

Taste In cultural theory, taste refers to the shared artistic and cultural values of a particular social community or individual. However, even when it seems most individual, taste is informed by experiences relating to one's class, cultural background, education, and other aspects of identity. Notions of good taste usually refer to middle-class or upper-class notions of what is tasteful, and bad taste is a term often associated with mass or low culture. Taste, in this understanding, is something that can be learned through contact with cultural institutions.

Technological determinism A position that sees technology as the most important determining factor in social change, positing technology as somehow separate from social and cultural influence. In this view of technology, people are merely observers and facilitators of technology's progress. Technological determinism has been largely discredited in favor of the view that technological change and advance is the result of social, economic, and cultural influences, and cannot be seen as either autonomous or outside those influences.

Television flow A term used by cultural theorist Raymond Williams to describe the way that television incorporates interruption, such as television commercials and the break between programs, into a seemingly continuous flow so that everything on the TV screen is seen as part of one single entertainment experience.

Text A term extended by French theorist Roland Barthes to include visual media such as photography, film, television, or painting, to suggest that they are constructed on the basis of codes in the same that way that language forms a text. Insofar as they are constructions, texts can be broken down into their component parts through the work of analysis. Barthes in particular distinguished texts from works, such as art works, to indicate an active relationship between the writer and reader or artist/producer and viewer. This is because the constructed nature of the text implies that its meaning is produced in relationship to the viewer rather than simply residing in the work itself. To treat an art work as a text means that we read it through codes rather than passively absorb or stand in awe of it.

Textual poaching A term used by French theorist Michel de Certeau to describe the ways that viewers can read and interpret cultural texts, such as film or television, that reworks that text in some way. This might involve rethinking the story of a particular film, or in the case of some fan cultures, writing one's own version of it. Textual poaching was referred to by de Certeau as a process analogous to "inhabiting a text like a rented apartment." In other words, viewers of popular culture can "inhabit" that text by renegotiating its meaning or by creating new cultural products in response to it.

Third World A term coined in the post-World War II period, which refers to the countries of Africa, Asia, and Latin America. This was in response to the concept in political theory of the world divided into West (First World) and East (Second World) with two major superpowers, the USA and the USSR. These countries established themselves as a "Third World" rather than taking sides with Eastern or Western superpowers. With the decline of the Cold War, the decline of the autonomous nation-state, and the expansion of new technologies and global media and information systems in many Third World countries, the concept of a Third World is losing currency, but continues to hold important historical meaning. See *First World*.

Trans-coding The practice of taking terms and meanings and re-appropriating them to create new meanings. For example, the Gay Rights and Queer Nation Movements re-appropriated the term "queer," which had been used as a derogatory term for homosexuals, to give it a new meaning, both as a positive term for identity and as a theoretical term indicating a position through which the norm is questioned, or "queered." See *Queer*.

Ultrasound A technique now used in medical diagnosis that uses sound waves to map soft tissue in the body, and which produces an ultrasound image. Ultrasound is derived from the technology of sonar devices that can measure objects in water.

Unconscious A central concept in psychoanalytic theory that indicates the phenomena that are not within consciousness at any given moment. According to Sigmund Freud, the unconscious is a repository for desires, fantasies, and fears that act upon and motivate us though we are not aware of them. Freud's idea of the unconscious was a radical departure from the traditional idea of the subject that could easily know the reasons for his/her actions. Since the unconscious and the conscious sides of a human being do not work in concert, psychoanalytic theory speaks of the human as a divided or split subject. Dreams and so-called Freudian slips of the tongue are evidence of the unconscious. See *Psychoanalytic theory, Repression*.

Use value The practical function originally assigned to an object, in other words, what it does. This is in contrast to its exchange value, which is what is paid for it. Marxist theory critiques the emphasis in capitalism on exchange over use value. For example, a luxury car and a less expensive compact car have the same use value of being means of transportation, but the luxury car has a much higher exchange value. See *Capitalism, Commodity fetishism, Exchange value, Marxist theory*.

Virtual Because electronic technology can simulate realities, the term "virtual" has come to indicate phenomena that seem to exist but in no tangible or physical way. A virtual version of something is thus capable of functioning in a number ways that are similar to its actual physical or material counterpart. For example, in virtual reality, users wear gear that allows them the sensations of a particular reality, and they can respond as if they were in that physical space. Hence, airline pilots can use virtual reality systems to train on the ground as if they were flying through space. Virtual images have no referent in the real, but can be both analog and digital. The term "virtual space" has been used broadly to refer to those spaces that are electronically constituted, such as space defined by the Internet, the World Wide Web, e-mail, or virtual reality systems, but that do not conform to the laws of physical, material, or Cartesian space. Many aspects of virtual space encourage us to think of these spaces as being similar to the physical spaces that we encounter in the real world (when they are referred to as "rooms" for instance), however virtual space does not obey the rules of physical space. See *Analog, Cartesian space, Digital, Internet, World Wide Web*.

Virtual reality See *Virtual*.

Visuality The quality or state of being visual. It is believed by some that visuality characterizes our age, because so much of our media and everyday space is increasingly dominated by visual images. Those theorists who consider visuality rather than images emphasize the generalized condition and place of visuality in a culture or era, not necessarily specific entities (like photographs, for example) that are designed to be seen. Visuality can concern how we see everyday objects and people, not just those things we think of as visual texts.

Voyeurism In psychoanalytic terms, the erotic pleasure in watching without being seen. Voyeurism is often seen in tandem with exhibitionism, or the erotic pleasure in being looked at, and has historically been associated with the masculine spectator. Voyeurism is also used to describe the experience of the cinematic spectators who in the traditional viewing context of the movie theater can view the images on screen while themselves being hidden. See *Exhibitionism, Psychoanalytic theory, Scopophilia.*

World Wide Web The Internet information server that uses hypertext as its primary navigation tool. The World Wide Web includes multimedia: images, graphics, audio, and video in the form of web sites and pages that can be accessed and downloaded by viewers through browsers. See *Hypertext, Internet.*

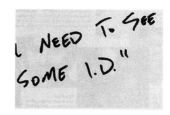

Picture Credits

p.11 *Their First Murder* (before 1945) by Weegee (Arthur Fellig), gelatin silver: 25.7 × 27.9 cm (10 1/8 × 11 in.). J. Paul Getty Museum, Los Angeles

p.14 *Still Life with Stoneware Jug, Wine Glass, Herring, and Bread* (1642) by Pieter Claesz, oil on panel: 30 × 35.8 cm (11 13/16 × 14 1/8 in.). Courtesy of the Museum of Fine Arts, Boston, bequest of Mrs. Edward Wheelwright, 1913

p.15 *The Treachery of Images (Ceci n'est pas une pipe)* (1928–9) by René Magritte, oil on canvas: 64.61 × 94.13 cm (25 7/16 × 37 1/16 in.). Los Angeles County Museum of Art, purchased with funds provided by the Mr. and Mrs. William Preston Harrison Collection. © 2000 C. Herscovici, Brussels/Artists Rights Society (ARS), New York. Photograph © 2000 Museum Associates/LACMA

p.18 *Trolley—New Orleans* (1955–56) by Robert Frank, gelatin silver: 22.9 × 34.2 cm (9 × 13 7/16 in.). © Robert Frank, courtesy Pace WildensteinMacGill, New York, print courtesy of the Museum of Fine Arts, Houston, The Target Collection of American Photography, museum purchase with funds provided by Target Stores

p.23, bottom © 1994, Newsweek, Inc., all rights reserved, reprinted by permission

p.25 © The Fonda Group

p.27, 41, 274, 275 Concept: O. Toscani. Courtesy of United Colors of Benetton

p.31 *Irises* (1889) by Vincent Van Gogh, oil on canvas: 71 × 93 cm (28 × 36 5/8 in.). J. Paul Getty Museum, Los Angeles

p.33, top © Pillsbury Co.

p.35 AP/World Wide Photos/Jeff Widener

p.37, left *The Small Cowper Madonna* (c. 1505) by Raphael, oil on panel: 0.595 × 0.440 m (23 3/8 × 17 3/8 in.). Widener Collection c 1998 Board of Trustees, National Gallery of Art

p.37, right *Virgin and Child* (1525) by Joos van Cleve, oil on wood: 70.5 × 52.7 cm (27 3/4 × 20 3/4 in.). Metropolitan Museum of Art, The Jack and Belle Linsky Collection, 1982 (1982.60.47)

p.38 *Migrant Mother, Nipomo, California* (1936) by Dorothea Lange, gelatin silver: 31.9 × 25.2 cm (12½ × 9 7/8 in.). © The Dorothea Lange Collection, The Oakland Museum of California, City of Oakland, gift of Paul S. Taylor, print courtesy of the Museum of Modern Art, New York. © 1999

p.39 ™/© 1999 the estate of Marilyn Monroe by CMG Worldwide Inc., Indianapolis, IN 46256 USA marilynmonroe.com

p.40 *Marilyn Diptych* (1962) by Andy Warhol, synthetic polymer paint and silkscreen ink on canvas: 6′ 10 × 57 in. © 1999, Andy Warhol Foundation for the Visual Arts/ARS, New York. Tate Gallery, London

p.42 Photo: Serge Thomann. Courtesy of Warner Bros. Records Inc.

p.53 © 1993 AT&T, reproduced with permission

p.55 *Untitled* (1981) by Barbara Kruger, photograph: 37 × 50 in. Courtesy of the Mary Boone Gallery, New York

p.60 *Read My Lips (girls)* (1988) by Gran Fury, poster, offset lithography: 16½ × 10 1/8 in. Courtesy of Gran Fury p.61 Photograph by Alastair Thain. Reproduced with permission of the Commission for Racial Equality.

p.62 *The Last Dinner of Chicano Heros* (1986–89) by José Antonio Burciaga, mural, Stanford University, Palo Alto, California. Photo: James Prigoff

p.64 Photo: Michel Torres. © Bettmann/Corbis

p.66 *Azteca* by Jorge and Rosa Salazar. Photo by Nathan Trujillo, courtesy of *Lowrider Magazine*

p.68 *The X-Files*, © 1996 Twentieth Century Fox Film Corporation, all rights reserved

p.77 *Rear Window*, © 2001 Universal City Studios, Inc. Courtesy of Universal Studios Publishing Rights, all rights reserved.

p.79 Courtesy of Canal + International. Photo: Museum of Modern Art Film Stills Archive

p.80, top *Woman with a Parrot* (1866) by Jean-Désiré-Gustave Courbet, oil on canvas: 129.5 × 195.6 cm (51 × 77 in.). Metropolitan Museum of Art, H.O. Havemeyer Collection, Bequest of Mrs. H.O. Havemeyer, 1929

p.80, bottom *Pygmalion and Galatea* (late 1800s) by Jean-Léon Gérôme, oil on canvas: 88.9 × 68.6 cm (35 × 27 in.). Metropolitan Museum of Art, gift of Louis C. Raegner, 1927

p.81, left *Venus and Cupid* (early 1500s) by Lorenzo Lotto, oil on canvas: 92.4 × 111.4 cm (36 3/8 × 43 7/8 in.). Metropolitan Museum of Art, purchase Mrs. Charles Wrightsman, gift in honor of Marietta Tree, 1986

p.81, right *Venus with a Mirror* (c. 1555) by Titian, oil on canvas: 1.245 × 1.055 m (49 × 41½ in.). Andrew W. Mellon Collection © 1998 Board of Trustees, National Gallery of Art

pp.82 top, 87, 106 Photo: Bruce Weber. Courtesy of Ralph Lauren

pp.82 bottom, 91, 124 Photo courtesy Levi Strauss & Co.

p.84, top *Gentlemen Prefer Blondes* © 1953 Twentieth Century Fox Film Corporation, all rights reserved. Photo: Museum of Modern Art Film Stills Archive

p.84, bottom *Thelma & Louise* © 1991 MGM—Pathé Communications Co., all rights reserved. Photo: Museum of Modern Art Film Stills Archive

p.88 Courtesy of the Coca-Cola Company

p.89, top left Courtesy of Land Rover North America

p.89, top right Courtesy of Conair Corporation

p.89, bottom Courtesy of Jockey International

pp.90, top, 105, 224 left Courtesy of Guess?, Inc.

p.90, bottom Courtesy of Coty Inc.

p.92 Courtesy of Reebok

p.96 *An Epileptic Boy*, Figure 14 from the book *Criminal Man: According to the Classification of Cesare Lombroso*, Gina Lombroso-Ferrero (1911). Courtesy of the San Francisco Museum of Modern Art

p.98 © Corbis

p.99 From *The Works of Jeremy Bentham*, vol. iv, John Bowring edition of 1838–1843, reprinted by Russell and Russell, Inc., New York, 1962

p.100 *License Photo Studio, New York* (1934) by Walker Evans, gelatin silver: 18.2 × 14.4 cm (7 3/16 × 5 11/16 in.). J. Paul Getty Museum, Los Angeles

p.101, bottom *Two Tahitian Women* (1899) by Paul Gauguin, oil on canvas: 94 × 72.4 cm (37 × 28½ in.). Metropolitan Museum of Art, gift of William Church Osborn, 1949

p.102 Photograph by Lady Broughton, 1935. Silver print. Pitt Rivers Museum, University of Oxford

p.103 Photograph by Thomas Andrew (?) c.1890. Albumen print. Pitt Rivers Museum, University of Oxford

p.110, left *Alice Liddell* (the daughter of Henry George Liddell, Dean of Christchurch, Oxford) (1872) by Juliet Margaret Cameron, albumen silver print from glass negative: 36.4 × 26.3 cm. Courtesy of the Metropolitan Museum of Art, David Hunter McAlpin Fund, 1963 (63.545)

p.110, right Photo: Geoff Kern

p.112, top *The Annunciation* (c. 1448) by Fra Carnevale, tempura (and possibly oil) on panel: 0.876 × 0.629 m (34½ × 24 3/4 in.). Samuel H. Kress Collection © 1998 Board of Trustees, National Gallery of Art

p.112, bottom *Funerary Papyrus of the Princess Entiu-ny, Daughter of King Paynudjem*, from the Tomb of Queen Meryet-Amun, at Bahri, Thebes, detail: The Judgement of the Heart. Metropolitan Museum of Art, Museum Excavations, 1928–1929 and Rogers Fund, 1930

p.119 *Rouen Cathedral: The Portal (in Sun)* (1894) by Claude Monet, oil on canvas: 99.7 × 65.7 cm (39 1/4 × 25 7/8 in.). Metropolitan Museum of Art, Theodore M. Davis Collection, bequest of Theodore M. Davis, 1915

p.120 *The Portuguese* (1911) by Georges Braque. Courtesy of Giraudon/Art Resource, NY © 1999 Artists Rights Society (ARS), New York/ADAGP, Paris, Kunstmuseum, Basel, Switzerland p.121 *Pearblossom Hwy., 11–18th April 1986, #2* (1986) by David Hockney, photographic collage of chromogenic prints: 198 × 282 cm (78 × 111 in.). J. Paul Getty Museum, Los Angeles

p.125 Warhol T-shirt from Ronald Feldman Gallery

p.126 *The Scream* (1893) by Edvard Munch. Courtesy of Scala/Art Resource, NY © 1999 The Munch Museum/The Munch-Ellingsen Group/Artists Rights Society (ARS), New York

p.128 Close-ups of early digital reproduction of the *Mona Lisa* (1965) by Andrew Patros, created at Control Data Corp. Digigraphics Labs in Burlington, Massachusetts. http://www.digitalmonalisa.com (Web reproduction accessed May 2000)

p.129 Mona Lisa tie by Ralph Marlin. Photo © Robert Baron, 1998

p.130 Artist: Dean Rohrer. © 1999 by Condé Nast Publications, reprinted by permission, all rights reserved

p.131 *Adolf as Superman: "He Swallows Gold and Spits Out Tin-Plate"* (1932) by John Heartfield. © 1999 Artists Rights Society (ARS), New York/VG Bild-Kunst, Bonn

p.132 *Silence = Death* (1986) by Silence = Death Project, poster, offset lithography: 29 × 24 in. Courtesy of ACT UP

pp.133, 134 Courtesy of California Department of Health Services

p.137 *Ashputtle* (1982) by John Baldessari, eleven black-and-white photographs, one color photograph, and text panel: 213.4 × 182.9 cm (84 × 72 in.). Collection of the Whitney Museum of Art, purchase, with funds from the Painting and Sculpture Committee

p.142 Gordon Gahan © National Geographic Society

p.143 *Untitled*, from *Dream Girls* series (1989–90) by Deborah Bright. Courtesy the artist

p.144 *Roy II* (1994) by Chuck Close, oil on canvas: 102 × 84 in. Photographer: Lee Stalsworth. Hirshhorn Museum and Sculpture Garden, Smithsonian Institution, Smithsonian Collections Acquisition Program and the Joseph H. Hirshhorn Purchase Fund, 1995

p.146 Courtesy of Dr. Richard A. Robb, Biomedical Imaging Resource, Mayo Foundation/Clinic, Rochester, Minnesota

p.152 *Restaurant, U.S. 1 leaving Columbia, South Carolina* (1955) Robert Frank, gelatin silver photograph: 8 3/4 × 13 in.

© Robert Frank, courtesy PaceWildensteinMacGill, New York, print courtesy of the Museum of Fine Arts, Houston, The Target Collection of American Photography, museum purchase with funds provided by Target Stores

p.154 *Retroactive I* (1964) by Robert Rauschenberg, oil on canvas. Wadsworth Atheneum, Hartford, gift of Susan Morse Hilles. © Robert Rauschenberg/Licensed by VAGA, New York, NY

p.155 *Drive-in Movie—Detroit* (1955) by Robert Frank, gelatin silver: 7 15/16 × 13 in. © Robert Frank, courtesy PaceWildensteinMacGill, New York, print courtesy of the Museum of Fine Arts, Houston, museum purchase with funds provided by Jerry E. and Nanette Finger

p.159 *Television Studio—Burbank, California* (1955/56) by Robert Frank, gelatin silver: 20.3 × 30.5 (8 × 12 in.). © Robert Frank, courtesy of PaceWildensteinMacGill, New York, print courtesy of the Museum of Fine Arts, Houston, museum purchase with funds provided by Jerry E. and Nanette Finger

pp.163, 249, 309, 329 Museum of Modern Film Stills Archive

p.167 3-D Movies, © UPI/Bettmann-Corbis

p.171 Courtesy of Electronic Arts Intermix

p.173 © Bettmann-Corbis

p.180 Photo: Donald Phelan

p.181 *The Eternal Frame* (1975) by Ant Farm/T.R. Uthco. Photo: Diane Andrews Hall

p.182 Photo: Adrian Dennis. Courtesy of AP/World Wide Photos

p.185 Courtesy of Artisan Entertainment

p.190 Reprinted by permission by International Business Machines Corporation © 1992

p.192 *Billboard, Birmingham, Alabama* (1936) by Walker Evans, gelatin silver print: 19.1 × 23.9 cm. © Walker Evans Archive, Metropolitan Museum of Art, purchase, The Horace W. Goldsmith Foundation Gift, 1990 (1990.1169)

p.195, top *Magasin, avenue des Gobelins (Store Window, avenue des Gobelins)* (1925) by Eugène Atget, matte albumen print: 23 × 16.8 cm (9 1/16 × 6 19/32 in.). J. Paul Getty Museum, Los Angeles

p.202 top *Two Hundred Campbell's Soup Cans* (1962) by Andy Warhol, synthetic polymer paint and silkscreen ink on canvas: 6′ × 8′ 4 in. © 1999, Andy Warhol Foundation for the Visual Arts/ARS, New York

p.202, bottom   *Drowning Girl* (1963) by Roy Lichtenstein, oil and synthetic polymer paint on canvas: 171.6 × 169.5 cm (67 5/8 × 66 3/4 in.). © 1999 The Museum of Modern Art, New York, Philip Johnson Fund and gift of Mr. and Mrs. Bagley Wright

p.204   Courtesy of Hitachi America, Ltd.

p.205   © General Motors Corporation

p.206   Courtesy of TBWA Chiat/Day

p.207   Courtesy of Bozell Wordwide, Inc.

p.208   Courtesy of Parlux Fragrances, Inc.

p.210   Courtesy of Volkswagen of America

p.211, top   Image by David Bailey. Reproduced with permission of Respect for Animals, PO Box 6500, Nottingham NG4 3GB

p.211, bottom   Reprinted with permission of the Henry J. Kaiser Family Foundation of Menlo Park. The Kaiser Family Foundation is an independent health care philanthropy and is not associated with Kaiser Permanente or Kaiser Industries. Courtesy of the Advertising Council, Historical File, University of Illinois Archives Record Series 13/2/207, Box 96 (February 1990)

p.212   Courtesy of Donna Karan Company

p.213   Courtesy of Bijan

p.214   Courtesy of Joseph Jeans

p.215, top   Courtesy of AdeM Cosmetic Companies

p.215, bottom   Courtesy of Clarins USA

p.216   Reprinted by permission by International Business Machines Corporation © 1998

p.218   Courtesy of Volkswagen of America

p.219   Courtesy of Motorola, Inc. © Motorola, Inc.

p.220   Courtesy of American Express

p.225   Courtesy of Maidenform Worldwide

p.226   Courtesy of Nike

p.228   Aunt Jemima sack quilt, Texas, 1940s. Collection of Shelly Zegart, Louisville, Kentucky

p.232   *The Right to Life* (1979) by Hans Haacke. © 2000 Artists Rights Society (ARS) New York/VG Bild-Kunst, Bonn

p.234, middle and bottom,   Courtesy of Billboard Liberation Front

p.242   © Corbis

p.244   *Broadway Boogie Woogie* (1942–43) by Piet Mondrian, oil on canvas: 127 × 127 cm (50 × 50 in.). © 1999 Museum of Modern Art, New York, given anonymously

p.245   *Number 1, 1948* (1948) by Jackson Pollock, oil and enamel on unprimed canvas: 172.7 × 264.2 cm (68 in. × 8 feet, 8 in.). © 1999 Museum of Modern Art, New York, purchase

p.247   *Model for the Monument to the Third International* (1919) by Vladimir Tatlin, wood, iron and glass: h 420 cm (165 1/3 in.). Collection of Centre Georges Pompidou/Musée national d'art moderne, Paris. Photo: Collection of Centre Georges Pompidou/Musée national d'art moderne, Paris

p.255   *Untitled Film Still #21* (1978) by Cindy Sherman, photograph: 8 × 10 in. Courtesy of the artist and Metro Pictures (MP #21)

p.261   © Corbis

p.262   *After Weston #2* (1980) by Sherrie Levine. Photo courtesy of Margo Leavin Gallery

p.264   Courtesy of Fred Wilson

p.265   Photo by Kelly & Massa Photography, reproduced with permission

p.266   Courtesy of McNeil Consumer Products

p.267   Photo: Linda Chen. © Miramax Films.

p.268   Used by permission of Eveready Battery Company, Inc. Energizer Bunny is a registered trademark of Eveready Battery Company

p.269   Courtesy of ABC Television Network

p.270   *The Simpsons* © 1992 Twentieth Century Fox Film Corporation, all rights reserved

p.272 left   Courtesy of Kenneth Cole

p.272 right   Courtesy of Moschino

p.273   Courtesy of Diesel USA

p.281   Courtesy of McLeod

p.283   Frontispiece from *Inquiries into Human Faculties* (1883) by Francis Galton

p.284   Figure 58 of Illustrations for *Mechanisme de la physionomie humaine* (1854) by Guillame Duchenne de

Boulogne/Adren Tournachon. Courtesy of the San Francisco Museum of Modern Art, gift of Harry H. Lunn, Jr.

p.285   Photograph made for John Lamprey, 1868. Albumen print. Pitt Rivers Museum, University of Oxford

p.286   © Rob Crandall/Stock, Boston/Picturequest

p.288   From The "Rodney King Case": What the Jury Saw in California vs. Powell, Court TV, 1992. Courtesy of Court TV

p.289   Woman, Kicking, Plate 367 from Animal Locomotion (1887) by Eadweard Muybridge, colotype: 19×51.4 cm ($7\frac{1}{2} \times 20$ 1/4 in.). © 1999 Museum of Modern Art, New York, gift of the Philadelphia Commercial Museum

p.293   Courtesy of Volvo

p.297   Photo: Lennart Nilsson/Albert Bonniers Forlag AB

p.298   Courtesy of Toshiba America Medical Systems

p.304   © 1993 Time Inc. reprinted by permission

p.306   Corps étranger (1994) by Mona Hatoum. Collection of Centre Georges Pompidou/Musée national d'art moderne, Paris. Photo: Collection of Centre Georges Pompidou/Musée national d'art moderne, Paris

p.308   The Government Has Blood on Its Hands (1988) by Gran Fury, poster, offset lithography: 31 3/4 × 21 3/8 in. Courtesy of Gran Fury

pp.311, 132   Reprinted by permission of Andrew Jergens Company

p.319   © Betty Press/Woodfin Camp/Picturequest, 1989

p.325   Courtesy of The Body Shop USA

p.330   Courtesy of the Centre for International Media Research, Netherlands

p.332   Courtesy Inuit Broadcasting Corporation

p.340   © 1998 Sun Microsystems, Inc., all rights reserved, used by permission. Sun, Sun Microsystems, the Sun Logo, the Java Coffee Cup Logo, Java, Solaris, The Network Is The Computer, We're the Dot in. Com, and all Sun-based and Java-based marks are trademarks or registered trademarks of Sun Microsystems in the United States and other countries

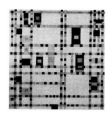

Index

Wiseman, Frederick, 351, 354

Woman's film, 73, 83

World Wide Web, 2, 5, 109, 128–29, 134, 138–39, 147, 152, 160, 172, 179, 194, 316–17, 321, 334, 338–44, 353, 356, 357–59, 369–70; advertising on, 184–85, 190–91; history of, 338–39; news on, 156

Worth, Sol, 328

X

X-Files, The, 67–68

X ray, 281, 291–92, 294, 301, 310

Y

Young, Robert, 311

Youth culture, 64–67, 229, 257, 350, 367; selling of, 68–70, 223–24, 352

Z

Zapata, Emilio, 62

Zapatistas, 341

Zapruder, Abraham, 180–81

Zapruder film, 180–81

Zines, 160, 179

Žižek, Slavoj, 296

Zola, Emile, 118